Stoltzfus

Iowa's Natural Heritage

Iowa's Natural Heritage

Tom C. Cooper, Executive Editor
Nyla Sherburne Hunt, Associate Editor

Published jointly by the
Iowa Natural Heritage Foundation
and the
Iowa Academy of Science

Iowa's Natural Heritage

Iowa's Natural Heritage is published jointly by the Iowa Academy of Science and the Iowa Natural Heritage Foundation.

THE IOWA ACADEMY OF SCIENCE is an affiliate of the American Association for the Advancement of Science, and shares the objectives of the AAAS in furthering work of scientists, facilitating cooperation among them, and increasing public understanding of the role of science in society, especially in Iowa. Most of Iowa's scientific community, both academic and non-academic, is represented in the Academy. Membership is open to anyone interested in the Academy's objectives.

IOWA NATURAL HERITAGE FOUNDATION

"FOR THOSE WHO FOLLOW"

THE IOWA NATURAL HERITAGE FOUNDATION is an independent, non-profit corporation dedicated to the preservation and wise management of Iowa's natural resources. Established in 1979 with support from Governor Robert D. Ray, the Foundation is a catalyst or facilitator, working cooperatively with governmental agencies, private groups, and individuals on programs that serve both short- and long-term natural resource goals. A board of trustees, representing a cross-section of Iowa's leaders, guides operations in three basic areas of assistance activity — land preservation and stewardship; public education and awareness, and long-range planning and research. The Foundation has had a significant role in a number of projects which will help to ensure a richer, fuller future . . . for those who follow.

Copyright ©1982 by the

**Iowa Natural Heritage Foundation
and the
Iowa Academy of Science**

All rights reserved. No part of this publication may be reproduced or utilized in any form without written permission from the publisher. Address all inquiries to the Iowa Natural Heritage Foundation, 505 Fifth Ave., Des Moines, Iowa 50309.

Designed by Morris McKnight, Chicago
Typesetting by Waddell Typesetting, Des Moines
Color Separations by Chroma-Graphics, Inc., Kansas City
Printing by The Graphic Corporation, Des Moines

Library of Congress Cataloging in
Publication Data

Iowa's Natural Heritage
1. Iowa — Description and Travel
2. Natural History — Iowa
I. Cooper, Tom C., 1936 -
II. The Iowa Natural Heritage Foundation and
Iowa Academy of Science

ISBN 0-943490-00-6

Second Printing — 1983

Acknowledgments

It took two organizations, many people, and four years to produce **Iowa's Natural Heritage**.

The idea for this volume was born in 1978 when Dr. Robert W. Hanson, executive director of the Iowa Academy of Science, suggested that the project be undertaken as the most ambitious publishing effort in the Academy's 103-year history. The Ohio Academy of Science had successfully published **Ohio's Natural Heritage**; the Iowa board gave the go-ahead for this project, to be patterned after the Ohio experience. Under Dr. Hanson's direction, several committees of Academy members were formed during the next two years to locate authors and an editor, outline the book's content, and seek funding.

A new Iowa organization, the Iowa Natural Heritage Foundation, appeared almost simultaneously. After several meetings, the Academy and the Foundation formed a partnership to share the copyright and to be co-publishers. The Academy took responsibility for developing the content; the Foundation took over financing, printing, and distribution.

A steering committee, representing both organizations, was formed to guide the project to completion. The Academy was represented by Dr. Hanson, Dr. Clifford McCollum, past president, and Dr. Richard Wacha. Representing the Foundation were Gerald Schnepf, executive director, and board members William Fultz and Dr. Glenn Leggett. These six individuals were heavily involved in the project from beginning to end, and spent many hours in meetings, and traveling to and from them. Clearly, whatever success this book achieves is the result of this steering committee.

Yet I must give special recognition to Bob Hanson, whose determination and confidence were most appreciated, and to Gerry Schnepf and Bill Fultz, who spent untold hours and days arranging for printing and marketing. Without their efforts, this book would not exist.

I wish also to acknowledge Governor Robert Ray for his continuing support of the Foundation, and for his commitment to this project.

The Des Moines-based Meredith Corporation, a revered giant in its field, provided valuable assistance early in the project to test marketing concepts.

The Des Moines advertising firm of Creswell, Munsell, Fultz & Zirbel, Inc., a Young and Rubicam Company, made available its resources several times during the project, including the development and production of a marketing study.

Dr. Leggett, president emeritus of Grinnell College, volunteered to do a most demanding and tedious task — proofreading the entire 352-page book.

Our designer, Morris McKnight, deserves a special acknowledgment. His design has produced a beautiful and practical volume. Morris waded through what must have been thousands of details over a nine-month period. Yet he never lost his sense of humor, even though pressured continually by deadlines.

And finally, I wish to express my appreciation to Nyla Sherburne Hunt, my associate editor. She researched, wrote, re-wrote, proofed, typed and indexed. Nyla's contribution to this book is immeasurable.

Tom C. Cooper,
Executive Editor

Alex B. Thiermann

Prologue

IOWA, located between two of the world's great rivers, is a name synonymous with agricultural fertility. Its good earth is the product of thousands of years of undisturbed prairie growth. It is a gently rolling land of wide horizons, wind-swept but with sheltering valleys — truly a land to nourish the soul as well as the body.

Its beauty lies not in the dramatic appeal of a Grand Canyon or Yellowstone. It has no mountains, and no sea. Rather, its beauty is more subtle. It lies in the towering bluffs of the Upper Iowa River, the ageless solitude of the Kettle Hole along the Little Sioux, the unchanging vistas of the Mississippi from the height of Pikes Peak. It can be found on a leisurely drive along a rural road amidst ripening fields of corn; a quiet canoe drift down a placid river; in a pinnacled summer thunderstorm, and even in the awesome power of a winter blizzard.

There is the orderly diversity of Iowa's cultural stock — the neat, clean streets of Dutch Orange City; the rugged pioneering spirit of Norwegian Decorah; the bustle of a Czech neighborhood in Cedar Rapids; the wooded hills of the Mesquaki Settlement; the solid self-assurance of the Amana Germans — all these and many more have fashioned here a state whose quality of life far outweighs its lack of scenic wonders.

This, then is a book about Iowa, a unique book by those best prepared to write it and illustrate it — some of the state's most knowledgeable scientists and competent photographers.

The 14 chapters have been arranged in three parts: Part I explains why the land looks as it does — how it got that way — and what the various natural factors are that influence its development. Part II covers the multiplicity of life on the land and in its waters, the plants, the animals, insects, birds, fish. Part III details the human experience.

The 32 authors have been selected from the state's three public universities and from many of its private educational institutions. Experts from some of the state's administrative agencies and from the private sector are also represented. All are recognized experts in their fields.

This book includes more than 325 photographs (315 of them in color) by 45 photographers. The pictures were chosen not only for their quality and beauty but for the ability to illustrate particular points in the text, and to add to the clarity of the exposition.

Though the articles are written by scientists, they are not couched in hard-to-understand scientific terms. Latin names have been avoided. The efforts of Executive Editor Tom C. Cooper have been aimed at ensuring that each article is scientifically accurate yet intelligible to the interested layman.

We hope that as you turn the following pages, you will find a volume worthy of representing the state of Iowa, a work that will retain its value throughout the years. Read and enjoy.

Otto Knauth

Tom C. Cooper

Contents

PART I
Iowa's Foundation 2

CHAPTER 1
Recorded in Rocks 8

CHAPTER 2
Glaciation 42

CHAPTER 3
Water 62

CHAPTER 4
Soils 78

CHAPTER 5
Weather and Climate 94

PART II
Living Iowa 116
    Iowa As It Was 122
    Natural Regions 126

CHAPTER 6
Plantlife 136

CHAPTER 7
Prairies 158

CHAPTER 8
Forests 180

CHAPTER 9
Wetlands 208

CHAPTER 10
Aquatic Life 230

CHAPTER 11
Wildlife 250

PART III
Man in Iowa 266

CHAPTER 12
Early Iowans 268

CHAPTER 13
Exploration and Settlement 284

CHAPTER 14
Evolution of a Conservation Ethic 304

Iowa Tomorrow 326
Epilogue 328
Authors 330
Index 332
Map of Iowa 342

PART I
Iowa's Foundation

geology,
glaciation,
water,
soils and
weather and climate.

Carl Kurtz

Tom C. Cooper

Carl Kurtz

CHAPTER ONE

RECORDED IN ROCKS
BY WAYNE I. ANDERSON

Carl Kurtz

Moss-clad sandstone bedrock is revealed in the Mississippi River bluffs in Clayton County. Polished and worn by running water in modern times, this sandstone was formed some 500 million years ago near the edge of a vast inland sea that covered most of North America.

(Previous Spread) Bold bluffs of limestone bedrock line the scenic Upper Iowa River in Winneshiek County, northeast Iowa. The fossilized remains of countless ancient sea creatures entombed in Iowa's bedrock reveal that our state has spent much of its past covered by warm shallow seas.

THIS LAND WE CALL IOWA has undergone dramatic changes in the 4.5 billion year history of the planet Earth. These changes produced a record of environments far different from that of present-day Iowa.

Our state once had a tropical climate and was covered by warm, shallow seas many times. Although we are now more than a thousand miles from the seas, hordes of marine creatures once crawled and swam in inland seas that washed over ancient Iowa. Beds of shark's teeth, mounds of coral, and many layers of sea shells have been unearthed in our state, mute testimony to the dramatic changes our land has experienced.

It may also be hard to imagine that Iowa, known the world over for its fertile land, was once a rocky terrain wrought by mountain building or that our state was at another time a salty tidal flat. Vast coastal swamps once occupied Iowa as well. Another fact about our state's past may seem equally incredible to some. Iowa has not always been situated at its present latitude! Our land was once much farther south, near the equator.

How do we know these things? The answer comes from the study of Iowa's foundation — our bedrock.

Carl Kurtz

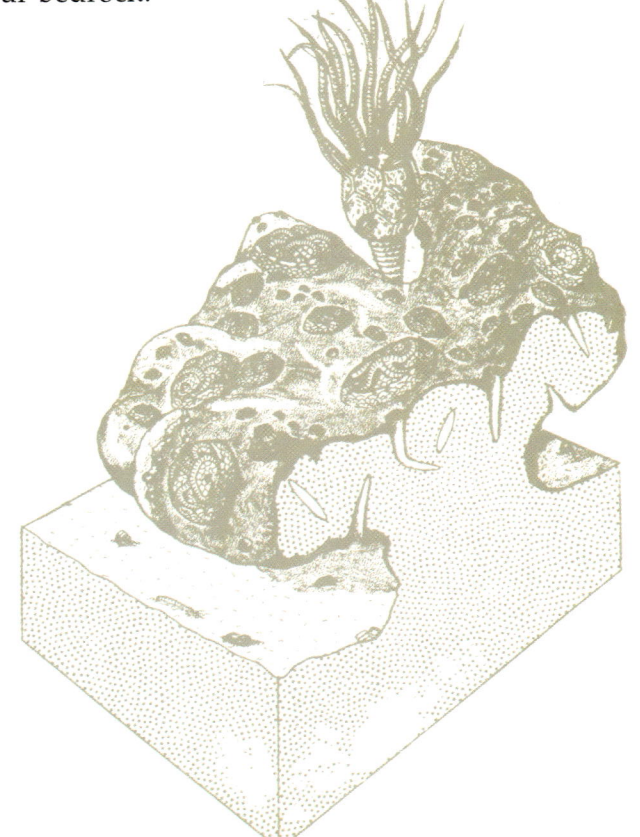

OUR LAYERED FOUNDATION provides important raw materials for Iowa's economy. It is the product of numerous geologic events. Most of our bedrock now lies buried beneath deposits of the Ice Age. In places, however, bedrock is exposed. For example, limestone is visible in roadcuts, cliffs, and in ravines and valleys throughout northeast Iowa; thick ledges of sandstone show up along the Des Moines River valley in central Iowa, and durable Sioux Quartzite is found at the surface in the prairie country of northwest Iowa. Gypsum, the bedrock at Fort Dodge, is quarried there for industrial uses. Limestone quarries abound in eastern Iowa, and several quarries in our state produce clay shale. Mines yield coal in southern Iowa.

Iowa's bedrock took hundreds of millions of years to form. The magnitude of geologic time is so great that it is difficult for most of us to comprehend. We measure human events in hours, days, weeks, months, years, and centuries, but geologic history is gauged by events that are most often measured in millions of years.

How fast does a sandstone rock crumble into grains of sand when exposed to the cycle of wind, rain, and freezing and thawing? It might take centuries before the accumulated change is detectable. How long does it take a 1-inch layer of limestone to accumulate on the floor of an inland sea. A century? A millenium?

How might we measure the rate of evolution of fossil fish found embedded in our bedrock? Certainly centuries will not do. Try millenia. Better yet, try millions of years.

This then is the pace of geologic time, in Iowa or anywhere on this planet.

The geologic time table is divided into four major eras — Precambrian (origin of life), Paleozoic (ancient life), Mesozoic (intermediate life), and Cenozoic (recent life).

In order to understand Iowa's geologic past, we must first fathom the geologic timetable. Let us compare events of geologic time, 4.5 billion years, to our 365-day calendar.

Most of the calendar year, Janu-

Slanted layers of sandstone in Dolliver State Park, Webster County, document the location and direction of flow of an ancient stream channel that coursed southwesterly across our state some 275 million years ago. Iowa's geographic setting then was similar in many ways to that of coastal Louisiana today.

Exquisitely-preserved crinoids, commonly referred to as stone flowers or sea lilies, are but one example of the remarkable fossil record preserved in our state's bedrock. Crinoids from Iowa, like these choice specimens from LeGrand in Marshall County, are displayed in many museums in this country and abroad.

(Far Right) These views show the position of continents in relation to each other and where the equator may have crossed them in the geologic past. The top view represents Late Paleozoic time (250 million years ago) when the landforms represented one giant super-continent. The bottom view is during Jurassic time (135 million years ago) when the continents were breaking apart and drifting toward their present locations.

Pete Krumhardt

ary to November 15, would be represented by the formation of rocks during Precambrian time. Iowa's oldest rocks are of Precambrian age, 1 to 2 billion years old. Iowa's abundant Paleozoic rocks are 230 million to 570 million years old and would be represented by a month's duration, November 15 to December 15. Mesozoic time was the Age of Dinosaurs and an interval for which Iowa's geologic record is somewhat incomplete. It would extend from December 15 to Christmas. Finally, Cenozoic time, heyday of the mammals, would comprise only one week of the calendar year. Iowa's Cenozoic record is incomplete and is represented by deposits of only the past 2.5 million years. On the scale of the calendar year, the Ice Age, a major event in Iowa's recent geologic past, is represented by only four hours. A mere five minutes represents the interval since continental glaciers melted from Iowa. Paleo-Indians were in North America then. Marquette and Joliet appeared at the confluence of the Wisconsin and Mississippi rivers on the eastern border of our state a few seconds before the end of our hypothetical year.

Geologists have reconstructed the positions of ancient continents, using a variety of data. In Paleozoic time, the continents were close together, forming a giant supercontinent. What is now North America was then near the equator. Much of Iowa's rock record formed there in warm shallow seas in tropical and subtropical settings. Later in Mesozoic time, the supercontinent split apart, and North America started to drift slowly toward its present position.

Looking backward to the time before Europeans settled Iowa, we see prairies and scattered forests as dominant elements of the landscape. Before that, during the Ice Age, glacial ice and evergreen forests alternately covered our state.

Before the Ice Age, in Mesozoic time, we see Iowa submerged beneath subtropical seas or occupied by salty lagoons and broad alluvial plains of great rivers. Coastal swamps and deltas, like those of present-day Louisiana, were present in Iowa in Late Paleozoic time. The thick deposits of dead vegetation that collected in these coastal settings later were transformed into coal. Warm, shallow seas invaded Iowa several times in Paleozoic time, leaving behind limestones and shales with exquisitely-preserved corals, shell fish, and other marine fossils.

The record of Iowa's oldest rocks, the Precambrian, is difficult to interpret, but events of the era are understood in general terms. Ancient Iowa was a sandy sea floor during part of Precambrian time. At other times, our state was a rift-valley system (a break in the earth's crust), somewhat comparable to the rift valley of present-day Africa. Dense dark rocks formed in the rift zone from lava flows and shallow bodies of molten magma. Still earlier in Precambrian time, Iowa was part of an ancient mountain belt in which granite and layered metamorphic rocks were formed. Yes, mountains in Iowa!

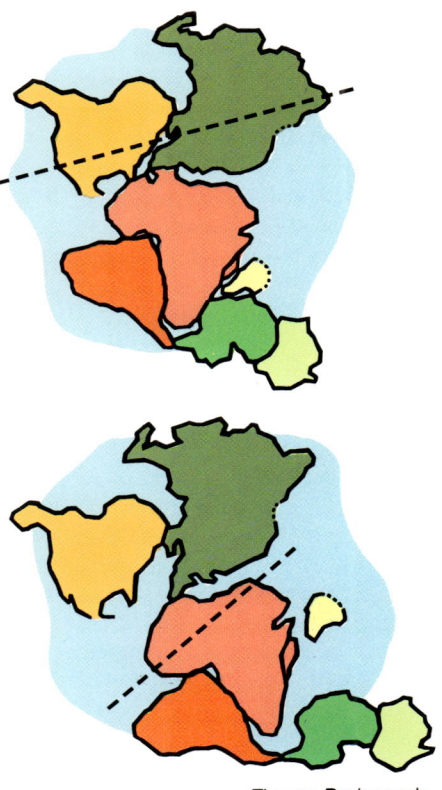

Thomas Rosborough

The Geologic Column

GEOLOGISTS have been able to piece together information about the thickness, distribution and composition of Iowa's sedimentary bedrock. Although the sedimentary rock record is thin and incomplete in northeast and northwest Iowa, it is nearly a mile thick in southwest Iowa. Remains of plants and animals embedded in the rocks and preserved as fossils help determine the relative ages of the rock layers.

Names for the divisions of geologic time (periods) and the rocks (systems) deposited during these periods of time make up the geologic column. Many of these strange-sounding names (Cambrian, Ordovician, Silurian, Devonian, etc.) came from the locality or tribal names in Europe where the geologic timetable was first established. Subsequently, these names were used elsewhere for rocks of similar ages.

Fossils tell us the relative age of rocks. For example, Devonian rocks in Iowa contain fossils nearly identical to those of Devonian rocks in Europe. Fossils found in Devonian rocks are more advanced than those in the underlying Silurian System, but less advanced than fossils in the overlying Mississippian System.

Although these fossils tell us that Devonian rocks are older than Mississippian rocks, or younger than Silurian rocks, the fossils do not tell us how many million years ago the Devonian rocks were formed. Information of this nature is obtained by studying radioactive chemical elements that occur in rocks. Some radioactive elements are like atomic clocks, and they can be used to date rocks. The dates are given in terms of millions or billions of years before the present. Special care must be taken to obtain samples that are suitable to use in radiometric dating. Most rocks cannot be dated by this method, but a sufficient number of radiometric dates have been applied to the geologic column so that we have a reasonably good understanding of the dimension of geologic time.

Our account of Iowa's geologic past will focus primarily on larger groupings of rocks (systems) deposited during vast time intervals. On occasion, specific rock formations, groups or series will be discussed to illustrate key points about Iowa's geologic past.

To geologists, formations are the basic unit used to work out the sequence of the earth's history in a region. They are mappable bodies of rock and have both vertical and horizontal dimensions. Formations are distinguished on the basis of their composition, and they can be traced laterally for some distance. The rocks that comprise a formation generally reflect deposition in the same or closely-related environments.

Geologists have divided Iowa's rock column into more than 100 formations, but we will not discuss all of them here.

ERA	PERIOD (Millions of Years Ago)
CENOZOIC	QUATERNARY 2.5 - 3.0
	TERTIARY
MESOZOIC	65 CRETACEOUS
	130 JURASSIC
	185 TRIASSIC
PALEOZOIC	230 PERMIAN
	265 PENNSYLVANIAN
	310 MISSISSIPPIAN
	355 DEVONIAN
	410 SILURIAN
	425 ORDOVICIAN
	475 CAMBRIAN
PRECAMBRIAN	570 PRECAMBRIAN
	Part of Precambrian Omitted
	4,500

Selected Series, Groups, or Formations	Major Gaps in Iowa's Rock Record		
			Rise of Man and the Great Ice Age
			Age of Mammals
Carlile, Greenhorn, Graneros, Dakota			Mountain Building Begins in the Western USA
Fort Dodge			Dinosaurs and Other Reptiles Rule the Earth
			Modern Atlantic Ocean Starts to Form and Continental Drift Begins
Virgilian Series, Missourian Series	Des Moinesian Series, Morrowan Series		Coal-Measures Flora Flourishes in Coastal Swamps
Warsaw, Keokuk, Burlington	Gilmore City, Hampton		Age of Crinoids
Yellow Spring, Lime Creek, Shell Rock	State Quarry, Cedar Valley, Wapsipinicon		Age of Fish
Gower, Hopkinton			Reefs Develop in Shallow Seas
Maquoketa, Galena, Platteville, St. Peter			Diverse Invertebrate Life in Widespread Seas
Prairie du Chien			
Jordan			Age of Trilobites
			Primitive sea life present
Sioux Quartzite			
			Formation of the Earth's Oldest Rocks

17

Iowa's Bedrock

IOWA'S BEDROCK was deposited in layers and resembles a large stack of pancakes. As seen in a roadcut or quarry wall, the layers appear flat but, in reality, most of them are gently inclined.

In eastern Iowa, bedrock layers slant toward the southwest. In extreme northwest Iowa, rock layers are inclined downward to the southeast. Because the state's bedrock has been gently tilted and subsequently eroded, different ages of rocks are exposed. In general, Iowa's bedrock gets progressively younger as we travel from northeast to the southwest. The oldest bedrock (Precambrian) is revealed in the extreme northwest corner of the state, but it is also present near Manson in north-central Iowa, an area that represents a puzzle to geologists.

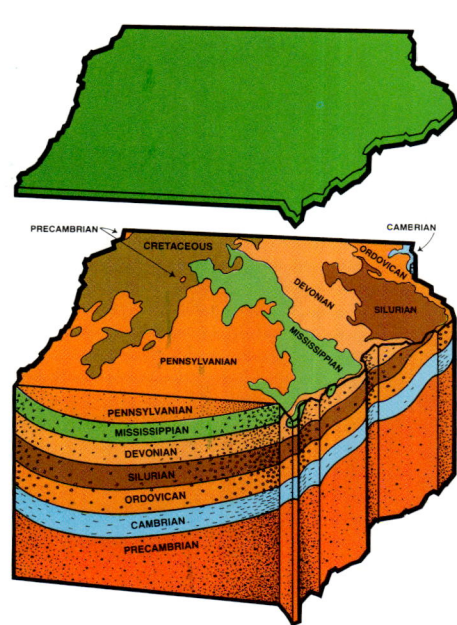

(Above) Block diagram showing distribution of our state's bedrock. In general, Iowa's rocks sag down to the southwest to form a large basinal structure.
(Right) Bedrock is a prime contributor to our scenery. Here at Woodman Hollow State Preserve in Webster County, sandstone ledges form picturesque cliffs along the Des Moines River.

Carl Kurtz

The Precambrian Era

THE PRECAMBRIAN SYSTEM is complex; it consists primarily of crystalline igneous (formed by molten rock) and metamorphic (compacted and altered) rocks. Often termed basement rocks, these rocks have a dense, nonporous texture and generally lie at considerable distances below the surface.

Approximately 40 wells have probed our state's Precambrian basement. From these wells, we learn that Iowa's Precambrian record contains quartzite, banded and layered metamorphic rocks, and assorted igneous rocks. Common igneous rocks include granite, basalt (fine-grained igneous rock), and gabbro (a more coarse-grained igneous rock).

Granitic rocks are associated with layered metamorphic rocks. Such rocks commonly form several miles below the earth's surface in the root zones of mountain belts under intense heat and pressure. Some of the granitic rocks have been dated radiometrically as 1.3 to 1.4 billion years old. Other granites are probably older still, perhaps as old as 2 billion years.

The occurrence of granite and associated metamorphic rocks in our state's subsurface reveals that ancient Iowa was once part of a complex mountain belt or belts. These mountains were leveled by erosion long before Paleozoic seas inundated our area some 550 million years ago.

Precambrian rocks are well exposed to the north of Iowa in northern Minnesota, northern Wisconsin, and Michigan's upper peninsula. Geological information obtained in these states can be applied to Iowa. The formation of basalt and gabbro was associated with an ancient rift zone (a linear depression where the Earth's crust was pulled apart). Dark-colored lava oozed out along the rift to form layer upon layer of basalt, while coarse-textured rocks like gabbro formed at the base of the rift zone from magma (molten rock material) that cooled more slowly. Radiometric dating has established that the rocks of this ancient rift system formed about 1 billion years ago.

In the Lake Superior area, copper occurs in rocks of the Precambrian

Wayne I. Anderson

(Below) **Iowa's oldest exposed bedrock, the Sioux Quartzite, can be viewed in Gitchie Manitou State Preserve in the northwest corner of our state. Sand grains that comprise this ancient and durable rock formation were deposited on the floor of a sandy basin more than a billion years ago.**

Carl Kurtz

rift system, and there is reason to expect that similar rocks in Iowa might also bear some mineral wealth. However, only limited exploratory drilling programs have been undertaken in Iowa.

The Sioux Quartzite, Iowa's only exposed Precambrian bedrock, peeks through the loamy soil in the prairie country of northwest Iowa. Exposures are visible in Gitchie Manitou State Preserve in Lyon County. In addition, quartzite has been recovered from fairly shallow wells in Lyon and Sioux counties.

Red mudstone, which is interbedded with Sioux Quartzite in southwest Minnesota 35 miles north of the Iowa border, has served as a source of pipestone for Indian craftsmen for centuries. Sioux Indians consider pipestone, highly prized as a trade good, a spiritual item, and Indian tribes long have attached spiritual significance to the pipestone region. Gitchie Manitou State Preserve derives its name from an Indian word for "God."

The Manson Disturbed Area, a puzzling occurrence of near surface Precambrian rocks, is found in Calhoun and Pocahontas counties in northcentral Iowa, where a 1.5-square-mile area of broken and crushed Precambrian basement rock lies less than 100 feet beneath the earth's surface, buried only by glacial deposits. Deformed Mesozoic strata, also occur in the area. Glacial deposits that overlie the disturbed Precambrian and Mesozoic rocks are not disturbed, however, so the date of the deformation can be placed in preglacial times.

Two explanations have been offered for the Manson Disturbed Area. Some geologists speculate that the Precambrian basement in the Manson area was shoved upward by forces from within the earth — perhaps by volcanic processes. Others suggest that the area was smashed by a meteorite in preglacial times.

Meteorite-impact craters do display battered and broken rocks similar to those recovered from well cores in the Manson area, but they also contain special minerals that form by impact. These minerals haven't been found in cores from Manson so the theory is not unequivocally accepted. The origin of the Manson Disturbed Area remains a mystery.

Regardless of their origin, the Manson area rocks are of value to man. These crushed and broken rocks serve as reservoirs for groundwater, and wells drilled into the Precambrian basement supply the town of Manson with an abundance of good, soft water. Precambrian basement rocks usually yield little water because they are dense and nonporous, but the Manson rocks are an exception.

Cambrian Era

WORN AND ABRADED by both wind and water, the sand grains that compose Iowa's Cambrian rocks (500 million years old) are made chiefly of well-rounded quartz. Quartz, a union of silicon and oxygen, is a stable and abundant mineral — the material of which common sand is largely composed. While other mineral grains deteriorate and decompose, quartz is so stable that it survives countless cycles of weathering and erosion. It is a major component of sedimentary rocks.

The sand of Iowa's Cambrian rocks was deposited in shallow water near the edge of a vast sea that covered North America some 500 million years ago. What was Iowa like then? The Gulf Coast of Texas serves as a model. There, sand is abundant, both as beach and shoreline deposits and on the adjacent continental shelf. Waves roll the sand around relentlessly, producing rounded grains of uniform size. Mud, kept in suspension by wave agitation, is carried out to sea. Thus, sand is concentrated along the beaches and at the edge of the sea.

We can see exposures of Cambrian sandstones in Allamakee County in extreme northeast Iowa where Cambrian rocks form the bedrock. Cambrian strata are also found in the subsurface throughout most of the state. The porous sandstones make ideal reservoirs for water, soaking up and storing water much like sponges. Many Iowa communities obtain their drinking water from wells drilled into Cambrian sandstones.

Sandstones of Cambrian age are exposed along the bluffs of the Mississippi River valley in Allamakee County in northeast Iowa. Deposited by wave action near the margin of a shallow sea, the sand grains of Iowa's Cambrian sandstones display remarkable purity and roundness. Many Iowa communities recover their drinking water from wells drilled into Cambrian sandstones.

Carl Kurtz

(Far left) **Limestone bluffs along the Upper Iowa River, near Bluffton in Winneshiek County reveal the layered nature of Iowa's bedrock. Rocks shown here belong to the Galena Group.**

(Left) **The St. Peter Sandstone holds up this scenic waterfall in Pikes Peak State Park in Clayton County.**

Carl Kurtz

Ordovician Rocks

THE ORDOVICIAN ROCKS (475 to 430 million years old), deposits of an extensive sea that covered most of the continent, reflect deposition in shallow water. Such rocks are well exposed in northeast Iowa as bluffs along the Mississippi, Turkey and Upper Iowa rivers. Galena Group, the middle portion of Iowa's Ordovician rock record, forms prominent cliffs and distinctive chimney-like columns along the Upper Iowa River in Winneshiek County. Many canoeists are familiar with this spectacular scenery. In addition, beds of the Galena Group make up the bold palisades along the Mississippi River near Dubuque and contribute to the beauty of the northeast Iowa landscape at several other locations.

Pioneer geologist David Dale Owen, who in 1839-1840 made one of the first geological surveys of Iowa, described the topography associated with the Galena beds as follows: "These mural escarpments, exhibiting every variety of form, give to the otherwise monotonous character of the landscape in Iowa a varied and picturesque appearance. Sometimes, they may be seen in the distance, rising from the rolling hills of the prairie like ruined castles, moss-grown under the hand of time."

Rocks of the Prairie du Chien Group, the base of our Ordovician record, display crinkly, cabbage-like forms, structures that represent sediment that was trapped on the surfaces of algal colonies and mats. Nearly identical algal structures form today on shallow, sunlit floors of subtropical seas; surely the ancient algal structures found in Iowa's Ordovician rock record formed in similar settings.

Rocks of the Prairie du Chien Group also contain oolites, another indicator of shallow-water conditions. Oolites are laminated deposits of lime that formed around a sand grain, shell fragment, or other particle. Oolites are roughly spherical in shape and sand-size in dimension. Normally, they are composed of concentric layers of calcium carbonate. Today, oolites form in warm, shallow seas, where waters are saturated with lime and agitated by waves.

After the beds of the Prairie du Chien Group were deposited, the seas retreated, and Iowa's setting became that of a low coastal plain, exposing these rocks to weathering and erosion.

In Middle Ordovician time, the sea again washed over Iowa. A blanket of clean, white sand was deposited along the leading edge of this sea, producing the widespread quartz sandstone known as St. Peter Sandstone. You can see the St. Peter Sandstone today at Sand Cave and Pictured Rocks in Pikes Peak State Park in Clayton County, where it is cemented with brightly-colored oxides of iron. Sand is excavated for commercial use from the St. Peter in Clayton County in more than 50 acres of underground excavations. Natural gas is stored underground in porous sandstone near Redfield in Dallas County and near Keota in Washington County.

As the Middle Ordovician shoreline inched slowly northward beyond our state, the sandy, beach environment that gave rise to the St. Peter Sandstone was replaced by a marine shelf, where muds and carbonates formed. These marine muds and carbonates (limestones and dolomites) now comprise the Glenwood Shale, Platteville Formation, and the Galena Group.

Rocks of these Ordovician units are literally crammed with fossils. All major invertebrate groups are represented. Common fossils include bryozoa, corals, brachiopods, snails, trilobites, and nautiloid cephalopods.

Carbonate rocks of the Galena Group have undergone extensive solution in northeast Iowa, producing caves and sinkholes. Spectacular Cold Water Cave in Winneshiek County is one such example.

Ordovician rocks have served as hosts for lead and zinc mineralization in the Dubuque area and in adjacent southwest Wisconsin and northwest Illinois. The Dubuque area was one of our nation's principal mineral districts in the mid-1800s. Though the area has no active mines today, zinc was mined in nearby southwest Wisconsin on a limited basis until just a few years ago.

Thin layers of altered volcanic ash are present in the Galena Group. Eight layers have been documented, and others may be discovered in the future. The ash apparently came from volcanoes in the Taconic Mountains, an active mountain belt situated along the east coast during Ordovician time.

In Late Ordovician time, the seas over Iowa grew murky as large quantities of mud were washed into them from the Taconic Mountains. Muddy deposits of this sea comprise the shales and impure carbonates of the Upper Ordovician Maquoketa Formation.

The thick shale sequence of the Maquoketa Formation is highly impervious to fluids and has been used to store liquified petroleum gas at three subsurface sites in Iowa. Two of the storage facilities are in Johnson County; the third is in Polk County at the southeast edge of Des Moines.

Colorful speleothems of massive flowstone decorate the walls and ceiling of Iowa's most spectacular cave, Cold Water Cave in Winneshiek County. This is a "living cave," where dripstone and flowstone features continue to form by an almost imperceptibly slow process.

Tom Wagner

"The Gallery" section of Cold Water Cave contains a majestic mass of flowstone; delicate sodastraw deposits hang from fractures in the ceiling.

Lead mining from the Galena Group in the Dubuque area during the mid 1800s is depicted in this drawing from the work of pioneer Midwestern geologist David Dale Owen. (From the Samuel Calvin collection, University of Iowa.)

Old red cedars on limestone palisades along the Cedar River in Palisades-Kepler State Park south of Cedar Rapids.

Carl Kurtz

Silurian — Abundance of Dolomite

(Top) Bealer's Quarry, about 1900. During the last half of the 19th century, building stone was quarried from several sites in Iowa. Today, a single stone quarry operates at Stone City. (From the Samuel Calvin collection, University of Iowa.)

THE SEA COVERED Iowa during much of Silurian time, leaving behind layers of limestone and dolomite (magnesium-bearing rock, similar to limestone). Water depth in the Silurian sea fluctuated in response to global sea level changes brought about by glaciation and deglaciation in the Southern Hemisphere.

The seas were clear and, as during Ordovician time, teemed with life. Brachiopods, cephalopods, corals, and crinoids were particularly abundant. Crinoids are often called "sea lilies" because they are plant-like in appearance. Actually they are cousins to the starfish. Crinoids and corals produced reef-like masses (bioherms) on the Silurian sea floor. The Cedar River cuts through the core of one such bioherm at Palisades-Kepler State Park in Linn County.

Silurian formations are more resistant to erosion than the soft shales of the Maquoketa Formation, which they overlie. The result is a resistant ridge-like landform called the Silurian Escarpment, one of northeast Iowa's most prominent landscape features. Resistant Silurian strata have a similar effect on the landscape in states to the east of Iowa. Niagara Falls in New York is the most notable example.

Silurian formations are responsible for scenic features in several of our state parks, such as Backbone, Bellevue, Bixby, Brush Creek Canyon, Echo Valley, Maquoketa Caves, and Palisades-Kepler.

At several sites in eastern Iowa, the Hopkinton Formation contains hordes of brachiopods. In some rock exposures, all of the brachiopods are oriented in the same way, with their shell margins upward; this suggests that the brachiopods were preserved in living positions, attached to the sea floor.

Most of the brachiopods are represented by internal molds, sediment that filled the interior of the shells. This sediment filling resembles, in a superficial way, a pig's foot, and it is not uncommon for a novice fossil collector to discover a fossil pig's foot in the Silurian rocks of eastern Iowa.

During the late 1800s and early 1900s, the Silurian Gower Formation was quarried for quicklime, which was used extensively as mortar in building.

Today building stone is quarried from the Gower Formation at Stone City in Jones County, as it has been for several decades.

When interior seas receded in North America at the close of Silurian time, Silurian and Ordovician strata were exposed to the forces of weathering and erosion. Iowa remained high and dry until Middle Devonian time, when an arm of the sea again covered the continental interior. Devonian rocks of marine origin were deposited in Iowa.

Most of the buildings of the Iowa Men's Reformatory at Anamosa were constructed from stone quarried from local Silurian bedrock by convict labor. The quarry industry at nearby Stone City once employed over 1,000 men and served as one of eastern Iowa's most important industries during the last half of the 19th century.

Devonian — Rise of the Fish

IOWA HAS NO Early Devonian rocks, because the state was above the sea then and its surface rocks were subjected to weathering and erosion. By Middle Devonian time, aproximately 375 million years ago, inland seas washed over the state again, leaving an extensive sedimentary record. As in earlier Paleozoic periods, the climate was warm, the setting subtropical, and the sea supported an abundance of life. Marine muds, carbonate sediments, evaporite minerals, and countless fossil remains were deposited in the warm Devonian seas and later converted into rock.

Today, Devonian rocks are exposed in a belt extending northwestward from the Mississippi River at Muscatine, to Iowa City, Waterloo, and Mason City. Devonian rocks are quarried for a variety of purposes. Clay shale is used in the manufacture of brick and tile; gypsum is used for plaster and building board, and limestone is crushed for road aggregate and for use in concrete, cement rock, and quicklime.

Rocks of the Wapsipinicon Formation formed on broad mudflats and in shallow restricted seas. At times, the sea was abnormally salty and devoid of life.

Gypsum deposits of the Wapsipinicon Formation are mined in southeastern Iowa near Mediapolis from 600 feet below the earth's surface.

Whereas, restricted seas and arid tidal flats existed during deposition of the Wapsipinicon beds, more typical marine conditions prevailed during the deposition of the Cedar Valley Formation. Limestone and dolomite constitute the bulk of the Cedar Valley Formation, although evaporites are known from the subsurface. Well-preserved fossils are common in the beds of the Cedar Valley Formation.

Locally in eastern Iowa (near Iowa City, Independence, and Waterloo), fossil corals and sponges are sufficiently abundant so as to constitute entire beds of rock. One of these beds can be traced for more than 40 miles and has a width of at least 20 miles. Occurrences like this are the remains of vast underwater "meadows," where corals and sponges flourished on the warm shallow sea floor.

Upper Devonian rocks of Iowa include the State Quarry, Shell Rock, and Lime Creek formations, and the Yellow Spring Group. The State Quarry Formation is found only in Johnson County and represents tidal-channel deposits that were laid down on the eroded surface of the underlying Cedar Valley Formation.

Named for exposures in a state-operated quarry, near North Liberty, the State Quarry Formation furnished part of the building stone used in the construction of the Old Capitol on the University of Iowa campus. Abundant fish fossils (bones, teeth, and spines) comprise "bone beds" in the State Quarry Formation. Fish remains are also known from other Devonian rocks in Iowa.

The Devonian Period is sometimes called the Age of the Fishes. Although many of the Devonian fish were small, some were whoppers. An armored fish from the Devonian of Ohio measured nearly 25 feet long.

Certain fish, such as sharks, had internal frameworks of cartilage, rather than bony skeletons. Cartilaginous material is not generally preserved in fossil record, but teeth are because they are composed of resistant calcium phosphate. Shark's teeth are common in Iowa's Devonian rocks.

The Shell Formation, named for exposures along the Shell Rock River in Cerro Gordo and Floyd counties, has a limited distribution; it is known only from a five-county region in northcentral Iowa.

A remarkably preserved fauna was recovered from the Shell Rock Formation near Nora Springs in Floyd County, where bottom-dwelling creatures were preserved in growth positions. Such deposits are relatively rare and especially treasured by scientists because they give many clues to the environment and habitat requirements of fossil organisms.

The Lime Creek Formation lies on the Shell Rock Formation where that formation is present and on the Cedar Valley Formation elsewhere.

Courtesy, Field Museum of Natural History, Chicago.

Composed of shale and impure limestone, the Lime Creek beds formed on a muddy marine shelf. Fossils weather free from the formation in Cerro Gordo and Floyd counties, providing some of the best fossil collecting in the state.

In addition to readily visible fossils, the Lime Creek beds also contain fossils that are too small to be seen with the unaided eye. These microfossils can be recovered on fine sieves

and studied by use of a microscope.

Iowa's Yellow Spring Group is represented by shale, siltstone, and impure dolomite. Known mainly from subsurface studies, these beds were deposited on a shallow muddy sea floor when large quantities of mud washed into the sea from a land area along the eastern edge of the continent. Limited surface exposures of the Yellow Spring Group occur in northcentral Iowa (Butler, Cerro Gordo, and Franklin counties) and in southeastern Iowa (Des Moines and Washington counties). Conodonts, spores, brachiopods, fish parts, and assorted microfossils are found in the Yellow Spring Group but, for the most part, the rocks are not abundant in fossils.

Restoration of a Middle Devonian seafloor, representative of conditions during time of deposition of the Cedar Valley Formation. The environmental setting shown contains crinoids, corals, bryozoa, nautiloid cephalopods, brachiopods, trilobites and snails.

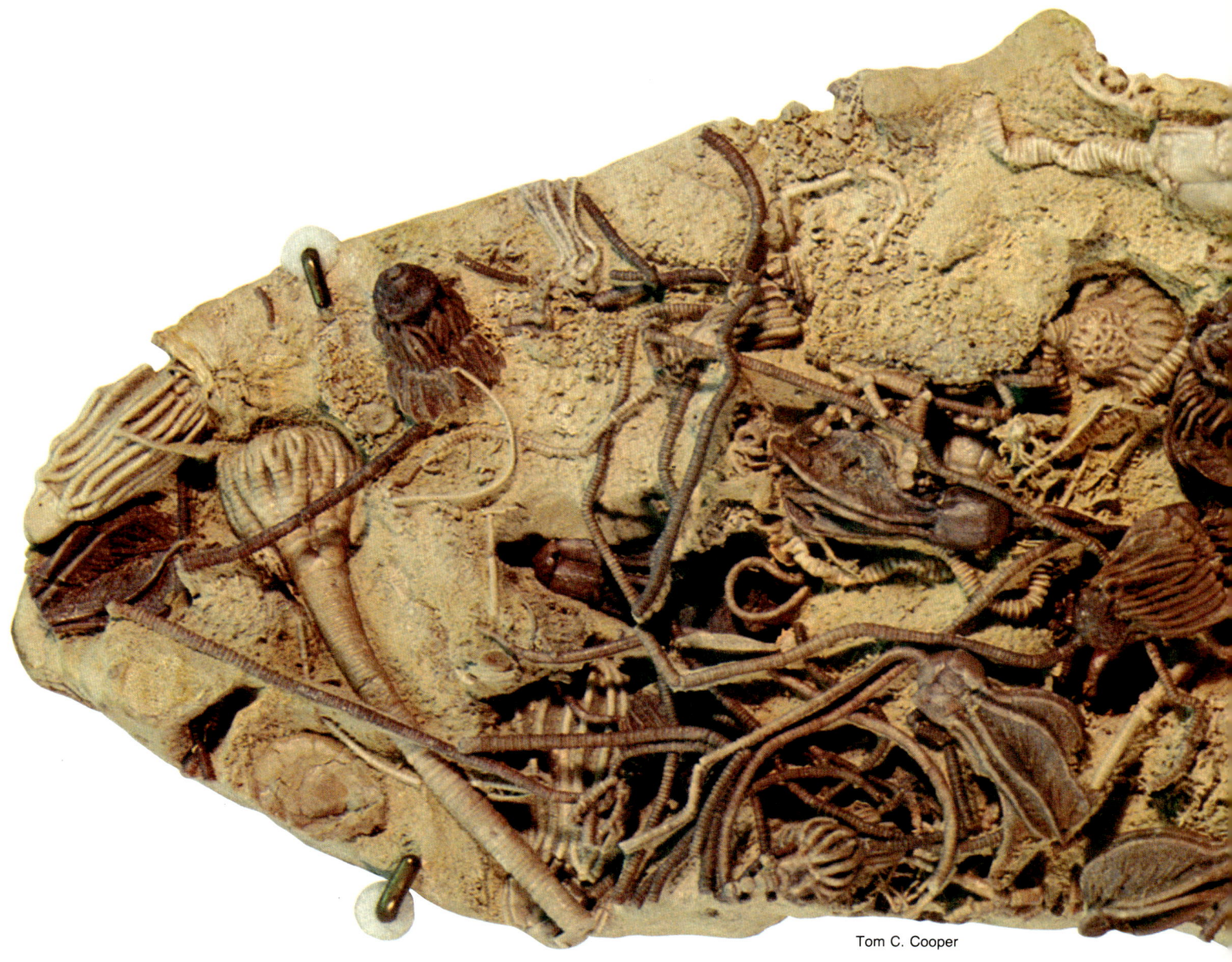
Tom C. Cooper

Mississippian — Age of Crinoids

SHALLOW SEAS occupied the interior of the North American continent once again during the Mississippian Period (350 to 310 million years ago). These were the last of the widespread limestone-producing seas to invade the interior of the continent. At later times, other seas covered portions of the continental interior, but they were not as widespread as the Mississippian seas.

Small quantities of mud, silt, and sand washed into the Mississippian seas from uplifted areas within the continental interior, but the seas were clear most of the time. Limestone was the chief deposit of these warm, shallow seas. Some of the limestones are composed almost exclusively of fossil fragments — the broken and crushed remains of brachiopod shells, bryozoan colonies, and crinoid stems. Portions of some of Iowa's Mississippian formations are composed almost exclusively of crinoidal debris. Oolites are also abundant in Mississippian rocks.

The Mississippian outcrop area constitutes a diagonal belt, 20 to 40 miles wide, extending from Lee and Des Moines counties in the southeast corner of the state, northwest to Hancock and Humboldt counties in northern Iowa. Exposures of Mississippian strata in southeast Iowa are particularly noteworthy. Together with exposures along the Mississippi Valley in western Illinois and eastern Missouri these rocks constitute important reference sections. The Mississippian System takes its name from these exposures.

Eleven formations constitute Iowa's Mississippian System. They are the McCraney, Prospect Hill, Starr's Cave, Hampton, Gilmore City, Burlington, Keokuk, Warsaw, Spergen, St. Louis, and Ste. Genevieve formations. We will describe five of them (space does not allow for a discussion of all eleven).

The Hampton Formation, named for exposures near Hampton in northcentral Iowa, is known for the many fine crinoids that it has yielded. Preeminent among crinoid collectors (who collected from the Hampton Formation) was B. H. Beane (1879-1966) of Le Grand.

Beane grew up on a farm adjacent to a limestone quarry near Le Grand. Crinoids, called "stone flowers" by quarry workers, were discovered in the quarry about five years before Beane was born. As a boy, he became curious about the work of paleontologists who visited the quarry to collect exquisite Le Grand crinoids. Later, Beane himself made some of the finest discoveries in all of paleontology. He recovered many slabs of limestone that contained crinoids preserved essentially intact, and he painstakingly removed the stony matrix from around them with simple tools such as needles and toothbrushes. Crinoid-bearing slabs that Beane collected and prepared are on display in museums all over the world. The rarest of Beane's discoveries was a large slab that con-

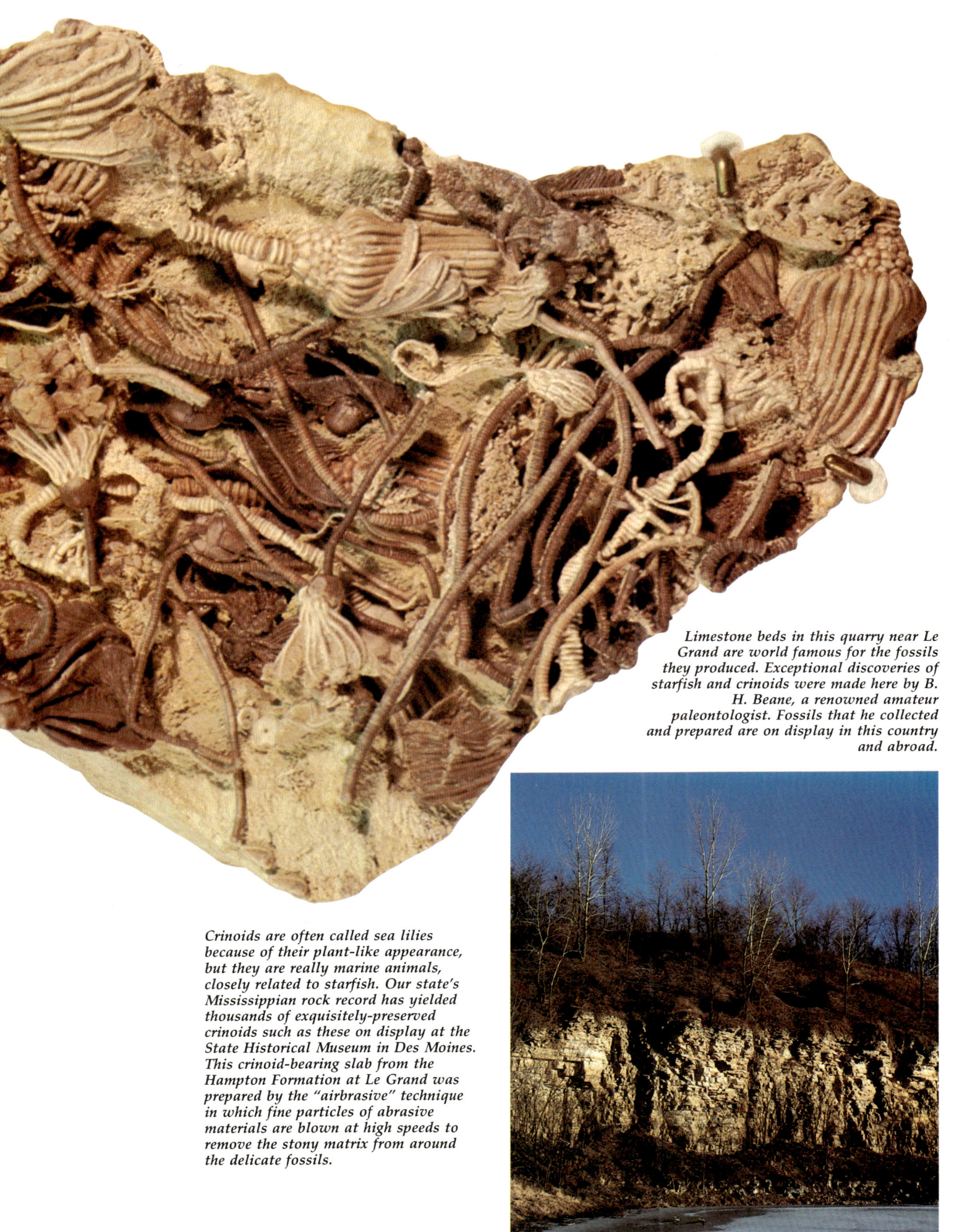

Limestone beds in this quarry near Le Grand are world famous for the fossils they produced. Exceptional discoveries of starfish and crinoids were made here by B. H. Beane, a renowned amateur paleontologist. Fossils that he collected and prepared are on display in this country and abroad.

Crinoids are often called sea lilies because of their plant-like appearance, but they are really marine animals, closely related to starfish. Our state's Mississippian rock record has yielded thousands of exquisitely-preserved crinoids such as these on display at the State Historical Museum in Des Moines. This crinoid-bearing slab from the Hampton Formation at Le Grand was prepared by the "airbrasive" technique in which fine particles of abrasive materials are blown at high speeds to remove the stony matrix from around the delicate fossils.

Tom C. Cooper

tained 183 starfish, 12 sea urchins, and 2 trilobites. This magnificent slab is now on display at the Iowa State Historical Museum in Des Moines.

The Gilmore City Formation overlies the Hampton Formation, and it, too, has yielded some exceptional crinoids. Spiny echinoids have been recovered also. Named for the town on the border of Humboldt and Pocahontas counties, the Gilmore City limestones are almost pure calcium carbonate. These beds are quarried for commercial uses near this town which bills itself as the limestone capital of Iowa. Gilmore City beds are quarried at Humboldt and Alden as well.

Rocks of the Burlington and Keokuk formations occur above the Gilmore City Formation. The Burlington and Keokuk formations were named for exposures along the bluffs of the Mississippi River in southeast Iowa. Both formations can be traced laterally into adjacent states, and their names appear often in the literature of Midwestern geology.

Crinoids from the Keokuk and Burlington formations drew Charles Wachsmuth and Frank Springer into paleontology. Both men, largely self-trained in paleontology, became intrigued by the curious sea lilies that were found in southeast Iowa. Springer (1848-1927) grew up in Wapello and later practiced law in Burlington. He collaborated with Charles Wachsmuth (1829-1896), a resident of Burlington, in a number of monumental publications on crinoids.

The noted nauralist and conservationist Aldo Leopold, author of *A Sand County Almanac*, and *Round River* described Wachsmuth, a fellow townsman, as follows:

"When I was a boy, there was an old German merchant who lived in a little cottage in our town. On Sundays he used to go out and knock chips off the limestone ledges along the Mississippi, and he had a great tonnage of these chips all labeled and catalogued. The chips contained little fossil stems of some defunct water creatures called crinoids. The townspeople regarded this gentle old fellow as just a little bit abnormal, but harmless. One day the newspaper reported the arrival of certain titled strangers. It was whispered that these visitors were great scientists. Some of them were from foreign lands, and some among the world's leading paleontologists. They came to visit the harmless old man and to hear his pronouncements on crinoids, and they accepted these pronouncements as law. When the old German died, the town awoke to the fact that he was a world authority of his subject, a creator of knowledge, a maker of scientific history. He was a great man — a man beside whom the local captains of industry were mere bushwhackers. His collection went to a national museum, and his name is known in all the nations of the earth."

Rocks of the Warsaw Formation overlie the Keokuk Formation. Composed largely of shale and impure dolomite, the Warsaw beds are loaded with geodes. In fact, the region around Keokuk is one of the most renowned geode localities in the world and is a favored collecting area for geologists, museum curators, and rock-and-mineral enthusiasts. In the Keokuk region, geodes weather free from the Warsaw Formation and occur in abundance in stream beds. Objects of remarkable beauty, geodes are coveted by collectors. A variety of minerals line the interiors of Keokuk geodes. The geode became the official state rock in 1967 after action by the Iowa General Assembly.

Mississippian time in Iowa closed with deposition of the Spergen, St. Louis, and Ste. Genevieve formations. All are of marine origin.

The seas withdrew from our state at the end of Middle Mississippian time, exposing rocks of Mississippian age to weathering and erosion in Late Mississippian and Early Pennsylvanian times. In Iowa, a major unconformity (erosion surface) separates the Mississippian System from the overlying Pennsylvanian System.

©Copyright 1949, Oxford University Press, Inc.

Intricate bands and colorful patterns characterize this "coldwater agate" geode from the Keswick area in Keokuk County. Geodes are abundant in the Mississippian bedrock of our state.

Bill Witt

Pennsylvanian — Battle of Land and Sea

Ledges of Pennsylvanian sandstone at Ledges State Park in Boone County are the deposits of ancient streams that developed their channels across broad alluvial and deltaic plains some 300 million years ago.

IN PENNSYLVANIAN TIME (310 to 265 million years ago), Iowa lay near the edge of a shallow sea. The climate then was tropical to subtropical, and lush vegetation grew in great coastal forests and swamps — almost at the water's edge and, for millions of years, the land "battled" the sea.

The shoreline shifted dozens of times. Some of these shifts were caused by worldwide changes in sea level brought about by the waxing and waning of continental ice caps in the Southern Hemisphere. Other shifts resulted when large fan-shaped deltas grew seaward. As a result, Iowa's Pennsylvanian record is comprised of both marine and nonmarine beds. In places the rocks occur interbedded, representing alternating episodes of marine and nonmarine deposition.

Iowa's Pennsylvanian record is complex and diverse, consisting of interbedded sequences of shale, siltstone, sandstone, clay, coal, and limestone. More than 70 formations are represented in the system, and the preponderance of formation names illustrate this rock record is indeed highly varied.

These Pennsylvanian formations have been assigned to larger units, called groups. Groups, in turn, are assignable to still larger divisions, called series. Iowa's Pennsylvanian rocks are in four series of ascending order: Morrowan, Desmoinesian, Missourian, and Virgilian.

Rocks of the Morrowan and Desmoinesian series are composed primarily of dark carbonaceous shale, clay, and siltstone. Massive sandstone beds, coal seams of commercial importance, and thin layers of limestone are known, too.

Sandstone beds form rocky ledges and prominent cliffs in Dolliver State Park in Webster County, Ledges State Park in Boone County, and at Wildcat Den State Park in Muscatine County. These sandstones represent complex stream channels developed on deltaic plains adjacent to the Pennsylvanian seas.

Most of Iowa's coal has come from seams found in the Desmoinesian Series. These seams represent altered vegetation of ancient coastal swamps that were once widespread in southern Iowa.

The Missourian Series is composed chiefly of shale and limestone. Only minor coal seams, unimportant economically, are known. Marine conditions dominated during deposition of the Missourian Series, and numerous brachiopods, corals, foraminifera, mollusks, conodonts, fish remains, and calcareous algae are known.

The Virgilian Series contains both marine and nonmarine strata. Shales, siltstones, and limestones are present. Coal from the Virgilian Series has been mined in Adams, Page, and Taylor counties.

Pennsylvanian rocks provide important economic products in our state. Limestone quarries in Madison County furnish rock for cement plants in Des Moines. Shale has been used in the manufacture of brick and tile products, and coal has a long history of use in Iowa and elsewhere.

The quantity of energy stored in the vast buried coal swamps of Pennsylvanian age is enormous. Energy derived from the combustion of such coal powered the Industrial Revolution in Europe and North America. Pennsylvanian-age coals still constitute one of the largest reservoirs of stored energy in the world; billions of tons of this valuable energy source are present in the bedrock of our state.

Lichen-covered sandstone beds of Pennsylvanian age constitute the bedrock at Woodman Hollow State Preserve in Webster County.

Carl Kurtz

Thin layers of coal and sandstone alternate in a repetitive manner in this exposure of Pennsylvanian bedrock, Iowa River valley, Hardin County. Our state's coal beds were formed in Pennsylvanian time in lush coastal swamps where vegetation grew the year around.

Carl Kurtz

Formation of Coal

COAL, a combustible rock which can be ignited and burned, forms by the transformation of vegetation. Formation of peat, partly-altered plant material, is a first stage in the process.

In Pennsylvanian time, peat formed in poorly-drained coastal swamps, where groundwater levels were high, protecting the vegetable debris of peat from decay. It is estimated that approximately 10 feet of peat are needed to produce a foot of bituminous coal. Surely the formation of coal seams of commercial value required enormous amounts of Pennsylvanian vegetation. What was the nature of this vegetation?

The Pennsylvanian coal swamps of Iowa supported a jungle-like growth of scaly lycopod trees (ancestors of modern club mosses), tree ferns, and mangrove-like trees. True ferns, seed ferns, and ancient rushes provided a luxurious undergrowth. Conditions were tropical to subtropical, and vegetation grew the year around.

In southern Iowa, coal deposits of economic potential occur in rocks of the Desmoinesian and Virgilian series. The coal occurs in seams of variable thickness, however, and individual seams are often discontinuous. In addition, much of Iowa's coal is relatively high in impurities, including sulfur compounds.

Iowa coals contain from two to 12 percent sulfur by weight. Approximately one-half of the sulfur occurs in organic chemical compounds and the other half is present in iron sulfide minerals, "fool's gold". Organic sulfur in Iowa coal was probably derived from plants that grew in the ancient coal swamps. The origin of the iron sulfide is not fully understood. Sulfur in the iron sulfide minerals may have come from the shallow Pennsylvanian seas that periodically buried the coal-forming swamps. Sedimentary rocks of marine origin often immediately overlie seams of high-sulfur coal in our state, suggesting that the marine beds may have contributed to the sulfur in the underlying coals.

The sulfur content of coal can be reduced by separating the iron sulfide minerals by gravimetric means, commonly called "washing." Washing also removes other undesirable constituents of coal such as sand, silt, and clay. The organic sulfur in coal is more difficult to remove. Removal of organic sulfur requires expensive and time-consuming chemical processes. At present, this treatment is not economically feasible.

Iowa coal has been mined since well before the turn of the century. In 1886, our state produced over four million tons of coal at a value of $1.25 per ton. Iowa's coal production peaked in 1917 when nearly nine million tons were produced from approximately 400 mines of various sizes. The coal industry in Iowa has declined steadily since the 1930s. Passage of the current state and federal environmental protection laws and regulations has restricted the use of Iowa coal because of its high sulfur content. Production of Iowa coal fell to 473,000 tons from four mines in 1980.

Iowa coal has always been difficult and expensive to mine, in comparison with other coals of the mid-continent region. Why is this so? Typically, Iowa coal beds are thin and discontinuous; many are lense-shaped bodies, rather than continuous tubular beds. This makes mining difficult and expensive.

Two modern beneficiating plants have been constructed in recent years to "clean up" Iowa coal. Coal produced from these plants demonstrates that Iowa coal can be competitive in both quality and cost with "washed" coal from neighboring Illinois and Missouri.

What, then, does the future hold in store for Iowa's coal mining industry? The soaring costs of energy sources such as oil and natural gas and the growing costs of transporting coal from other states, provide the economic climate for Iowa coal to be competitive in the local marketplace. Iowa's coal industry has a chance to stage a comeback. Time will tell if such a revitalization takes place.

A Major Gap in the Record

JUST AS AUGUST and September follow July in our yearly calendar, Permian and Triassic follow the Pennsylvanian in geologic chronology. Permian and Triassic rocks, however, are completely absent in Iowa. Rocks of these ages are known in the plains states to the west of Iowa, and they are spectacularly displayed in Arizona, where Permian strata compose the rim rock of the Grand Canyon and Triassic layers make up the Painted Desert and Petrified Forest. Permian and Triassic rocks also occur to the east of our state in the Appalachian Mountains.

Why are Permian and Triassic rocks missing in Iowa? What was going on in our state during this 80 million year span? The answer is almost certainly erosion.

Iowa was probably a low-lying, arid plain, subjected to weathering and erosion during Permian and Triassic time. Apparently, Iowa remained emergent through most of Jurassic time as well, for the state's Jurassic record is quite limited.

Iowa's Paleozoic rocks were warped and uplifted in Late Paleozoic time, forming part of a large regional fold. In general, the Paleozoic strata of our state slant down at a gentle angle to the southwest. Erosion of these inclined beds has produced an outcrop pattern characterized by northwest-southeast trending belts of Paleozoic bedrock. Mesozoic rocks were deposited on the eroded edges of these Paleozoic strata when seas invaded Iowa for the final time during the Cretaceous Period.

Tom Wagner

Moine Creek is eroding Silurian bedrock in Brush Creek Canyon State Preserve in Fayette County. Our state's bedrock was subjected to the forces of weathering and erosion during all of Permian and Triassic time, a duration of nearly 80 million years.

Buried and discovered near Cardiff, New York, the "Cardiff Giant" was passed off as a fossilized creature from an ancient age. Today, the original "Cardiff Giant" can be viewed at the New York State Historical Association, Cooperstown, New York. A replica is on display at the reconstructed fort at the west edge of Fort Dodge.

Mesozoic — Last of the Inland Seas

THE MESOZOIC ERA of geologic time (230 to 65 million years ago) consists of the Triassic, Jurassic, and Cretaceous periods. Iowa has no Triassic record and only a partial record of Jurassic.

Mesozoic means middle life and, at the time it was named, the Mesozoic was thought to be the middle portion of earth history. We now know the great age of the Earth (4.5 billion years), and that the Mesozoic Era is but a part of its late history.

The Mesozoic Era is often called the Age of the Dinosaurs. The era also saw the first birds, mammals, and advanced flowering plants. Dinosaurs, birds, and mammals have not been discovered in Iowa's Mesozoic rocks. Dinosaur remains have been reported in Nebraska, North Dakota, and South Dakota, however, and their eventual discovery in Iowa cannot be ruled out. Fossils of large sea-going reptiles (plesiosaurs) have been reported from western Iowa.

The Jurassic is represented in Iowa by a single formation, known as the Fort Dodge. Exposures of the Fort Dodge Formation are found only in the northern part of Webster County, although the formation at one time may have been more extensive. The formation contains gypsum and shale, and minor amounts of sandstone and conglomerate.

The gypsum beds probably formed by evaporation in a restricted sea that extended into Iowa from the west. When sea water evaporates, its salinity increases and eventually gypsum salts precipitate from the briny concentrate. Evaporation of this type is often associated with a arid or semi-arid climate.

Iowa's first gypsum mill was erected at Fort Dodge in 1872. Since then, the industry in the Fort Dodge area has grown to its present size, producing nearly 2 million tons of gypsum a year. The Fort Dodge area consistently ranks as one of the nation's leaders in gypsum production. Iowa generally ranks from second to fourth among the states in annual gypsum production.

How long will this valuable resource last? Recent estimates indicate that gypsum reserves in the Fort Dodge area will be depleted within the next 50 years. Abundant gypsum reserves are present, however, in southeast and southcentral Iowa.

Gypsum has many uses. It is used in the manufacture of portland cement, plaster, plaster board, and other building products. It is also used as a soil conditioner and as an ingredient in blackboard chalk.

Gypsum from the Fort Dodge area provided the raw material for one of history's greatest hoaxes when George Hull purchased a large block of it in Iowa and had it shipped to Chicago. There it was carved into the form of a sleeping giant 10 feet long and 3 feet wide. Subsequently, the giant was taken to New York state and buried near the village of Cardiff on the farm of George Hull's brother-in-law, William Newell.

The giant was "discovered" in 1869 when Hull and Newell were digging a well. Newell soon erected a tent over the well site and charged curious visitors 50 cents to see the mysterious stone giant. Supposedly some 50,000 sightseers visited the Newell farm to see the "Cardiff Giant."

Some scientists recognized that the giant was not truly a fossil, but they did think it was old, perhaps representing a statue of some ancient civilization. Eventually the Cardiff Giant was exposed as a hoax, but not before Hull turned a handsome profit and demonstrated P. T. Barnum's popular maxim that people are gullible.

A variety of depositional environments are represented in Iowa's Cretaceous record. Sandstone, shale, conglomerate, and lignite (a low-grade coal) occur in the Dakota Formation of western Iowa. Much of the lower portion of the Dakota was laid down by streams. Later, deltaic and coastal settings prevailed when Iowa lay along a large arm of the sea. This sea advanced into Iowa from the west and eventually, marine beds were laid down some 100 million years ago.

The Graneros, Greenhorn, and Carlile formations represent deposits of this sea, the last marine incursion to affect Iowa.

Cenozoic — A Lengthy Period of Erosion

IN CENOZOIC TIME (63 million years ago to the present), the Atlantic Ocean basin grew wider, continents continued to drift slowly toward their present positions, and climatic and faunal diversity increased on a global scale. In Late Cenozoic time, climates grew cooler; huge, continental ice sheets formed in North America and Europe. The Cenozoic Era, often known as the Age of the Mammals, is divided into two periods: Tertiary and Quaternary. The Tertiary represents some 63 million years of earth's history; the Quaternary encompasses the last 2.5 to 3 million years.

Iowa, above sea level in Tertiary time, was subjected to weathering and erosion. Except for a few patches of stream-laid sands and gravels in western Iowa, where a few mammal bones have been discovered, Tertiary deposits have not been found here. To the west, in the Badlands of South Dakota and Nebraska, Tertiary rocks are rich in mammal remains.

In Tertiary time, the Mesozoic rock record was largely removed by erosion, and streams carved deep valleys into the Paleozoic bedrock. Iowa's topography was later buried by unconsolidated deposits of Quaternary age. The Quaternary Period is represented by the Pleistocene Ice Age and recent time. Recent or Holocene time, the interval since the continental ice sheets melted off North America and Europe, encompasses 10,000 to 15,000 years.

Although the Ice Age (2.5 to 3 million years in duration) represents only .05 percent of all of earth history, it was a most significant event in our state — an event of such magnitude that it deserves expanded discussion, for the comings and goings of massive bodies of glacial ice have left an enduring mark.

We have traced nearly 2 billion years of geologic change in Iowa. Although some of these changes have produced results that are astonishingly prominent, others remain almost imperceptible. The sum of these geologic events and processes make Iowa what it is today in terms of its natural resources, its elevation, its relationship to major rivers, and its position with respect to the equator and the oceans.

It is events of the Ice Age and recent time, a relatively short geologic span, that have provided Iowa with the wherewithal to become one of the most fertile regions on this planet — a breadbasket for the world.

Pete Krumhardt

Large boulders are revealed in the Des Moines River in Boone County during a time of low stream flow. Stream erosion played a significant role in Iowa's geologic past during Tertiary time, when a rugged stream-dissected topography was formed and streams cut deep valleys into bedrock. Later this landscape was largely buried by deposits of the Pleistocene Ice Age.

Tom C. Cooper

CHAPTER TWO
GLACIATION

BY JEAN C. PRIOR, RICHARD G. BAKER, GEORGE R. HALLBERG, AND HOLMES A. SEMKEN

The gentle contours of the land and patterns of crops in the fields bring a nod of familiarity and a feeling of home to many Iowans. Though we think of these landscapes as some of the most durable, unchanging features in our lives, they have evolved from distinctive origins traceable to some of the most interesting and diverse events of geologic history.

(Previous Spread) Farmers work into the early evening hours to finish harvesting oats in central Iowa. The low-relief landscape is the result of glacial activity approximately 14,000 years ago.

Tom C. Cooper

OUR RURAL IOWA LANDSCAPE, through the seasons, has all the appearance of a well-tended garden. Nearly every square mile seems accessible and parcelled out to some purpose. All is not as it appears, however. We can sense something unknown about this familiar land just by sifting through the soil beneath the neat rows of corn and soybeans; examining unearthed bones, teeth, and shells from extinct animals; noting the lakes and marshes clustered in northcentral Iowa; breaking open worn, weathered boulders strewn about the farms; gazing across broad valleys that interrupt the geometric patterns of fields and roads; or losing ourselves among the unruly tracts of hills in western or northeastern Iowa. These features catch our attention and tantalize our imagination, for they are natural relics from a history beyond our experience. But, though distant from us by eons of geologic time, this past is not as unknown or secretive as it might seem.

Geologists working in Iowa have compiled a remarkable record of the events that shaped our state's landscape. They have documented dramatic contrasts in the state's physical environments throughout geologic time. Chapter 1 introduced Iowa's most ancient origins, those periodic encroachments of tropical seas which, in the course of hundreds of million years, produced thousands of feet of sedimentary strata. These rocks compose the basic geologic skeleton of our state, and in scattered, often picturesque localities, outcrops of these strata may be seen. For the most part, however, this skeleton is hidden beneath younger sediments that arrived in Iowa recently by geologic standards and fleshed out new forms and contours to yield the modern Iowa landscape.

In sharp contrast to the marine environments represented by the state's bedrock strata, these younger materials are loose, uncemented, and the products of a completely different geologic process — glaciation. In the Great Ice Age, repeated advances of massive sheets of glacial ice reached into the northcentral and northeastern United States. In addition, sub-Arctic climates, torrential rivers of glacial meltwater, forests of pine and spruce, a native fauna that included muskox, reindeer, mammoths, mastodons, and giant beaver, and even volcanic eruptions in Wyoming left their imprint on Iowa during this remarkable interval of time. To understand something of this past link to our present landscape is to see and appreciate Iowa from a new perspective.

These steep, sharply ribbed slopes in Harrison County near Little Sioux are part of Iowa's famous loess hills. Loess is a common and widespread glacial-age deposit; these hills, however, are a rarity among the world's landforms.

Carl Kurtz

Glacial Events

IT IS IMPORTANT to realize that glaciation, like the inundations of the seas earlier, took place no faster than the day-to-day, season-to-season progression of time with which we are familiar. In the course of thousands of years, however, dramatic changes did occur, and from the perspective with which we regard past geological events, glaciation must have been an awesome spectacle, both in the rest of the world and here in Iowa.

Other episodes of glaciation are recorded in the Earth's geologic record, but only that series of advances and retreats which took place during the Quaternary Period and, more specifically, the Pleistocene Epoch — a span of time from approximately 2.5 million years to about 10,000 years ago — profoundly influenced our modern landscape. In fact, we are so closely tied to the events of the period that this Ice Age may be considered as still in progress. Vast ice sheets still cover Antarctica, Greenland, and Iceland, and our present climatic regime is well within the range of other interglacial stages that punctuated the major periods of Pleistocene ice advance.

The natural events which trigger these episodes of glaciation are not totally understood. We do know there must be continental masses at high latitudes, and that only slight shifts in the world's temperature, and precipitation increases in polar regions can have remarkable cumulative effects. These shifts are attributed in part to changes in the seasonal amounts of solar radiation falling at high latitudes, changes in the general positions of air masses, and the wobble in the motion of the earth's axis. Other contributing factors may be migration of the magnetic pole, and changes in the planet's ocean temperatures and currents which result from the shifting of continental "plates" and the opening or closing of land barriers between oceans.

Pleistocene cooling of the northern latitudes and the increased precipitation and accumulation of snow and ice eventually produced thick mounds of glacial ice. Under pressure, ice behaves as a plastic, and the base of the glacier began to move outward under the stress of its own weight. Continental glaciers coalesced and expanded southward from the Hudson Bay region in the Canadian Arctic, moving into more moderate climates until melting along the ice margins kept pace with the rate of advance. The blanket of glacial ice at its maximum extent may have been as much as two miles thick as far south as the Great Lakes' northern shores. The great weight of this ice actually caused depression of the Earth's crust, and the "rebound" that followed the melting of the ice continues today, especially in the Great Lakes vicinity and northward. Water to form the ice came from the sea, and the growth of the glacial mass, therefore, caused a dramatic, worldwide lowering of sea level by as much as 300 feet below its present position.

In spring and summer, vast floods of muddy, sediment-laden meltwater discharged from the ice margins down the ancestral valleys of the Missouri, Mississippi, and the Ohio. These rivers deepened their valleys as sea level fell and their downstream gradients steepened. In contrast, melting slowed in the winter and sediment, temporarily halted in its downriver journey, was left exposed to dry on the flood plains. Windstorms, enhanced by the differences in air-mass temperature and pressure between the land and adjacent invading ice, swept the finer material from the valleys and dispersed it over large, ice-free areas of the mid-continent, forming the extensive silt deposits known as loess.

With the passage of thousands of years, the climatic system that supplied moisture to the glaciers changed, accumulation diminished, and the ice began to thin and stagnate. Undoubtedly some ice lingered in low protected areas long after the bulk of the glacier melted away. Sea level rose in quick response as water previously locked up as ice returned to the sea. Gigantic meltwater floods coursed through river valleys which in turn became clogged and filled with sediment as ocean levels rose and stream gradients leveled.

Iowa was partly or completely covered with glacial ice many times during the Pleistocene. Each glacial advance obliterated river valleys, deranged and diverted other streams, created new rivers, eroded and filled valleys that persisted, and added significant accumulations of ice- and wind-deposited sediments to the landscape. As we will see later on, this potpourri of Ice Age activity that Iowa experienced has given our state a special place in the history of glacial investigations and Quaternary science.

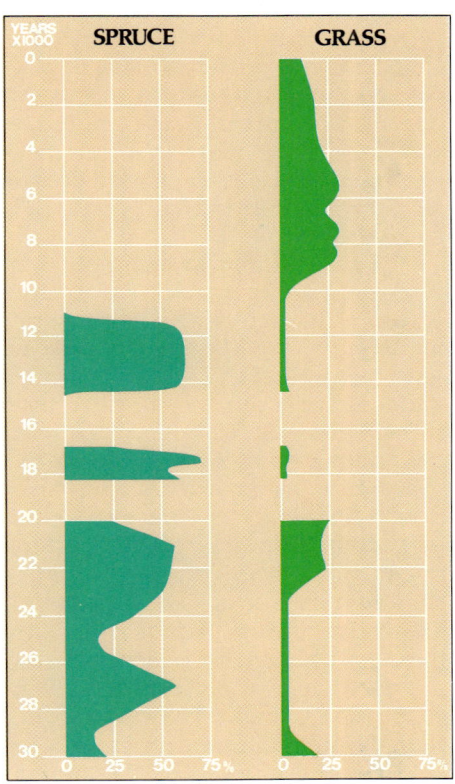

Pollen diagrams are an interesting method of illustrating changes in vegetation through a measured interval of time. Pollen collected from bogs in glaciated landscapes can be studied to determine which plants were present as the ice melted and how species changed in response to moderating climate. This diagram with spruce (on the left) and grass (on the right) shows the comparative shifts in pollen percentages reflecting the change from cool, forested conditions to a more open vegetative cover, and especially the shift to warmer, dryer conditions as the prairies expanded in more recent time.

Glacial Signatures

THIS DRAMATIC SEQUENCE of events now seems far removed from our experience, except perhaps during the most severe Iowa winters. The evidence for this story is found in both ocean depths and continental interiors. Cores taken of deep-sea sediments provide vital information about changing cycles in water temperature because sea-water chemistry, plant life and animal populations all responded to changing environments. Their record accumulated continuously in the sea-bottom muds. Land-locked areas, such as Iowa, provide a completely different set of clues to the interpretations of past Ice Age environments. Much of this evidence lays before us in the landscapes we see, in the materials found beneath the land surface, and in the fossil flora and fauna that occasionally come to light.

One of the most common signs of glacial activity in Iowa is the glacial erratics strewn about the state's landscape. These boulders with their worn edges and their dull weathered surfaces are too heavy to have been transported by water and provide abundant evidence of the power of moving ice. When broken open to expose a fresh surface, these rocks display colorful suites of interlocking crystals not seen in Iowa's native sedimentary rocks. These minerals are characteristic of igneous and metamorphic rocks which are now exposed only in Minnesota, Wisconsin and Canada. They are part of a tremendous volume of rock and soil scooped and plucked by the advancing glaciers, suspended within the dense ice, and transported far south of their natural areas of occurrence — hence the name "erratics." Pilot Rock in Cherokee County is a particularly prominent example, but erratics of all sizes exist throughout the state. Fields best known for corn and soybeans are also known for the crop of boulders that periodically works to the surface through seasonal freezes and thaws and through soil erosion. Well-drillers too, occasionally report unexpected encounters with enormous, resistant glacial erratics.

Less often seen are actual scars left on the state's rock surfaces by glacial action. Long linear tracks called glacial grooves, series of parallel furrows etched into the bedrock, were created by ice dragging cobbles and boulders as it inched across the surface. This grinding action left the grooved surface smooth to the touch and almost polished in appearance. Smaller scratches — striations — and planed or beveled surfaces — facets — also appear on cobbles and pebbles carried by the ice. Glacial grooves in Iowa usually are seen when they are temporarily exposed as glacial sediments are stripped from a bedrock surface before quarrying. A small expanse of glacial grooves, inscribed on a pedestal of State Quarry Limestone, is on permanent display at the Stainbrook Geological Preserve in northern Johnson County. These grooves lie parallel to the direction of the ice flow and provide important information about the direction of ice movement within local areas to investigating scientists. Striated and faceted igneous and metamorphic pebbles also can be found here.

Soils are another easily observed and important link to our glacial past. Our highly prized, fertile soil is the weathered exterior of materials left by glacial action. In the thousands of years that have elapsed since the ice sheets disappeared, moderating climate, physical and chemical weathering, accumulation of prairie and woodland plant litter, root systems, and organisms have all contributed to the transformation of raw glacial deposits into the rich soils that are the basis of Iowa's agricultural wealth.

The soils we use today, however, are but the latest in a series. Ancient buried soils — paleosols — developed on earlier land surfaces. These paleosols represent significant intervals of weathering and exposure and are among the best indicators in the geological record for multiple stages of glaciation during the Pleistocene. These paleosols are most easily observed in the southern half of the state in the spring and fall when soil colors are most noticeable. Reddish-orange zones on freshly plowed hillslopes, clay-rich zones of sticky gumbo, and linear seeps and springs

Bill Witt

Glacial erratics, the field stones of Iowa's farmland, are known to nearly every observer of the Iowa countryside (below). Some of these, such as St. Peter's Rock in Chickasaw County (right), are immense boulders and well known local landmarks.

Wayne I. Anderson

Other erratics, smaller in size, are piled by landowners onto unused ground such as this Fayette County sinkhole (below). Erratics, frozen in place at the base of the moving glacier, scraped against Iowa's bedrock surfaces with such grinding force that parallel grooves were etched in the rock as seen at the Stainbrook Geological Preserve in Johnson County (bottom photo).

Mary R. Howes

along the sides of hills are all characteristics of a buried soil profile.

Rivers and their valleys also provide clues about Ice Age events. Consider for a moment the appearance of the Missouri Valley, the lower Mississippi Valley, and the other major river valleys which drain Iowa's interior. These valleys and their flood plains are unusually broad compared to the width of the river flowing through them. Only during occasional major floods do we see how it is possible for the rivers to transport large quantities of material and laterally expand the sides of the valleys. This was precisely the case during deglaciation when enormous volumes of meltwater and sediment were continuously released down these natural corridors and wide valleys were necessary. The valleys today do not function as meltwater channels, but the underfit appearance of their streams is a good indicator of the dominant role they played in the state's recent geologic past.

Finally, the landscape itself reveals its glacial origins. It is not only the soils, but also the slopes that have enhanced Iowa's agricultural development. The gently rolling character of much of the state's terrain means easy access for farm machinery to those fertile acres. The subdued nature of the topography is a far cry from the rugged terrain of the underlying preglacial bedrock surface. The difference between the two landscapes is the additional accumulation of glacial drift — material derived from glacial ice or its melted water — that buried the older, rugged landscape with softer sediments.

The thickness of this mantle varies widely over the state — from more than 600 feet in westcentral Iowa to almost nothing in the northeastern corner. As successive sheets of glacial drift were left behind and post-glacial drainage patterns were established, these younger sediments were eroded into the gentle contours we recognize as the modern Iowa landscape.

Glacial, wind-blown, and waterlaid deposits cover about 97 percent of the land surface of Iowa, and affect all our daily lives. The nature of the materials determines many properties of our state's rich soils, supplies foundations for buildings, and affects water supplies. The investigation of these deposits is of great concern to scientists and engineers.

Glacial deposits also have played a significant role in the development of scientific thought about the Pleistocene Ice Ages. The sequence of these deposits, or their stratigraphy, was first analyzed nearly a century ago. Much of the classical scientific work that unraveled the geologic evidence for multiple glaciations in the Midwest was done in Iowa. This work originally defined four glacial stages, separated by intervals of time (interglacials) thought to be similar to the present. The classical early Pleistocene stages — the Nebraskan glacial, the Aftonian interglacial, and the Kansan glacial — were all defined from work in southern Iowa and eastern Nebraska, particularly in the Afton-Thayer region of Union County (hence, the name AFTON-ian). The next youngest interglacial stage, the Yarmouthian, was defined from evidence around the village of Yarmouth, Des Moines County, in southeast Iowa. The work in these areas established the framework and geologic terminology used in most of North America.

In recent years in Iowa, however, the sequence of glacial deposits has been found to be much more complex. Many of the classic descriptions of these glacial deposits came from exposures along streams or in roadcuts and quarries, and many of these sections in southern Iowa described the entire Kansan and Nebraskan sequence in 30 to 40 feet of exposure. As noted, however, the thickness of glacial deposits in some of these areas ranges up to 600 feet. In recent years, discovery of deeper exposures and the use of new drilling techniques have allowed more complete observations of the stratigraphy of the glacial deposits. Evidence from wells and core drilling have revealed as many as four distinct till deposits below the classic Nebraskan till. This has complicated the older view that the Kansan and Nebraskan represent the earliest glacial episodes.

Another aspect of technology that has changed the perception of Pleistocene geologic history has been the development of radiometric age-dating. Radioactive elements breakdown or decay into somewhat different elements at a constant rate over long periods of time. With careful measurement of the by-products of decay, the age can be estimated for certain kinds of materials. Radiometric dating has been applied to different materials associated with glacial tills in Iowa: volcanic ashes, wood, and sediments rich in organic matter, such as peat. Volcanic ashes millions of years old can be dated by fission-track methods. Wood and other organic compounds can be radiocarbon-dated back several tens of thousands of years. These techniques allow the establishment of an actual chronology for glacial events.

Volcanic ash deposits have been recognized for many years within the classic Kansan and Nebraskan deposits of southwest Iowa. These ashes,

Bob Coyle

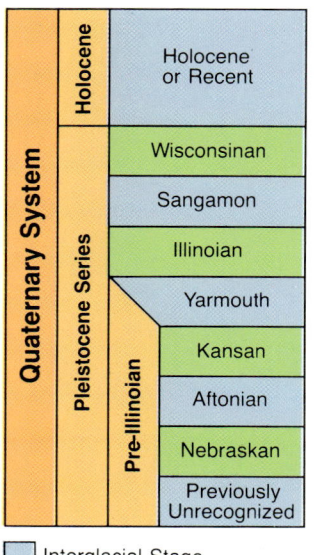

This scenic view from the Balltown Ridge in Dubuque County illustrates the importance of bedrock formations and erosional history in the landscapes of northeastern Iowa, and it contrasts sharply with the more subdued landscapes dominated by glacial deposits in the rest of the state.

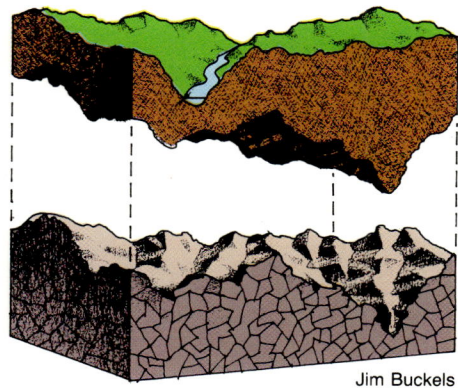
Jim Buckels

The Ice Age in Iowa gave the state a geological facelift. Before the glaciers appeared, the state's terrain was more rugged, with steep hills, abrupt bluffs, and deep valleys — the result of erosion on sedimentary rocks during many millions of years. Later, when the glaciers melted, their deposits masked this older landscape. The differences in topography between Iowa's present and buried landscapes, as well as variations in thickness of these glacial deposits, have important implications for water and mineral investigations, drilling activities, and engineering design.

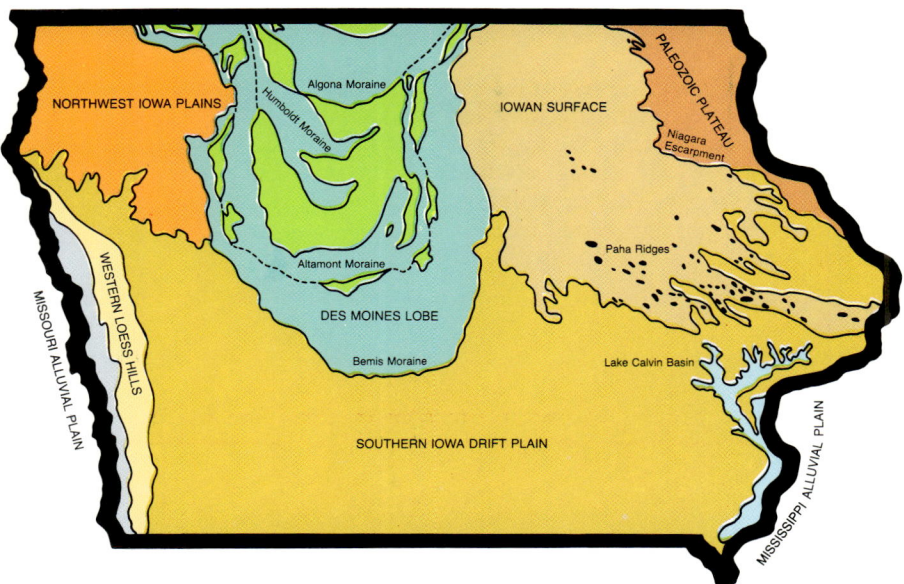

This map outlines the principal landform regions of Iowa. As portions of the state were released from the glacier's grasp, steam erosion took over as the dominant geologic process. These regions, recognizable to any Iowa traveller, each contain distinct landscape patterns and forms which developed as erosional processes took place at different times on varying thicknesses of loess, glacial drift, bedrock, and old valley alluvium. The column at the left identifies the sequence of glacial and interglacial episodes, from oldest (bottom) to youngest (top), that have left deposits in our state.

51

wind-blown materials consisting of volcanic glass and minerals from explosive volcanic eruptions in the Western United States, are widespread and buried within the glacial deposits. (The eruption of Mt. St. Helens in 1980 produced ash falls over a wide area and, when buried, this ash will mark a specific geologic event.) In earlier geologic studies, these ash beds were called the Pearlette Ash and all were considered to be the same age and the result of a single eruption. Detailed chemical and mineralogic analyses and radiometric dating show, however, that actually four separate ash falls occurred in western Iowa and adjacent areas. These ash deposits are approximately 600,000, 700,000, 1,200,000, and 2,200,000 years old and were formed during eruptions of now-extinct volcanoes in Yellowstone National Park in Wyoming, roughly 850 air miles to the west. These deposits occur in Adair, Audubon, Cherokee, Guthrie, Ringgold, Union and Woodbury counties and near the Harrison-Monona County line.

The age-dating of deposits and the recognition of more glacial and interglacial episodes than classically recognized has caused many changes in the conceptual framework of the Pleistocene Epoch. As with all aspects of science, comfortable and familiar concepts must be put aside in the light of new discoveries. Classical Kansan and Nebraskan terms have become obsolete because of the new evidence. These older Pleistocene deposits will be referred to as Pre-Illinoian until the details are worked out.

Within these older Pleistocene deposits, at least five or six glacial-interglacial periods occurred. The volcanic ash dated at 2.2 million years old occurs on top of the oldest recognized glacial deposits. This places the beginning of glaciation in Iowa at more than 2.2 million years — considerably older than most previous estimates. The youngest of these older Pleistocene deposits is somewhat younger than ashes dated at 600,000 years.

The Illinoian and Wisconsin glacial stages also are now recognized as complex periods. The Illinoian is thought to span a time period between perhaps 125,000 and 500,000 years and also to represent several glacial and interglacial cycles. Only the oldest of the Illinoian glaciers entered eastern Iowa; it was an auxiliary lobe of a larger eastern ice sheet.

The Wisconsin glacial stage is the best understood — because it is the youngest and the most completely preserved. Abundant material which can be radiocarbon-dated has allowed development of a detailed chronology. The Wisconsin stage was also complex; glacial ice advanced and retreated several times, but did not completely disappear from North America until about 6,000 years ago. Some regard the Greenland ice cap as a remnant of this episode. Wisconsin glacial deposits are present only in northcentral Iowa. The youngest of these deposits is represented by the Des Moines Lobe, and ranges in age from about 14,000 years at its outer margins to about 12,500 years old near the Minnesota border. An earlier episode of Wisconsin glaciation, buried by the younger Des Moines Lobe, is recorded by deposits which date between 20,000 to 25,000 years old. These are exposed at the surface in part of northwest Iowa, west of the Lobe. Most of the loess deposits that mantle much of Iowa are also a product of this Wisconsin stage. These wind-blown silts were deposited across the state between about 28,000 and 14,000 years ago.

The dating and development of a systematic understanding of these deposits allows correlation of glacial-age events here with those in other parts of the world. This may enable scientists to understand the causes of the Ice Ages — past and future.

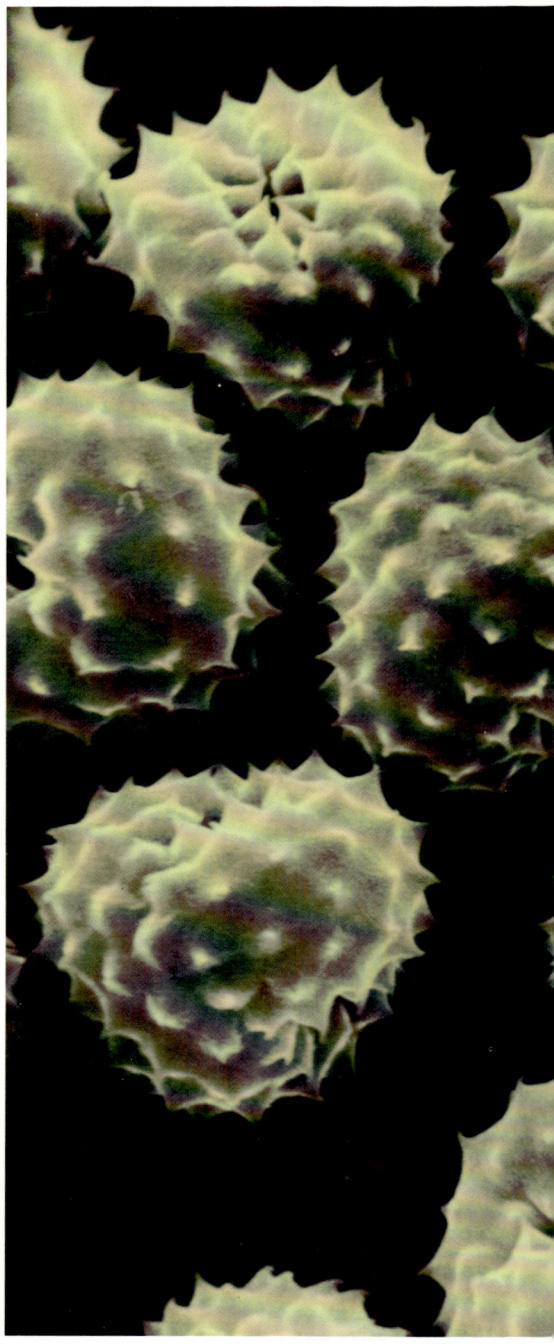

Richard Baker

Flora and Fauna of the Glacial Environment

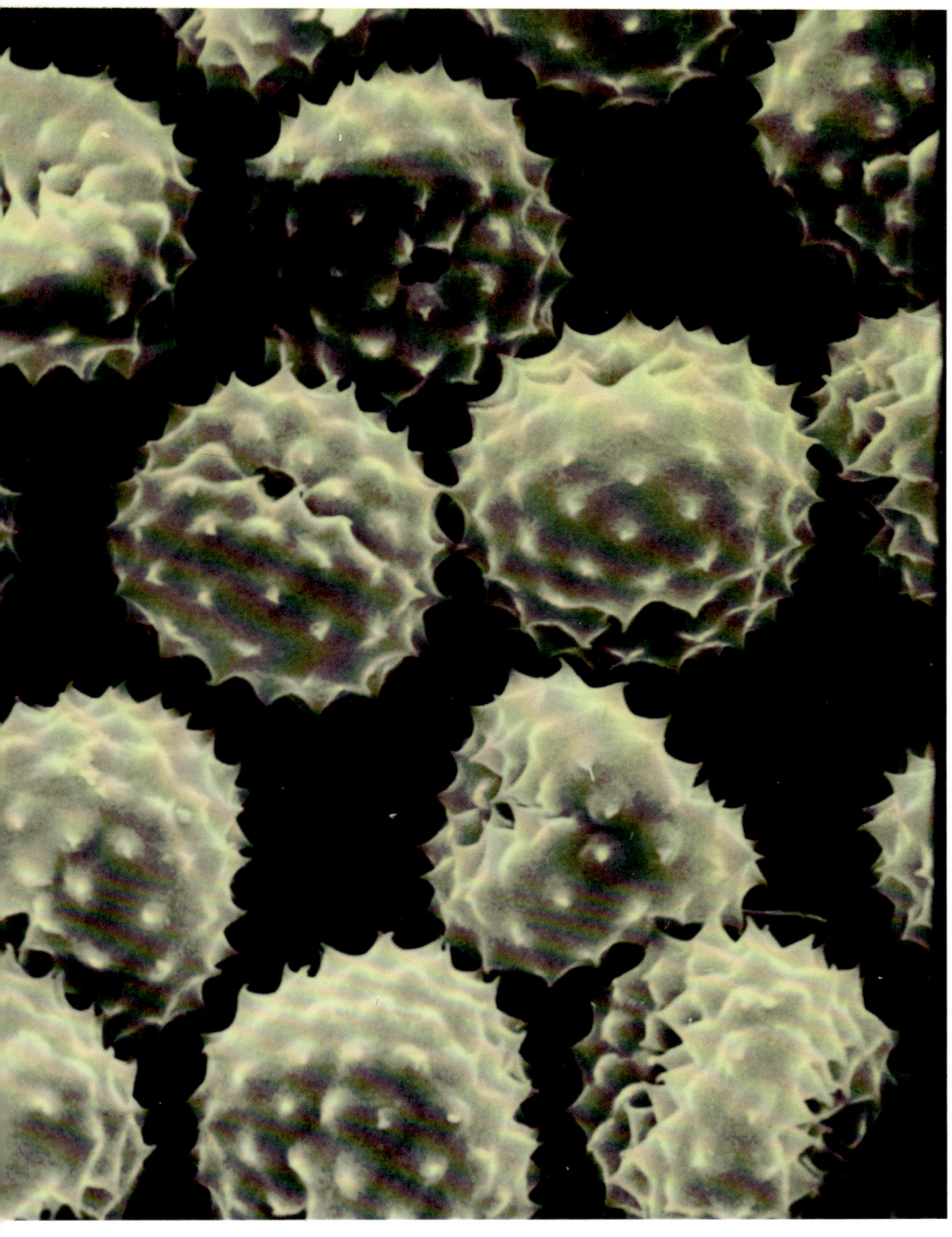

Views of microscopic pollen grains collected from glacial-age sediments provide important records of the vegetation and climate that existed during this period as well as the sequence of changes that followed. This photograph of ragweed pollen was taken through a scanning electron microscope which magnified the grains 2,100 times. The increase of ragweed in the pollen record marks the disturbance of natural vegetative associations brought on by the activities of man and settlement.

SOME OF THE most intriguing aspects of Iowa's glacial record stem from interpretations made about the paleoenvironments — that is, climate, flora, and fauna that existed coincidentally with glacial advances and retreats. Distribution of native vegetation over Iowa in the late 1800s shows that most of the state was covered by prairies, with smaller amounts of woodland present along river valleys and on some eastern upland divides. How long has this pattern prevailed? What was the sequence of vegetative change from the time glaciers last entered the state 14,000 years ago until the vast prairies were seen by the state's first pioneers? These questions address the history of vegetation.

Information on this aspect of Iowa's heritage is available from the study of fossil plant remains preserved in sediments found in various parts of the state. Leaves, seeds, or fruits of plants are occasionally preserved intact in these deposits, but the most abundant plant fossil is pollen. These microscopic reproductive cells have resistant coats that survive indefinitely in sediments found in lakes, marshes, and bogs. Pollen is produced abundantly by many plants, is widely distributed by the wind, and is well preserved when it lands in the proper environment.

By examining a peat deposit layer by layer, scientists can determine the changing sequence of plant cover in the surrounding geographic area. Each layer also can be radiocarbon-dated, and the changing percentages of pollen can be compared through a measured interval of time. (See diagram, page 47.)

Information on the glacial-age vegetational history of Iowa is sparse. Only a few poorly dated sites are available from which to interpret this history before 30,000 years ago. These sites do indicate that spruce and pine forests were often present, and evidence at only one early site suggests that prairies were widespread over the state. For the past 30,000 years — the latest portion of Quaternary time — enough dated pollen records are available to assemble a generalized sequence.

Carl Kurtz

The Iowa landscape 30,000 years ago apparently was an open pine forest, accompanied by spruce, with grasses in open areas. From about 28,000 to 23,000 years ago, vegetation changed to a closed spruce-pine forest, with perhaps a few birch trees here and there. This forest resembled modern forests in southern Canada implying that our climate was considerably cooler than at present.

About 23,000 years ago, pine diminished in the forest; spruce became dominant, and larch appeared. The increase in grass pollen again tells us that the trees in the forest were more widely separated. This combination of plants today grows further north in Canada than the preceding group, and implies that the climate was getting even colder.

Evidence from between 20,000 and 14,000 years ago is sketchy, but it suggests a very open spruce parkland. Remains of tundra plants are found with spruce needles, indicating an environment much like the present Arctic treeline in central and northern Canada. Glaciers were fully expanded in the Midwest, and climate was apparently at its coldest.

About 14,000 years ago, spruce, fir, and larch joined grasses and scattered deciduous trees to form an open parkland environment. Although this assemblage also indicates a very cool climate, the modern counterpart is farther south than the Canadian Arctic. The climate had begun to warm, and beginning about 14,000 years ago glaciers began to retreat in central Iowa.

By 11,500 years ago, spruce and larch disappeared from the Iowa landscape; birch and a variety of other trees formed a deciduous forest (see Chapter 8) across the state. By 10,000 years ago, oak and elm were the dominant forest trees. But as climate continued to become warmer and drier, these trees were subjected to moisture stress, and they yielded to plants better adapted to dry climates — the prarie plants (see Chapter 7). Grasses, the chenopods — such as pigweed — and the composites — such as daisies, wormwood, sunflowers, and ragweed — began to vie for space in the forest. By about 7,700 years ago, prairie had become well established across the state. Deciduous trees were probably confined to scattered upland stands in northeastern Iowa. This was the warmest, driest period in our present "interglacial" climate. One consequence of this aridity was that the state's groundwater and lake levels were lower; for example, the surface of Lake Okoboji was 30 feet lower than it is today.

About 3,000 years ago, deciduous trees, particularly oak, began to re-establish themselves in Iowa, though not as abundantly as they were about 10,000 years ago. This latest change reflects a return to slightly cooler and more moist climates characteristic of the present. Judging from other climatic records for the past million years, some experts feel that this change is the first indication of a slow cooling that may eventually lead to another glacial period. Only time will tell.

A diverse group of mammals also lived in Iowa during the Ice Age. These animals can be divided into four categories: (1) Large, now extinct species, with no direct living descendents. Members of this group include mastodons, short-faced peccaries, stag-moose, giant armadillo, shrub oxen, woodland musk oxen, stilt-legged deer, giant beaver, and ground sloths which were at least the size of an ox. (2) Animals now extinct in North America but which survived on other continents. The mammoth, camel, llama, and horse are the best known members of the group. Why the horse disappeared from North America approximately 10,000 years ago, but spread rapidly after being reintroduced by the Spanish in the 1500s is still a mystery. (3) Species with tundra or boreal affinities which survived extinction, but are now found only in the tundra or northern conifer forests. Reindeer and barren-ground musk oxen are common as fossils throughout the state. Also significant are a number of rodents and insect-eaters which fall into this group. These include the collared lemming, heather vole, Arctic shrew, and the northern bog lemming. (4) The fourth group, frequently overlooked because of familiarity, survived the extinction process and inhabited the state at least until historic times. Large members of this group include the pronghorn, bison, moose, wapiti or American elk, bears, both white-tailed and mule deer, otter, and

Following the last glacial episode, coniferous and deciduous trees stressed by the increasingly warmer and drier climate gave way to the prairie plants, such as big bluestem shown here. These plants and their root systems helped to transform the exposed surface of the underlying glacial deposits into rich soils.

This Pottawattamie County roadcut contained a tusk, teeth and other skeletal fragments of a mammoth. A colder climate and coniferous flora existed in southwest Iowa at the time the mammoth roamed the region 20,000 years ago.

the wolf. Most of the small mammals presently residing in the state also lived here in late-Pleistocene time. Squirrels, chipmunks, red fox, deer mice, marmots, beaver, and rabbits are a few representatives of this group.

The modern fauna of Iowa is thus the impoverished remnant of a highly diverse late-Pleistocene community that suffered from extinction, immigrations to more northern regions, or restriction of range to other continents. The greater number of species that lived during late-glacial time suggests more ecological niches were present then than are now available. Small mammals, such as rodents, are particularly valuable indicators of the total environment because they are too small to migrate seasonally to avoid adverse conditions. The late-Pleistocene fossil fauna shows that small mammals — such as the pine vole (a forest species), the collared lemming (a tundra species), and the prairie vole (a Great Plains prairie species), all lived together in Iowa. Today, however, their ranges are almost mutually exclusive. These vertebrate-fossil associations of mammals which do not coexist today indicate that the glacial environment of Iowa does not have a comparable modern analog, and that climatically, this environment consisted of cool summers, and winters similar to or only slightly colder than those of today, except perhaps at the immediate border of the ice. "Glacial cold" then, was most likely a summer phenomenon.

Small land snails also contribute to our understanding of Ice Age environments. Like the mammals, many live today only north of the state. However, several species that were widespread in glacial times now are found exclusively on cold-air slopes in northeastern Iowa. These slopes are bathed in cold dense air that seeps out of ice caves and flows downslope modifying local conditions so that summers are cooler than those in surrounding areas. The survival of these Ice Age relicts in these specialized habitats suggests that the Pleistocene climate was similar, with cooler summers and with winters much like those of today. This interpretation supports that proposed from both the mammalian and pollen record.

Two of the more interesting large animals of the Pleistocene fauna are mammoths and mastodons. They were common inhabitants of the Ice Age Iowa landscape, and fossil remains, primarily teeth, of one or the other have been recovered from practically every county in the state. Mammoths were directly related to the living Indian elephant, and some specialists regard these elephants as a remnant of a population that once ranged throughout North America and Europe. Two species, Jefferson's mammoth and Columbian mammoth, are known from Iowa. Jefferson's mammoth, named after Thomas Jefferson (an avid fossil collector), is similar in form to the wooly mammoth of Siberia and northern North America. It also was the most common elephant in Iowa during the late Pleistocene. The Columbian mammoth, which was larger and generally predated Jefferson's, is relatively rare. Only one species of mastodon is known from the late Pleistocene of North America. Unlike the mammoths, the mastodons have no living representatives.

Between 9,000 and 12,000 years ago many of these large Ice Age mammals became extinct. The cause of these extinctions is not fully known, but they occurred at the same time as the major environmental change that defined the end of the Ice Age. The conifers, deciduous trees, and grasses no longer formed a complex, amalgamated ecosystem, but diverged into the modern tundra, northern boreal forest, eastern deciduous forest, and prairie biomes. Each occupies a distinct geographic region. The small mammals which were adapted to specific plants or plant associations retreated with their food supply to their present habitats. Perhaps the large mammals, such as the mastodon, required the diverse foods present in this large parkland environment and became extinct when their habitat was partitioned into the environmental scheme we see today. Their fossilized remains are mute monuments to the effect of environmental change.

Iowa native Grant Wood (1891-1942) had his own interpretation of the Iowa landscape, as seen in this image entitled "Young Corn," painted in 1931. Wood said he painted the Iowa landforms, not because they were necessarily the most beautiful in the world, but because he knew them best.

Courtesy of the Cedar Rapids Art Center, Cedar Rapids School District Collection.

Modern Landscapes

TO APPRECIATE the effect of Iowa's glacial history on today's landscape, we should become familiar with some of the state's major natural divisions, for the two are closely related. Broad topographic patterns can be observed, and in various regions certain chapters of the geological record dominate the terrain.

The state's oldest landscapes are found in northeastern Iowa. This is an area of unusually high topographical relief, unexpected scenic beauty, numerous rocky bluffs and cliffs, rivers entrenched into steep-sided valleys, level upland summits, and abundant woodlands. It is a deeply dissected landscape dominated by durable sedimentary bedrock formations such as sandstone, limestone and dolomite. Fracture traces, or joints, in the carbonate (lime-rich) rocks control the sharp-angled courses of streams flowing through the area. Underground waters also move along these natural partings in limestones and in places have enlarged the crevices into major cavern systems, such as Cold Water Cave in Winneshiek County. Sinkholes and springs are other natural features observed at the land surface that result from the combined effects of underground drainage and near-surface carbonate bedrock. This region has been popularly described as "Little Switzerland," and for many years geologists referred to it as part of the Driftless Area, owing to an apparent lack of evidence for glaciation. Though remnants of glacial drift prove that the area was ice-covered during the earlier part of the Pleistocene, the landscapes of this region today are dominated by plateau-like uplands and deep, narrow valleys with a long history of erosion into the underlying Paleozoic-age strata. This bedrock-controlled topography is mantled with loess, and thin deposits of glacial drift occur between the bedrock and loess in the western half of the region. The western and southern boundary of this region is marked by a more or less continuous line of prominent, east-facing bluffs known as the Silurian Escarpment. The Balltown Ridge north of Dubuque is an exceptionally scenic segment of this interesting physiographic feature.

The rolling plains of glacial drift in south, northwest and northeast Iowa come next in age. These areas are covered with glacial deposits that represent all ice advances into Iowa except the most recent. These deposits have buried the high-relief, preglacial landscapes that are exposed to view in extreme northeastern Iowa. The glacial deposits are loose and uncemented, and thus they erode into a landscape of softer, flowing contours. Artist Grant Wood had a special eye for capturing this landscape form on canvas. These plains are old, composed of glacial drift which has weathered well over 500,000 years. Because they have been exposed for so long, streams are well established and effectively drain the entire area. They have carved deeply into the once-fresh glaciated surfaces and have removed all remnants of landforms created by contact with ice. The drift sheets are now changed into landscapes dominated by slopes, alternating hills and valleys, mile after mile of billowing ocean-like swells and troughs. The only later addition to these weathered rolling hills is a younger (Wisconsin-age) covering of wind-deposited loess. Some streams have eroded completely through these glacial-age sediments into the older bedrock formations beneath. State and county parks throughout this region are often in these deeper valleys, where scenic rock exposures form the valley sides. Geologists have many good topographic and geologic reasons to further divide this area, particularly into a northeastern and northwestern component and though significant, in terms of their erosional history, they are basically variations of the theme presented here.

The loess hills in western Iowa consist of deposits that buried the landforms described above. They are composed of a mantle of uniform silt-sized particles which covers rolling drift plains. But here, the layer of loess dominates the form and substance of the terrain. This region is an exceptional example of the strong influence of wind, both in the geologic past and as a significant contributor to our modern landscape. Loess in itself

Carl Kurtz

The Freda Haffner Kettlehole Preserve, shown here, is probably the most striking ice-contact feature in our state. Located along the Little Sioux River Valley in Dickinson County, this steep-sided, bowl-shaped depression was formed by the melting of a large, isolated block of partially buried glacial ice. The marsh in the middle shows that the kettle has no drainage outlet. All sediments shed by the side slopes since the ice melted are still held within its interior.

is not unique. It occurs in varying thicknesses as the uppermost geologic unit throughout the state, except for northcentral Iowa, and in fact exists over much of the Midwest and south along the Mississippi Valley. The loess has accumulated in unusual thicknesses, however, along the western Iowa border, a result of the proximity to its source — the adjacent valley of the Missouri River. Remembering the role of this valley during episodes of glacial melting, it is not hard to visualize the vast amount of sediment that lay exposed to the winds during winter. In the course of 15 or 20 thousand years of late-glacial time, these sediments were carried out of the valley and redeposited on the adjoining uplands to depths ranging up to 200 feet. Loess, reflecting the narrow size range of particles that can be moved by wind, is a very uniform-textured silt, loosely compacted, porous, and light-weight. When eroded or excavated, it retains remarkably vertical slopes. Subsequent stream dissection of the loess has carved an intricate, sharp-featured, corrugated landscape of peaked hills, steep slopes, narrow ridge crests, and intersecting spurs. Natural slumping of the hillslopes has marked them with characteristic horizontal benches

Iowa Geological Survey, Jean C. Prior

The loess hills along the western Iowa border are one of the state's most distinctive landform regions and most interesting natural areas. These hills were carved from great thicknesses of wind-deposited silt which was winnowed from glacial debris lodged in the adjacent Missouri River Valley during meltwater flooding. This segment of sharp-featured hills in Monona County north of Turin is one of many tracts that have been the focus of interest because of their scenic appeal and scientific value.

known as "catsteps." The most prominent bluffs and ridges of this unique landscape are found along the Iowa side of the north-south course of the Missouri Valley from Sioux City south to west central Missouri. The contrast in terrain and elevation between the valley and adjoining hills is abrupt and spectacular. Within three to ten miles east of the Missouri Valley these distinctive hills gradually merge into the familiar rolling glacial plains described earlier.

The landscapes of northcentral Iowa, more than those of any other part of the state, show clearly the direct effects of glacial action. A lobe of glacial ice, an appendage of the vast Wisconsin ice sheet, intruded into this area between 14,000 and 12,500 years ago — quite recently in terms of geologic time. Iowa's capitol, now situated near the southern margin of this ice advance, lends its name to the region — the Des Moines Lobe. Ice occupied this area toward the end of the major period of loess deposition, so the glacial drift here has no cover of wind-blown silt, and instead, buries deposits of loess. This drift sheet is also younger by hundreds of thousands of years than the older drift sheets to the east, west and south, so stream erosion has barely begun to establish well defined patterns. In fact, the lack of stream drainage results in numerous marshes and lakes, which are some of the most obvious natural features of this region. The Freda Haffner Kettlehole Preserve in Dickinson County is an outstanding example of the closed, undrained depressions that can be seen. From sediments in such features, the important pollen samples described earlier are taken. Many of the state's rivers also have their origins in boggy swales on the surface of the Des Moines Lobe. Hills in this region of our state are irregular knobby hummocks of debris which accumulated as stagnant glacial ice melted. Ocheyedan Mound in Osceola County and Pilot Knob in Hancock County are prominent examples. They are part of widespread aligned bands of ridges and hills called moraines, which resulted from deposition of glacial debris along the ice margins and from changing conditions beneath the ice. Variability, but variability with a definite pattern, best describes the Des Moines Lobe, both in terms of its topography and the unsorted, ice-deposited material beneath its surface.

No matter which of these regions of our state we examine, precipitation falls, runoff gathers into channels, and rivers flow, slowly changing the appearance of the land. Whether a small creek or a major river, running water erodes the landscape and carries sediment from the uplands to the lowlands. River valleys or alluvial plains are the distinctive landscape corridors where this transportation process takes place and where sediment is temporarily stored until sufficient water volume or velocity is available for the journey to continue. Large river valleys have a vertical history of deep scouring and filling, which reflects response to the Pleistocene events described earlier. They also have a horizontal history of continually migrating meanders. These rivers can shift course many times, leaving the flood plain etched with abandoned-channel scars, sloughs, and oxbow lakes as landmarks of the old routes. Iowa's largest alluvial plains, the Missouri and Missisippi flood plains, define our western and eastern borders, while the state's interior is drained by numerous smaller valleys. Together they represent the latest chapter in Iowa's geologic record and the most significant geologic activity presently at work on the state's landscape. The valleys we observe today may be old, especially those excavated into the bedrock of northeastern Iowa, or they may be young, barely discernible landscape features, such as those found on the Des Moines Lobe, but the river channel and its adjoining flood plain, wherever found, are the most youthful geologic features we can observe here in Iowa.

The contrasts in terrain between this rock-lipped waterfall in Pikes Peak State Park and the grassed waterways draining these central Iowa farm fields underscore the topographic diversity that exists within our state. The natural materials which underlie these landscapes, whether sedimentary rock or loose mixtures of clay, silt, sand and boulders, are important factors in determining the land's appearance and the effect that stream erosion will have. The geologic past, from shallow, tropical seas to the frozen grip of glacial ice, may be read from these landscape records.

Tom C. Cooper

Tom C. Cooper

Our Land is Shaped

THE IOWA LANDSCAPE now has new meaning. It is a record of successive geological events and processes — a record of ancient seas of which only rock and fossils remain; a considerably younger, shorter, but more visible and detailed record of glacial and interglacial environments, and a recent, almost instantaneous record in geologic terms, of modification by streams. Some Iowa landscapes are clear illustrations of a single portion of this record; most display a combination.

The results statewide are landscapes of remarkable diversity. The variations depend upon whether bedrock strata are exposed and, if so, what kind; whether glacial drift is present, and, if so, for how long; whether loess is present and, if so, how thick; and whether streams are present and, if so, what is being eroded. Ask these questions of any Iowa landscape — the rocky, sentinel bluffs high above the Mississippi at Pikes Peak State Park south of McGregor in Clayton County, the cool seclusion of Starr's Cave sheltered in the Flint Creek Valley near Burlington, the steep alternating swells and troughs between Des Moines and Council Bluffs, the high treeless plains north to Gitchie Manitou in Lyon County, the gently sloping inclines of Grundy County, the angular peaks and pitches that guard Preparation Canyon in Monona County, the knobby hills and prairie potholes of the Spirit Lake country, or the broad lowlands that surround DeSoto Bend in Harrison County — and the answers will be an intriguing combination of time, materials, and natural events, an absorbing account of earth history, and a lesson in landscape appreciation. So often we think of states other than Iowa as having important things to say about the earth's history. Mountain peaks and deep canyons certainly do speak with authority, but think about the special places you know in Iowa. Whether they are tracts set aside as state or county parks and preserves or just favorite natural areas you like to visit, in almost every instance these places are out of the ordinary because of particular geological conditions. They are scenic oases where geology speaks with a firm voice. These geological conditions in turn determine habitat, and habitat determines the distribution of plant and animal communities.

Iowa's bedrock and glacial history are indeed the foundation of our natural heritage.

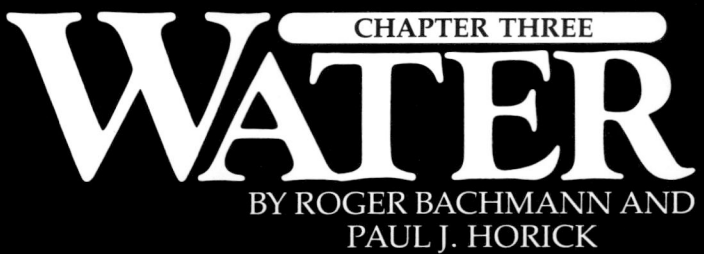

CHAPTER THREE
WATER

BY ROGER BACHMANN AND
PAUL J. HORICK

Carl Kurtz

Water cascading down the face of the spillway of the dam at Beeds Lake State Park in Franklin County makes an inviting scene for prairie-bound Iowans. The lake and dam were constructed by the Civilian Conservation Corps in the 1930s. The Iowa Conservation Commission has constructed numerous other lakes and recreational areas providing opportunities for boating, fishing, swimming, camping, and hunting.

*Previous Spread
Water is basic to all life. With it we prosper; without it we perish. The importance of water is becoming increasingly evident to each generation. This tranquil scene of the Cedar River at Palisades-Kepler State Park in east-central Iowa reminds us of the fundamental concept that we are merely stewards with the responsibility of preserving and passing on our natural heritage.*

IOWA IS A BOUNTIFUL LAND, blessed with abundant water resources. As testimony, our state lies between two of the world's great rivers — the Mississippi and the Missouri, boundaries that are the envy of many states.

We are also blessed with ample supplies of good quality subsurface water or groundwater.

Most of the water flowing in Iowa's border rivers is unused except for some used in hydroelectric power generation and a bit taken by a few cities for municipal supplies. Iowa has many streams in the interior that are also available for water supply development, either directly from the stream or from alluvial sand and gravel deposits beneath the valley floors.

The surface water resources include several natural lakes in northcentral Iowa. The most notable are Okoboji and Spirit lakes in Dickinson County, Clear Lake in Cerro Gordo County, and Storm Lake in Buena Vista County. Generations of Iowans have enjoyed these beautiful lakes.

Many artificial lakes have been constructed in the state to meet our recreational needs. Some of these occur as lovely wooded oases surrounded by fields of fertile cropland. Most were created by building dams across the tributary valleys of large streams. Other lakes along the flood plains of river valleys are old meander swaths or oxbows that are intersections of the water table. The total storage capacity of all these lakes is not great, and their value is primarily esthetic. The state also has four major impoundments that are U. S. Army Corps of Engineers reservoirs: Coralville, north of Iowa City, on the Iowa River; Red Rock, near Pella and Saylorville, north of Des Moines, both on the Des Moines River; and Rathbun, north of Centerville, on the Chariton River. Although these reservoirs were built mainly for flood control they are used extensively for recreation.

Enormous quantities of groundwater are stored in alluvial deposits beneath the broad valleys of the Missouri and Mississippi rivers and smaller interior streams, in sand and gravel layers interbedded in glacial deposits, and in deep bedrock aquifers. These underground sources have great importance in meeting our water demands. Approximately 75 percent of all Iowans and most of our rural residents rely on groundwater for their source of supply; and 58 percent of our industries, excluding electric utility generating plants, use groundwater for cooling and processing.

This is the hydrologic cycle, whereby precipitation falls to earth, then much of it runs off to our oceans, and finally evaporates into the atmosphere where it will be available again as precipitation.

Storm clouds darken the sky and herald an approaching thunderstorm over beautiful Lake Geode in southeast Iowa. About 32 inches of precipitation falls on the state each year, providing ample water to grow crops and to recharge our rivers, lakes, and underground reservoirs.

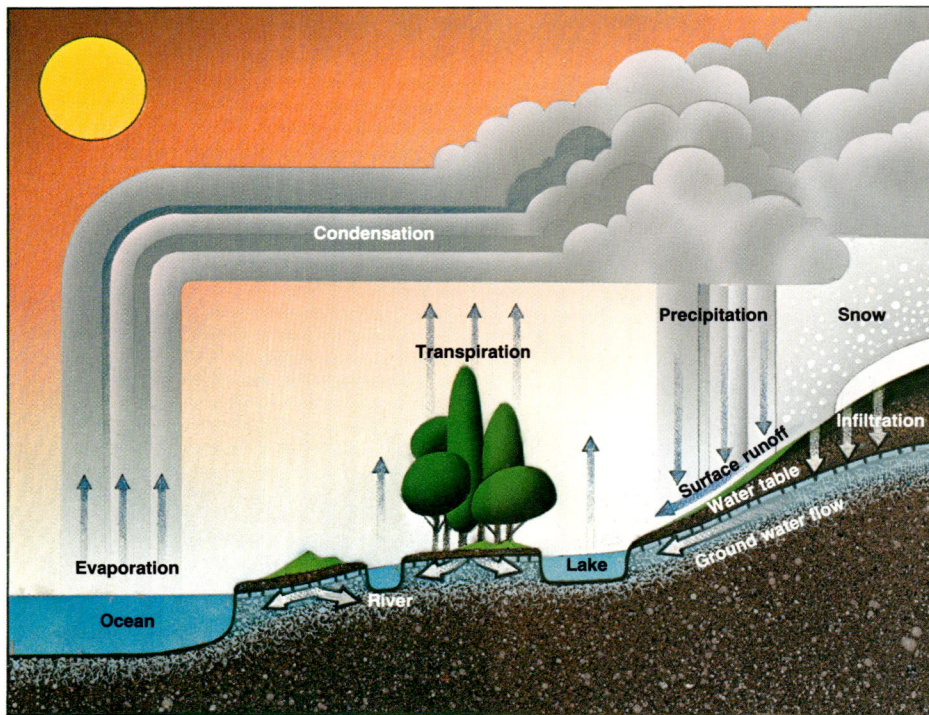

Jim Buckels

Iowa's first white settlers concentrated their dwellings along streams for easy access to water — both to consume and to use for transportation. A good water supply was as important as food. Man can exist many days without food, but he will live only a short time without water. As the population grew and agriculture expanded, people moved to upland areas and dug or bored wells for their water needs. With undrained land and abundant marshy areas, groundwater levels were high, and water was relatively easy to obtain for the limited requirements of small family farms.

In the first half of this century, a rapid growth of water-thirsty industries and electric utilities occurred, and water demands increased manyfold. Exact figures on water use in Iowa are not available, although the U.S. Geological Survey has made estimates at five-year intervals since 1950 for major categories of use — public supply, rural, irrigation, industrial, and electric utilities. These estimates indicate water use for all purposes in Iowa, except hydroelectric power generation, was about 3.5 billion gallons a day in 1975. That is a tremendous amount of water, but only about 1 percent of daily fresh water use of the nation.

Hydroelectric plants use another 28 billion gallons a day to drive turbines. It is obvious that very large quantities of water are required to keep abreast of our growing water demands. Water use projections indicate our water intake may increase by 2 percent or more per annum until the year 2020 to support population growth and economic output. The heaviest water users in Iowa will be in the electric utility, manufacturing, and agricultural sectors.

Water is constantly moving between the earth, the oceans, and the atmosphere because of the heat of the sun and the pull of earth's gravity. Water evaporates from lakes and ponds, from wet ground, and growing plants — even animal and human bodies — and is carried in the air as vapor or gas. When air cools, water vapor condenses to become liquid and falls as rain. Some of this precipitation runs off as streams of surface water to the ocean, some evaporates back to the atmosphere again, and a small percentage seeps into the porous ground, infiltrates to the water table and becomes groundwater as shown above.

Carl Kurtz

Surface Water

THE WINTER BLIZZARD, the spring rain, and the summer thunderstorms all act to water the land — the basis for life in Iowa. On the average, about 32 inches of precipitation falls on the state in a year, with about 90 percent of this falling as rain. This represents about 11 million gallons of water for each person in the state, although only a fraction of this is actually available for use. Many losses of water occur before it appears in rivers or streams. About 2 inches of the annual precipitation that falls on the leaves of trees and other plants is evaporated back into the air before it ever reaches the ground. Of the water reaching the ground, 4 inches will run over the surface to contribute directly to the flow of creeks, streams, and rivers. The rest soaks into the ground, contributing to soil moisture. During the growing season, most of this water, however, is taken up by the roots of plants and transported up to the leaves where it is evaporated through small openings called stomata in a process called evapotranspiration. About 24 inches of water a year are consumed in this process. The remaining 2 inches left in the soil are available to circulate in the groundwater and may eventually recharge stream flow through springs or by direct seepage into the beds of streams or lakes. Thus of the original 32 inches, only about 6 remain as surface runoff.

Water running over the surface of the land collects in small channels or rills that in turn join with others to form headwater streams that join with other streams to form the larger rivers. Two of the largest river basins in Iowa are the Iowa-Cedar and Des Moines rivers. Both move across the state from the northcentral border with Minnesota to the Mississippi River in the southeast. These two basins — along with the Skunk River basin — account for more than half the annual runoff in the state. The rest comes from the flows of the smaller streams in northeast, western, and southern Iowa.

The average annual runoff from the interior streams of Iowa amounts to about 18 million acre-feet a year (an

The Delta Queen, a modern version of an old steamboat, regularly plies up and down the Mississippi River between St. Paul and New Orleans during the summer, recapturing some of the nostalgia of riverboating days.

acre-foot of water is a unit of measure equal to one acre covered by one foot of water). By comparison the Mississippi River at McGregor has an average annual discharge of 24.5 million acre-feet and the Missouri River at Sioux City 23.1 million acre-feet. Both these rivers drain large land areas upstream from Iowa and receive the runoff from some interior Iowa streams as well.

It is perhaps misleading to speak of the average flow in a river because flow varies considerably from place to place and from time to time. Because of differences in precipitation and evaporation across the state, runoff in northwest Iowa is only 2 inches a year while it is more than 9 inches a year in the east near Dubuque. Even greater variability is encountered in the flow of an individual stream within a year and from year to year. For example, the highest recorded flow in the Iowa River at Marshalltown of 39,400 cubic feet a second (cfs) is 4,000 times greater than the lowest recorded flow of 9 cfs. Iowa rivers have their highest flows usually in the period from April to July because of higher precipitation rates then.

Most natural lakes in Iowa were formed by glacial action that left depressions as the ice retreated. These depressions filled with water to form lakes or ponds. In time lakes tend to fill with sediment or outflowing streams lower the water level. With time — often many thousands of years — a lake may eventually disappear because of these processes. This has happened in southern Iowa where lakes created by early glaciation have long since disappeared. In northcentral Iowa, the story differs because the landscape is much younger, and many natural basins formed by more recent glaciers remain. Indeed, many parts of this area could not be cultivated until drainage systems were developed.

How important water is in Iowa may be illustrated by the fact that we use about 150 gallons per person per day for domestic purposes, including water system losses and public services. Of course, water is also used in many kinds of industries, as well as in energy production. In pioneer days, dams were built to impound water to turn waterwheels so mills could grind grain or saw logs. Later water power from small rivers throughout the state was used to produce electricity. In recent years most of these power plants fell into disuse as they became uneconomical in comparison with fossil-fuel plants. At present only 5 hydroelectric plants operate on interior streams, and one plant remains on the Mississippi River at Keokuk. Water is used, however, to cool condensers of steam power plants that use either fossil or nuclear fuels. In fact, this is Iowa's largest category of water use, accounting for about 68 percent of all surface and ground waters withdrawn in the state. Fortunately only about 2 percent of this water is lost to evaporation; the rest is available for reuse.

In drier years, precipitation may be too low to produce agricultural crops. Then rainfall is often supplemented by irrigation. Water is pumped from a river or from the ground and used to provide necessary moisture for crops. To control the water being removed, the state requires permits for water withdrawals and regulates amounts taken.

Iowa's rivers have served as a transportation network since before

the arrival of the first settlers. The Indians used canoes, as did the first explorers and trappers. The Lewis and Clark expedition went up the Missouri River by boat as it moved along what is now Iowa's western border on the journey to the Pacific. Steamboats plying the Mississippi and Missouri rivers played an important role in the early settlements of those areas of Iowa, and attempts were made to extend boat service as far as Fort Dodge on the Des Moines River but the river was too small to be dependable.

Even in an age of interstate highways and jet planes, water transportation still plays an important role in Iowa. Barges loaded with such bulk cargoes as grain, coal, and oil make heavy use of the Mississippi River where systems of locks and dams have been built to insure sufficient water depth for navigation. Water transportation continues to be the cheapest and most energy efficient for moving relatively large cargoes at slow speeds.

For most of us, rivers, lakes, and wetlands seem most important for the recreation they can provide. Fishing is the favorite water-related activity of Iowans, with 50 percent of the population making an average of 14 trips a year. Pleasure boating, water skiing, and swimming are also important activities on Iowa lakes and reservoirs, while canoeing is rapidly becoming a popular activity on the fast streams of northeast Iowa. Water is also an important attraction for picnicking and camping, so it is no coincidence that most of our state and county parks are situated on lakes or rivers. The state preservation of undeveloped lakeshores and river banks is important to insure water-based recreation for future Iowans.

Northbound barge traffic on the Mississippi River approaches the Marquette Bridge, as seen from Pikes Peak State Park in this telephoto view.

Water skiing on the Mississippi River at Dubuque is one of the more exhilarating forms of recreational activity on our large streams and lakes.

Recreation on Iowa's water is not limited to the warmer months as evidenced by this activity at Hickory Grove Park in Story County.

French Creek, a rapid flowing trout stream in northern Allamakee County, runs through a rocky valley carved in the Jordan Sandstone with ledges of Oneota Dolostone capping the wooded slopes.

Like any other important resource, some problems exist in the use of water in Iowa. Some of these problems involve too much or too little water. Floods that sometimes occur on all of our streams — from the smallest creek to the great Mississippi — can cause property destruction and loss of life. We are trying to solve this problem in two ways: one, building structures such as dams and levees to control floods, and two, preventing people from building in low areas that are likely to flood, thus reducing damages that would occur when inevitable floods do come.

The other extreme is drought. Prolonged periods without adequate rainfall can have devastating effects on our crops, and on surface and underground water supplies. We cannot control the amount of rainfall, but sensible water management practices can lessen the impact of too little rainfall.

Iowa also has some problems with water quality. Our heavy concentration of row crops leads to erosion and loss of soil to rivers and streams. These soil particles can settle out on the streambed and destroy fish habitat and eventually fill in lakes and reservoirs. Widespread adoption of soil conservation measures could reduce this problem.

Wastes from cities and industries can also contain materials that are harmful to aquatic life. Fortunately, Iowa has been a leader in the adoption of modern pollution-control measures and is continuing to improve the degree of waste treatment throughout the state.

In summer, many lakes and ponds in the state develop heavy growths of algae, which make the water appear green and reduce the underwater visibility. This growth is a result of high nutrient concentrations that promote plant growth in the water, just as fertilizers stimulate growth of crops. While in some cases pollution sources may contribute some of these nutrients, runoff from fertile prairie soils contains sufficient nutrients to cause problems — particularly in shallow lakes, where there is little dilution of inflows. Algae is less of a problem in deeper lakes, such as West Okoboji and Big Creek, or in lakes fed mainly by groundwater, such as Blue Lake on the Missouri River flood plain, or the numerous gravel pits and quarries that are fed by seepage rather than runoff.

Tom C. Cooper

Groundwater

WHAT IS GROUNDWATER? What distinguishes it from surface water? Where does groundwater come from? How does it occur? Where does it go? These are elementary questions, but groundwater is still a big mystery to many of us.

Most people understand that precipitation is the source of water in our rivers and lakes. But what keeps the rivers running or the lakes full when it is not raining? The answer is groundwater, which seeps into streams and lakes and maintains the base flow of streams and the level of the lake surfaces.

Sediments that comprise the Earth's crust, the loose surface materials, and the consolidated rock formations at varying depths below land surface contain porous sands and gravels, sandstones, and creviced limestones and dolostones that act like a huge reservoir or sponge. Below a certain depth, the porespaces and openings in these formations are filled with water. This is known as the zone of saturation, and the top of this zone is called the water table. Between the water table and the land surface is a zone of aeration in which the formation openings are filled with air and water. Groundwater therefore is mostly water filling the voids and cracks in the rocks below the top of the saturation zone. It is water that can be retrieved by wells. At great depths, no groundwater is found because the rocks are under such great pressure that openings in them are very small and practically watertight.

Water in the ground is constantly moving through the zone of saturation to a point of outlet such as a spring or streambed. It is this water that is free to move into wells. The water moves through the tiny openings between the sand grains and through the interconnected joints in limestones. Movement may be slow or rapid, depending on the formation's capacity to transmit water. Eventually groundwater moves into streams or is drawn from wells and is exchanged to the atmosphere again.

The Geologic Framework

IT IS HELPFUL in understanding our groundwater resources to review briefly the geological structure and formational units of our state described in *Chapter 1*. The materials covering Iowa are loess, a wind-deposited silt, and glacial till, a pebbly clay deposited by glaciers. Except for a small area in northeastern Iowa, these deposits spread across the entire state. The average thickness exceeds 100 feet, but may range up to 600 feet in parts of western Iowa. Sand and gravel bodies of varying thicknesses and extent are scattered irregularly through the till. Below the till lies a thick succession of sedimentary rocks — primarily shales, siltstones, sandstones, limestones, and dolostones. These rock layers reach a maximum thickness of about 5,200 feet in southwestern Iowa and wedge out to zero thickness against crystalline rocks of Precambrian age near Iowa's northwestern corner. At the northeastern corner the sedimentary column is about 800 feet thick.

Iowa's dominant geologic structure is a broad trough, formed in Paleozoic time, called the Iowa Basin. Set between three major structural features — the Transcontinental Arch on the northwest, the Wisconsin Dome on the northeast, and the Ozark Uplift on the south — the Iowa Basin plunges southwest, with its axis running from eastcentral Minnesota through Mason City to the southwest corner of the state. Erosion has beveled the surface so that the oldest strata are now found in the northeastern and northwestern corners of the state. Flat-lying sediments that are primarily sandstone or shale were spread across the dipping Paleozoic rocks in the northwestern part of the state during the Cretaceous Period. The Cretaceous rocks may be as thick as 550 feet in places.

These sedimentary formations contain several aquifers that are valued for the development of public water supplies and for industrial, irrigation and rural use.

Many Iowans are surprised to learn there are numerous waterfalls in our state. Most are located in northeast Iowa. This view is of Falling Spring in northern Fayette County, near Douglas.

Carl Kurtz

Winneshiek County is known for the number of its springs that furnish a perennial supply of water to the clear-running creeks. The chief source rock is the basal Galena Limestone just above the Decorah Shale as in these two photos of Malanaphy Springs waterfall northwest of Decorah along the Upper Iowa River.

Carl Kurtz

Carl Kurtz

The Aquifers

BEGINNING AT THE SURFACE and going to deep underground, the principal aquifers are alluvial and glacial sand and gravel bodies, Cretaceous sandstones, Mississippian limestones and dolostones, Silurian-Devonian dolostones and limestones, Cambrian-Ordovician sandstones and dolostones, and deep-lying Cambrian (Dresbach) sandstones.

Variability on virtually all dimensions characterizes aquifers. They may range in thickness from a few feet to hundreds of feet. They may lie just beneath the surface of the earth, or they may occur at great depth. (Some Iowa wells are more than 3,000 feet deep.) An aquifer may be merely local in size, or it may extend for hundreds of miles.

The two basic types of aquifers are unconfined or water-table aquifers and confined or artesian aquifers.

In an unconfined aquifer, water is in contact with atmospheric conditions through the unsaturated zone. The water level in the formation may rise in response to percolating water or decline during a prolonged dry spell. No relatively impermeable confining layer lies above this kind of aquifer.

In confined or artesian aquifers, water occurs between layers of thick clay or shale or dense limestone. These confining layers — both above and below — hold the water under pressure. When a well drill penetrates such an aquifer, the water will rise in the bore hole above the top of the aquifer. If the pressure is sufficient, water may even flow at the surface. These aquifers and the wells themselves are called "artesians." The name comes from Artois, France, where many flowing wells once occurred.

Surficial aquifers occur as alluvial deposits along stream valleys, in buried bedrock channels, and as scattered, irregular layers in the glacial drift. Such aquifers provide irrigation water for corn and soybeans along the Missouri River between Sioux City and Council Bluffs and for industrial purposes in the area near Fort Madison, Clinton and Muscatine. Indeed, alluvial deposits in

Carl Kurtz

Sunrise over beautiful Pine Lake State Park northeast of Eldora in Hardin County. This man-made lake typically has all the facilities for water-based recreation and for camping, picnicking, hiking, golfing, and snowmobiling. It shows how foresighted Iowans improved the opportunities for recreation in areas where natural lakes are not present.

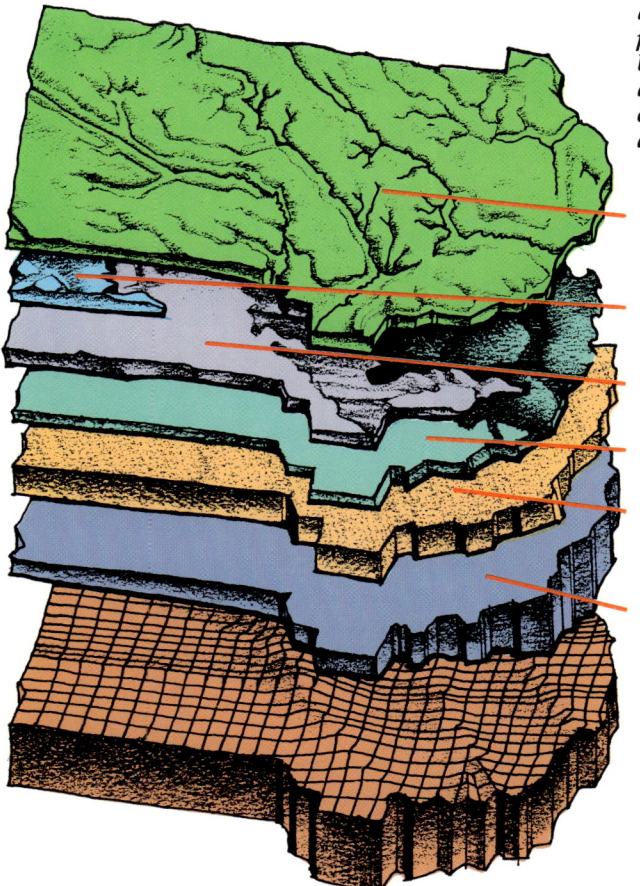

Illustration of the principal aquifers in the east-central portion of Iowa. The bedrock aquifers are actually separated by confining beds of shale or dense carbonate rock.

our state's river valleys comprise one of the best sources of water for larger capacity wells throughout Iowa. Unconsolidated layers of clay, silt, sand, and gravel make up these deposits, and the porous sands and gravels are the main water-bearing units. Yields of a few hundred to a few thousand gallons a minute (gpm) generally can be obtained from individual wells. The thickness of these deposits varies from 100 to 160 feet along both the Missouri and Mississippi rivers, but may be only from 25 to 75 feet thick on interior streams.

Cities which rely entirely or in part on surficial aquifers for their water supplies include Ames, Cedar Rapids, Des Moines, Dubuque, Muscatine, Newton, Sioux City, Spencer, and Waterloo.

Among Cretaceous Rocks, the Dakota Formation contains the chief bedrock aquifer of northwestern Iowa and, to a lesser extent, in western and southwestern Iowa. The most productive wells occur in northwestern counties, where the sandstone ranges in thickness from 250 to 300 feet. Municipal and irrigation wells produce as much as 750-1,000 gpm. Thickness and character of the Dakota Formation show considerable local and regional variation because the rocks were deeply eroded in post-Cretaceous time.

Water from the Dakota aquifer generally is classified as fair to poor in chemical quality. It is widely used, however, for municipal, domestic, and irrigation purposes in areas of the state which do not have better supplies.

The Mississippian aquifer is confined by Pennsylvanian shales above and Devonian shales below and consists of a thick succession of sandy and cherty limestones and dolostones. The average thickness ranges from 250-350 feet. Yields of 100-200 gpm are common in north-central Iowa and only 5-10 gpm in southeastern Iowa. In the north-central counties artesian wells have produced exceptional yields ranging as high as 500-900 gpm. One of the best flowing wells in our state was completed along the South Skunk River Valley at Story City in October, 1945. The final depth of the bore was 261 feet, and water spurted 20 feet above ground before the well was capped. Water quality in this well was rated as good. Overall, in the principal area for developing wells from this aquifer — from the Keokuk-Burlington area northwest to Wright and Humboldt counties — quality and well efficiency varies considerably.

Except for a few counties in the northeast and northwest corners of the state, the Silurian-Devonian aquifer underlies about 85 percent of Iowa. Consisting of a thick succession of limestone and dolostone formations, this aquifer is also confined between strata of shale or dense carbonate rock. Maximum thickness of the aquifer is about 650 feet with an average of 200-350 feet. A variable thickness of glacial drift clay overlies the principal formations in the eastern Iowa outcrop area.

As with other aquifers, chemical quality of Silurian-Devonian water varies. Quality is generally good in the northeast; however, nitrate concentrations appear to be increasing in areas where overburden is thin and where sinkholes are abundant. In central and southern Iowa, the water is highly mineralized and extremely hard. Yield from wells also varies considerably, with best results obtained in the northeast. An irrigation well drilled in January, 1980, about four miles north of Cedar Falls went to 315 feet and produced about 1,400 gpm with less than two feet of drawdown. The most productive area for developing wells is in a broad area from Wapello to Clinton northwest to the Minnesota border between Cresco and Northwood. As many as 175 Iowa communities rely on the Silurian-Devonian aquifer for their water, with wells producing 100-600 gpm or more.

In the eastern two-thirds of the state, the Cambrian-Ordovician aquifer is important because of its larger yields and because, in many places, overlying formations produce only small quantities of water of poor chemical quality. Yields of several hundred gallons a minute on up to 2,000 gpm have been obtained from individual Cambrian-Ordovician wells. The aquifer averages between 400 to 500 feet thick in Iowa.

The Jordan Sandstone is the chief water-producing unit in the Cambrian-Ordovician aquifer. Statewide, about 200 wells draw water from this unit, and it has been the subject of detailed study recently because the artesian head has declined — in some places as much as 175 to 200 feet.

Chemical quality of the water from the Cambrian-Ordovician Aquifer ranges from good to unusable, becoming increasingly mineralized to the west.

The deepest water-bearing unit in Iowa is the Cambrian-age Dresbach aquifer, a thick sequence of coarse- to fine-grained sandstone. This aquifer is separated from the overlying Jordan Sandstone by 250 to 375 feet by silty dolostone and a fine-grained sandstone. The Mt. Simon Sandstone occurs in the lower part of the aquifer, is approximately 1,200 feet thick and is the most important water source. Individual wells are capable of delivering 2,000-3,000 gpm. The Dresbach aquifer is used only in the eastern part of Iowa at Bellevue, Clinton, Dubuque, Lansing, and Maquoketa.

At Clinton, as many as 18-20 deep wells, including five municipal wells, tap Mt. Simon Sandstone water. Total withdrawal from the aquifer there may be in the range of 5 to 6 billion gallons a year, and the cone of depression there is the largest in the state.

Chemical quality of water from the Dresbach aquifer in the few cities mentioned is good. Elsewhere in the state, the aquifer yields water unsuited for public supply.

Few rivers in the world can match the mighty Mississippi for grandeur, beauty, power, usefulness, ugliness, and destructiveness. It is constantly changing but is still the same — the same "old man river" seen here with a full moon rising over the distant Wisconsin shoreline.

The Future

IOWA HAS A REPUTATION as a land of plenty, with beautiful green prairies and wooded valleys, largely because of its rich soils, abundant water resources, and long growing season. Unfortunately, we now find ourselves faced with mounting prospects of pollution in our rivers and lakes. In fact, we have just about reached the limits we can tolerate in some surface water systems.

Human activity is the biggest cause of pollution. Agricultural chemicals are being spread on our farmland in huge quantities, and some eventually reach our water supplies. A number of industrial dumps still leach into rivers and endanger surface-water and shallow well-water supplies. We cannot continue to pollute our streams and shallow aquifers without suffering grave consequences to public health and the environment.

Iowa has regulations to safeguard surface water and groundwater resources. These must be periodically reviewed and upgraded. As faithful and responsible stewards, we must provide the support to assure compliance with these laws to guarantee the quality of our water resources. Indeed, without ample supplies of good quality water, we will have little cause to be concerned about the other elements of our natural heritage. This calls for sensible and careful management and continued research into our water supplies to meet the demands that lie ahead.

Carl Kurtz

CHAPTER FOUR
SOILS

BY THOMAS E. FENTON
AND GERALD MILLER

(Previous Spread) **Forage production on gently, moderately, and strongly sloping landscapes on thick loess deposits of the Marshall soil association area of western Iowa.**

Oats and soybean crops on moderately sloping terrain in Guthrie County add a touch of color to the landscape.

Tom C. Cooper

MANY PEOPLE CONSIDER Iowa's soil resources to be our most precious natural heritage. Thick, nutrient-rich soils, blessed with favorable temperatures and ample rainfall, have made Iowa agricultural production the envy of the world. No other state has a higher proportion of land in food production than our state; three of every four acres are devoted to cropland.

Our soil is a unique resource, comprising the greatest concentration of prime farmland in the world. Recent USDA inventories report that nearly one-fifth of the best cropland in the United States is found in Iowa. Fertile, black topsoil, reaching an average depth of 14 inches or more, is the "black gold of Iowa."

The largest part of our rich inheritance of soil was formed under great expanses of tall grass prairie that once covered the state. The fibrous root systems of grasses and forbes contributed plant material to the soil that decomposed, releasing abundant nutrients. These soils have a strong granular structure that allows them to remain workable even after many years of cultivation. However, breaking up the prairie sod often required as many as seven yoke of oxen to pull a single plowshare.

Large areas of prairie were poorly drained and thought to be unfit for farming by early settlers. In prairie sloughs and potholes, vegetation grew so well that the process of decay fell behind and peat bogs were formed. These peat deposits, sometimes up to 20 feet deep, often caught fire and burned out of control for years. The smell of burning peat was a familiar one to early settlers in central Iowa. As methods of draining land were developed and clay tile became available, these wet prairie areas became some of the most productive of the prairie soils.

Soils found under forest vegetation make up the second largest portion of our state's soil resources. Early settlers chose these woodlands over the less familiar prairies. Availability of firewood and logs to build cabins influenced their choice, but this land also was much easier to break up for farming than the deep prairie sod. Topsoil developed under woodlands is thinner and often lighter in color than that developed under prairie. A gray subsurface layer is often associated with soils developed under forest vegetation. For this reason, these kinds of soils were called "white oak soil" by the early pioneers.

Soil between these rows of soybeans in northcentral Iowa is susceptible to erosion caused by rains, although the corn residue from the previous season's crop will help control some of the soil loss.

FERTILE BOTTOMLANDS, lying along Iowa's many rivers, were the first to be settled by immigrants to our state. Overflowing waters, carrying sand, silt, and clay from the above watershed spread out across flood plains year after year, century after century, depositing thick layers of dark-colored soil material. These farmlands are today some of the richest in our state.

Agriculture is our state's major industry. In 1980 Iowa ranked first in the United States in corn production, accounting for 22 percent of the nation's corn crop. Our state was second in soybean production. Iowa also led the nation in all livestock marketing. Each swine producer raised enough pork to feed 840 Americans and each beef producer provided enough beef to feed another 741. One-tenth of the nation's food supply comes from Iowa.

Our state contributes heavily to the food supply exported to food deficient countries. Iowa ranked second in the nation in agricultural exports, and revenue from all crop production for 1980 was second only to California.

Tragically, Iowa also has the distinction of having the greatest amount of soil erosion of any state in the Corn Belt. The average loss is estimated at 9.9 tons of topsoil per acre per year. This translates to 261 million tons of sediment each year, much of which finds its way into rivers and is carried away. The loss of topsoil through erosion, when combined with the reduction in organic matter content brought about by aeration of the soil through cultivation, results in a significant decline in the thickness of topsoil. Statewide, an average of one-half of the thickness of the original topsoil has been lost.

How Soils Form in Iowa

PARENT MATERIALS we see today could provide the soil material that could feed future generations of the world's population. Weathering of parent materials results in a loose mass of mineral particles that can be mixed with living things and their remains. Both mineral and organic solids are present to a varying degree, dependent upon how and from what material they were formed.

Pore spaces, containing air and water, occur between the individual soil particles or aggregates of these particles. Thus solids, liquid, and gas are present in all soils. The percentage of each varies among soils and even within a soil type.

The soil-forming factors — parent material, climate, organisms, topography, and time — work together in many ways to give us the different kinds of soil we have today. Whenever these five soil-forming factors are the same on any part of the landscape, the soils should be similar. Whenever there is a significant change in any factor, the soils will be different.

This scene north of Dubuque consists of moderately to very steep slopes covered with thin loess and glacial drift over shale and limestone rocks. The Mississippi River is in the distance.

Tom C. Cooper

Parent Material

PARENT MATERIAL is the loose, weathered mineral and rock fragments from which soil is formed. These fragments make up the framework of the soil. They are to the soil what a skeleton is to an animal. As they weather, nutrients are released — phosphorus, potassium, calcium, magnesium — all essential to the growth of plants. Clay is formed from the minerals. The size of particles in the soil helps determine its ability to hold water and plant nutrients.

Most soil parent materials in Iowa are unconsolidated deposits, originally left as a direct or indirect result of glacier activity. This material, called *glacial drift* is an unsorted mixture of clay, silt, sand, gravel, and boulders. Glacial drift varies greatly in its composition. That material left in place by retreating ice is called *till* and can be very sandy, silty, or clayey but commonly is a mixture of these textures. Water running out from glaciers carries materials with it. This material is called *outwash*. The moving water has partially sorted this material. It is composed of gravel, sand, or silt depending on characteristics of the meltwater and the distance of the deposit from the source. Outwash deposits in Iowa commonly have sandy or gravelly layers.

A large part of Iowa's glacial drift has been covered with wind deposited particles called *loess*. Loess consists primarily of silt and clay-sized materials. These materials were deposited by rivers or glacial meltwater, picked up by wind and redeposited elsewhere. The major source area for much of the loess deposited in Iowa was the flood plain of the Missouri River (*see Chapter* 2). Certain properties of the loess-derived soils were determined by the distance from the source. Coarse particles were deposited close to the source area while the content of finer particles increases with distance from the source. Thickness of the deposits decreases in a south-southeasterly direction, the direction of the prevailing winds across Iowa. Loess deposits of 100 feet or more may be found on hills adjacent to the Missouri River.

Alluvium is that material laid down by rivers or streams on bottomlands or flood plains. Some of the richest soils in Iowa are along our rivers. Alluvium in Iowa consists mostly of sediments from uplands carried down across the watershed over a period of many years.

Sedimentary rocks, bedrock, organic deposits, and *colluvium* (material that has accumulated at the bottom of steep slopes) make up the remainder of Iowa's parent material.

Climate

CLIMATE HAS AFFECTED both the deposition of parent material and the types of soil that have been formed from these deposits. Freezing, thawing, sunshine, rainfall, and wind are all climatic factors that act upon parent material to form soil through the process called weathering. Both physical and chemical weathering are hastened by high temperatures and adequate rainfall. Leaching and erosion are important factors determining the kinds of soils formed.

Iowa has a climate of warm summers, rather cold winters, and moderate rainfall. Not only is the weathering process hastened under these conditions, but vegetation types are influenced as well. Also, different types of soil are formed under different types of vegetation.

Climatic changes have also played a role in the history of our soils. Glacial advances are generally associated with lower temperatures and increased precipitation, while retreat of the ice sheets is associated with higher temperatures and decreased precipitation.

Recent studies in the Midwest indicate that there have been marked changes in climate even in the postglacial period. In the past 13,000 years, the climate has changed from cool (and probably moist) through warm and dry to present-day conditions. Soils formed since our last glacial period have been influenced by these changing environmental conditions.

Organisms

LIVING ORGANISMS and their remains are a source of organic material that is an important part of the soil. Animals, plants, insects, worms, bacteria, fungi, and other organisms all affect the formation of soil.

Of all these, plants play the dominant role. The kind of vegetation that grows on the soil determines what and how much organic matter will be returned and also affects the rate of decay.

In Iowa two types of vegetation have covered most of the landscape. Forest vegetation was most prominent in eastern Iowa and along the major streams in other parts of the state. The remainder of the state was covered primarily by tall prairie grasses.

The difference in the amount of organic carbon present in soils developed under different types of vegetation is striking. A soil known as "Tama" is a soil developed under prairie vegetation. The upper 4 feet of this soil contain approximately 68 tons of organic carbon per acre, while "Fayette," a soil formed under forest vegetation, has approximately 42 tons per acre. The soils differ not only in the amount of organic carbon present, but also in how deep the organic carbon is distributed in the soil. The annual addition of organic matter from the above-ground portion of trees and prairie grass is not greatly different. The underground portion of prairie vegetation contributes much greater amounts than trees.

This deciduous forest on strongly sloping terrain is common in northeastern Iowa. Slope of the land affects soil development due to the stability of the land surface. Thin soils occur on these landscapes due to the strongly sloping terrain.

Tom C. Cooper

Tom C. Cooper

This is Iowa's "black gold" — thick, dark colored topsoil high in organic matter formed under native prairie grasses.

Topography

TOPOGRAPHY, or lay of the land, affects soil formation primarily as it influences run-off and drainage. Rainfall on hilly land may result in erosion and leaching of nutrients. In poorly drained areas, water inhibits aeration. Those chemical processes that require little or no oxygen, form black and greyish soil horizons. On gently sloping lands, enough aeration occurs to form brown or yellowish-brown soils.

The direction a slope faces is also a factor in soil development. In Iowa, south-facing slopes are normally warmer and drier than north-facing slopes. This can affect the kind and amount of vegetation that grow in an area. For example, in northeastern Iowa in areas not presently cultivated, south-facing slopes are more commonly grass-covered, while north-facing slopes have a timber cover.

The topography of Iowa is most often characterized in terms of slope gradient (percent slope). Slope of the land affects soil development due to the stability of the land surface. More developed soils are often in level areas, while sloping areas show less development. About 60 percent of the land area in Iowa has slope gradients of 5 percent or less.

Time

TIME IS NEEDED to form soil. In evaluating the effect of time on soil formation, the other four factors must be considered. A stream may deposit alluvial material in a matter of days, but centuries are needed to weather and form a soil from bedrock. The amount of time needed to form a well developed soil may be drastically different in a cold, dry period than that of a warm, rainy period. Parent material also differs in stability due to its environment, greatly influencing the amount of time needed for soil formation. Soils formed under different vegetations also require varying periods of time to develop. The time factor of soil formation may vary widely within the same area as well as among different areas across the state.

Soil Profile and Classification

The traditional method of moldboard plowing has been blamed for some of our soil erosion. New methods of conservation tillage are encouraged now, whereby crop residue is left to protect the soil from erosion by wind and rain.

ALL SOILS have acquired certain characteristics as a result of soil-forming processes. Chemical, physical, and biological changes have occurred, determining, for example, color, acidity, nutrient content, and the amount of organic matter present. Combinations of these characteristics are in horizontal layers within the soil called "horizons." The horizons or layers occur in a vertical sequence from the surface down to a depth of several feet and make up the "soil profile." Each soil has a unique profile that varies in the kind and number of horizons.

Three major horizons are present in most Iowa soils. These are designated as A, B, or C, moving from the surface downward.

The thick, dark-colored A horizon is known as "topsoil." It is the zone of the soil that has the maximum biological activity. Bacteria, fungi, plant roots, insects, and small animals all contribute to horizon development. Native prairie grasses, with extensive root systems, were important sources of organic matter for many of our Iowa soils. Well decomposed organic matter (humus) coats the mineral particles in the A horizon and is responsible for the dark color.

The B horizon occurs immediately below the topsoil and is commonly referred to as "subsoil." The subsoil is lower in organic matter and biological activity than the topsoil. It is usually harder when dry and stickier when moist than the A horizon. These properties result from lower organic matter content and an accumulation of clay part of which moved down from the A horizon. Color of the B horizon results primarily from the presence and oxidation state of iron coatings on the exterior of the mineral particles. If iron and organic matter are absent, the color will be that of the mineral particles.

Parent material directly below the subsoil is referred to as the C horizon. It may be the same kind of material from which the A and B horizons developed or it may be different.

Horizons can be subdivided by putting a number after the letter. Additional horizons can be identified. If a thick layer of partially decayed organic matter is present on the topsoil it may be designated as an "O" horizon. Underlying bedrock may be identified as an "R" horizon.

Soils are classified and grouped according to their profile properties. The present system of classification has six categories — with the soil series being the lowest class. In Iowa, soil scientists have classified approximately 450 soil series. A soil series is named for a town or geographical location near which it was first identified or mapped. Tama is a well drained loess-derived soil formed under prairie vegetation in a humid climate. Any soil that has a similar profile and properties within a given range will be called Tama whether it is in Iowa or any other state. Normally, soil series have a limited geographical extent because of changes in one or more of the soil-forming factors over a large area.

Features that affect the use and management of a soil are called phases. These designations may be added to the soil type name. Slope groups and erosion classes are examples of phases; for example — Tama silty clay loam, 5-9 percent slopes, moderately eroded.

The pattern of soils across Iowa forms a patchwork of intermingled soil types. The kind of soil may vary with each rise or gully within a field. However, certain combinations of soil types are repeated from field to field and often across whole sections of the state. These combinations are called soil associations. One or several soil series may be included in an association.

This is a soil profile of Nicollet loam with approximately 20 inches of topsoil. The dark colored vertical lines in the subsoil resulted from animal burrows and subsequent filling with topsoil material.

Soil Survey Program

INFORMATION about soils has been organized in a way not only to name and characterize them, but also to predict their behavior when used for agricultural, construction, engineering, or other purposes. Soils surveys must be done to gather this information.

The soil-survey program in the United States began in the 1890s. The earliest published soil-survey reports in Iowa were those of the Dubuque area (1903), and Cerro Gordo (1903), Story (1903), and Tama (1904) counties. Since that time, our knowledge of soils has greatly increased, methods have been improved, and the surveys are more detailed and accurate.

At present, the soil-survey of Iowa is a cooperative effort of various agencies of county, state, and federal government. The agencies involved in various aspects of this program are the U.S. Soil Conservation Service, the Iowa Agriculture and Home Economics Experiment Station and the Cooperative Extension Service, Iowa State University, the Iowa Department of Soil Conservation, and the County Conference Boards.

Approximately 12 person-years are required for the soil-survey field work of an average-size county. Many of the counties being surveyed have a staff of 3 soil scientists, so approximately 4 years are required from initiation to completion of the field work. With present available resources, field work is being completed at the rate of approximately 4 counties per year.

In 1982 field work for modern county soil surveys had been completed in over two-thirds of our state. Field work was in progress in another 17 counties and the remaining counties were scheduled to commence field work by the middle of the decade. By the late 1980s all the field work was projected to be completed for modern soil surveys in all 99 Iowa counties.

The practice of contour and strip-cropping on this moderately sloping landscape in eastcentral Iowa helps reduce loss of fertile topsoil.

Tom C. Cooper

Soil Conservation

OUR HIGHLY PRODUCTIVE soils provide no guarantee that over the next 50 to 100 years or longer, Iowa will continue to lead the nation in food production. Early in Iowa's history the people of our state began to realize that soil and other natural resources could be exhausted. In 1882, Dr. Thomas H. MacBride, who later became the president of the University of Iowa, delivered a series of imaginative lectures setting forth the objectives of conservation. His vision and ideas grew in the minds of landowners and farmers throughout the state who saw the need to preserve our natural resources.

In response, the State Board of Conservation was organized, along with the Fish and Game Commission to provide a state park system and insure the rights of the people to fish and hunt in our state.

In accomplishing this objective these agencies soon discovered that good fishing could only be provided in streams and lakes where siltation and pollution had been brought under control; that hunting could only be provided where land users had left suitable cover for wildlife. The beautiful landscapes of the state could only be preserved and maintained by woodland conservation programs.

These realizations prompted the Iowa General Assembly in 1931 to adopt a joint resolution, approved by the governor, instructing the State Board of Conservation and the State Fish and Game Commission to collaborate on a long-term conservation plan and program. This resolution called for a 25-year program that would also include soil conservation.

Iowa's first 25 Year Conservation Plan was issued in 1933. Involved in this early organization were Aldo Leopold and J. N. "Ding" Darling, who both later became well-known conservation advocates.

Drought and dust bowl conditions of the early 1930s prompted the federal government to assist state governments in soil conservation work. Iowan Henry A. Wallace, U.S. Secretary of Agriculture at the time, assisted in drafting model legislation

Soils formed in alluvial deposits, such as these along the Skunk River Valley in Story County, are some of our state's most productive soils.

Tom C. Cooper

Tom C. Cooper

for states to use in establishing Soil Conservation Districts. This model law was sent to all governors in 1937 to be studied by state legislatures. The Iowa General Assembly enacted our state's Soil Conservation District Law in 1939.

The Soil Conservation District Law provided for the formation of a State Soil Conservation Committee. This committee consisted of seven members and an advisory member and had the task of supervising the establishment of the Soil Conservation Districts.

The first district to be established in Iowa was the Marion County District in 1940, the last was Howard County in 1952. Each district consists of one county except Pottawattamie which is divided into two — East and West. After the districts were established technical assistance was provided by the U.S. Department of Agriculture.

Soil Conservation Districts were founded on the principle of local citizens working to solve their problems, whereby the organization of each district was to be initiated by the farmers of the district. Twenty percent of the landowners within the area had to petition the State Soil Conservation Committee to hold a hearing. If a need was established at this meeting and the committee determined it was feasible to form a district, plans were made to hold a referendum. The referendum had to be approved by 65 percent of the landowners before the district could be formed. Each district selected three Soil Commissioners at the referendum and election. They formed the governing body of the district.

Cost-sharing incentives for landowners became available from the federal government in 1938 with passage of the Agriculture Adjustment Act. Various programs have been available since then and have been administered under several names. The USDA Soil Conservation Service has provided the technical assistance to establish eligibility, and to design and implement these programs.

As soil conservation districts came into existence, the demand for funds soon exceeded federal appropriations. Therefore, the Iowa 53rd General Assembly voted to provide funding directly to the Soil Conservation Districts, making Iowa the first state in the nation to appropriate money for this purpose.

Soil Conservation Districts in Iowa are local divisions of state government and now have jurisdiction not only over agricultural lands, but all other Iowa land as well. In 1970 the name of the state agency became the Department of Soil Conservation. The governing body continues to be called the State Soil Conservation Committee, however.

In 1971 the Iowa General Assembly enacted an Iowa Conservancy District Law. Six conservancy districts were formed, set apart by the boundaries of major river basins of the state, the purpose being to approach soil conservation problems from a watershed approach. The legislature also gave authority for commissioners to establish soil loss limits. Under this authority a system was established whereby a landowner receiving excessive sediment from erosion from someone else's land may file a com-

This landscape in eastcentral Iowa shows soil conservation practices on gently-sloping terrain.

Iowa Department of Soil Conservation

plaint against the landowners. If a review of the complaint shows significant erosion is occurring, corrective measures must be taken.

In 1973 Iowa became the first state to provide cost-sharing funds for installing corrective measures for erosion control.

It has been recognized that the tremendous costs of protecting our soil from erosion cannot be carried by the farmer alone. For example, in expensive erosion control programs such as terracing, the farmer who needs it the most is usually the one with the hilly, sloping land which provides a marginal or insufficient economic base to do the terracing.

Even though Iowa has been a leader in conservation programs, it is estimated that only one-third of the state's cropland is adequately protected from erosion (that is, loss does not exceed 5 tons per acre per year for most of our soils). Soil scientists estimate that topsoil will replace itself at that rate each year. This leaves approximately 18 million acres of cropland unprotected and in need of soil conservation practices.

The need for conservation efforts was described in a 1976 speech presented to the Iowa Seed Dealers' Association by William H. Greiner, Director, Department of Soil Conservation, State of Iowa:

"What does conservation protection mean? Let us look at an example of a typical southern Iowa soil and we will use that 8 inches of topsoil left. The example being used is an 8 inch topsoil layer of Grundy silt loam on a 2 to 5 percent slope, which is not terribly steep. If the farmer plants corn year after year, plows in the fall up and down the hill, and leaves no crop residue on the surface, he will lose the entire 8 inch layer of soil in 36 years.

"If the field is contoured, but still fall plowed, the topsoil will last twice as long, or 72 years.

"The topsoil will last 104 years if the farmer builds terraces on the contour, and continues to plow without leaving crop residue on the surface.

"If he plows on the contour in the spring, and leaves as little as 2,000 pounds of residue per acre on the

Blizzard conditions cause both topsoil and snow to form large drifts in this Boone County rural area.

Though our Iowa soils are some of the richest in the world, fertilizers such as anhydrous ammonia are applied to corn to produce even greater yields.

ground, the soil will last 176 years.

"Finally, if he practices no-till farming, with contour terraces and crop residue on the surface all year long, the 8 inches of topsoil will last 2,224 years — long enough, our soil scientists say, to make some new topsoil.

"Think about that. Farming in the most careless way, this valuable topsoil will last only about one-third of a century. Using the best soil conservation system, the original soil lasts 22 centuries, with more produced to take its place."

These figures are estimates, based on average annual soil loss predictions. In any one year, of course, soil losses could be less or much worse.

Iowa is the first state in the nation to have a soil conservation policy statement and 5-, 10-, 15-, and 20-year long-range goals that have been adopted by the legislature. This program enacted in 1980 has been named "Iowa Soil 2000" and has the objective of reducing erosion losses to nondepleting levels by the end of the century. "Iowa Soil 2000" was developed in the process of responding to the Soil and Water Resources Conservation Act (RCA) passed by the United States Congress in 1978 which required each state to conduct an appraisal of its soil and water resources. Iowans chose to carry out their task at the grassroots level and held local and regional meetings to gather citizen input. RCA Committees and Task Forces were formed and reported their recommendations to the State RCA Committee in July, 1979.

In 1980, the State RCA Committee issued an *Iowa Five-Year Resource Conservation Plan*. In this plan the Committee concluded:

"Soil erosion must be reduced to the allowable soil loss limits before the current productive capability of the soil is permanently impaired. This will require commitment at all levels of government and by the private sector, in a vastly accelerated conservation effort."

The continual removal of topsoil by erosion, increased energy costs for on-farm production as well as increased production costs of fertilizers and chemicals, conversion of cropland to nonagricultural uses, and the uncertainty of continued favorable weather patterns may have a major impact on our state's ability to achieve record crop yields in the future.

Scientists and farmers are increasing their efforts in the one area that can be controlled — topsoil erosion. New tillage techniques are being studied by researchers and applied by farmers. One readily available and adaptable technique to slow topsoil erosion is conservation tillage.

The future potential of reaping high yields from our productive soils, depends upon our ability to preserve our soil resource. Thamon Hazen, Assistant Director of the Iowa Agriculture and Home Economics Experiment Station says, "Where conservation tillage is concerned, the scientists we look to for miracles are telling us something by their actions. They are not devoting their time to search for a soil replacement. They believe our future lies in preserving the soil."

Carl Kurtz

CHAPTER FIVE
WEATHER & CLIMATE
BY PAUL WAITE AND ROBERT SHAW

Previous Spread
A storm-threatening summer sunset sky. Seldom seen cumulonimbus mamma clouds, a harbinger of thunderstorms sometimes associated with floods, windstorms, hail and or tornadoes.

Tom C. Cooper

A typical mid-summer shower in Story County replenishing Iowa's thirsty crops with water. (Below)

WE IOWANS ARE well aware of the stimulating effects of our ever changing weather and climate upon our activities. We cannot escape the fact that our climate — the summation of our daily weather — profoundly affects our food supply, energy needs, transportation, water supplies, shelter, and economic well-being. Neither are we surprised that our weather guides us in our choice of recreation, choice of occupation, moods, health, and even, some say, the kind of literature we read. Our weather is sometimes blamed for the discomforts of the physically handicapped, seizures of the mentally ill, and for the occurrence of crime against our society.

Most of us well remember the two long, cold, snowy winters of 1977-78 and 1978-79, which, persisting well into spring, brought on cabin fever epidemics among our winter-weary populace. Nor will we soon forget the intense heat of the dry 1980 summer with its costly discomfort upon our lives and the near dessication of our countryside. While humans have been successful at harnessing most natural forces, our climate remains almost entirely out of control. For the present we must remain content to claim such local modifications as building shelter belts and heating our homes. Rainfall and hail modification research may, in time, provide us our first controls over our state's weather and climate. But presently our greatest hope is that our climatic influences will become well enough understood that climate forecasts can be significantly improved for planning our general activities a year or so in advance.

Iowa's weather is well known for its variety and, on occasion, its destructive fury. No one who has ever seen the awesome spectacle of an Iowa tornado will forget the savage fury of the twister.

As the tornado is to the warm season so is the blizzard to winter, with its numbing cold winds full of blinding snow that sifts through our homes and into the smallest cracks; truly the blizzard is an arch-foe of human and beast.

By contrast, Iowa's weather can be as gentle as a lamb and as beautiful as the newly emerged butterfly. One of those occasions is that first mild spring day with its warm southerly breezes wafting billowing white cumulus clouds overhead, floating lazily somewhere between the azure blue skies above and the greening meadows below. Every season has its beauty; be it the dewy quiet summer morning, the crisp dry sunniness of autumn or the gentle snow sifting over the whitening countryside.

A summer evening rainbow over Slater, Story County.

Tom C. Cooper

Measurement and Use of Climatic Data

IOWA'S CLIMATIC information is available to everyone because of the wisdom and foresight of our forefathers, who well over a century ago began measuring our state's daily weather. U.S. Army surgeons at Fort Calhoun near Council Bluffs made the first measurements, beginning October 19, 1819. Weather records were kept at a number of Midwest Army forts before the Weather Bureau was established in 1870.

Iowa's corps of citizen weather observers began in 1838, when Iowa Territorial Governor Robert Lucas' private secretary, Theodore Sutton Parvin (1807-1901), arrived in Muscatine with thermometers and barometers. Other citizen observers followed in the 1840s, '50s and '60s. In 1870 the Army Signal Corps was charged with establishing a national weather service, which was transferred to the Department of Agriculture in 1891 and to the Department of Commerce in 1940.

Iowa's own weather service began October 1, 1875, under the direction of Professor Gustavus Hinrichs, then at the State College in Iowa City. This was the first state weather service established west of the Mississippi River and now is the nation's oldest state service in continuous operation. Since 1890 it has enjoyed varying degrees of cooperation with the National Weather Service.

The National Weather Service supervises the official cooperative climatic network of nearly 270 Iowa observers, some of whom have kept weather records for more than 40 years — even longer than 50 years in a few instances. The National Weather Service provides daily forecasts for periods of a few days and weather outlooks from five days to seasonal length in advance.

The Iowa Department of Agriculture maintains an official archive of weather records from the last century, analyzes climatic data and prepares climatic probabilities, summarizes and provides climatic data and studies for Iowans. The Iowa State University Meteorology/Climatology Section conducts climatic researches and is one of our nation's leading schools in preparing students as climatologists and meteorologists.

Almost everyone uses Iowa's climatic resources for all kinds of plans: selection of a date for an outdoor event; design of a bridge to withstand all floods; spring-planting density of corn; when to plant tomatoes; design of an energy efficient home, or date to put on snow tires. While not neglecting other elements in the economy, the major efforts of climatology are directed toward the eight of every ten Iowans who depend directly upon agriculture for their livelihood.

Three factors — soil, climate, and technology — are the prime contributors to Iowa's leading role in agriculture. Climate causes the greatest variation in agricultural production. Iowa's normal climate is nearly perfect for agriculture, but the normal is observed rarely. When our weather becomes too hot, too wet, too windy, or too dry, our plants and animals suffer stress, and our agricultural economy usually suffers. At certain times some stress may actually be beneficial but, in excess, climatic stress reduces plant yields and livestock gains even to the point of destruction.

Carl Kurtz

Elements of Our Climate

The golden glow of an Iowa sunset and the sparkling wintry ice on a farm fence.

SOME SAY climate is Iowa's most valuable environmental resource. In times past it helped create our countryside and our legacy of excellent soils. Its changeability stimulates our people, whose literacy and longevity scarcely are exceeded anywhere in our nation. In spite of occasional weather-caused destruction and adversity, our climate is a valuable resource.

Iowa's climate, a result of latitude and interior continental location, is characterized by marked seasonal variations. In the warm half year, the prevailing southerly flow of air from the Gulf of Mexico region provides about 70 percent of our annual precipitation. In the colder half year, winds are usually from the northwest in masses of cold dry Arctic or polar air, sometimes relieved by milder Pacific polar incursions.

Iowa lies at the crossroads of our nation's air mass movement — cold air from polar and Arctic regions arrives from the north and northwest; mild Pacific air moves eastward across the state; warm desert air comes from the southwest United States, and warm humid air from the Gulf of Mexico. The seasonal prevalence of the air masses — largely cold and dry in winter and warm and moist in summer — creates great variability in our climatic elements.

Air and soil temperatures are important controls for plant and insect development. All the weather changes that we observe are related in some way to one single element — heat. And the source of almost all the earth's heat is the sun with surface temperature of about 10,000 degrees F. By virtue of distance, earth tilt, and interior continental location, Iowa receives enough solar energy to average a very pleasant 48.5 degrees, varying from about 45 or 46 in the north to 51 or 52 in the south. In the course of a year, monthly variation is about 55 degrees, varying from 19.2 in January to 74.0 in July, while the average extreme range is about 115 degrees. In central Iowa, that's from 99 to -16 degrees F. Iowa's most extreme temperatures were measured decades ago — 47 below 0 in northwest Iowa in 1912 and 118 above in southeast Iowa in 1934, a record range of 165. In the average year, Iowa temperatures drop 34 below somewhere in the state and by summer reach 104, most often in the southwest, for an average state range of 138 degrees.

Temperature change is typical. On a daily basis, temperatures vary about 15 degrees F in the cloudier winter months to 20 or more in the long, sunnier days of summer and sunny, dry autumn days. Typically we experience 1 or 2 changes of air masses a week, which are particularly abrupt in the colder half year. We can experience changes of 20 degrees in a few hours or 40 to 50 degrees in a single day. Yes, our weather does change rapidly and frequently.

Few weather events are more noteworthy to Iowans than the last spring and the first autumn freeze, since some 94 percent of Iowa is devoted to farms and, in the rest, urban dwellers grow flowers and gardens. The intervening growing season of some 145 days in the north to 170 days in the southeast amounts to less than half the year, but hardier plants such as grass and winter wheat usually are green until mid-November and green up again in late March, leaving a dormant season of about 18 or 20 weeks.

On the average, the last spring freeze occurs around May 3 — varying from about April 20 in the south to about May 10 in the north. The first autumn freeze occurs from about September 30 in the north to October 10 to October 15 in the south.

Many plants grow and develop by a fairly precise relationship to temperature. Corn is one. It develops at an increasing rate with each degree of daily average temperature above 50 degrees F until the day averages over 86, at which temperature stress adds no more to the growth rate and may even slow it down. Similarly, peas develop with temperatures over 40 degrees, and grass and small grains begin growth at about the same point.

The beautiful frosty touch at the end of a growing season.

Carl Kurtz

Many weed seeds also develop with cool temperatures. Spring flowering and tree leaf development frequently are directly related to spring temperatures, the aggregation of which is termed growing degree days. Our forefathers recognized these facts and kept records of plant development. In the same vein arose weather proverbs such as "when the oak leaf is as big as a squirrel's ear, it's time to plant corn."

Engineers learned a half century or more ago that heating requirements in homes, factories, and businesses could be directly related to the number of degrees below a certain base (usually 65 degrees F). The daily average temperature is subtracted from the base and this remainder is added day after day to give monthly and seasonal totals. From the same 65-degree base, cooling-degree-day (CDD) requirements are figured for our hot-weather season. The measure of cooling-degree days is directly proportional to cooling costs, with the number increasing from less than 600 CDD in the northeast to as many as 1,200 at Keokuk in extreme southeast Iowa.

The importance of soil temperature is evident when we realize that most heating is accomplished by the sun striking the earth. In turn, heat radiating upward from the soil provides most of the warmth to the overlying air, thereby dominating the environment.

Since 1937, soil temperatures have been continuously measured in Ames at the Iowa State University Agronomy Farms. Since 1950, the network has expanded, numbering 17 sites in 1981; this is one of the longest and best-continuing state soil-temperature programs in the United States.

101

Clouds

FOR IOWA'S FARMER, fisherman, or aircraft pilot, clouds are signals of weather to come. Knowing clouds provides major assistance in making your own weather forecasts. Clouds form from gaseous water vapor in the atmosphere. This gas, when cooled to saturation, condenses into droplets or ice crystals and forms one of the types of clouds typical for Iowa, the puffy white cumulus — clouds that grow into towering cauliflower-shaped cumulo-nimbus characteristic of Iowa summers. Sometimes alone, cumulus more often are accompanied by the high, thin, wispy cirrus and some stratified clouds as well. It is those familiar cumulo-nimbus — flashing with lightning and rumbling with thunder — that produce most of our rain. In the four-month period of May through August, cumulo-nimbus produce more than half the annual rainfall and most of the season's hail storms, windstorms, floods, and tornadoes.

In the colder half year, stratus-like clouds are the dominant types with attendant lighter rain, drizzle, and snow. Occasionally the stratus forms at ground level as fog. In Iowa's colder half year, dense fog is twice as frequent as in the warmer half.

Iowa's monthly cloudiness pattern averages some 65-70 percent from November through May, with December and March the cloudiest. From June through October cloudiness decreases to 50 to 60 percent. October and often September and August are the least cloudy Iowa months.

Summer's cumulus clouds are often the most spectacular and inspiring, particularly after a storm has passed eastward and the lower afternoon sun produces a spectacular rainbow of water droplets from the departing storm. Winter is not without its spectacular views either. Often parhelia, popularly termed "sun dogs," are seen with cirrus clouds and the sun at a low level. On rare occasions, the parhelion may be viewed when the sun is at higher elevations. The cirrus, composed of ice crystals, will produce lunar and solar haloes. Perhaps most often in winter and early spring, the atmosphere's clarity enables us to see some spectacularly colored skies. Striking cirroform or semi-stratified clouds from below the horizon, the sinking sun's rays transform them first to yellows, then to pinks or reds, and finally fade them to grays as the earth rotates. For many of us, glowing pink aircraft contrails pencilled across the azure western sky are evening beauties, even though they are artificially made clouds.

Parhelia or sundogs, occasionally seen in winter. (Right)
A low sun with suspended ice or snow crystals. (Below)
Ominous clouds 30 minutes after the Jordan tornado in 1976 in Boone and Story counties. (Bottom)

Carl Kurtz

Bill Gillette

Pete Krumhardt

The setting sun illumines the sky and colorful cumulus.

Precipitation

IOWA'S RAINFALL variability is more closely related to its crop yields than any other climatic element. Our best crop years coincide with normal to above-normal precipitation. For example, the above normal rainfalls in 1972-73 and again in 1978-79 coincided with record yields. Lack of rain, particularly in 1976 and in central counties in 1977 illustrates the crippling effects of drought upon crop production. Agricultural losses in 1977 cost Iowa $1 billion.

The importance of our precipitation cannot be overstated. It regulates the flow of our streams and springs, the level of our water tables, lakes and ponds, and the soil moisture reserves with which we begin our growing season. Our precipitation serves as an atmospheric cleanser and as a source to flush pollutants from our streams. Increasingly, pressure upon our water supplies necessitates care and planning to maintain our agro-economy.

Precipitation — the most measured of weather elements in Iowa, with nearly 300 official sites providing data — includes rain, snow, sleet, drizzle, hail, and other falling hydrometeors. It does not include moisture gained from dew, frost, or fog. Snow and related frozen forms constitute about 10 percent of our precipitation; almost all of the remaining 90 percent is rain. Fortunately more than 70 percent falls during the growing-season months of April through September. Much of the precipitation that falls on frozen soils in most of December, January, February, and March runs off as it melts.

Iowa precipitation is quite variable. Besides the typical seasonal variation, average precipitation varies annually from as little as 25 inches in the extreme northwest to around 35 inches along southern and east central counties, with a state average near 32 inches. Within Iowa, calendar-year totals have varied from 12.11 inches at Clear Lake in 1910 and Cherokee in 1958 to 74.50 inches at Muscatine in 1851. On a state-wide basis, the driest single year was 1910, with an average of 19.89 inches, and the wettest was 1881, with an average of 44.16 inches

Tom C. Cooper

High winds fan cumuloform clouds over Iowa's green and growing countryside in Story County.

Iowa Weather Extremes

Temperature
    Highest Day: 118° F at Keokuk, July 20, 1934
    Hottest Month: 83.3°, July 1936
    Hottest Summer: June-August 77.6°, 1936
    Warmest Year: 53.2°, 1931
    Coldest Day: -47° F at Washta, January 12, 1912
    Coldest Winter: December-February, 11.8°, 1874-75
    Coldest Year: 43.3°, 1875
    Worst Winter (prolonged cold and snow): 1935-36
    1978-79 coldest winter since 1935-36
    1977-78 and 1978-79 coldest consecutive winters of Iowa record

Precipitation
    Greatest One Minute: 0.69 inch, 11 miles north of Jefferson, July 10, 1955
    Greatest Day (official): 12.99 inches, Larrabee, June 24, 1891
    Greatest Day (unofficial): 21.70 inches, Boyden, Sioux County, September 18, 1926
    Greatest Month: 22.18 inches, Red Oak, June 1967
    Greatest Month (state average): 10.33, June 1947
    Greatest Year: 74.50 inches, Muscatine, 1851
    Greatest Year (state average): 44.16 inches, 1881
    Driest Month (state average): 0.02 inch, October 1952
    Driest Year: Cherokee, 12.11 inches, 1958 and Clear Lake, 12.11 inches, 1910
    Driest Year (state average): 19.89 inches, 1910
    Worst Drought Years: 1936 and 1894, recent years, 1976-77

Snow
    Heaviest 13 Hour Snowfall: 24.0 inches, Northboro (Page County), February 25-26, 1912
    Heaviest Single Storm: 30.8 inches, Rock Rapids, February 17-21, 1962
    Snowiest Month: 42.0 inches, Osage and Northwood, March 1951
    Snowiest Month (state average): 23.2 inches, March 1951
    Snowiest Season: 90.4 inches, Northwood, 1908-09
    Snowiest Season (state average): 59.0 inches, 1961-62
    Earliest Snowfall: September 16, 1881, amounts to 6 inches between Stuart and Avoca and 4 inches in Algona. Measurable snow west half state
    Latest Snowfall: May 28, 1947, amounts up to 8 inches at Cherokee and 7½ inches at Waukon, a trace of snow at Fayette on May 29, 1927

Frost
    First killing frost autumn: Average, September 25-30 north to October 10-15 south
    Earliest General: September 8-9, 1927
    Earliest in north: August 1 and 8, 1927
    Last killing frost spring: Average, May 10 north to April 20-25 south
    Latest General: May 29, 1947

Blizzard
    Worst in Western Iowa: January 12, 1888
    Worst in Eastern Iowa: January 31, 1863 and January 1, 1964

Tornado
    Worst: Hardin County through Camanche into Illinois, June 3, 1860, 141 killed, 329 injured, 160 mile long path

Hail
    Worst Storm: Grinnell across southeast Iowa near Burlington into westcentral Illinois, August 18, 1925
    Largest Hailstone: Dubuque, June 16, 1882, 17 inches circumference, weight 1.75 pounds

Barometric Pressure
    Lowest: 28.66 inches, Sioux City, March 26, 1950
    Highest: 31.09 inches, Sioux City, December 29, 1917

Wind
    Highest (not in a tornado): Over 100 mph with gust exceeding 115 mph at Ottumwa, June 25, 1960 and 105 mph at Waterloo, July 9, 1980

Tom C. Cooper

Iowa's awesome lightning as seen approximately 50 days or nights per year. Bethesda Lutheran Church, Ames. (Left) A silver lining to a summer storm cloud. (Below)

Pete Krumhardt

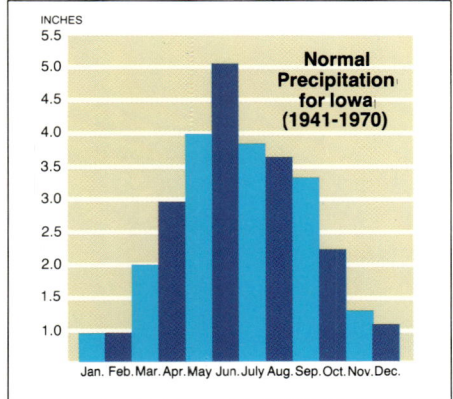

of rain. In recent years (since 1955) the driest year was 1976, with 23.61 inches, and the wettest was 1973, with 42.95 inches.

On about 50 days a year, thunderstorms produce most of our warm-weather violence. Nearly two-thirds of our thunderstorms are reported during the third of a year from May to August. And, of course, in this same period we get most of our tornadoes, floods, hailstorms, windstorms, and soil losses from erosion.

On 80 percent of the days with measurable rain, amounts are less than a half inch, and on the average, only one day a year produces more than two inches of rain. But on September 17-18, 1926, the greatest rainstorm of record in Iowa was reported at Boyden in Sioux County. This storm deluged the area with 21.7 inches of rain in a 24-hour period. In the first 6 hours 15.1 inches fell with an additional 5.6 inches being received in the next 6 hours. Excessive rainfalls are costly in terms of soil erosion, crop and property losses and, on occasion, loss of livestock or human lives.

The atmospheric phenomenon which kills most often in Iowa is lightning. It takes its toll largely from farmers and others involved in outdoor activities. Tornadoes, while far more dramatic, kill somewhat fewer Iowans — except during those few times when a savage storm cuts through some population center. This is partly explained by the fact that lightning can be expected to strike within each square mile 20 to 30 times in a year while a tornado strike in each square mile is expected only once every 250 to 300 years. A human death from hail has never been reported in Iowa, but substantial property damage is sustained every year. In 1980, the worst in decades, crop and property losses from hail were set at about $100 million or more.

Perhaps the most unusual hail storm in Iowa history took place in Dubuque in 1882. A military officer stationed there wrote this report:

"Dubuque, Iowa, 16th (June 1882). For thirteen minutes, commencing at 2:54 p.m., the largest and most destructive hailstones fell that were seen at this place. The hailstones measured from one to seventeen inches in circumference, the largest weighing one pound and twelve ounces. Washington Park was literally covered with hailstones as large as lemons, and large basketfuls could be gathered in a few minutes. They exhibited diverse and peculiar formations, some being covered by knobs and icicles half an inch thick; others were surrounded by rings of different colored ice with gravel and

Carl Kurtz

The calm winter serenity on Honey Creek in Reece's County Park in Hardin County after an early winter snow and heavy frost. (Left)

Winter's icy beauty in a central Iowa stream. (Below)

Carl Kurtz

blades of grass imbedded within them. The foreman of the Novelty Iron Works, of this city, states that in two large hailstones melted by him were found small living frogs. A number of persons were severely cut and bruised by falling hailstones. The damage inflicted is estimated at $5,000. One florist lost 2,387 panes of glass. Hundreds of windows of south and west exposure were broken, including twenty windows of heavy French plate glass."

Drought, the lack of adequate precipitation, often is intensified by heat and dessicating winds. It is the most costly atmospheric phenomenon of all to Iowa's agro-economy. On the average, drought is twice as costly to farmers as flood, hail, or wind. Remarkable droughts in Iowa and the Great Plains include 1894, 1934, 1936, mid-1950s, and mid-1970s. Major droughts have occurred 20 to 22 years apart, and from this sequence, we would predict the next major drought period to be in the mid-to-late 1990s.

Snowfall, despite its small contribution to water, is important for its insulating qualities over soil and over wintering crops. It is also a source of joy and activity for winter-sports enthusiasts and, in late winter, as a source of water to recharge stream flows. Snow combined with rains occasionally causes major spring flooding at the end of March or in early April; snow deters transportation and lowers winter temperatures, increasing energy use and livestock care and indirectly causing numerous deaths among snow shovelers. Almost always snow produces mixed reactions because it is a costly, inconveniencing benefactor.

Coupled with strong winds and cold, snow can be deadly. The term blizzard originated in Iowa, first appearing in print in the Estherville (Iowa) *Vindicator* to describe a storm that swept across the Dakotas and Iowa March 14, 1870. Iowa normally experiences one or two blizzards a year and, every few years or so, a particularly devastating blizzard is recorded. The April 8-10, 1973, storm with its 5 to 20 inches of snow driven by 40 to 50 mph winds, gusting to 65 mph, caused 14 storm-related deaths and livestock losses of $19 million. It will not soon be forgotten, nor will the blizzard of January 12, 1888, in western Iowa, and the December 31, 1863-January 1, 1864, blizzard in eastern Iowa. The savage fury of a blizzard is to winter as the tornado is to summer.

Agricultural Water Balance

WATER USED by crops comes from summer rains or from moisture stored in the soil. Iowa State University has been conducting a survey of soil-moisture conditions since 1954. The amount of moisture available to plants is determined for the upper five feet of the profile. In mid-April available soil moisture typically ranges from less than 5 inches in northwestern Iowa to almost 11 inches in eastcentral Iowa. The reserve helps (carry) the crops through dry periods in the summer. Soil moisture reaches a minimum in early September, and then increases with fall rains. By early November, the reserves average from near 4 inches in northwestern Iowa to 9 inches in eastcentral Iowa.

Another important factor in the agricultural water balance is water lost by evaporation and transpiration. The demand for water by the atmosphere — what we call the potential for evaporation — is greatest in the west and least in the east. Measured pan evaporation from mid-April through October ranges from 43 inches in southwestern Iowa to 36.5 inches in eastcentral Iowa. Although the potential for evaporation is greatest in the west, water lost by crops (evapotranspiration) shows only a small gradient across the state — and is highest in the east because of the greater availability of water (more soil moisture reserve and more summer rain). Northwestern Iowa has an average loss of almost 21 inches for the period; southeastern Iowa has a loss of 22 inches.

Carl Kurtz

A central Iowa shower typical of Iowa's warm season.

A low sun lights up a towering anvil top of a cumulonimbus cloud.

Larry Stone

Wind — The Atmosphere in Motion

HAVE YOU BEEN asked by a small child, "What makes the wind blow?" It is the sun which makes the wind blow, because of its differential heating of the earth's surface. Wind has come to command a special respect once more as a possible energy source for Iowans. Where windmills once dotted the countryside, sleeker more efficient wind chargers are appearing today. But wind is more than a source of energy.

Our winds transport heat, energy, water vapor, insects, dust, pollen, spores, pollution, and snow. The cooling power of a summer breeze and the freezing chill of a wintry blast are well known, and so is the destructive sweep of winds in a storm, toppling trees, stripping shingles from roofs, and flattening crops to the ground. Winds erode our top soils quite in contrast to the soil-building of our loess hills formed by winds some 13,000 to 29,000 years ago. Snow fences are set and shelter belts are grown to evade the wind effects on farms. In spring, kites are flown and, in summer, sails are unfurled to power our boats. No doubt about it: winds are important. Without them, pollution would stagnate into a cloud over our land.

Our monsoon-like pattern provides a prevailing flow of air from the south for the six months from May through October and from the northwest from November through April.

Typically Iowa winds are strong-

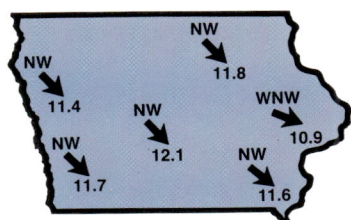

Winter winds and velocity.

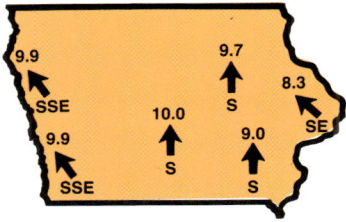

Summer winds and velocity.

111

The cumulo-mamma clouds formed minutes after a tornado in Boone County.

est in March and April, averaging about 13 miles an hour, and weakest in August, averaging near 8 miles an hour. On a typical day, wind speeds are least from midnight until shortly after sunrise, averaging 7 or 8 miles an hour, and increase to 12 to 15 miles an hour from noon until about 3 p.m.

Violent winds and the greatest windstorm losses are reported during the months of April through July and are associated with severe thunderstorms. At roof-top level of most houses (15-20 feet), we can expect 80 mile-an-hour winds once a century.

Our most dreaded winds are those associated with tornadoes. The tornado is recognized by its rotating funnel of condensed moisture, dust, and debris. The average Iowa tornado is a few hundred yards in diameter, with internal wind speeds varying from 100 to 500 miles an hour. Its life span is usually but a few minutes as it travels a path of a few miles. The forward speed is usually 30 to 35 miles an hour. During the average season, about 30 tornadoes and more than 100 funnel clouds aloft are reported, mostly during April through July over our state. Iowa lies along the northeast side of the world's greatest tornado belt.

It was the Lewis and Clark Expedition moving up the Missouri River along southwestern Iowa, which observed the first tornado of Iowa record. The year was 1804.

According to historical documents, the first of Iowa's outstanding tornadoes moved southeastward passing south of Iowa City on the afternoon of May 24, 1859. The Iowa City tornado claimed five lives, injured six persons seriously, and a dozen or more were less seriously hurt.

In the next year, Iowa's greatest killer of record swept away most of Camanche, a small hamlet south of Clinton, on the evening of June 3, 1860. Called the "great tornado" it was said to have begun in central Iowa west of Cedar Rapids and to have ended in Michigan. Its toll along its path in Iowa totaled 134 dead, 81 injured and 2,500 persons homeless — mostly in Camanche, which was nearly obliterated. Its path was described as erratic; its speed varied; it skipped and sometimes appeared as two or more funnels. Perhaps the Camanche tornado was really a whole family of tornadoes.

The Grinnell tornado the evening of June 17, 1882, was Iowa's first million-dollar tornado. Loss of life was placed at 100, and injuries were borne by about 300 persons. The heaviest losses were sustained at Grinnell and Malcom. The tornado was reputed to have originated in Greene County near Jefferson, passing south of Ogden. It traveled about 57 miles an hour, reaching Grinnell near 8:45 p.m. In Grinnell 60 persons were killed, 150 were injured, and property losses totaled $600,000. Another 40 deaths, 150 injuries, and $500,000 in losses were reported elsewhere along the path, which included Malcom, Brooklyn, and Mount Pleasant.

Iowa can be accurately called "the tornado state," because more tornadoes for its area occur in Iowa than any other state.

Bill Gillette

(Top) Aftermath of the Jordan tornado that ripped through Boone and Story counties in 1976. (Above) Three photos showing the size and movement of the Jordan tornado. National Weather Service officials called this the most devastating tornado of 1976, yet no lives were lost. ©1976 by Charles Barthold and the Palmer Broadcasting Company

Major Iowa Tornadoes (1803-1980) with Five or More Fatalities

Tornado Location	Date	Number of People Killed	Injured
Iowa City, Johnson Co.	May 24, 1859	5	18
Camanche, Clinton Co.	June 3, 1860	134	81
Keokuk and Washington Cos.	May 22, 1873	8	15
Monona Co. to Buena Vista Co.	April 21, 1878	10	28
Crawford Co. to Pocahontas Co.	April 21, 1878	18	29
Macedonia, Pottawattamie Co.	June 9, 1880	20	
Wheelers Grove, Cass Co.	June 9, 1880	Many (20)	
Hancock Co. to Cerro Gordo Co.	June 11, 1881	9	
Grinnell, Poweshiek Co.	June 17, 1882	100	300
Dunlap, Harrison Co.	April 21, 1883	Some (5)	
Pomeroy, Cherokee Co. to Calhoun Co.	July 6, 1893	89	Many
Clay County	Sept. 21, 1894	53	
Sioux, Lyon & Osceola Cos.	May 3, 1895	15	35
Polk to Jasper Co.	May 24, 1896	20	
Stanwood, Cedar Co.	May 18, 1898	19	40
Salix, Woodbury Co.	June 11, 1899	5	
Pottawattamie Co. & East Harrison Co	March 23, 1913	33	100
Pearl Rock to Calmer, Butler Co. — Winneshiek Co.	May 9, 1918	8	20
Denison to Stanhope, Crawford Co. — Hamilton Co.	May 21, 1918	6	35
Berkley to Wellsburg, Boone Co. — Grundy Co.	May 21, 1918	10	91
Council Bluffs, Pottawattamie Co.	Sept. 28, 1923	6	5
Ionia, Chickasaw Co.	April 23, 1948	5	25
Belmond, Wright Co.	Oct. 14, 1966	6	172
Charles City, Franklin Co. — Howard Co.	May 15, 1968	13	450
Oelwein-Maynard, Fayette Co.	May 15, 1968	5	156
Grinnell, Jasper & Poweshiek Cos.	Sept. 16, 1978	6	45
Algona-Manson & 8 other tornadoes Emmet & Kossuth Cos. to Dallas Co.	June 28, 1979	5	70

Solar Radiation

THE ONLY LONG-TERM, solar-radiation station in Iowa today is at Iowa State University. Radiation peaks in the late June-early July period, shortly after the summer solstice due to decreasing cloud cover. The minimum radiation values occur in December, near the time of the winter solstice.

Agriculture has always been dependent upon solar energy since crops are produced by photosynthesis with sunlight. Now, solar radiation is being considered as a supplementary energy source along with wind, the latter used for decades to pump water by windmills dotting our countryside.

Wind offers the greatest potential for energy in the spring, while solar radiation has the least energy on a horizontal surface in winter. By orienting solar receptors properly, the amount of solar energy can be significantly increased in winter. If the two sources are combined, the highest potential energy period would be the spring, with summer and fall having the minimum amount of potential energy.

Early morning sunrays diffused by fog.

Climate Change

OUR CLIMATE is undergoing constant change, fluctuating from year to year and decade to decade and suggesting some patterns that may be useful to us in planning for the decades ahead.

A cooling trend began after the 1930s, reversing a remarkably strong, half-century-long warming trend. Average temperatures rose 3.5 degrees F in the 1930s over the decade of the 1880s. A 2.2 degree F cooling since the 1930s made the 1970s comparable to the decade, 1900-09. And, with year-to-year fluctuation, it will be difficult to say when this cooling pattern has come to an end — perhaps not until quite some time after the pattern has ended. Iowa's warming-then-cooling pattern has been in agreement with worldwide change, particularly in the higher latitudes of the Northern Hemisphere.

Iowa's past autumn, winter, and spring temperatures followed the same general climatic pattern as previously described, but summer temperatures tend to oscillate by alternate decades without significant long-term, warming or cooling trends. Thus, it is that the summers of 1970s, 1950s, 1930s, 1910s, 1890s, and 1870s are warmer than decades adjacent to them (for the 1873-1980 period of study). This is explained, at least in part, by droughts in those same decades.

Precipitation, too, seems to oscillate — apparently being closely related to a 22-year-long, double-sunspot period. Since 1873 unusually dry periods occurred from 1886 to 1899, from 1930-39, and from 1953-58. In more recent years, 1975 to mid-1977 was a seriously dry period.

Neither climatic changes nor their causes are well understood. Explanations may be based upon such widely differing things as variations in solar radiation; volcanic ash floating in the upper atmosphere; man-made alterations to the countryside; or atmospheric pollution. Granted an expanding population with growing needs, atmospheric scientists must learn as much as they can about probable — even possible — future climatic trends.

Tom Wagner

PART II
Living Iowa

plantlife,
prairies,
forests,
wetlands,
aquatic life
and
wildlife.

Carl Kurtz

Carl Kurtz

Carl Kurtz

Iowa as it Was

BY LARRY EILERS

ONE HUNDRED and fifty years ago, Iowa was essentially virgin territory — wild and undisturbed. A few explorers had penetrated our land, particularly along the Missouri and Mississippi rivers, but Iowa was still Indian territory. Settlement had not begun in earnest.

What was Iowa like then? What did the early settlers see? An excellent description of how Iowa appeared shortly after settlement was written by Bohumil Shimek (1861-1937), an early professor of natural sciences at the University of Iowa and a lifelong naturalist *(see Chapter 14)*. In the Foreword to *The Plant Geography of Iowa* (1948), Shimek wrote:

"A native of Iowa, the writer had an opportunity to observe many of the earlier natural conditions which have become a mere tradition. Born and reared at the edge of the woods extending north from Iowa City, the contact with the earlier conditions of this really fine piece of inland woods became an intimate part of his earliest experience . . .

"There were then still miles upon miles of almost undisturbed timber, fine white oaks predominating on the uplands, the hard maple occasionally dominating the river-bluffs, and the red cedar finding an anchorage on the limestone ledges, while the black walnut and various softwood trees occupied the narrow bottom lands. The upland woods were carpeted in early spring with hepaticas (chiefly on the steeper slopes) and the rue anemone, while the ravines were decked with beautiful ferns, interspersed with pink and yellow ladies'-slippers and many other wild flowers, all in great profusion, while the lowland woods displayed their gorgeous raiment of spring-beauties, *Mertensia*, buttercup, *Phlox* and *Isopyrum*, the whole making a wonderful flower garden.

"Nor did plant-life furnish the only interest. The wild turkey persisted, at least as late as 1886, the drumming of the ruffed grouse, now almost extinct, was one of the most familiar sounds in our woods, and the passenger pigeon still came in great clouds to seek shelter amid the oaks of

This view along the Mississippi River bluffs shows a rich, mature upland forest characteristic of the once-extensive forests of eastern Iowa.

Cedars are adapted to harsh environments. Our oldest Iowa tree is a cedar growing in a similar situation. This scene is of the Upper Iowa River in northeast Iowa.

This delicate flower is a harbinger of spring in Iowa's woodlands. Its color varies from white- to lavender-to blue. Hepatica is sometimes called "liver leaf" because the old leaves are wine colored and three-lobed in shape.

our uplands. (The writer saw the last pair of passenger pigeons in 1887. The male was shot.)

"Nor were primitive conditions displayed in the forests alone. There were still remnants of prairies, even in eastern Iowa, and in the year 1882 the writer found large areas of native prairie in the counties north and northwest of Wright County, and for more than 20 years thereafter (in constantly diminishing amount) in the northwestern part of the state . . .

"The waters, too, were largely unchanged. The mania for draining every wet spot had not fully developed, and there were oxbow lakes along our streams, then still undisturbed and unpolluted, and the "thousand-lake" region of north-central Iowa, with the countless kettle holes and lakes, was still true to the name bestowed upon it by the early pioneers.

"Something of the primeval conditions of that region is suggested further by the fact that in 1882 the writer still found much of the territory north and northwest from Wright County without roads other than uncharted prairie trails, and that not only was the flora of the prairie and the prairie "sloughs" and lakes but little affected by the white man's invasion, but bird-life still occurred in old-time profusion. Prairie-chickens were found in countless thousands and their nests often covered acres of the prairie; the long-billed curlew, now unknown in Iowa, everywhere hovered over the prairie, an easy mark for every pot-hunter; great clouds of golden plovers, or "prairie-pigeons" swooped down seemingly out of nowhere, apparently to alight, but only to sweep away again like a turbulent wave; the white and the sandhill cranes danced merrily (and awkwardly) before their mates; the borders of swamps and "sloughs" were often lined with the nests of ducks of several species; pelican eggs could be collected in favored spots by the boat-load; and practically every muskrat house supported the nest of a wild goose."

Professor Shimek describes the three major types of natural vegetation that were widespread in the

Iowa of his youth: tall-grass prairies, eastern deciduous forests, and wetlands. Remnants of each still exist in Iowa. Other minor but striking vegetational types that remain in our state include the sand plants, rock inhabitors, aquatic plants of cold-water springs, and several tiny clusters of plants that are far removed from their normal ranges. The latter are often called relict communities and will be discussed later. All of these several types of native vegetation show variation in the kinds of plants and animals they contain, depending on the available moisture, soil type, exposure to sun and wind, latitude, longitude, and other factors. Thus the prairies in western Iowa are somewhat different from those in eastern Iowa, and the forests of southern Iowa differ from those in the north.

Prairies

WHEN THE EARLIEST settlers first saw Iowa, 85 percent of the land was covered with tall-grass prairie (*see Chapter 7*). From a hilltop they could literally view a "sea of waving grass."

The prairie had a great influence on the lives of the first settlers: game there provided food; grasses provided grazing; sod provided housing; and flowers provided beauty. Our richest soils were formed from the deep prairie sod. Once the dominant vegetation of our region, it is now so scarce that one has to drive many miles to find even a small patch of native prairie. Yet these small pieces are very important as living remnants of early Iowa, and they remain as a part of our heritage.

In early Iowa many unusual and beautiful plants thrived. Now some species are gone altogether, and many others, such as monkshood shown here, are endangered.

Dean Roosa

Forests

THE FORESTS of Iowa were largely confined to the eastern and southern parts of the state, except for the strips of woodland that extended up the major rivers and streams (*see Chapter 8*). These narrow "gallery forests" were predominantly along the eastern banks and adjacent waterways because frequent prairie fires, driven before the westerly winds, effectively trimmed back any woody growth along the western banks.

Of Iowa's original vegetation, forests are the most plentiful today. They can be divided into three types, each characterized by its dominant tree species. These subdivisions are not always clearly distinct, and all three types integrate considerably.

Oak-hickory woods occupy the exposed uplands and south and west slopes. On the moist, sheltered north and east slopes and the adjacent ravine bottoms, maple-basswood forests are most often found. Alluvial woodlands (gallery forests) are restricted to the lowlands along rivers and larger streams.

Carl Kurtz

*(Above)
The major Iowa rivers often have forested banks that extend nearly the length of the river. These strips of woodland are the only type of vegetation in Iowa that provides a nearly continuous habitat for many birds and mammals.*

*(Left)
Sedges are grass-like plants that are common in wet areas. Sedges provide food and nest sites for many wetland animals.*

Wetlands

WETLANDS were most abundant in northcentral Iowa in the region covered by the last glacier to enter the state (*see Chapter 9*). This is the "thousand-lake" region referred to by Professor Shimek. This area was once peppered with small lakes, potholes, kettle holes, marshes, wet draws (sloughs), and sedge meadows.

Once abundant, wetlands were drained and tiled to such an extent that only a small fraction remains. Fortunately, some of the best that remain are being preserved as wildlife areas.

Postglacial Plant Migrations

WE KNOW that parts of Iowa were covered by ice sheets several times during the glacial era and that the last glacier left Iowa around 12,500 - 14,000 years ago (*see Chapter 2*). No prairies, deciduous forests, or wetlands were there then. When did these plant communities arrive? Where did they originate?

As the climate warmed and the glaciers melted, plants from the west, south, and east of the glaciated areas slowly migrated into our state. As the glacial margin retreated, the deciduous forest from the east and south slowly replaced the boreal coniferous forest that occurred along the margin. The maple-basswood forest moved into Iowa from the similar forests of the east. The upland oak-hickory woodlands of Iowa originated in the widespread forests of the south and southwest which still exist. Most of our prairie plants came from the plains region of Colorado, Nebraska, and Kansas. However, the tall grasses — big bluestem, little bluestem, Indian grass — migrated from the southeast, where they and their closest relatives still remain. Our wetland plants also moved in from the south and southeast, where they are abundant today.

The living Iowa we know today has changed dramatically, but we are indeed fortunate to have remnants of early Iowa to study and appreciate.

Natural Regions of Iowa

BY DEAN M. ROOSA

THE FORCES OF NATURE, working in concert with time, have sculpted the Iowa landscape — here pulling bedrock to the surface, there burying it beneath many feet of soil. As you travel across Iowa, the scene is continually changing. In some cases the change is remarkably subtle, but the differences do exist for the discerning traveler.

In her book *A Regional Guide to Iowa Landforms*, published by the Iowa Geological Survey, Jean C. Prior has divided our state into landform regions based on glacial history and topography. If biological attributes, such as distinctive flora and fauna, are considered, these landform regions may be called natural regions and subdivided into sections. The following pages describe some of these regions and their distinctive plant and animal inhabitants.

Sioux Quartzite Region

IN THE VERY NORTHWEST corner of Iowa is a small outcropping of ancient bedrock, the Sioux Quartzite (*see Chapter 1*). More than a billion years old, this rock occurs mainly in Gitchie Manitou State Preserve. Here, in the thin soil among the rocky outcrops, soil lichens grow intermingled with some of Iowa's rarest vascular plants — buffalo grass, fameflower, and prickly pear cactus. Although seldom encountered elsewhere in Iowa, spikemoss, a tiny relative of coal age giants, abounds here. Colorful crustose lichens adorn the pink quartzite bedrock, which is in places worn smooth by centuries of wind erosion. A number of unusual and hardy mosses pioneer this harsh, exposed environment. No wonder this small area has been a regular stopping place for botanists for over a century.

Carl Kurtz

The broad flood plain of the Missouri River resulted from eons of silt deposit by a wild and restless river. The river has since been straightened and diked and this alluvium converted to agriculture. It still acts as a major migration corridor for waterfowl.

Alluvial Regions

BEFORE SETTLEMENT, Iowa rivers flowed wild and free, periodically flooding the valley floors and depositing silt; due to this rich soil, these areas became lush with flood-tolerant plants. Through the years, these bottomlands became biological treasure-houses of plant and animal diversity that could exist nowhere else than in this specialized niche. Although the native communities are today much reduced in size and quality, extensive areas along the two border rivers still show the rich soil and flat character that has made them so valuable for agriculture.

Missouri River Alluvial Section

Up to 12 miles wide in places, the vast Missouri River flood plain has generally been converted to farmland. Old oxbows, a reminder of times when the river was free-flowing, are a prominent feature of the flood plain.

The area, rich in crops today, was once a biological treasure — ever-flooding, ever-changing. The same waters that caused destructive flooding deposited the soil which made the region prized for agricultural production.

The flood plain lies along a major migration pathway for waterfowl. Large concentrations of such birds — especially snow geese — may still be seen each spring and fall, particularly at DeSoto Bend National Wildlife Refuge north of Council Bluffs.

Years ago, eons ago, low prairie grasses grew here in profusion, and here danced the prairie chicken and the sharp-tailed grouse. The western spadefoot toad and the grasshopper mouse are still found here.

Mississippi River Alluvial Section

In scattered spots along the Mississippi River, the native character of the flood plain may yet be seen. The undisturbed alluvial community is one of Iowa's endangered community-types. In this community occur the only Iowa nesting sites for the red-shouldered hawk, the brown creeper and the bald eagle. Numerous plants, including sycamore, pecan, and arrow arum, are restricted to alluvial deposits. These alluvial communities also serve as a buffer between the stream and the upland agricultural community. Most of this alluvial section is now artificially drained and protected by a system of levees.

Loess Hills

Finely ground material washed out of melting glaciers was picked up by prevailing westerly winds and deposited in a band of hills which resemble huge snowdrifts, starting at the eastern edge of the Missouri River Alluvium. The area is called the Loess Hills Region and today is perhaps the most significant natural area remaining in Iowa. To early native Americans these bluff-tops overlooking the broad Missouri were sacred land.

While loess is fairly common in the world, it rarely reaches the depth and relief of the western Iowa loess. The rugged nature of these hills has prevented their conversion to cropland and has protected them from overgrazing. Some of the hills today appear as the first pioneers saw them. Much of Iowa's remaining native prairie is found in these hills where one may yet find the plains pocket mouse, the grasshopper mouse, southern bog lemming, showy yucca and the Chuck-will's-widow; here, too is excellent habitat for rare prairie skippers, like ottoe's skipper. On the dry blufftops are found numerous Great Plains plant species that occur nowhere else in Iowa. Soil lichens grow, almost invisibly, among the prairie grasses. Occasionally, with luck, one may find a stalked puffball. As the Missouri River orientation changes near Sioux City, the loess becomes shallower, but it continues along the Big Sioux River and forms the western boundary of the Northwest Iowa Plains Region.

Northwest Iowa Plains Region

This region, largely treeless, lies at the highest altitude and has the lowest rainfall in Iowa. The gently rolling surface, once covered with tall-grass prairie, is now devoted to agriculture, although scattered prairie remnants remain. Not as old as some or as young as other Iowa surfaces, this region is further divided into the Tazewell Swell and Swale Section and Western Iowa Plains Section. An erosion cycle affected both sections and resulted in a similar drainage pattern across the entire region. Loess mantles the entire region, but is thicker in the western part, where it obscures the boundary between this region and the Western Rolling Hills Section.

Tazewell Swell and Swale Section

This is the youngest of the two sections in this region and has a gently undulating surface, now converted to agricultural purposes. Scattered tall-grass prairie remnants persist and the Richardson's ground squirrel has recently been found in the northern portion of this section.

Western Iowa Plains Section

The western part of this section, rugged and capped with thick loess, still contains prairie remnants and woodlands. Some unusual species such as the prairie rattlesnake and the western spadefoot toad still exist here. The valley of the Big Sioux River provides an important migration path for waterfowl and raptors. The prairies of the bluffs near the Big Sioux are important for prairie skipper butterflies and some Great Plains plant species.

The poorly-drained landscape characteristic of the northern part of the Wisconsin Surface Region contains many wetlands. Some are permanently wet, some periodically wet — and many have farm fields immediately adjacent. They are biologically important and esthetically pleasing.

Tom C. Cooper

Wisconsin Surface Region

APPROXIMATELY 30,000 square miles of Iowa were covered by the most recent glacier, the Wisconsin. Because this glacier's southernmost reach halted where the city of Des Moines is now located, geologists call this area the Des Moines Lobe. As it retreated, the glacier left several visible marks on the land. Examples include moraines and prairie potholes or marshes. Such features help divide the region into the Prairie Pothole Section, the Oak Savanna Section, and the Moraine and Plain Section.

At the interface of this region and the Northwest Iowa Plains are several small glacial "fens". These are upwellings which usually occur on hillsides with constantly flowing cold water high in sulfates and carbonates. Plants unknown elsewhere in Iowa, including arrow grass, northern green orchid and grass-of-parnassis, flourish in this unique habitat.

Prairie Pothole Section

Glacial ice generated incalculable forces on the land — gouging out materials, depositing them nearby, leaving a gravelly knob or ridge here, dropping a block of ice in a depression there, gradually forming the varied landscape destined to become the biologically rich Prairie Pothole Section. For nine millenia, this part of Iowa lay under a mantle of diverse and complex prairie vegetation. Ice-age relics are visible today in this section in the form of prairie potholes, kettleholes, moraines and lakes. At one time Iowa's wetlands totaled about 1.5 million acres and were the dominant feature of the landscape in this section. Not realizing their value — in fact, considering them wasteland — we have tiled and drained them, plowed and planted them, reduced them to less than 55,000 acres. Not content and still not recognizing their significance, landowners continued to drain them in recent years; some are being drained today.

The Prairie Pothole Section, extending south to northwest Humboldt County and east to Kossuth County, is a region of prairie potholes, glacial knobs and ridges, depressions and kettleholes, forming a southern extension of the prairie pothole region of the Dakotas and western Minnesota. Here is Iowa's waterfowl "factory," its deepest lakes and their associated species, and its prairie nesting birds like the bobolink, upland sandpiper, grasshopper sparrow and, occasionally, burrowing owls. In the prairie potholes are found many wetland species including the yellow-headed blackbird, marsh wren, least bittern, black tern and several species of rails. Some of the interesting, but rare plants found in the potholes, include wild rice, bog bean, mare's tail, bog cotton, as well as an extensive complement of common wetland species. In this section are some of Iowa's finest examples of tall-grass prairie, where one of the world's rarest vascular plants, prairie bush clover, reaches its greatest abundance; also on these prairies a different complex of fungal species occur and one may find showy puffballs in the genus *Disciseda*. The state's finest example of a kettlehole and all of the glacial fens occur in this section.

Oak-Savanna Section

Oak-savannas are areas where scattered oak trees grow in a prairie environment. This situation has arisen because protection from prairie fires allowed the fire-resistant oaks to persist, protected somewhat from the fires by depressions which were usually wet. In Iowa, these savannas are on glacial knobs and occur as a prominent feature in the Wisconsin Surface region, in Hancock, Winnebago and Worth counties. Savannas are quite widespread in Iowa, but these are the most striking. In most, the prairie grasses have been removed by grazing.

Pilot Knob, a glacial knob, is a prominent feature of this section; in a depression at the base of the knob is the state's only sphagnum bog. Among the sphagnum moss grows the glistening, beautiful insect-eating sundew plant. In the bog waters are found an array of jewel-like desmids, the most beautiful of the green algae. Earth-tongues are among the unusual fungi that occur near the bog. In nearby woods lives the red-backed vole, a boreal relict species. In the northeast part of this section, large areas of peatland occur. Once wetlands, these have since filled up with moss and sedges. Most are now farmed, although a few are mined for peatmoss to be used in greenhouses or as packing material.

Moraine and Plain Section

The Wisconsin Glacier left a terminal moraine in Des Moines, marking its maximum advance. It also left recessional moraines as it paused in retreating. These are prominent in Wright and Dickinson counties, and northeast Boone County. These are called the Altamont, Humboldt, and Algona moraines.

The moraines, often dry and gravelly, have sideoats, blue grama, Junegrass and pasque flower growing on the tops. The entire section has been mainly converted to agricultural purposes.

Potholes and kettleholes are also found here occasionally, but not in the abundance they are in the Prairie Pothole Section. Examples of marshes in this section are Elm Lake in Wright County and Goose Lake in Hamilton County. In these depressions are found an array of marsh plants, much diminished today, but which occasionally contain such interesting reminders of the past as bog-bean, small white lady's-slipper and whitetop grass.

Dean Roosa    Carl Kurtz

Southern Iowa Drift Plain

ONE CAN STAND on the lawn of the State Capitol in Des Moines — a surface that is approximately 14,000 years old and look generally southward and see a surface which is a half-million years old. One would be looking at the Southern Iowa Drift Plain, last covered by the Kansan Glacier some 500,000 years ago. Historically, this portion of Iowa was heavily wooded, and today it contains a significant part of the Iowa's remaining forest cover. This very large region, covering most of southern half of Iowa, can be divided into the following sections: Western Rolling Hills Section, Rolling Hills Section, Tabular Uplands Section, and Eastern Tabular Uplands Section.

Western Rolling Hills Section

This section abuts the loess hills on the west; the deep loess gradually thins as one travels east and the rugged hills flatten out to become rolling hills. The ancient character of the landscape is shown by the absence of marshes and moraines, which have long since succumbed to erosional forces. In this section there are few flat uplands; the only flat terrain occurs in the river valleys. The mature landscape provides good habitat for wintering birds such as sparrows and raptors, and long-eared owls occasionally nest here. Dickcissels reach their greatest Iowa abundance in this section and the largest example of a lowland prairie is found here.

Rolling Hills Section

Compared with the previous section, the Rolling Hills Section is more heavily forested, has shallower loess, and is more level on the uplands. The Iowa Conservation Commission has extensive tracts of State Forests here. Where rivers cut deeply into the bedrock, cliff-dwelling plants cling to the canyon walls. Gallery forests bordering the streams include species which have migrated north from the Ozark Plateau — kingnut hickory, sassafras, pecan, and sycamore.

The network of small tree-lined streams winding through the dissected landscape create an important breeding ground for bats, including the endangered Indiana bat. Such a mature landscape provides good terrain for nesting and wintering raptors, as well as habitat for significant populations of reptiles and amphibians.

Tabular Uplands Section

The varied Tabular Uplands Section extends from Hardin County, where three regions converge, east to the Mississippi River bluffs. Flat, tabular uplands are a noticeable feature of this relatively mature, dissected landscape where significant woodlands remain. Here the eastern decidous woodland met the tallgrass prairie in a broad transition area. Southern affinities of flora and fauna express themselves in this section, where various species terminate their ranges. Numerous sedges, trees, and animals such as the small-mouthed salamander, and several species of snakes are examples.

Eastern Tabular Upland Section

This rugged part of Iowa, historically replete with prairie-covered flat uplands, scenic entrenched rivers like the Maquoketa, wooded ravines and abundant rock outcrops, is an important meeting ground for plants with southern and northern affinities. For example, white pine, ground pine and Canada yew, all representative of northern regions, and goat's beard, and paw paw, which normally appear farther south, are found here.

Forests in Iowa have been dramatically reduced from pre-settlement times and in much of the state they are found mainly along streams. The basswoods, shown here in Dolliver State Park, are common, especially in the Paleozoic Plateau.

(Far Left)
Marshes in Iowa are restricted to the young landscape of the Wisconsin Surface Region. Shown here is Goose Lake, in Hamilton County, near the southern terminus of this glacial surface.

Prairie marshes dot the young landscape left by retreating glaciers. These marshes are among the most productive communities known, and provide the only Iowa habitat for many wetland species of flora and fauna. This view is of Big Wall Lake in southern Wright County.

Carl Kurtz

Iowan Surface Region

THIS LARGE REGION, situated between an ancient and a young landform, is divided into three sections: the Northern Swell and Swale Section, the Swell and Swale Section, and the Paha Ridge Section. A varied region, it ranges from intensive agriculture to rich woodland, and from prairie to bog. Though it is geologically complex, it serves as a transition zone between the deciduous woodland to the tall-grass prairie, and is important to the study of Iowa's natural history.

Northern Swell and Swale Section

The Northern Swell and Swale Section contains a botanically varied landscape, from tall-grass prairie to ancient aspen bogs to streams with submerged aquatic plants. In the northwest part, scattered oak-savannas are among remnants of the state's native condition. Extinct aspen bogs provide excellent habitat for orchids, adder's-tongue fern and bog willow.

Swell and Swale Section

As with the other sections of this region, the mature landscape has been eroded sufficiently to expose glacial erratics. Although still a prominent feature of the landscape, they are slowly being removed or blasted to facilitate farming. In this large section are the only Iowa sites for the wood turtle, silky prairie clover, and water shield. Prairie remnants, some with shooting star and prairie smoke are found here and occasionally the yellow trout lily and twinleaf, both exceedingly rare, may be found.

Paha Ridge Section

This section is named for elliptical, loess-capped hills called paha. Heavily farmed in the west, this area becomes more forested toward the east. This section provides good habitat for the blue-spotted salamander and ornate box turtle.

Similar to a great flowing marsh, the Wapsipinicon River traverses the entire length of this region. Along its banks today are sizable marshes. Here large stands of river birch are found and a few marshes contain the massasagua rattlesnake.

The Cedar River crosses much of the region. Along this stream are found numerous sandy areas that provide sites for the blue-spotted salamander, adder's tongue fern, and dwarf birch.

Paleozoic Plateau Region

BORDERING THE LARGE Iowan Surface Region on the northeast is the heavily dissected and scenic Paleozoic Plateau. This region is dissected by erosion, forming a rugged landscape dominated by bedrock. Many microhabitats are found here, from dry hill prairies to cool, moss-covered hillslopes, many with boreal or northern plant and animal species. This region is divided into two sections — the Driftless Ridge and Valley Section and the Turkey River Section.

The Driftless Ridge and Valley Section

So named because it lacks glacial deposits or drift, the topography here is Iowa's most rugged and scenic, and a considerable portion of Iowa's remaining forestland is found here. Because of the extremely dissected nature of the landscape, many microhabitats also occur in this area. Often, the cool, north-facing, talus slopes contain ice caves, from which cold air flows, creating a boreal habitat. Northern remnants such as golden saxifrage, monkshood, and bunchberry grow here. Small landsnails, holdovers from the Ice Age and found nowhere else in the world, survive here. Two rare lichens, lungwort and *Umbillicaria* grow nowhere else in the state. Most of Iowa's trout streams are also in this section.

The Turkey River Section

The Turkey River flows the length of this section. Although the area is not as rugged and scenic as the Driftless Ridge and Valley Section, it is still rugged and contains cool slopes with cold air drainage from ice caves and harbors some disjunct species. Examples are bearberry, twinleaf, shinleaf, and partridge pea. Trout streams are frequent throughout the region. Some public areas which show off the beauty of this region are Pikes Peak State Park, Yellow River State Forest, Mt. Hosmer at Lansing, and Bellevue State Park.

Carl Kurtz

Dolomite, which has resisted erosional forces throughout time, creates scenic escarpments in the Paleozoic Plateau. Certain plants cling to a tenuous existence here. Shown is a view from atop the Turkey River Ridge along the eastern Iowa border.

Sandy Provinces

SCATTERED throughout Iowa are areas of pure sand, deposited by stream action in our geological past. Some have been altered forever by silt deposited by floodwaters; others still have shifting dunes. On these sandy areas are found some exceedingly rare plants and animals.

The largest and most spectacular sandy area is Muscatine Island. Here the shifting sand dunes and varied topography provide habitat for about 30 species of plants and animals that are "threatened or endangered" in Iowa. One, the Illinois mud turtle, numbers only a few thousand in the world and most are found in Iowa's sandy areas. Other unusual species are the ornate box turtle, plains pocket mouse, hognose snake, water snakes, and lark sparrow.

Another large sandy area is in and near DeSoto Bend National Wildlife Refuge along the Missouri River. Here nest the least tern and piping plover; here, too, lives the western spadefoot toad.

Sandy areas are found along the Cedar River in Cedar, Linn, and Black Hawk counties. Here occasionally are found the royal fern, sphagnum moss, and meadow beauty. Earthstar fungi and British soldier lichens find these sandy areas excellent habitat.

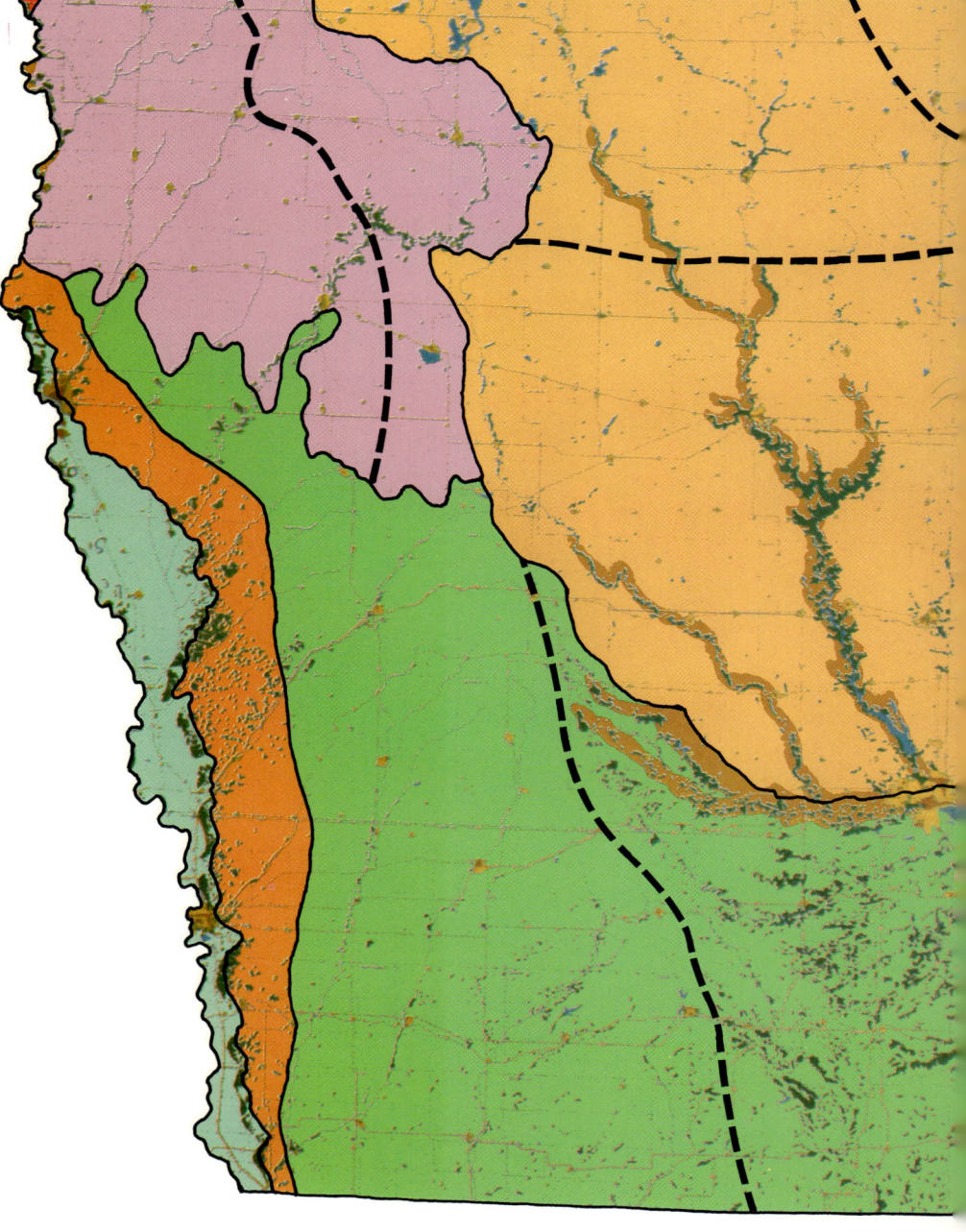

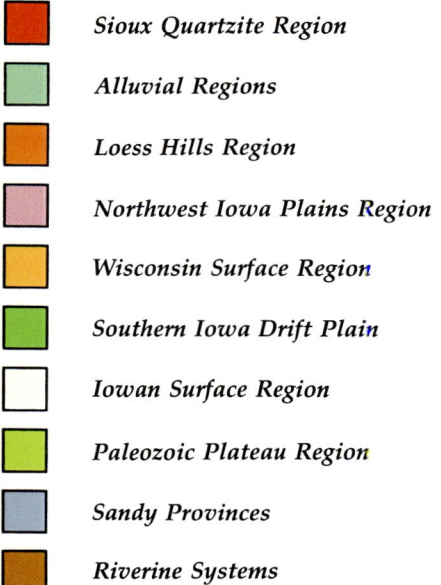

- Sioux Quartzite Region
- Alluvial Regions
- Loess Hills Region
- Northwest Iowa Plains Region
- Wisconsin Surface Region
- Southern Iowa Drift Plain
- Iowan Surface Region
- Paleozoic Plateau Region
- Sandy Provinces
- Riverine Systems

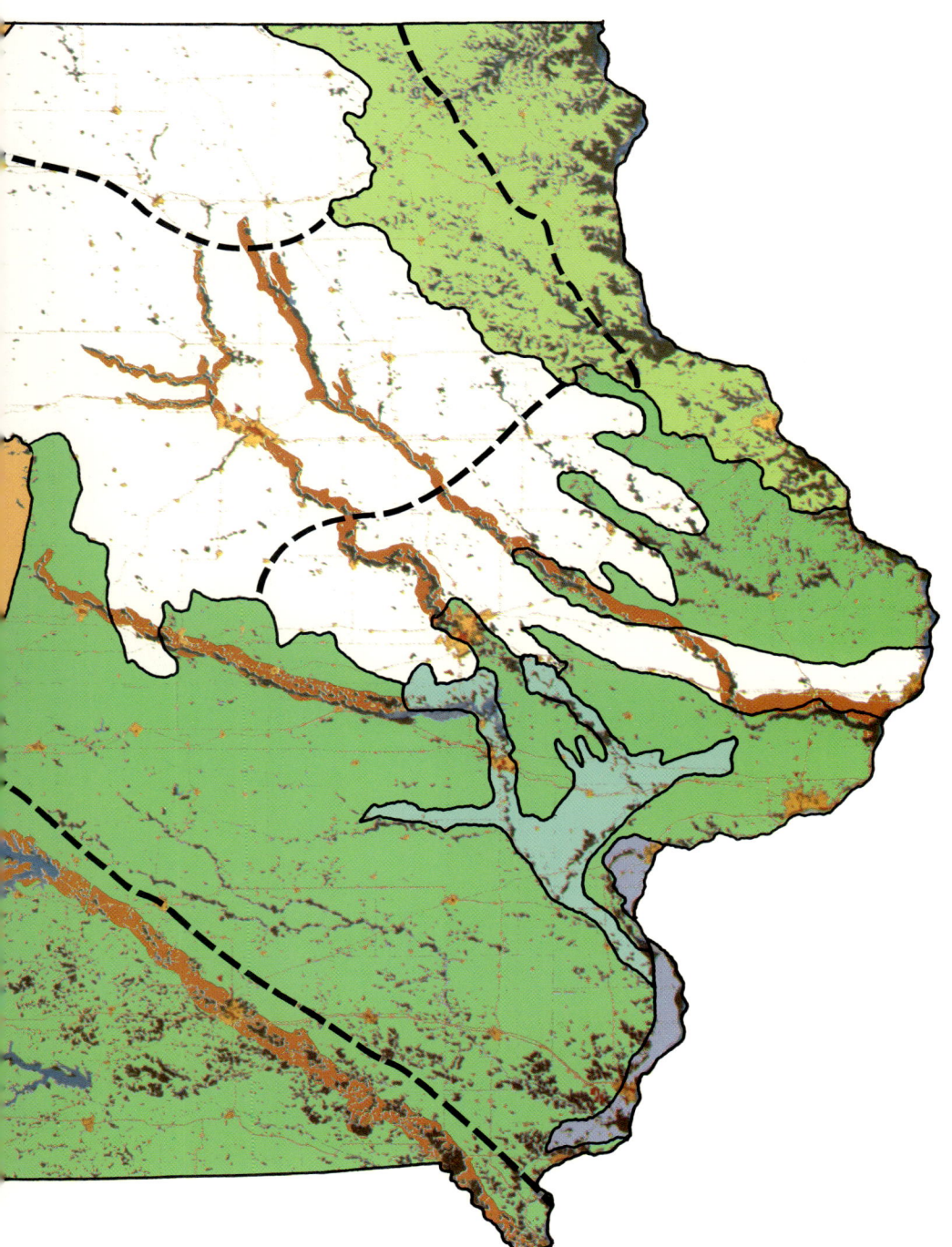

Riverine Systems

IN THE DEEP valleys formed by the major rivers are wooded, moist habitats that provide migration pathways for animals, especially birds, each spring and fall. They were also a migration pathway for plant species during interglacial periods. In addition, these riverine systems afford habitat for many of our vanishing species or our remaining wild species. Here you expect to find nesting hawks, many other birds and squirrels. The true flood plain forest is an endangered community in Iowa, and many animals are threatened because of the loss of these specialized niches.

Lake Calvin Region

A large glacial lake, Lake Calvin, is thought to have been impounded when the Illinoian Glacier blocked the waters of the Iowa and Cedar rivers. This ancient lake basin is located in portions of Louisa, Muscatine, Johnson, Cedar, and Scott counties. The terraces of the lake are still visible, sand dunes are frequent and the broad flood plains often have oxbows and sandy depressions where unusual species are found. The only Iowa station for the royal fern is found in one such sandy depression; a disjunct population of skunk cabbage and ornate box turtles are also found in this region.

Iowa may appear at first to be a monotonous land with little variety in landforms, animal, and plant life. To those willing to study the face of our state and get acquainted with its wildlife, it is a surprisingly exciting place.

An understanding of the distribution of plants and animals, and their relationship to the landscape left by geological forces can make Iowa a vastly more interesting place to live. A true feeling for the importance of natural areas, and how they came to be and now relate to the natural regions, and the subsequent transferring of this feeling to the next generation will assure a continuation of the high quality of life Iowans have enjoyed in the past.

Bill Witt

Skunk cabbage plants grow in colonies in shaded seeps. They bloom very early because the purple-hooded flowering buds have an elevated internal temperature which thaws the frozen soil. Relatives of the Jack-in-the-pulpit, they contain the same poisonous properties.

(Previous Spread) A prairie shrub, the wild rose was well-chosen as Iowa's state flower. It is the ancestor of some of our cultivated roses.

Thousands of different strange and beautiful native plants still grow wild in Iowa. If you look closely at these plants, you see a great variety of sizes, shapes, and colors. Some plants are woody, while some are soft-stemmed; some are tall, and others grow nearly flat on the ground; some have a single stem, and some have many stems. Within each of these groups, we can see additional differences in the shapes of the leaves, the arrangement of the branches, and in the kinds of flowers and fruits they bear. If we look at a sufficient number of plants, however, we may begin to notice patterns of similarities. Within the flowering plants, for instance, the beans, peas, and clovers all have similar features and are called legumes. Also, the grasses, the maples, and the sunflowers are familiar groups of plants. Within these groups the flowers all resemble each other.

There are groups of nonflowering plants, too, such as the cone-bearing woody plants — pines, spruces, and cedars. The spore-bearing ferns are also easily recognized. Many people are familiar with aquatic algae because some algae can pollute ponds and lakes. A few people even know the delicate mosses and liverworts, which are common, but generally unrecognized.

Because of their similarities and differences, it is possible to classify plants to make it easier to study and discuss them. We will use the following informal classification system for the plants of Iowa:

Seed producers
  Flowering plants
  Cone-bearing plants (conifers)

Spore producers
  Green plants
    Ferns, horsetails, club mosses, etc.
    Mosses, liverworts, and hornworts
    Algae

  Non-green plants
    Fungi (mushrooms, rusts, smuts, mildews, etc.)
    Lichens

139

Flowering Plants

MOST OF THE PLANTS we see around us are flowering seed plants. All of our crops, including corn, soybeans, small grains, and alfalfa have flowers, as do our garden plants such as potatoes, tomatoes, beans, and carrots. Cultivated flowers belong here of course, but so do most trees and shrubs, the great majority of prairie and wetland plants, and even the weeds. If you see a green plant growing in Iowa, the odds are very high that it is a flowering seed plant. More than 1,800 kinds of native flowering plants have been found in Iowa.

Flowers are reproductive structures. The parts essential for reproduction are the stamens that produce pollen and the pistils which form fruits that contain the seeds (*see drawing*). However, fruits and seeds are not formed unless the proper kind of pollen is received on the stigmas.

Wind-pollinated plants (oaks, walnuts, grasses) do not have petals which would interfere with the air currents that carry the pollen. Flowers with petals and often distinctive odors are insect-pollinated. Their bright colors and pleasing aromas are to attract insects, not to please people.

Insect-pollinated flowering plants are more common than wind-pollinated plants because they reproduce more efficiently. Insects direct the transport of pollen from flower to flower; the wind does not. Thus less pollen is produced by insect-pollinated plants, resulting in higher efficiency and less energy use. Higher efficiency translates directly into a competitive advantage over less efficient plants.

Large leaves that are flat and thin are typical of flowering plants. Food production takes place in the leaves and their shape is beautifully suited for this purpose. Large leaf surfaces also permit the loss of large amounts of water vapor, however, and in cold weather this loss cannot be replaced from frozen soil. Consequently, plants of northern climates either lose their leaves in winter — as do many trees — or die back to the ground — as do grasses and other soft-stemmed plants.

Flowers form seeds within some kind of fruit. Some seeds are highly nutritious and edible (beans, peas, nuts, peanuts, pumpkin seeds). In some cases, the entire fruit is edible (apples, cherries, grains, tomatoes). These edible seeds and fruits provide much of our food, and most of the remainder of our vegetable food is supplied by the shoots (celery, asparagus), roots (carrots, turnips), tubers (potatoes, Jerusalem artichoke), and even the buds of flowering plants (onions, cabbage). Since most of the animals we eat also get their food from flowering plants, we would find it impossible to survive without them. We also obtain lumber (ash, oak, walnut), clothing (cotton, linen), medicines (digitalis, atropine, quinine), and flavorings, spices, and seasonings (lemon, chocolate, mints, sage, dill) from flowering plants. Finally, our lives would be much less pleasant without the wild and cultivated flowers that brighten our woods, prairies, gardens, and homes.

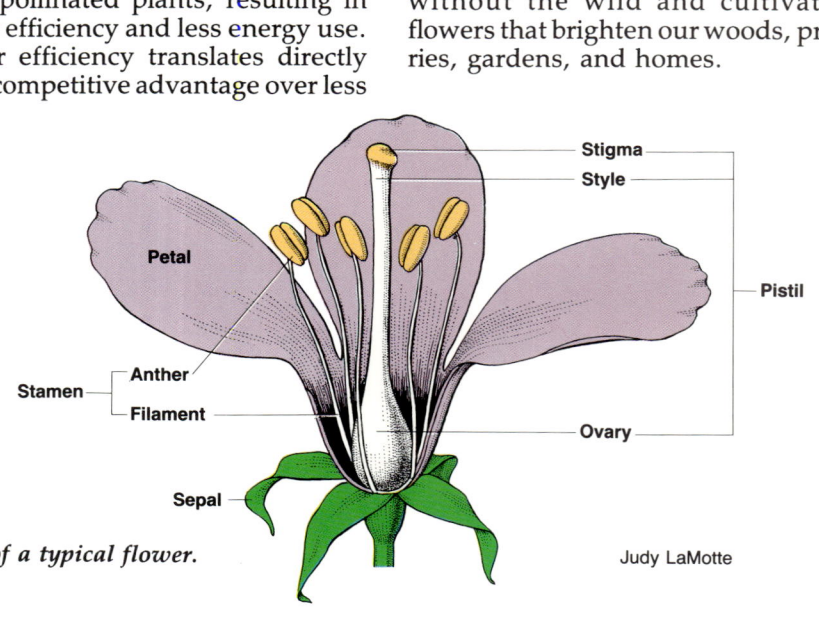

Parts of a typical flower. Judy LaMotte

Ron Sarson

Brenda and Ken Formanek

Interesting and Unusual Plants

A NUMBER of Iowa plants have features that attract our attention. Some appeal to us because they are beautiful, others are edible, and a few are poisonous. While most of our plants are not parasites, a few are either partly or wholly parasitic on other plants. We even have a few plants that get a part of their food by trapping and "eating" small animals — they are partly carnivorous, in other words. Finally, some plants are of interest because of their striking appearance or because they exist far from their closest relatives.

Because we have so many interesting plants in Iowa, only a representative sample will be discussed.

(Left)
Blue-flag Iris is a native plant of wet prairie draws. The large, showy flowers indicates an insect-pollinated plant and the visiting bumble bee confirms this diagnosis. The colored markings form a pattern that attracts only certain insects.
(Above)
Ironweeds, moist prairie plants, attract pollinators to clusters of small, highly-colored flowers. These clusters of flowers (heads) are characteristic of the sunflower family.

Showy Plants

MANY IOWANS will be familiar with some of our attractive and showy plants because they are now cultivated or are familiar wildflowers. However, other beautiful plants are now so rare that they are seldom seen, while others have disappeared.

Iowa's woodlands are prettiest in April and May when one can first find the white, pink, or blue flowers of *Hepatica* and the white flowered bloodroot. Shortly after, we find *Trillium*, spring beauty, rue anemone, and Dutchman's breeches carpeting the forest floor; wild ginger on the slopes, and bluebells and false rue anemone in the lowland woods. In May, we commonly see bellwort, wild geranium, mayapple, *Phlox*, and Jack-in-the-pulpit, and if we are fortunate, we may find a clump of yellow ladies' slipper. Years ago we might have found the beautiful pink ladies' slipper orchid, but now it is almost extinct. Providing texture to the woodland floral view are lovely ferns. The most striking are the interrupted, lady, maidenhair, ostrich, and rattlesnake ferns.

Other Iowa plants that catch the eye include the white prairie fringed orchid, wood and Michigan (sometimes called turk's cap) lilies, shooting stars, blue-flags, beard tongues, *Monarda*, tall bellflowers, cardinal flowers, and the New England aster. Most familiar, perhaps, is the beautiful wild rose, our state flower.

Ron Sarson    Ron Sarson

Edible Plants

IT IS POSSIBLE to mention only a few of the many Iowa plants that have been used for food in the past. Several popular books are available on this topic; only a few common edible plants will be mentioned here. Most of these plants should only be considered emergency food sources because they are usually not very tasty and because there is danger of eating similar, but poisonous, plants. Probably the safest (and most delicious) sources of wild foods are the berries and cherries. Even here you must be sure of the identification of the plant and eat only fully ripened fruit. Berries that can be eaten are the wild strawberries, raspberries, blackberries, dewberries, the fully ripe choke cherries, and ground cherries. Some nuts that are edible and tasty are the black walnut, butternut (not bitternut!), shagbark hickory, kingnut hickory, and the hazelnut. Other nutlike fruits should be avoided. American Indians and early pioneers ate many other plants, but they knew them intimately and they knew when they were edible and how to prepare them. The fact is that many of these food sources were only marginally nutritious and not very palatable.

Carl Kurtz

Ron Sarson

(Far Left)
This showy plant, the Michigan lily, is restricted to moist prairies. The parts of the nodding flowers are in threes, or multiples of three. Like most members of the lily family, the sepals and petals look much alike.
(Middle)
The attractive wood lily is a prairie plant that is restricted to eastern and central Iowa.
(Above)
It is always a welcome treat to find a patch of wild strawberries! Occurring in prairies and woodland openings, they are smaller, but tastier, than cultivated varieties.
(Left)
Bellworts are woodland plants with yellow, nodding flowers. They are related to the lilies and their strap-like sepals and petals look alike. An odd feature of their leaves is that they completely encircle the stem.

143

Poisonous Plants

It is worth a spring trip to the woodlands just to see mayapples in flower. The leaves occur either singly or in pairs, but only those with two leaves bear flowers. Except for the ripe fruit, the plants are poisonous.

THE PLANTS listed below are poisonous and should be avoided. Only a few of the more common poisonous plants are discussed here; for further information, consult one or more of the books available on this subject. The parts of the plants that contain the poisonous chemicals are in parentheses after the plant name.

Black nightshade *(entire plant, especially unripe fruit)*. This is a very common plant of gardens and waste places. Ripe fruits are blue-black.

Deadly nightshade *(entire plant, especially unripe fruit)*. Related to the black nightshade, this plant is a vine with lobed leaves that has tempting red fruits. It grows in fence rows and waste places.

Black cherry *(all parts, unripe fruits, seeds)*. A common tree of eastern Iowa, it produces many shiny, dark, blue-black fruits. The fruits are edible when fully ripe.

Elderberry *(entire plant, unripe fruit)*. The fruit is edible when ripe.

White snakeroot *(entire plant)*. This innocent-looking plant of the open woods is the cause of the "trembles" or milk sickness, a disease that killed many people in earlier years.

Larkspur *(seeds and young plants)*. Often planted in Iowa, it is also a native prairie species.

Mayapple *(all parts, unripe fruits)*. A well-known woodland wildflower. The fruit is edible when yellow and soft.

Bloodroot *(entire plant)*. The orange-red sap of the early-flowering woodland plant is poisonous.

Water hemlock *(entire plant, especially the roots)*. Sometimes found in wet, roadside ditches, it can be mistaken for wild parsnip or Queen Anne's lace. It can be deadly.

Jack-in-the-pulpit *(all parts)*. This is a common woodland plant. If even a small part of it is eaten, it causes swelling of the mucous membranes, and intense biting pain.

Several plants (blue cohosh, moonseed, Virginia creeper) produce grape-like fruits that have been eaten by mistake.

Be absolutely certain that the plant you wish to eat is non-poisonous.

(Above) Because they are bright red and shining, Jack-in-the-pulpit fruits are often spotted by woodland hikers. Though they are attractive and appear edible, they are poisonous.
(Right) Bloodroots are one of our earliest woodland wildflowers. Their pure-white flowers and notched, veiny leaves accent the spring landscape.

The Indian pipe does not produce its own food and the entire plant is white. It grows in clusters in the woods and frequently catches the attention of hikers. It is related to the blueberries.

Plants That Cause Dermatitis

A FEW IOWA PLANTS can cause swelling of the skin, intense itching, and blisters. Everyone knows of poison ivy, but not many can recognize it. A woody shrub or vine, it can be found along the edges of woods, in hedges, or even climbing high on other trees.

Poison oak is not found in Iowa. It occurs in the eastern and southern United States, as well as along the West Coast.

Wild parsnip can cause a poison ivy-like reaction when handled with moist hands in the sunlight. Stinging nettle and wood nettle have hairs on their stems and leaves that cause an unpleasant stinging or itching when they are touched by the skin. However, the sensation soon goes away and there are no after-effects.

Parasitic Plants

FLOWERING PLANTS that parasitize other plants are rare in Iowa. Indian paintbrush is a colorful plant that is a partial root parasite on other prairie plants. It has green leaves, however, and obtains most of its food in the normal way. Another partial root parasite is the bastard toadflax, a small prairie plant. It, too, is green and does little damage.

The dodders and cancer-roots are completely parasitic and have lost their green color. Dodders (morning glory relatives) have yellow-orange twining stems that attach to native plants, often of the sunflower family, and rob the host plants of some of their sap. Generally, neither of these two plants cause any great harm to their hosts.

Indian pipe, a woodland plant with glistening white stems and leaves, often attracts the eye in summer or early fall. Not only does it have an unusual appearance; it also has an unusual parasitic relationship. It is an indirect parasite that gets its food from a mycorrhizal fungus that obtains its nutrients from the roots of trees.

Cone-bearing Plants

CONE-BEARING plants are commonly called evergreens or just pines. A better common name for the group is conifers, because all of the Iowa plants in this group produce cones. Seeds are formed within these cones, and the cones protect them until they are released. Another distinguishing conifer trait is needle-like leaves. Though many kinds of conifers are cultivated in the state, only five are native to Iowa, and they form only a small part of our vegetation. The eastern red cedar is the only conifer that occurs in every county in Iowa. Cedar wood was used extensively in earlier times for fence posts because of its rot-resistant properties. Cedar chests and pencils also are made from this tree. Our largest conifer, the eastern white pine, is restricted to northeastern Iowa, although it is cultivated elsewhere. This tree was once widely distributed in the northeastern United States and adjacent Canada, and the soft, durable wood was used for many purposes. Since it was so useful, the original, widespread white pine forests are nearly all gone. Significant Iowa stands of this beautiful tree are found in White Pine Hollow State Preserve (Dubuque County), Pine Lake State Park (Hardin County), and Twin Springs City Park (Winneshiek County).

The three remaining conifers, all restricted to northeastern Iowa, are the balsam fir, the Canada yew, and the prostrate juniper. The balsam fir, primarily a northern tree, occurs in a few stands in Iowa's extreme northeastern corner, where it can be recognized by its spire-like growth form. The Canada yew is a sprawling shrub and can be found in cool, shaded, steep ravines. The prostrate juniper is rare and occurs on exposed rocky outcrops in moist woods. All three are likely relics of a much wider distribution in glacial times.

Carl Kurtz

There are places in Iowa containing unexcelled scenery. This stand of native white pines in Dubuque County probably remains from the time when Iowa was extensively glaciated. Pines bear no flowers, but reproduce from seeds formed in cones.

This orchid-like bladderwort flower protrudes from a submerged aquatic carnivorous plant. Tiny bladders on the plant trap aquatic insects which serve as a supplemental source of nitrogen.

Carnivorous Plants

THE SUNDEW and the bladderworts are very unusual Iowa plants in that they trap and digest various small animals. The sundew, an acid bog plant, has sticky hairs on its rounded leaves that ensnare insects, while the aquatic bladderworts produce many tiny bladders that trap small organisms. Both use the animal food sources to supplement their nitrogen intake but are not dependent on them for survival.

The sticky hairs on the tiny sundew ensnare small insects which are used as supplemental food sources. Sundews are restricted to acid bogs and are only found in one place in Iowa.

Ferns

ONLY ABOUT 60 kinds of plants in this group are found in Iowa, but they are beautiful and interesting. They have a long history, and once — in that ancient time when Iowa's coal fields first began to form — were the dominant vegetation in part of our state. Many fossils of the fern group have been found in Iowa coal beds. Like flowering plants and conifers, they have green leaves or fronds; unlike them, however, they do not produce seeds. They produce spores, minute reproductive structures that scatter far and wide in the wind. At one stage in their life history, these plants produce sperm that require a moist environment to enable them to swim to an egg cell. This requirement for moisture is a factor in limiting the distribution of ferns primarily to moist woods and other damp places.

This lovely lady fern can be found in upland woods in most of Iowa. Ferns do not bear either flowers or seeds, but reproduce by minute spores which are often formed on the undersurface of their leaves (fronds).

Mosses, Liverworts, and Hornworts

THE PRECEDING groups of plants are all large enough to be seen easily with a casual glance. The mosses, liverworts, and hornworts are much smaller, and you have to be within a few feet of one to see it. Thus many people are not aware of them, even though they are common. Like the ferns, these plants produce swimming sperm and usually require a moist environment. Often they grow in tufts or patches and are closely pressed against soil, logs, or rocks. Because of this growth pattern and because of their many hair-like roots, they are very effective in preventing soil erosion. Some are also soil-formers, since those that inhabit rocks slowly dissolve them into their constituent minerals.

The mosses are the most common of the group and, with a little magnification, their delicate leaves, stems, and roots can be seen clearly. Liverworts and hornworts are less abundant and are often strap-like or plate-shaped in appearance. All members of this group form swollen capsules in which many microscopic spores are produced, and these tiny reproductive structures can be blown over vast distances.

This large mass of broom and haircap mosses forms a beautiful scene in miniature. The cushiony tufts help prevent erosion while the tiny plants slowly dissolve the rock to form soil. Like the ferns, mosses reproduce by microscopic spores.

Morels, sponge mushrooms, may be found on the ground in woodlands throughout Iowa in early spring.

W. H. Bragonier

Algae

THE ALGAE are a diverse group of primarily aquatic plants that vary greatly in size and shape (*see Chapter 10*). Some types are microscopic single-celled individuals; others are barely visible colonies of cells in flattened, globular, or ribbon shapes. Still others are clearly visible and could be mistaken for flowering plants. Most of us are acquainted with some types of algae, but we may not recognize them as such. Those that grow in stock tanks or other stagnant water are mistakenly called moss; floating stringy algae are often called pondweeds or scum; algae that pollute ponds or lakes are frequently called unprintable names.

Though small in size, algae are of great importance to us. Like all green plants, algae produce energy-rich compounds. Since they are eaten by many animals that are eaten by other animals, they serve as a primary source of food for all aquatic animal life. In the process of food production by algae, oxygen is released as a by-product. Because algae are so numerous, they contribute a significant portion of the oxygen that we breathe. In a process called nitrogen fixation, some kinds of algae can use nitrogen gas directly from the atmosphere to form nitrogen compounds that enrich the water or soils they inhabit. Consequently, even though some types of algae can cause noxious water pollution, it is clear that they are so important to us that we could not live without them.

Fungi

MUSHROOMS, toadstools, puffballs, earth stars, stinkhorns — these names call to mind distinctive things each of us has seen in the woods, on a lawn, or pictured in magazines or books. And the words "sponge mushrooms" have a special meaning" for many Iowans.

A hunt in the woods for the distinctive tan sponges atop their hollow stalks when the slopes are bright with wildflowers is one of the special treats of spring. Every Iowa mushroom hunter, and we are many, has a special set of clues for favorable places to search and particular signs to observe. The lure of good eating, the challenge of the hunt, and the dramatic emphasis of a short season all add to the experience. Each hunter soon learns that chances of a successful hunt are reasonably good if last year's good harvest areas are revisited. But why? How can the mushrooms be there each May when no evidence of them exists during the other 11 months of the year? Why do they occur some years and not others? To answer these questions, we must understand more about these particular fungi. Other fungi also may affect us, directly if we are involved in agriculture, more indirectly if we are not farmers.

The active vegetative portion of any fungus is tiny and inconspicuous. It consists typically of long branched threadlike filaments or occasionally single small cells. We often become aware of the presence of a fungus when we see the result of the activities of these filaments — a dead spot on a rose leaf, a greenish-white overgrowth on a corn ear, or the wilting and death of an elm tree. Occasionally we see fruiting bodies develop — a sponge mushroom on the ground on a wooded hillside, the dry powdery mass of a mature corn smut gall, a fairy ring of mushrooms in a lawn, or a group of puffballs on a rotten log.

All fungi must get their food, their energy supply, directly or indirectly from other organisms, living or dead. Individual fungi have distinctive ways of doing this, and they may occupy some peculiar niches.

Each fungus eventually produces special structures, called

Bracket-like mushrooms, like this one (Phyllotopsis nidulans), develop on soggy logs in the woods during summer and fall. Thin knife-like gills on the lower surface of the cap characterize all mushrooms.

(Left)
The distinctive fruiting bodies of jelly fungi like this Tremella are common on down logs in moist woods in summer.

(Below)
Fungal filaments feed and grow throughout a food source. Sometimes the filaments are grouped into cords.

Lois Hattery Tiffany/George Knaphus

Lois Hattery Tiffany/George Knaphus

Bob Coyle

spores, from which new individuals develop. Basically, each fungus spore has a living protoplast, a reserve of stored food (fats and oils), and usually a protective wall. Spores may be blown in the wind, carried along in flowing waters, splashed about by raindrops, even moved with soil or carried by animals. When spores land in a place where they have moisture and a favorable temperature, they will germinate and form new vegetative filaments that must contact a usable food source before the stored food reserve of the spore is depleted.

Most fungi develop in one of three basic food-relationship situations. Many common fungi can be included in the first group as "saprophytes" because they can get food only from dead organic materials such as dead leaves and stems on the soil surface, fallen branches or logs, leaves resting on the bottom of a stream, and dead roots and other plant or animal debris in the soil. The fungal filaments grow at the tip and probe into and through these dead tissues. Digestive enzymes produced in the living cell move out into the tissues and act to break them down. Many of the soluble products are absorbed by the fungus filaments and used in growth. We say that the leaves decay and the logs rot. Other living things benefit because, as a result of these fungal activities, materials that were tied up in the dead tissues are released for use by other generations of living organisms.

If the litter at the surface of the soil in a forest is turned over, we see an interwoven network of white, brown, or even blue or orange cord-like branched strands. These are the organized threadlike elements (hyphae) of particular fungi. When conditions are right, such hyphae produce fruiting bodies, large visible structures on or in which spores are produced. We call these fungus fruiting structures by various common names: mushrooms or toadstools, boletes, corals, puffballs, brackets, earth stars, birds nest fungi, cup fungi, stinkhorns, and sponge mushrooms or morels. Sometimes these fruiting bodies, with their distinctive shapes and brilliant colors, seem to have been produced singly at random on the ground. Some seem to develop in arcs or rings, particularly in lawns or pastures. Some cluster on logs.

Still other groups of mushrooms and boletes seem always to be in association with particular trees. These fungi are likely to have a very special relationship to the trees under whose canopy they develop, and are examples of the second basic kind of food relationship situation. The hyphae of these fungi are growing in the roots of the trees, actually among or within the root cells. As a result of these special arrangements, these fungus roots (mycorrhizae) can absorb certain nutrients more effectively from the soil than could the plant roots alone.

Many saprophytic fungi and mycorrhizal fungi are always present

151

Clusters of this mushroom (Flammulina velutipes), often called "winter mushroom" or "velvet stem", may occur on dead wood at any time during the year except the coldest winter months.

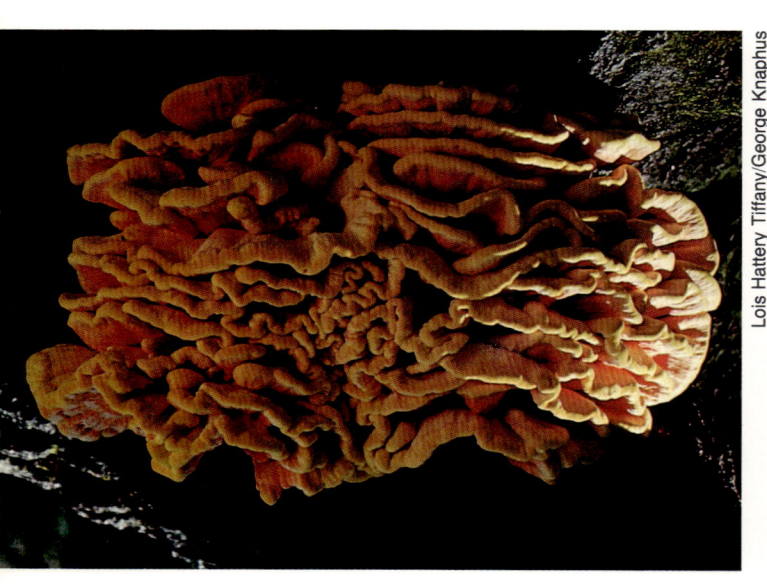

(Above) "Sulfur mushroom," technically not a mushroom because it lacks gills, forms clusters of orange shelf-like brackets on dead or living trees in summer and fall.
(Right) Shaggy mane is a common mushroom of lawns and pastures. It digests itself quickly, the entire cap dissolving into a black liquid.

Crimson cups, developing from sticks buried in leaves in the woods as early as the first week in March, are one of the welcome signs of spring. They also may be seen in late fall in some years.

Lois Hattery Tiffany/George Knaphus

and active in their particular habitat, even though they do not produce fruiting bodies. Only when all conditions are right — enough reserve food, adequate moisture, and favorable temperatures — will fruiting bodies develop. Even given favorable situations, the fruiting bodies of some fungi will develop only at a particular season, such as the sponge mushrooms in early spring or the giant puffballs in the fall.

The third kind of basic food relationship develops between a specific fungus and a particular living green plant. When the fungus enters the plant, it may directly kill host cells which it then uses as food, or the fungus may by some other means establish a way to obtain food from the living plant. These fungi are called parasites, and the results of their activities are plant disease. Sometimes only a limited number of cells are killed, and a leaf spot may form or a fruit may rot. In other situations, the fungus may plug the conducting tissues of the living plant, and the plant will die, as with elm wilt or oak wilt. Sometimes cells of the plant are stimulated to **overgrow, and grotesque distorted stems** or leaves develop. Less spectacular, but often more dangerous, **are the parasitic fungi that do not directly kill host cells**. Instead they establish special feeding systems with living cells, such as are developed by the rusts or powdery mildews. The host plant will survive, but much of the food it manufactures is stolen and used by the fungus. All of these kinds of plant parasitic fungi develop on our native plants, on introduced ornamental plants in our lawns and gardens, and, most economically significant, on our crop plants.

One of the most peculiar of fungus-plant relationships forms the unique plants we call lichens, which are a combination of a particular fungus and a particular alga. The fungus hyphae form the framework of the lichen body. The algal cells are concentrated in a layer near the middle of the lichen plant. The two organisms grow in a balanced association, forming a plant completely unlike that formed by either one alone.

Many lichens are large and obvious, growing on the trunk bark or branches of living trees, on any kind of rock surface, and even on soil in woods or prairies. Variously colored, from dull browns and gray-greens to bright orange, their forms are intriguingly diverse, too, ranging from flat plate-like structures to upright branched spires to long dangling stringy masses. Lichens can survive long periods without water, becoming dry and crisp. When moisture is again available, they absorb it rapidly, becoming greener, soft, and pliable.

New lichen plants develop when pieces of an old lichen, sometimes only a tiny fragment containing cells of both the lichen fungus and the lichen alga, blow in the wind or float in water to a new site. Lichens slowly may alter the surface on which they grow, separating rock particles to form pockets of new soil. On undisturbed soils, alone or with mosses, they may form a plant cover that absorbs water and stabilizes the soil surface.

Relict Areas — Reminders of the Past

AS THE OVERALL climate and vegetation of the state have changed, topographical differences have allowed certain small areas to maintain an environment which is a remnant of an earlier time. This provided refuges for plants and animals reminiscent of a different climatic time. For example, a steep, north-facing slope in northeastern Iowa escapes the sun's drying rays and provides a refuge for plants which otherwise occur only in cool, moist regions much farther north. In western Iowa, southwest-facing slopes absorb an abnormally high amount of the sun's rays and are subjected to dry, southwest winds. Such areas maintain plants and animals typical of regions much farther west or southwest. These refuges house relict communities. They are preserves, waiting, ready to expand whenever climatic shifts make conditions more favorable for them.

Iowa has a number of relict areas. These can be recognized by the plant or animal species that occur there. The Bluffton Fir Stand in northern Winneshiek County, has a large stand of the balsam fir, a boreal evergreen tree, as well as white pines and white birch. White pine, which is basically a northeastern United States species, also occurs at Wildcat Den State Park in Muscatine County and in the lovely Hardin County Greenbelt along the Iowa River between Iowa Falls and Eldora. Other typical northern species that are found in these relict areas include ground pine, bearberry, shinleaf, monkshood, yellow birch, Canada yew, mountain maple, twinflower, and dwarf scouring rush.

Often these northern remnants contain ice caves that bathe the slopes with cold air all summer. When this happens, another complex of species is found. This may include the Iowa Pleistocene snail found nowhere else in the world, and golden saxifrage, found only in a few places in the world, mostly in Iowa. All were probably widespread in the Ice Age, but now persist only in tiny areas with a microclimate similar to earlier conditions.

Iowa Conservation Commission, Ken Formanek

Fens characteristically have upwelling cold water high in carbonates and sulfates. Because of this, numerous plants are found there that occur nowhere else in Iowa. Silver Lake Fen, shown here, is located in Dickinson County.

(Left)
The gleaming white bark of the paper birch is a notable feature of the "driftless area" of northeast Iowa. A relict area in Hardin County, shown here with the scenic Iowa River in the background, contains a detached population of this species.

(Top)
The fragile cactus growing in the thin, dry soil of Gitchie Manitou State Preserve, is found nowhere else in Iowa, but is widespread in the southwest United States. These special habitats often provide a place for the state's rarest species to live.

(Above)
Relict areas often harbor plants far out of their present range. One such Iowa plant is fameflower, widespread in the southwestern states, here shown growing in the dry soil of Gitchie Manitou State Preserve in very northwest Iowa.

The sphagnum bog at Pilot Knob in Hancock County is another holdover from a much earlier age. Its insect-eating sundew plant, rare bog-cotton, and the red-backed vole in the nearby woodlands makes this one of Iowa's most unique spots.

In Muscatine County, the Big Sand Mound is a fascinating and important biological treasure. Shifting sand dunes, perhaps the only ones remaining in Iowa, provide suitable habitat for a number of very rare species, among them the Illinois mud turtle, plains pocket mouse, ornate box turtle, and a dozen or so of the state's rarest plants. This environment is perhaps a remainder of an Iowa dry period.

One of the most unusual places in Iowa is Gitchie Manitou State Preserve in the very northwest corner of our state. Occurring here among the billion-year old Sioux Quartzite rock outcrops are prickly pear cactus, fameflower, and buffalo grass, all found nowhere else in Iowa.

The Loess Hills of western Iowa are remnants of the conditions which prevail on the Great Plains. These steep, west-facing loess bluffs harbor some of the most unusual and rare plants and animals in Iowa. For example, yucca is fairly abundant and the night-flowering mentzelia is big and beautiful. Also the southern bog lemming and plains pocket mouse have been found there recently. These bluff-tops, sacred to the early native Americans, are Iowa's most unusual landform and among the most extensive loess deposits in the world. The state-owned Loess Hills Wildlife Area and the Turin Loess Hills State Preserve are classic examples of this interesting landform.

The eastern deciduous forest extended across most of northeastern North America, west to where the tall-grass prairie began. Iowa is in this transition zone and in the eastern third of the state we find remnants of this biome. Good examples of the eastern deciduous forest are White Pine Hollow in Dubuque County, Mossy Glen in Clayton County and Palisades-Kepler State Park and Preserve near Mt. Vernon. The maple-basswood community is the typical expression of this forest type. Other major components are the oak-hickory community, present on dry uplands, and Canada yew, present on the steep, north-facing slopes.

The prairie pothole biome extended into northwest Iowa; this resource has largely been lost and beautiful marshes continue to be drained. A few excellent examples of the prairie potholes are Elm Lake in Wright County, Cheever Lake near Estherville, Goose Lake near Jewell, and Jemmerson Slough near Spirit Lake. These highly productive areas usually contain white and yellow waterlilies, cattail, river bulrush and occasionally bog cotton, bog-bean, mare's tail and wild rice.

The magnificent tall-grass prairie biome reached its zenith in Iowa, truly the "tall-grass prairie capital of the world" at one time. Climatic changes now favor woodland formation in Iowa; this coupled with the agricultural activities of man, have caused the demise of the prairie. Thus, even Iowa's dominant native vegetation type has become a relict, a pathetic reminder of yesterday. Our largest state-owned prairie is slightly over 200 acres and perhaps less than 5,000 acres of prairie remain in the entire state. These remnants are priceless and needed if we are to interpret what our ancestors met as they crossed the Mississippi River on their way to a new life.

Some of our prairie remnants are Cayler Prairie near Lake Okoboji, Hayden Prairie near Lime Springs in Howard County, and Kalsow Prairie in Pocahontas County, northwest of Manson. Visit a tall-grass prairie and see what our ancestors faced; these prairie remnants are foreboding, intimidating, tough, yet fragile, beautiful and priceless.

These reminders of the past should be zealously guarded against destruction because they serve as scientific markers of environmental conditions of the past eras, because they provide habitat for exceptionally rare species which lend diversity to our state, and because they will be valuable educational areas in the future.

CHAPTER SEVEN

PRAIRIES

BY DARYL SMITH AND PAUL CHRISTIANSEN

(Previous Spread)
Slough grass and mountain mint compete for space in a swale of Hayden Prairie. The mosiac of grasses and flowers is typical of the tall-grass prairie.

Old-timer recollections of childhood on the tall-grass prairie have in common stories of grass so tall that it obscured a man walking or a person riding on a wagon seat.

Daryl Smith

IF YOU TRAVELED across Iowa during the 1830s, the view was astounding. Tall-grass prairie dominated the landscape. As far as you could see there was grass. It must have been an awesome sight.

The journals of early travelers often compared Iowa prairies with the oceans. Phrases such as "a sea of waving grass" or "earth oceans" were common. Settlers in southcentral Iowa talked of traveling through prairie from Oskaloosa to Des Moines without seeing a single tree. Today, as we motor across our state's fertile agricultural region on ribbons of concrete, it is difficult to conceive that it was once possible to wander from river to river, border to border, without leaving tall-grass prairie. Even in most forests you were not far from the prairie edge.

The height of the grasses in late summer and early autumn also made a lasting impression on settlers. Almost every prairie recollection refers to grasses so tall that people in them were hidden from view.

Before settlement, 30 million acres of Iowa was prairie. Forests were limited to the major stream valleys and the northeast corner of the state. Iowa's prairie landscape was part of a vast composite of grass, wind and sky occupying over 640 million acres of mid-continent North America. The tall-grass part of this vast grassland formed a triangle with its apex at the Wabash River in northwest Indiana. It radiated over northern Illinois, southwestern Minnesota, Iowa, northwestern Missouri, southern Manitoba, the eastern Dakotas, Nebraska, and Kansas and extended south across part of Oklahoma into Texas.

Today the Iowa prairie is an illusion. An active imagination and a little nostalgia are required to strip away a century and a half of civilization's artifacts and envision the former landscape. It is hard to believe that this panorama of farmland was once all tall-grass prairie. In the autumn of 1830, before settlement, almost any area was covered by miles of wine-colored big bluestem, interlaced with golden Indian grass — without a single tree. Man tamed this prairie wilderness to feed a hungry, developing nation. In less than a century after settlement, the Iowa prairie was converted to cropland. The rich black soil formed by the prairie plants caused the prairie's demise. Iowa prairie was plowed and planted into oblivion. Of the original 30 million acres of native prairie, only a few hundred acres remain, remnants of the past scattered across the agricultural landscape.

Carl Kurtz

(Left)
Colorful flowers dominate the prairie scene before the tall grasses take over in late summer. Kalsow Prairie in early July features a purple-to-white patchwork quilt of prairie phlox with splashes of orange butterfly milkweed and yellow ox-eye.

Larry Stone

Origin of the Prairie

THE QUESTION of prairie origins has been hotly debated since explorers and settlers first observed them. In the 19th century, many writers on the subject said they believed that awesome prairie fires were primarily responsible for the treeless grasslands. Beginning at the turn of the century, more emphasis was placed on water stress and on the concept that vegetation was influenced greatly by climate. Dr. Bohumil Shimek, University of Iowa botanist and student of the prairie in the early part of the century, placed great emphasis on evaporation and water stress. In the vicinity of Missouri Valley in Harrison County in 1908, he studied evaporation rate in relation to weather conditions, and this work convinced him of the key role evaporation played in the extent of prairie vegetation.

At about the same time, Dr. Frederick Clements was developing a theory of vegetation with climate as the key factor influencing the vegetation type present at any particular place.

Post-glacial climatic history may have played a key role in the initial establishment of tall-grass prairie. Pollen analysis documents a very warm, dry period which fostered the spread of the prairie. Once established, prairie was difficult to dislodge, and with the prevalence of fire, held its own against woody invasion.

In the past 30 or 40 years, ecologists have begun to favor the concept of a variety of factors — including climate, soil, and relief — all interacting to determine vegetation type. In this scheme fire emerges as a considerable influence in determining prairie vegetation.

(Above) ***In early June the plumes on each seed of*** **Geum trifolium** ***indicate that its seed is wind dispersed. This showy plant has many common names — prairie avens, prairie smoke, grandfathers whiskers and three sisters.***

Billowing smoke from prairie fires can be seen for miles. Prairie fire riding a strong headwind struck terror in the staunchest heart of the early settlers who ventured onto the open prairies.

Fire

EACH GROWING SEASON, tall-grass prairie produces far more vegetation than grazing animals eat. The stems and leaves of this vegetation are killed by frost and dry in winter. Over the next few years, this litter slowly decomposes and returns to the soil. Several years' growth may fall and accumulate on the ground, but each spring new shoots from prairie plants must fight their way up through the litter to reach sunlight. Consequently, seedlings have a difficult time getting established.

Fire relieves the prairie of this burden of litter. Litter build-up is also a fuel build-up, and when sufficient fuel has accumulated, the litter can easily be ignited if it is relatively dry. Across Iowa, one or two years' litter accumulation is sufficient fuel for a fire. When large stretches of unplowed prairie existed, the spark may have been provided by lightning or deliberately set by man. The greatest frequency of lightning bolts occurs in July, but strikes are likely from spring through fall, so many prairie fires might have been started by a single storm, especially if little rain accompanied the lightning.

American Indians apparently set prairie fires for a variety of reasons. In the spring fresh grass would appear first where the litter from previous years' growth had been removed, and this would attract grazing animals for the hunters. At other times, herds of animals could be driven by a fire and perhaps killed as they jumped from an embankment. Lewis and Clark, as they traveled up the Missouri River in 1804, noticed that Indians often set fire to the prairie to attract attention. They might do so, for example, to call scattered villages together for a meeting.

Today we usually equate fire with disaster. With the prairie, however, fire acted in a different way. Because almost all of the plants were adapted to fire, they could grow back from root stocks after a fire. Therefore, very few prairie plants were killed. Even prairie shrubs resprouted after burning. A fire in the spring would frequently hasten the growth of the prairie vegetation. Even if the fire occurred later in the growing season, within a few days green shoots would begin to appear and, within two or three weeks, the landscape would once more be green. Fire was undoubtedly instrumental in maintaining prairie along forest edges because it could kill many woody species. Today fire can be used in prairie management to control woody and non-native species which are not fire-adapted.

There are other types of fire adaptation on the prairie. For example, prairie plants seem to burn better than most plants. Once a fire gets started in the summer, even the green leaves of the grasses will burn well and keep the fire going.

Carl Kurtz

Prairie fire quickly removes the litter and dead plant material without harming the living roots or soil. Even the mice can survive when flattened close to the ground below the intense heat higher in the vegetation.

Daryl Smith

Prairie Plants

GRASSES DOMINATE the vegetation of the prairie. Except in spring, grasses are the primary visual aspect of the prairie and account for more than 90 percent of the total weight of annual plant growth. Several species begin growth soon after the snow melts in the spring. The early flush of cool-season grasses (those which prefer cool conditions for growth and seed production) is completed by the first of July. Porcupine grass, rosette panic grasses, Junegrass, and Canada wild rye are all important.

The most significant prairie grasses begin their growth somewhat later and do not produce seeds until late summer. These warm-season grasses include big bluestem, the most important of tall-grass prairie grasses. Often called turkey foot because the three spikes of the seed head resemble a bird's foot, big bluestem produces seed stalks 6 to 8 feet tall.

Indian grass, another notable warm-season tall grass, has a plume of seeds at the top of the seed stalk. Indian grass was a partner with big bluestem in providing most of the tall-grass growth on the prairies of our state.

Prairie dropseed is a bunch grass that is found along with big bluestem and Indian grass in the better drained portions of upland prairies. Each plant produces a mass of long narrow leaves that spread out in a circle. The seed head forms a fine branching plume.

Given wet soil conditions, other tall grasses take over. Blue-joint grass, cordgrass and switchgrass are the most prominent. Because undrained wet prairie was impossible to cultivate, these low areas were often used for wild hay. Cordgrass was not a favorite of haymakers. First of all, the leaf edges were very sharp — if the leaf was rubbed from top to bottom, it would cut like a sharp knife. Secondly, cordgrass hay was slippery, and many a load "slid out," leaving the top of the load on the ground.

Where soils are drier due to rocky or sandy conditions, several other grasses dominate. In mild dry conditions, little bluestem and sideoats grama are most abundant. These species are called mid-grasses because of their intermediate height when mature — about knee high. Tall dropseed, another midgrass, often dominates on sandy soils.

On the driest sites, muhley grass and blue and hairy grama dominate. These grasses are short (not more than a few inches tall), with narrow, wiry leaves.

The mid- and short-grasses are all bunch grasses; that is, the original grass plant does not form new plants, but rather grows in a tight bunch which increases in diameter only slightly each year. This produces a clumping effect, quite different from the sod of Kentucky bluegrass in a lawn, for instance. After a bunch grass prairie is burned, it is evident that the plants occupy only a small portion of the ground surface, leaving bare soil between. However, the roots reach into the spaces between plants and extract moisture and nutrients, and the grass leaves drape over the open spaces and shade them, preventing other plants from growing there. In addition, the leaves help prevent erosion by breaking up rain drops before they reach the soil.

Not only do grasses dominate prairie vegetation, but they also dominate the prairie underground. The roots of prairie grasses branch, producing a dense network of fine roots. These roots penetrate deeply into the soil, often 6 or more feet below the soil surface. These roots, present for thousands of years, are responsible for the high organic content of prairie soil, giving it the black color.

Big bluestem, or turkey foot grass as it was sometimes called, was the dominant plant on the tall-grass prairie reaching 6-8 feet in height on the richer, more moist sites.

Carl Kurtz

A late summer scene on a dry prairie remnant in Black Hawk County. A purple carpet of blazing star forms a backdrop for little bluestem, Missouri goldenrod, and prairie bush clover.

Not only are prairie plants specialized in the growth of their stem and leaves but also in their roots. Some root systems are shallow and diffuse while others penetrate deeper into the soil to tap water and nutrient sources. Up to 90% of a prairie plant's mass may be underground.

About 72 species of grasses are found on Iowa's prairies. Not only do grasses dominate the visual aspect of the prairie, but the grass family has more species among the prairie vegetation than any other plant family.

In addition to grasses, two other plant families are prominent in the tall-grass prairie: the daisy or sunflower family and the pea or legume family. More than 50 species of the daisy family and 25 species of the pea family are found on the Iowa prairie.

All members of the daisy family have flowers in heads; that is, numerous flowers make up what we normally think of as one flower. The sunflower is a good example. The outer flowers of each head produce long strap-like petals, while the rest of the flowers across the face of the head have fine, tiny petals arranged in a circle. Each individual flower produces its own fruit, a sunflower seed. Not all daisy family species are as easily recognized as sunflowers or asters. Goldenrods and blazing stars have only a few flowers per head, but still they belong to this family.

Distinct characteristics also distinguish the pea family. Flowers are often similar to the sweet pea or garden pea. The banner and wings provide a signal for pollinating insects that a droplet of nectar awaits. The pod is also distinctive because it splits into two halves, similar to a garden pea pod or peanut.

Several other families also contribute substantially to prairie flora. The rose, buttercup, milkweed, mint, sedge, and parsley families are included in this group.

Wild strawberries provide a tasty treat for prairie visitors in June. Early travelers on the prairie found that they "sure beat hardtack and beans."

Blazing star provides a good illustration of the composite nature of the flowers of the daisy family.

The loess hills form a spectacular western border for our state. With the decline of prairie fires after settlement, trees moved up the draws while prairie plants continued to dominate the exposed slopes.

Loess Hills

ACROSS OUR STATE diversity in the environment has produced several distinct prairie community types. Soil type and depth, water availability, and topography are some of the major factors accounting for the variation in Iowa prairies.

Perhaps the best known of the distinct prairie communities are the loess hill prairies on the far western border of our state *(see Chapter 2)*.

As in all prairies, grasses are the most important part of the vegetation in these hills. Little bluestem is by far the dominant grass. Even though it is a bunchgrass, its extensive root system and matted dead leaves are a major factor in stabilizing the steep slopes of wind-deposited soil. Other grasses which contribute significantly to the cover are muhley and side-oats grama. Where moisture conditions are more favorable — near the base of slopes or on the east or north-facing slopes — big bluestem mixes with little bluestem. Where conditions are most harsh — on vertical west-facing exposures — sand dropseed is able to find growing space.

Yucca is a distinctive flowering species found in the loess hills. Relatives of this species are the Joshua tree and other large yuccas of the Southwest. Even though this yucca is not a large plant, it stands well above the prairie grasses with its slender flower stalk bearing large, white flowers in June. Later, the short, stout seed pod is infected with the larvae of the yucca moth. After dark, when the flowers open, they are pollinated by the yucca moth which then lays eggs in the flower's ovary. The eggs hatch, and the larvae eat the developing seeds. Usually, the few seeds not eaten are shed to provide for establishment of new plants at other locations.

In the loess hills, three more distinctive species that vary greatly in size and blooming periods are large-flowered beardtongue, skeleton weed, and bluets. Bluets are low, bushy plants with tiny, white flowers blooming in early summer. Large-flowered beardtongue also blooms in early summer, but is a tall plant with large, lavendar flowers. Skeleton weed is a leafless, branching plant with very few flowers in each head and with white petals. It blooms in late summer.

Several other more western species have their eastern-most range in the loess hills. Gaura, cut-leaved goldenweed, and sand lily join yucca on the steep slopes. Gaura is a pioneer species coming into areas where the soil has been exposed by erosion or digging. Cut-leaved goldenweed, in the daisy family, also invades bare soil on the driest sites. The sand lily is occasionally found on steep west-facing slopes along with yucca.

Hill Prairies

Hill prairies along the Mississippi River persist due to a combination of southern exposure and thin soil over bedrock.

OPENINGS on forested slopes called "hill prairies" or "goat prairies" form the eastern Iowa counterpart of the loess hills. Occurring in rugged areas, typically forested, these prairies may at first look like artificial clearings, but closer scrutiny will show that the vast majority are natural openings of long standing. Some people called them "goat prairies" because they are on such steep slopes that only a nimble goat could graze them. The size of the openings varies from small patches to several acres. Hill prairies typically occur on prominently exposed ridges or points or on steep, exposed, south to west-facing bluffs. They are caused by a combination of factors which result in droughty, well-drained or somewhat excessively drained soil. The substrates that permit rapid drainage are loess, glacial drift, or gravel rock outcrops. The location on a hilltop or south and west slope is exposed to the full impact of the hot, midafternoon sun and prevailing southwesterly summer winds. Periodic fires have maintained many hill prairies. Moderate grazing may also help maintain them, but heavy grazing will result in an abundance of juniper.

Hill prairie vegetation is of the bunch grass type, with little bluestem the dominant species in most stands. Side-oats grama is usually present and may occasionally dominate. On a few hill prairies, Indian grass or another grass such as big bluestem may dominate small areas or, rarely, the entire stand. Overall the types of plants are similar to those of the Iowa tall-grass prairie. Plants most characteristic of hill prairies are little bluestem, side-oats grama, purple prairie clover, yellow flax, scurf pea, and yellow puccoon.

Before settlement, hill prairies formed only a small part of the vast Iowa prairie. Because the steep slopes were not cultivated, hill prairies are now the least disturbed and most frequent type of prairie in Iowa. A large number of hill prairies are within Dubuque's city limits.

Autumn comes early in a moist swale of the low prairie. Sensitive fern (upper left corner) derives its name from being easily affected by the first light frost.

Carl Kurtz

Low Prairies

IN THE DRAINAGE ways and depressions where prairie soils are constantly wet, a distinctive plant community develops, dominated by mostly tall, moisture-tolerant plants. Slough grass and blue-joint grass are common. Often they produce large patches, where one or the other dominates to the exclusion of all other plant species. Sedges, grass-like plants, also are common, especially where the soil is more moist and standing water is found in the depressions among the plants. Often in these very wet soils small mounds topped by a thatch of grass or sedge will be lifted above surrounding soil.

The wet prairies are often colorful with a variety of flowers blooming. In the spring a familiar blossom, the blue flag or wild iris, is prominent. Often it grows in thick stands in a band just above the standing water line around the edge of a marsh or prairie pond. Other spring blooming species in this plant community are white lady-slipper, buttercup, swamp saxifrage, golden alexanders, and meadow rue.

In the summer, tall poison hemlock of the parsley family opens its tiny white flowers on stalks arranged like the ribs of an umbrella. In the eastern part of our state, bunch-flower produces bouquets of small, white, lily-like flowers. Prairie loosestrife, unusual in that it is a rather short plant producing blooms far down in the vegetation, has bell-shaped yellow flowers. Wild quinine's tiny white heads spring from large-leaved rosettes at this time. Smooth rose, without prickles on the stem but with typical pink blooms, also prefers the low prairies. Swamp milkweed pushes clusters of rose-pink flowers above its neighbors while, nearer the ground, the sensitive fern is producing spores on green-brown stalks.

Late in summer, the flat-topped white aster displays umbrella-shaped groups of white-rayed heads. At the same time, the deep purple of iron-weed can be seen for long distances. Sprawling among the taller plants are the smartweeds, with a variety of leaf-shapes, flower stalks and flower colors. Generally the colors are pink to red and the flowers are tiny, in tight elongated clusters.

Later, several yellow-flowered species provide color for the low prairie community. Sneezeweed has heads with yellow ray flowers whose petals are rather wedge-shaped with a slight notch on the outer margin. Smooth goldenrod has tall, slick, reddish stems and bunches of small, yellow-rayed heads. Spanish needles or sticktights with yellow heads produce distinctive fruits — flat and rectangular with two long, barbed needles at the outer end. The end of the flowering season is signaled by the pale purple blooms of bottle gentian, which flowers until freezing temperatures of fall end the growing season.

To humans, the low prairie is usually an uninviting place. Hummocked, uneven ground makes walking difficult. In the spring, water often stands in low places. In the hot summer, a combination of high temperature, high humidity, and high insect populations often make it unbearable. The low prairies are a haven for mosquitoes that caused considerable distress to early settlers. And, in the fall, the tangle of the season's growth of plants also makes walking difficult. Yet, many plant species find the low prairie an ideal habitat and respond with an abundance of growth and reproduction.

(Top) The hour-glass shape of the showy milkweed flower is typical of the milkweed family which has many species on the Iowa prairie.

(Right) Even with its roots in the moist soil of a wet prairie, water hemlock shows signs of wilting on a hot day in late June.

Paul Christiansen

Sand Prairies

SAND PRAIRIES are distinguished by their soil substrate. The sand may have been deposited by either water or wind. Soil moisture varies from dry to wet, but the limited water-holding capacity of the coarse-textured sand generally results in a rather dry habitat. Consequently sand prairies support a sparse covering of vegetation. Grasses mostly are low-growing and scattered in tufts or bunches with spaces of bare sand. The appearance as well as the vegetation of the drier sand areas resembles the sand-hills of Kansas and Nebraska. For example, sand reedgrass and western ragweed are rather abundant on Iowa sand prairies, but that is the only place in our state where they are found. Dominant grasses of the dry sand prairie are little bluestem, sand reedgrass, Junegrass, tall dropseed and needlegrass, along with characteristic flowers like partridge pea, sage, dotted mint, and prickly pear. As moisture availability increases the bare areas are filled in by plants, with big bluestem and Indian grass appearing among the dominant grasses along with blazing star, birdfoot violet, Missouri goldenrod, and savory-leaf aster.

Like hill prairies, sand prairies originally were a small component of the total Iowa landscape. They are not generally suitable for cultivation, however, and, consequently, a larger percentage of them remain than of the true prairie.

Sand prairie flora and fauna are unique in Iowa. The Big Sand Mound south of Muscatine probably contains more rare plants and animals than any other single locality in our state. In addition, other sand prairies in the state also harbor rare plants. For example, only one locality is known in Iowa for each of the following: silky prairie clover, northern panic grass, and slender sedge, but all are associated with sand prairies.

Succession to a sand prairie starts as sand reedgrass (foreground) and other grasses begin to stabilize a blow-out on Muscatine Island.

Carl Kurtz

(Left)
"What a thousand acres of Silphiums looked like when they tickled the bellies of the buffalo is a question never again to be answered and perhaps not even asked."
Aldo Leopold,
A Sand County Almanac

The Prairie Year

Early-Season Prairie Flowers
a. (left) Compass plant, July
b. Pasque flower, April
c. Purple coneflower, June
d. Ragwort, May
e. Purple prairie clover, June
f. Shooting star, May
g. Blue-flag iris, June

THROUGH THE SEASONS, the prairie reminds you of a poorly kept perennial flower garden. It looks unkept because blooms are not removed as they wither, and dead leaves and stalks of last year's growth remain. Yet this plant community provides a spectacular display of flowers with rich variety in color and shape from early spring when snow banks disappear to late fall when killing frosts put an end to the display. The beauty of the prairie continues into winter when various grasses create a mosaic from golden brown to rust, and frost and snow turn spent plants into sculptures.

The flowers of early spring are usually short, with their leaves and flowers close to the litter, and often they have fuzzy stems and leaves which slow down air movement that would cool the tender plants excessively. The pasque flower begins the parade in April with its large, deep blue flowers. In northeastern Iowa, prairie avens with its red flower bud scales (sepals) follows pasque flower.

In the western half of Iowa, ground plum — a legume with pink flowers — blooms early, and later produces its characteristic round pods about the size of large grapes. Following close behind are prairie avens, the early buttercup, and several violets.

Puccoons, with their coiled flower stalks and bright orange to orange-yellow flowers, blossom across Iowa in May. Eastern Iowa is treated to shooting stars with flowers ranging from purple to pink. Another bright spot in the spring flora is the lousewort's pale yellow, beak-like flowers.

Early summer begins with a flash of yellow from the prairie ragwort and golden alexanders. Purple coneflowers, prairie phlox, and American vetch furnish darker hues, while Canada anemone provides the white. In the low ground around the rims of the mashes, blue flag, the wild iris, will be blooming.

From the middle of June until late July the variety of flowers increases. Ox-eye, a false sunflower, furnishes large, yellow heads for sev-

Mid- and Late-Season Prairie Flowers
a. Black-eyed Susan, July
b. Wood lily, July
c. Goldenrod, August,
d. Downey gentian, September

A.
Ron Sarson

B.
Paul Christiansen

C.
Ron Sarson

D.
Ron Sarson

Prairie gay-feather, rattlesnake master and black-eyed Susan dominate a moist prairie swale in mid-July.

Carl Kurtz

eral weeks. Shortly, black-eyed Susan and yellow coneflower also open large heads with yellow ray flowers. In early July, compass plant begins flowering. Its tall flower stalks rise up to 6 feet tall and forecast the height of the prairie as the season progresses. The habit of aligning its leaves so they face east-west provides a crude compass for prairie visitors.

Through the summer, the legume family furnishes lead plant, a prairie shrub which has spikes of tiny purple flowers with yellow pollen. Purple and white prairie clover bloom in July. Their flower heads are elongated on stalks raised above finely divided leaves. Two companions which bloom at the same time are tick trefoil and wild pea. Both have white to pink flowers. Tick trefoil is easy to spot later in the season because it develops tiny hooked hairs on the surfaces of its pods, which easily catch and stick to clothing or animal fur. Wild pea uses another device to spread its seeds. As the long pod dries, it begins to twist, and when it finally splits into two halves, the seeds are thrown far from the parent plant.

One legume which is more notable for its leaves than its flowers is silverleaf scurf pea. A layer of fine hairs over the surface of the leaves gives them a bright, whitish cast. The dark blue flowers are small and obscure. Sage has similar leaf characteristics.

Several species of milkweed bloom in mid-summer. First out, the butterfly weed, is the showiest, with its large clusters of bright orange flowers. Very few of its flowers are successfully pollinated because a plant often will not produce a single pod.

Other milkweeds include the green milkweeds whose flowers are light green; the common milkweed with pink, very fragrant flowers, and Sullivan's milkweed with smoother leaves and fewer flowers in a cluster than the common milkweed.

The late summer display is heralded by the bloom of the Missouri goldenrod. After it blooms, a large number of other goldenrods, sunflowers, asters, and blazing stars, as well as several other beautiful species, put on a floral display.

Where the soil is more moist, the late goldenrod is dominant, and on rocky or sandy soils, the gray goldenrod is found. Numerous other species of goldenrod grow, with variations in their display of tiny, yellow flowers, stem heights, and habitat preference.

At the same time, the asters are producing an equally varied show. The uplands sport the panicled, sky blue, and New England asters. Where the soil is more moist, the smooth and flat-topped asters are common. Where moisture is less, the silky aster is more likely to be found.

The fall prairie also displays the sunflowers. The sawtoothed and showy sunflowers grow statewide, while Maximillion's sunflower grows in the western part of the state. All are perennials, much better behaved than the weedy, annual sunflower.

Not all the fall flowers are yellow. The blazing stars are a beautiful exception. These daisy-family members have small purple heads seated directly on long flower stalks. The prairie blazing star, or gay-feather, has heads clustered at the upper end of the flower stalk, producing a cattail-like effect. The rough blazing star spaces its heads at 1- or 2-inch intervals. In western Iowa the blazing star is shorter, with numerous stalks on each plant and with flower heads clustered near the stalk ends.

To find the field milkwort among the tall fall flowers, you must part the grass leaves and look for a plant less than 6 inches tall with a cluster of light pink flowers at the top.

The last of the prairie flowers in the fall is likely to be the gentians. In low, moist ground, the light purple closed gentian will be blooming, while in upland prairies, the downy genetian with dark purple blooms will be found. Sandy prairies will have still another — the delicate fringed gentian.

The Surviving Prairie

THE COMBINATION of a climate suitable for agriculture and the deep, rich soil built by prairie vegetation has led to the virtual destruction of the tall-grass prairie in Iowa. Today, only a few areas of significant size remain. Some of these in public and private hands are held with the intention of preservation. Several notable prairie remnants are preserved by County Conservation Boards.

The State Preserves Advisory Board and the Iowa Conservation Commission are attempting to preserve representatives of the various types of prairies in Iowa. Among the earliest prairies designated for preservation were Hayden Prairie, Cayler Prairie, Kalsow Prairie and Sheeder Prairie.

The Nature Conservancy, a private preservation organization has prairie preserves in Dickinson, Howard, Johnson, Jasper, and Story counties. The Freda Hafner Preserve is a few miles west of Milford, and the Ames High School Prairie is adjacent to the school.

Many small prairie areas still exist in railroad rights-of-way, odd field corners and old settler cemeteries, but more than 99.9 percent of the Iowa tall-grass prairie has been destroyed by cultivation or grazing. Therefore, the few remaining protected prairies become more significant.

The State Preserves Advisory Board and the Iowa Conservation Commission are attempting to preserve representatives of the various types of prairies in Iowa. Among the earliest prairies designated for preservation were Hayden Prairie, Cayler Prairie, Kalsow Prairie and Sheeder Prairie.

Iowa prairies preserved or being protected

Name	Size Acres	Ownership	County
Ames High School Prairie	7	Ames Community School	Story
Bergman Prairie	100	Private	Dickinson
*Cayler Prairie	160	State Conservation Commission	Dickinson
*Clay Prairie	3	University of Northern Iowa	Butler
*Crossman Prairie	10	Nature Conservancy	Howard
*Dinesen Prairie	20	Private	Shelby
Dock Prairie	25	Private	Allamakee
*Doolittle Pothole Prairie	25	State Conservation Commission	Story
*Emmet County Prairie	200	State Conservation Commission	Emmet
*Freda Haffner Kettlehole	110	Nature Conservancy	Dickinson
*Gitchie Manitou	40	State Conservation Commission	Lyon
*Hayden Prairie	240	State Conservation Commission	Howard
*Kalsow Prairie	160	State Conservation Commission	Pocahontas
*Kisk-Ke-Kosh Prairie	17	State Conservation Commission	Jasper
*Liska Stanek Prairie	20	Webster County Conserv. Comm.	Webster
Loess Hills Wildlife Area	200	State Conservation Commission	Monona
Lageschulte Prairie	4	Wartburg College	Bremer
Mark Sand Prairie	35	Private	Black Hawk
Ray Prairie	8	Private	Bremer
*Sheeder Prairie	25	State Conservation Commission	Guthrie
Siles Prairie	10	Private	Cherokee
Steele Prairie	200	Private	Cherokee
*Stinson Prairie	32	Kossuth County Conserv. Comm.	Kossuth
Turin Loess Hills Prairie	100	State Conservation Commission	Monona
Waubonsie State Park	50	State Conservation Commission	Fremont
Wearin Prairie	60	Private	Mills
*Williams Prairie	21	Nature Conservancy	Johnson

*Dedicated as a state preserve

Prairie Reconstruction

INCREASING INTEREST has been shown since the 1950s in rebuilding prairies. Using seeds and transplants, many small areas now provide Iowans with facsimiles of tall-grass prairie, while furnishing a largely maintenance-free ground cover. Grasses and the more vigorous forbs have generally been seeded, while species with less vigor or unusual requirements have been transplanted. With careful weeding, the planting may resemble prairie after a season of growth. Without special care — except an occasional mowing in the first year — the planting may require three years for prairie species to dominate.

Prairie reconstructions have been used for home landscaping, for educational uses at schools and colleges, for roadside cover, and for large-scale landscaping. Two notable examples in the latter category are landscape designs using prairie species at Salisbury Laboratories in Charles City in Floyd County and the headquarters of the Iowa Farm Bureau in Des Moines. When time and energy savings are important concerns in soil stabilization and beautification of grounds, prairie reconstruction is an attractive and potentially educational alternative.

We will, of course, never see "a sea of waving grass" stretching to the horizon. But many Iowans are determined to preserve the small niches of prairie we have remaining. They are like gems in our lush land, and are truly a part of our natural heritage.

Paul Christiansen

Prairie reconstructions provide an attractive landscape alternative as well as stimulating interest in a vanishing heritage.

Jim Brandenburg, ©1980

CHAPTER EIGHT

FORESTS

BY BENJAMIN F. GRAHAM AND
DAVID GLENN-LEWIN

WHEN THE FIRST SETTLERS crossed the Mississippi into Iowa, they found broad plains — rolling grassy prairie, interspersed with wetlands — and woods. Although the grassy area dominated the landscape, about a fifth of our state was tree-covered. Stands of white oak decorated ridges along the horizon, while a wide variety of trees crowded onto flood plains and stream banks.

For the pioneer, the Iowa woods provided an abundance of lumber and fuel. Where there were forests, men used them, and so the total decreased.

At one time, dense woods had covered our state. The earliest evidence of forests in Iowa comes from the Pennsylvanian Period some 300 million years ago, that time in our geological history when the state's massive coal deposits were formed. Tree-sized ferns and club-mosses abounded in the extensive swamp forests that grew here then — even before dinosaurs had evolved. Fossils of such primitive trees have been found for instance, in Marion County, and many others may be found with coal deposits in the central part of our state. Experts estimate that, to produce a foot-thick seam of Iowa coal, a 20-foot layer of accumulated organic remnants had to be compressed and dehydrated over a period of about 65,000 years. Today, not far beneath our much less extensive forests, lie immense stores of energy derived from sunlight that fell on those swamplands hundreds of millions of years ago.

Studies of such ancient and extensive photosynthetic systems as Iowa's Pennsylvanian swamps make up the field of paleobotany. This field deals in units of time which are difficult to comprehend and recalls plant species the likes of which are rarely seen today. Let's leap ahead, however, to a time in the history of our woodlands when species found there were more familiar.

Summer's green gives way to autumn's gold as these white ash leaves signal the change of seasons.

(Previous Spread)
Tall, slender balsam firs occupy a suitable cool moist habitat on this north-facing bluff above the Upper Iowa River near Bluffton.

Carl Kurtz

Among the largest in the world, the wind-deposited loess bluffs of western Iowa support an interesting variety of forests and grasslands.

Glacial Influence

THERE IS NO more appropriate or influential reference event in the development of Iowa's natural heritage than the retreat of the last great glacial ice sheet after it had scooped, scraped, and scoured more than 10,000 square miles of northcentral Iowa. As the ice receded, the relatively harsh climate around the glacial border moderated, setting the stage for hardy and aggressive plants and animals that would follow the retreating ice northward. Evidence is good that even today the slow northward movement of the ice is continuing, and the Greenland icecap represents a last remnant of that most recent or Wisconsin ice sheet that covered the northern half of what is now Iowa.

A consideration of the Pleistocene Ice Age (*see Chapter 2*) can make it easier to understand the variations in soils that, with the climate, have been so influential in determining distribution patterns of Iowa's natural vegetation. In the Pleistocene Age, Iowa was covered or partly covered by glacial ice on four successive occasions over a span of two million years.

Each ice invasion slowed, stopped, and then retreated. The result of these ponderous oscillations was the deposition of a deep mass of mineral material over most of Iowa's native and much-eroded bedrock (*see Chapter 1*). This mineral over-burden, in some places more than 600 feet deep, can be likened to a cake with four layers of coarse rocky glacial till topped and interspersed with generous frosting layers of very fine, wind-deposited loess soil blown across the state from the Missouri River flood plain by prevailing westerly winds of the warm, dry, interglacial periods.

Subsequent soil development on this stratified mineral substrate has left Iowa with extremely productive loess soils on her uplands and level ground, except in northcentral Iowa, where the rich prairie soils formed on glacial materials deposited after the major periods of loess deposition. On the steeper slopes and in the stream channels, the fine soils have been eroded by wind and rain, exposing underlying sands and gravels dropped by glacial ice.

This continuing loss of our fine soils through natural erosion — so often accelerated by careless mismanagement — poses our most serious conservation challenge today.

Clues From the Past

OUR PICTURE of the trees that grew in Iowa shortly after the Wisconsin ice invasion is like a giant picture-puzzle — one that is gradually taking form through the efforts of numerous investigators who have worked over the past century. The most obvious clues have been plant macro-fossils — pieces of wood and other preserved segments of plants recovered, frequently, in construction excavations and during well-digging. Conditions near the glacial margins were seasonally quite wet, and numerous lakes, ponds, swales, and bogs were formed from melting ice and precipitation. In such environments, low temperature, low oxygen supply and, often, high acidity provided for incredibly effective preservation of plant and animal remains. Normal decay organisms just could not operate under such conditions.

The relative (and sometimes actual) ages of such exciting discoveries have been determined from their position in the profile of stratified mineral drift laid down in Pleistocene times. A piece of charred log may date a prehistoric forest fire, or a beaver-worked stick may indicate the existence of a beaver-pond environment at some time in the past. From leaf, twig, and fruit fragments, species lists have been compiled which tell us much about the past vegetation and, indirectly, about the climatic conditions which supported it.

Equally fascinating is the history provided through the ingenious techniques of pollen analysis. Lennart von Post, a Swedish geology professor, is credited with introducing pollen analysis as a useful technique in 1916. To understand how it works, we must think again of our glacial history. As the most recent glacial ice sheet retreated, it left behind thousands of scoured out depressions and dammed valleys which, having filled with abundant melt waters, became the lakes of northern North America. Very gradually, over subsequent centuries, forest species changed in response to fluctuations in local climate. And, each spring through the centuries, winds wafted millions of microscopic pollen grains from trees and other plants to the surfaces of nearby lakes. There, year after year, century after century, they mixed with other organic debris and settled to the bottoms of the cold, glacial lakes. Today, after thousands of years, some of these lakes have become completely filled with layer after annual layer of accumulated dead organic matter. These are the sphagnum bogs of the northlands, and the sedge bogs of northern Iowa. Some of the larger and deeper lakes are still filling, mostly by sedimentation, but also by growth enrichment as the lakes age. Lying chronologically stratified within the peat of these bogs, is Nature's diary of changes in local vegetation over the past 15,000 years. Von Post said that samples of peat taken at intervals from the bottom to the top would permit us to identify and to count the microscopic pollen grains from different species of trees. Pollen grains are not only tough and durable, but also differ enough in size, shape, and surface ornamentation to be uniquely characteristic of the plants from which they come.

From such pollen studies, workers in Iowa have discovered that approximately 14,000 years ago, as the last ice retreated, spruce, fir, and pine trees dominated our forests. There is less evidence of oak, elm, maple, alder, birch, walnut, hazel, and basswood. Within 5,000 years, the spruce and fir had nearly disappeared, and oak, elm, maple, and basswood had assumed an important role. Presumably the advent of a warmer drier climate about 9,000 years ago discouraged even the deciduous forests and set the stage for the herbaceous plants of the prairies which were still here when the pioneers arrived. Represented among these more modern pollen grains are numerous grasses as well as several members of the sunflower, goosefoot, and pigweed families. Fossil pollen grains from ragweed are also present. Perhaps Sac or Fox Indians or their predecessors may have begun to sneeze in mid-August as many of us do now.

Carl Kurtz

Much of eastern Iowa's bedrock is covered by trees. Here the upper cave entrance can be seen from beneath the Natural Bridge at Maquoketa Caves State Park.

An intricate network of veins carries water and minerals to the photosynthetic cells in this maple leaf where life-supporting sugars are manufactured.

Pete Krumhardt

Raindrops fall softly to the thick mat of needles beneath this white pine at Pine Lake State Park in central Iowa.

Carl Kurtz

Tom C. Cooper

Alert and strong, this beautiful white-tailed buck prefers riparian forests where browse is plentiful.

Some pine seems to have been present over this whole span of time and, at least in the record from one bog near McCulloch, appears to have increased beginning about 3,000 years ago — perhaps reflecting a change to a more northerly prevailing wind. Although pine is not now a conspicuous part of Iowa's forests, small relict stands have persisted, accompanied by other boreal forest species, in restricted microclimates.

The wonderful reminiscences of such early Iowa naturalists as T. H. MacBride (*see Chapter 14*) also provide windows through which we can look back and see Iowa's forests and prairies as they used to be. In the following passages from an 1895 newspaper (reprinted in *The Palimpsest*, published by the State Historical Society, 1926), MacBride describes things as he recalled them from his youth some 60 years earlier:

"The primeval woods were confined to two very dissimilar locations; to ridges of clay, sand, or rock and to flood plains of streams, flats more or less wide, subject to overflow. All the richest most fertile areas of the state were prairie . . . not infrequently the streams were found shaded with only a fringe of their characteristic species while groves of forest trees covered isolated hilltops far away.

"The primeval forests in these diverse localities were very different in character. The species were different. Down by the streams the wild plum, wild cherry, box-elder, soft maple and elm made, with the grape and Virginia creeper, thickets almost or wholly impassable, with shade so dense that the ground beneath was absolutely bare. Where by the junction of two streams the flood plain was widened with richer alluvial soil, walnuts, hackberries and cottonwoods with an occasional bur-oak, gave to the woodland more of the appearance of an eastern forest, and here and there on rocky banks were groves of hard maple rivalling those of Pennsylvania and Vermont. But on the clay ridges the white oak flourished sometimes to the exclusion of all else; while the most striking peculiarity of the Iowa upland forest was its openness. One could drive through it anywhere. To one following some long clay ridge the trees opened on every hand as in a royal park, and out past their clear white weathered boles on a summer day the emerald prairie gleamed and shone to the horizon's edge.

"Changes in the animal world are of course even more radical than those seen in the world of plants. Deer that were once abundant are entirely gone and many a smaller species is quite extinct. . . .

"Even parrots once enlivened the groves and meadows of our southern counties. Great flocks settled in spring on leafless trees and lit them up with the colors of the rainbow, easy mark, alas! for every idle vagabond with wit enough to carry a gun.

"To the old regime . . . contributed likewise the annual fires which swept all grass-grown regions, forest and prairie alike, keeping down the natural increase of the forest so that only the hardiest individual under exceptional conditions managed to thrive at all . . . Such trees are now, owing to the absence of forest fires, wholly surrounded by 'second growth' . . . but if one be privileged to walk through such a surviving bit of woodland and can for the once imagine the smaller trees removed, and the ground beneath the remaining lofty white oaks carpeted with grass, he may even yet at least in imagination see the woods of Iowa when through their shades the Sacs and Foxes 'pursued the panting deer'."

189

Autumn's blaze of color in Iowa is packed in the passing leaves and presages the black and white winter season.

Tom C. Cooper

Riparian Forests

THE TREES OF IOWA'S native forests are a mixture of broad-leaved, deciduous species characteristic of the great southeastern forest, with a very light mixture in northeast Iowa of conifers that have persisted in locally hospitable habitats. In this predominantly prairie state, the general pattern of forests is largely a product of the rivers and streams that drain the land. A dozen tributaries of the Mississippi River reach back to the northwest and drain about three quarters of the state as they flow south and east. Approximately an equal number of Missouri River tributaries, flowing southwest, drain the western quarter of the state. Along these riverbanks, where the stress of drought has been reduced and protection from fire increased, long fingers of riparian forest have ventured out across the prairie to provide shelter, timber, and fuel from prehistoric times.

The one exception to the association between forest and streams is the Driftless Area of northeast Iowa which was virtually unaffected by the last glaciation. The Driftless Area is characterized by rolling, hilly terrain, a cooler, more moist climate than most of Iowa, and forests that extend westward from the Mississippi to form a lush and verdant blanket up the slopes and over the hilltops.

Indescribable October beauty along the Des Moines River in Boone County.

191

Nature decides where each plant grows best, as evidenced by the conspicuous zonation of these trees from wet bottom to higher ridge.

Kinds of Iowa Forests

Tom C. Cooper

TO IDENTIFY general forest vegetation, the most common and perhaps the most convenient method is to use the dominant woody species as the key character — sometimes supplementing this with some conspicuous habitat characteristic. Upland forests, for example, are those occupying a position above the reach of standing water or floods. There is, of course, a substantial range of slope positions even within this definition of upland forests. Also recognizable are clear differences in vegetation occupying flood plains. The general differences between upland and flood plain forests are so striking, however, that this broad distinction will serve our purposes. These differences may include such things as the species present, the structure and appearance of the vegetation, the type of soil, growth and reproduction habits of the trees, the plants comprising the ground layer, and even the animals present.

Throughout most of Iowa, upper slopes, ridges, and hilltops are the sites for forests dominated by white oak and shagbark hickory, along with other associated species. Lower down, in moist protected areas, the white oak forest gives way to a woodland in which red oak, sugar maple and basswood predominate (although their relative proportions vary from one site to another). In general, the amount of maple increases toward the north and east.

As with all forests, the transition from one type to another is subtle and not sharply defined. In many places, as you walk up a slope from a protected ravine, it is impossible to tell exactly where the change takes place from red oak/maple/basswood to the white oak/hickory forest on the hilltop. Each species, with its individual behavior and distribution, sometimes produces confusing patterns of vegetation. Basswood, for example, may abandon the low slopes and protected areas and — as in the Ledges State Park in Boone County — grow on hilltops and flat uplands along with white oak. Some hardy, less common species — such as the chinkapin oak and the red cedar — seem to have met the challenge of survival through their ability to cling to cracks and crevices of rocky bluffs above the rivers in northeast Iowa. Both of these species prefer alkaline soils or a limestone substrate. Red cedar glades are often found on overgrazed pastures and abandoned fields.

Along rivers and streams, where high water may flood the forest at least occasionally, the kind of woodland is quite different from the upland forest. Although the trees are deciduous (similar to the upland species), the structure of the forest and its species composition are almost entirely different.

Species distribution in the lowland forest depends in part upon the intensity and frequency of flooding. Sand bars and shores that are accumulating new soil are often covered with a young and vigorous growth of willow or cottonwood saplings. It is not uncommon for these species to be so dense, and their branches so tough and pliable, that they are virtually impenetrable. These common lowland species actually require beds of bare mineral soil for their seeds to germinate. They rarely prosper where they have to contend with sod or a deep humus layer on the soil's surface.

The fox squirrel, impertinent forest resident and industrious planter of oaks, hickories and walnuts.

Pin oaks stand out among the hardwoods on this flat land along the Mississippi River in Des Moines County. In Iowa, autumn's colors are golds, reds and browns, and the maple's contribution is dramatic.

Being sensitive to minor differences in the drainage characteristics of the soil, trees of the flood plain often exhibit marked variations in growth rate that are obviously related to their distance from the stream channel. During flooding, swifter water near the channel lifts and transports larger mineral particles, frequently depositing them in marginal ridges parallel to the stream's banks. Shallower floodwaters which spread out across the flood plain are less energetic; their flow slows more and more as they get farther away from the channel. One result of this diminishing energy pattern is the finer aluvial soils of the flood plain. Away from the main channel, large trees may grow without being uprooted by the force of the current in flooding. More important, on the flood plain, trees have to contend with periodic lack of oxygen for their roots. Tolerance to flooding is probably the most important factor that distinguishes lowland from upland forest species. Many flood plain species' life histories show adaptation to recurrent floods. The common trees, for example, produce large quantities of light, easily dispersed seeds well suited for colonizing new beds created by flooding. Once dispersed, the new seeds germinate and grow rapidly.

The predominant tree species in a lowland, flood plain forest are eastern cottonwoods, silver maple, green ash, and boxelder. Before 1950 the American elm was common in this marginal flood plain habitat and in better-drained sites uphill. But then Dutch elm disease fungus found its way into Iowa and brought about the catastrophic demise of one of our truly magnificent trees. The virulent parasite, which killed its victims by causing plugs to form in their water-conducting cells, came to us from Holland. Its most prolific and vigorous carrier, the small European elm bark beetle, also came from Europe.

Like several lowland species, the cottonwood may grow to be enormous. Its impressively tall, straight trunk is frequently branchless, except near the top, and its girth can challenge that of any of the eastern trees. The tall uncluttered trees of the lowland forest, open and airy, often penetrated by shafts of sunlight, led some early writers to call them "cathedral forests." In this inspiring setting, cottonwood and poplar leaves rustling incessantly in the prairie breeze provide an audible dimension to the riparian community and set it apart from the quiet of other woodland communities. The flattened leafstalks of these species produce their peculiar leaf oscillations.

The interior of the cathedral forest is not quite as benign as its name would indicate, however. Knee-high clusters of waxy white berries surrounded by brilliantly beautiful, red, fall foliage identify poison ivy, which must be treated with respect. Further, this highly variable species often takes the form of rugged woody vines, some the size of an arm, that festoon the column-like treetrunks. On the forest floor, the rich carpet of herbaceous plants often contains an abundance of the painful stinging nettle.

Because its trees are scattered and the canopy quite open, it is appropriate to give another kind of Iowa woodland vegetation a name other than "forest." This is the savanna. An open park-like stand of oak trees (most often bur oak or white oak), the savanna characteristically has trees so dispersed that an assemblage of typical prairie species flourishes among them. Something of an ecological mystery, those prairie oaks may have been spared the trauma of prairie fires until they were large enough to tolerate and survive the heat of a burn. Under such circumstances, large, wide-branching, open-grown oaks have co-existed with grassland species for centuries.

Cottonwoods, dressed in autumn colors, stand guard along Iowa's waterways. These are in Marshall County.

195

The peace and beauty of this lowland forest in the early morning sunlight must be experienced to be appreciated.

Carl Kurtz

Forest Structure

A FOREST IS MUCH MORE than the tall trees that dominate it. A number of other plants grow at various predictable positions beneath its canopy. In very complex forests — a tropical rain forest, for example — there are five or six layers of plants, each consisting of many species. In Iowa forests, in addition to the dominants, there are four distinguishable strata: the understory, the shrub layer, the herb layer, and the ground layer. Each forest stratum has slightly different physical conditions to which its species have been able to adapt. Within a stratum, each species has evolved a special set of characteristics that make it better able than any other species to survive and prosper in its own special niche.

The understory of an Iowa forest usually contains some young canopy trees, but many of its characteristic species are different. Probably the most representative and widespread understory tree is ironwood. Also called hop-hornbeam, ironwood is frequently a crooked tree up to eight inches or more in diameter and approximately twenty feet tall. It is especially easy to identify early in the fall, when it bears pendulous dry fruits resembling clusters of hops. On lower slopes, where there is more moisture, the American hornbeam (also called blue beech and, confusingly, ironwood), may be found. Closely related to ironwood, its sinewy trunk is covered with smooth gray bark. Another small tree, sometimes found in the understory, is the alternate-leaved dogwood. Reminiscent of the flowering dogwood of the southeast, it is not nearly as spectacular in flower, but is completely redeemed by its splashy red, autumn foliage.

The shrub stratum of the mature forest is usually not a continuous layer, but consists of clumps of various shrubs scattered more or less at random. Sometimes these shrubs appear to be more prosperous where patches of sunlight have leaked through the tree canopy. In Iowa they may include such common and easily recognized species as the gooseberry, with its prickly stems and edible fruits, and the viburnum with its arrow-straight stems. Also likely to be found are the coralberry, sometimes called buckbrush, its crimson foliage adding to the fall colors near the ground; several species of dogwood with interesting fruit clusters and often, brightly colored stems, and the curious hazelnut, its male flowers in pendulous catkins remaining on the bush through winter.

Pete Krumhardt

Gary Hightshoe

The herb layer is composed of nonwoody species that grow above the ground and beneath the shrubs. Most Iowa forest herbs die back to the ground or below in winter and are renewed in spring either from seeds or from underground parts that tolerate winter subsurface temperatures.

Among various herb forms are the grasses and the grass-like sedges. Sedges, in fact, are often the most abundant species in the herb layer. To distinguish them from the grasses, look closely at the lower stem and the way in which its leaves are attached. The sedges are distinctly triangular in cross-section, while the grasses are round.

In the herb layer, Iowa's incomparable spring wild-flower display occurs, only to give way in a few weeks to the less spectacular summer woodland plants. Here, too, woodland ferns appear, growing best in more moist and protected spots. In this dense and busy forest stratum, you may learn about the medicinal plants, the poison plants, the dye plants, and the edible plants. Alternatively, your curiosity may be piqued by the bees' favorites or by wild herbs and spices, or by plant potions and remedies from folklore. The herb layer can be the most fascinating of the forest layers and is also the most diverse.

Emerging through the herb layer, and making their way into the crowns of the dominant trees, a group of aggressive vines make up a conspicuous part of the forest's structure. Dependent upon the larger plants for support, the vines often spread from tree to tree, in a sense sewing the canopy together. Most common among these curiosities are poison ivy, the Virginia creeper, and the wild grape.

Lowermost of the structured Iowa forest's definable strata is the ground layer. Here fungi break down dead plant and animal tissues and start the return back into the natural nutrient cycle. Here, too, to the mushroom hunter's delight, following spring rains, morels push up among the dead leaves.

Mosses, liverworts, lichens, and other small ground layer plants are often overlooked as we walk through the woods. They do much to stabilize and enrich the forest soil but, because they are relatively inconspicuous, few people are aware of them.

A once proud tree, draped in a green mossy blanket, returns to the earth whence it came.
(Right) Bigtooth aspen leaves and those of quaking aspen, brighten the forest floor in eastern Iowa.

Seasonal Change

WE HAVE BEEN CONSIDERING forests as groups of plants growing in response to local environmental conditions, but the forest changes as seasons change, too. Everyone has seen the forest green up as winter gives way to spring and summer, or its warm fall colors signal the approach of winter. Many more subtle changes also occur, differing for each species.

Trees leaf out in the spring. Timing differs among species, but most come out within a few weeks of each other. Tree flowers, on the other hand, appear on a much more varied schedule. Several oaks flower before their leaves even appear; the flowers are in long pendulous catkins that hang from the branches. Other species flower throughout the spring and early summer, and witch hazel, found in northeastern Iowa, does not flower until late fall.

Shrubs also have seasonal differences. Gooseberry, for instance, flowers in the spring, while coralberry blooms in the summer.

In the herb layer, however, seasonal changes are most dramatic and conspicuous. Early in spring, before the leaves come out on the trees, masses of ephemeral wildflowers bloom. The delicate lavendar of the hepatica contrasts with its tough, leathery, brownish-green leaves that have lasted through winter. Sprays of white or light pink flowers on the Dutchman's breeches dangle like so many upside-down harem pants. Spring beauties appear — their small, whitish, cup-shaped flowers, with light blue streaks, perched on slender stalks, dog-tooth violets — not violets at all, but members of the lily family — produce single, nodding, white, bell-shaped flowers on leafless stalks, and their leaves are mottled spatulas that disappear before summer begins. While the air is still crisp, and traces of snow linger in the shade of moss-covered logs, these and numerous other species of spring wildflowers carpet the sunlit forest floor in an early announcement of life's annual renewal.

The delicate leaves of the honey locust are in strong contrast to its vicious thorns.

Dutchman's breeches decorate Iowa's woodlands in the spring.

(Top) A frosty morning in November gave these fallen oak and elm leaves the delicately beautiful appearance of etchings in the early morning light.

The colorful cap of the fly amanita belies its poisonous nature.

A stately oak dominates this winter forest in Reece's County Park in central Iowa.

Mosses and shield ferns have resisted early November frosts in this yellow birch stand in Hardin County.

Carl Kurtz

Forest Succession

IMAGINE THAT WE CAN compress time so that 50 years becomes one day. We will look at three parcels of land: one an abandoned pasture; another a stand of honey locusts, elms, ashes, junipers, and big-tooth aspens; and the third a stand of white oak and shagbark hickory, with ironwood in the understory. What will we see tomorrow?

Changes on the abandoned pasture are dramatic. No longer open, it has become a forest. We find some fairly large trees, a rather dense shrub layer, and some typical forest herbs. Most of the trees are honey locusts, elms, ashes, junipers, and big-tooth aspens — all very much like what we saw yesterday (50 years ago) on the second site. Noting that some of the trees and shrubs — such as honey locust, hawthorne, and gooseberry — are spiny and knowing that the area used to be a pasture, we infer that the two facts are related: grazing tends to favor spiny species. If we are right, we can also deduce that the second site we observed yesterday probably had been a pasture 50 years earlier.

What has happened to the second site we observed yesterday? It still looks like a forest, but substantial changes have taken place. We see fewer elms, ashes, and locusts. Some hickories and oaks have grown up. The shrub layer appears less dense, and the herb layer seems better developed.

Yesterday's third site appears to have undergone little change. It is still a forest; the tree species are the same, but the trees are larger. Only when we look carefully do we note some subtle increase in the abundance of oak and hickory. We see, also, that some of yesterday's dominant trees no longer are there, and others of the same species have grown in new places. We see some very old trees, partly dead, and some young trees that have not yet reached the canopy. The ground underfoot is soft and spongy with a thick layer of leaf litter. There have been changes, not in the kinds of plants, but in the degree to which they have come into balance with each other and the environment.

Our imaginary compression of 50 years into one day illustrates the process of ecological succession. The rate of change is greatest early in the process; it slows down as the forest approaches its more stable, climax condition. Also, earlier pioneer species are relatively short-lived; many of these have light, easily dispersed seeds, well-suited for colonizing young, disturbed habitats. The trees of the mature forest are longer-lived, and many have heavier, less readily dispersed seeds, which can provide the extra energy for seedlings to get started beneath an already established forest canopy.

The idea of the process of ecological succession assumes one important thing: that no disturbance occurs to start the process over — or to set it back to an earlier stage. The examples in our compression of time actually covered only a portion of the usual time it takes for succession to occur. In many forests, succession proceeds over several hundred years and, within that time, it is highly probable that some disturbance will disrupt the otherwise orderly process. Fire, wind, and the ravages of disease or insect invasion are examples of events which can affect succession. Although destructive in themselves, such events are, in a sense, regenerative. They renew natural processes, and they contribute to the dynamics of forest succession.

Tom C. Cooper

Trees of Special Interest

GROWING IN OUR STATE are a number of isolated small stands of trees of unusual interest. For instance, the white pines are holdovers from a time when our climate was much cooler. Such magnificent pines grace the hilltops and precipitous slopes at White Pine Hollow State Forest Preserve two miles northwest of Luxemburg in the northwest corner of Dubuque County. Some obscure circumstance of soil or local climate has enabled not only the pines, but also numerous other species, representative more of the northwoods than of prairie country or deciduous forest, to survive and prosper here. For example, stands of Canadian yew thrive on some of the north-facing slopes; both white and yellow birch, and the green and white leaf-whorls of rattlesnake plantain can be seen. Also present are trillium and yellow lady's slipper, as well as innumerable mosses and ferns, kept cool the year around by air from the deep limestone caves and ravines characteristic of the area.

Pines and white birches also have persisted just northeast of Eldora in Hardin County. Here, in and near Pine Lake State Park, their graceful green boughs reaching out from straight black trunks provide colorful relief from the black-and-gray background of the winter deciduous forest. In October, much enhanced by the reflective beauty of two man-made lakes, the fleeting autumn colors are accentuated by the scattered verdant pines and the stark white trunks of clustered, curving birches.

In a 1903 report on Iowa forests, L. H. Pammel described as the most southerly distribution of pine a stand in Wildcat Den State Park in Muscatine County. There, in Montpelier Township, the pines remain, doing best on a steep bluff, and satisfying the ultimate test for biological success — natural reproduction. Pine reproduction has been most successful on very steep slopes where the tree's critical need for bright sunshine can be satisfied.

Balsam fir, an important component of the northern spruce/fir forest (perhaps the most sought-after Christmas tree before the advent of the tree-farm) still lives in a few hospitable habitats in northeast Iowa. As rare as it is in Iowa, balsam fir may not survive the encroachment of axe and saw. In 1938, Henry Conard described six areas of fir in Winneshiek and Allamakee counties. At some of these sites, the beautiful, fragrant evergreen persists, primarily on the cool, moist, north-facing bluffs along the Upper Iowa River northwest of Decorah.

Since the tree species that push out across the prairie along Iowa's rivers represent the more aggressive and hardy of the southeastern broad-leaved forest, it is not surprising to find a few that have already reached their northern limits in some southern counties. Although they are but a small part of our natural heritage, they are among the most interesting of our trees. For instance, a few miles west of Muscatine a natural grove of pecan trees now grows, protected as the Pecan Grove State Preserve. Said to be the largest of the hickories, the pecan makes its way into southeastern Iowa only in this area along the Mississippi.

A dozen or so American chestnut trees demonstrate the tenacity of nature and the importance of chance. Although they were undoubtedly planted in central Jasper County, where they stand, they are of great interest because they may be the largest such stand to have survived the devastating chestnut blight which came to this country from Asia in 1906. While scattered individual trees can be found from Iowa to the east coast, many are merely persistent stump sprouts which grow for a decade or so and then die. The survival of these Jasper County trees might be a result of some miracle of genetic immunity but, realistically, it seems more likely that they escaped the blight because of their isolation. Once an important component of the eastern deciduous forest, the American chestnut ranged from the east coast westward to the Ohio River. Today the Jasper County trees prosper and bear fruit prolifically.

Carl Kurtz

Old native white pines, rare in Iowa, stand proud and tall in White Pine Hollow State Forest Preserve in Dubuque County.

The Oldest and the Biggest

A certain mystique exists about superlatives in any area of interest. What's the oldest tree? What's the biggest? These are questions that some Iowans' have pursued recently. Professor Roger Landers, a former member of the Iowa State University faculty, has counted the growth-rings from many trees across our state. Among the oldest trees are a white oak in Pammel State Park and a bur oak in O'Brien County, both of which were living well back into the 17th century. A white pine tree at Backbone State Park is 208 years old, and a white oak at Ledges State Park has now been growing for 294 years. But the current state champion, an eastern red cedar in Palisades Kepler State Park, is 455 years old and, we hope, still growing as it clings to a steep limestone bluff above the Cedar River near the Mount Vernon area.

To find Iowa's largest trees, the *Des Moines Register*, the State Forester, and Iowa State University foresters undertook a survey in 1978. Nominations and measurements for each species were invited from citizens across the state. A point system used by the American Forestry Association to score the nation's champion trees was adopted. The point score for a given tree is the sum of three numbers: (1) the circumference, in inches of the tree trunk four and one-half feet above the ground, plus (2) the height of the tree in feet, plus (3) one fourth of the crown spread in feet.

The survey succeeded not only in establishing 45 state champions, but also in regaining a place for Iowa on the American Forestry Association's National Register of Big Trees. An eastern cottonwood in Tama County reported by Mrs. Frank Behounek was declared the national champion. Its impressive dimensions are: circumference, 34 feet 1 inch; height, 78 feet, and crown spread 126 feet. Total points, 518.5.

The initial state winners established by the survey, with their circumference measurements, include:

white oak – 17 feet 1 inch
elm – 19 feet 6 inches
weeping willow –
    15 feet 6 inches
ginkgo – 11 feet 7 inches
sycamore – 18 feet
tulip-tree – 14 feet 6 inches
hackberry – 18 feet 4 inches
pecan – 9 feet 4 inches

There are, of course, many others, and the challenge to identify new champions continues. If you would like to take up the challenge, examine the complete list on page 3C of the *Des Moines Register* for August 13, 1978. If you make an exciting find, you may wish to report it to the office of the State Forester in Des Moines.

Carl Kurtz

Deeply furrowed bark of eastern cottonwood plays host to numerous species of tenacious lichens.

This majestic gnarled bur oak, patriarch of the loess bluffs of western Iowa, could tell us of the Indians who held council there.

Carl Kurtz

Conservation and Forestry

From 1850, when nearly 18.5 percent of Iowa was forested, to the present, with only about 4.3 percent still wooded, the trend has been toward clearing and reduction of woodlands. In this period, however, far-sighted citizens have addressed the need to protect Iowa's forest heritage.

The Iowa State Agricultural Society was among the early organizations to recognize the progressive deterioration of the forests which was accelerated by the selective harvest of only the best trees for lumber, ties, posts, and poles. For two decades in the mid-19th century, the society actively promoted forestry and encouraged tree-planting in the state.

Beginning in 1866, the Iowa Horticultural Society assumed the important role of educator and advocate for protection and propagation of our forests. In 1873, the society declared: ". . . the 20th day of April 1874, and the same day of each succeeding year, to be Arbor Day for the State . . ."

Also in 1873, the horticulturists recommended establishment of a Board of Forestry Commissioners and the appointment of a State Forester.

Still active, The Iowa Horticultural Society recently opened its 340-acre Iowa Arboretum southeast of Boone. Here, nature trails for visitors have trees and shrubs clearly marked, and woody plants potentially useful for landscaping in Iowa are on exhibit.

Open every day of the week, The Iowa Arboretum serves students at all levels and provides a versatile facility for the preservation of wildlife and endangered plant species.

The Iowa Academy of Science, organized in 1875, has been consistently supportive of all areas of conservation and preservation of Iowa's forest heritage. The Academy's committee on conservation and preserves is charged, among other things, with the responsibility to "support and encourage the identification, assessment and protection of natural resource areas . . ."

The State Forest Nursery at Ames, an important service of the Iowa Conservation Commission, has done much to slow the rate of decline in our forested lands. A modern facility covering some 98 acres, the nursery provides seedling material not only for forestation, but also for erosion control, Christmas-tree plantations, and wildlife habitat improvement. Nurturing as many as eight million seedlings at any one time, the nursery distributes, at minimal cost, approximately three million seedlings each spring. In one recent year, for example, the distribution included more than 1.5 million evergreens, approximately 606,000 broadleaved trees, and more than 730,000 shrubs for wildlife cover. Visitors are welcomed at the nursery.

The golden maples in Allamakee County add to the spectacular autumn display which draws thousands of admirers to northeast Iowa each year.

Tom C. Cooper

Iowa's autumn forests hold out an invitation to come, enjoy, cherish and protect.
This mischief-maker of the forest, the raccoon, moves about mostly at night and feeds on a varied diet of plants and animals.
The spectacular pileated woodpecker, sometimes nearly a foot and a half long, resides in dense woods along our major rivers.

Diminishing Forest Cover

A comparison of Iowa's presettlement forests with those of today brings to light some encouraging as well as some disturbing changes. Evidence is good, for example, that total woodland area has declined from nearly 7 million acres in presettlement days to approximately 1.5 million acres today. Most of the decline is due to land-clearing for agriculture. Ironically, some settlers who were accustomed to clearing trees and pulling stumps to make room for their crops in the eastern forests proceeded to do the same thing in Iowa and almost ignored the unfamiliar treeless grasslands which were to become the world's most productive cornbelt. But, even when farmers began to move out onto the prairie and sod-busting steel plows began to change the face of the land, ready access to woodlands remained critical for fuelwood, lumber, fencing, and shelter from incessant prairie winds. By the late 19th century, as the railroads pushed across the Mississippi and onto the prairie, for each mile of new track four to six acres of woodland were being stripped of their mature oaks to provide ties. Additional trees were cut for trestle timbers and telegraph poles.

Even as many settlers attacked the forests as an inexhaustible source of timber and a troublesome if not hostile environmental obstacle, some newcomers arrived in Iowa with a sense of conservation acquired in western Europe.

In 1849, writing to friends and family in Holland, for example, an early settler in the Pella area commented:

"In this state there is much more prairie than wooded areas. There are not as many trees as one could wish for. In the first place, because a great deal of lumber is needed for building; then there is so much needed to fence the land, and finally because there is always a great need for fuel. However, if a person uses common sense there is always plenty. After all, one need not go about it as carelessly as the Americans." (Robert D. Swierenga, Annals of Iowa, Vol. 38, fall, 1965).

Recent figures indicate that (1) Iowa is losing more than 40,000 acres of commercial forest annually, (2) three-fourths of our commercial forest is inadequately stocked with trees, and (3) only approximately one-fourth of Iowa's timber removals go to useful products — the rest is left in the woods as logging residue, cut or killed but not used, or left on land withdrawn from commercial forest use. Now, the woodstove fad in our state has pushed the price of firewood so high that immature trees are being harvested to satisfy the demand.

As petroleum derived products become scarcer and their costs become more prohibitive, almost certainly our need for wood cellulose and its derivatives will increase dramatically. We should plant now, so that the trees will be there when we need them. Patience and trees go together.

What greater gift can nature provide than a renewable resource which provides such value at maturity, with such priceless serenity and sustenance for the soul in the interim?

CHAPTER NINE
WETLANDS
BY RICHARD A. BISHOP AND ARNOLD VAN DER VALK

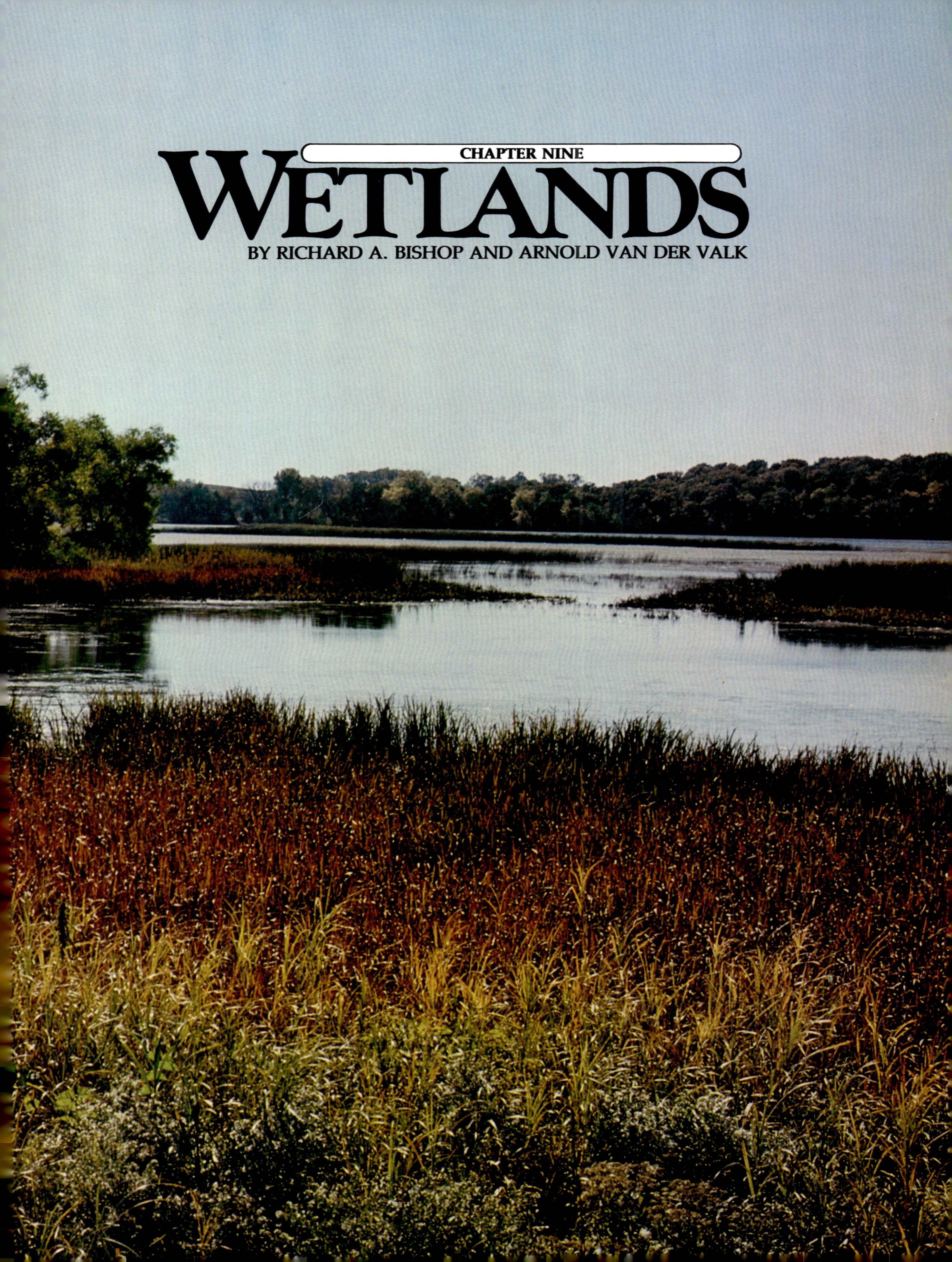

Tom C. Cooper

SETTLERS WHO CROSSED the Mississippi River into what is now northern Iowa were confronted by an almost endless sea of prairie intermixed with myriad lakes and marshes. This great expanse of wetlands must have been an awesome sight to our pioneers. Along with this seemingly endless sea of marshes waves of ducks, geese, and shore birds, and prairie chickens, buffalo, and other wildlife greeted the newcomers. Cries of flushed wildfowl, surprised on a prairie marsh, would nearly deafen an intruder.

This was our heritage — a vastness of wetlands with a bounty of wildfowl that man apparently could never exhaust.

This wonderland of water, heavily laden with nature's riches, was the footprint of the Wisconsin Glacier. This glacier left behind 7.6 million acres of mixed prairie and marshland, extending from what are now Polk and Dallas counties northward to the Iowa-Minnesota border, eastward to Worth, Cerro Gordo and Franklin counties, and westward to Osceola, O'Brien, and Cherokee counties. It leveled the land and gouged out holes and basins that were filled with water when this great ice mass retreated. Some basins were large and fairly shallow, such as Spirit Lake and Clear Lake, while West Okoboji was deep. Many more wetlands ranged in size and depth from shallow lakes down to small, seasonally flooded potholes of an acre or less. In parts of northwest Iowa, our ancestors would count up to 200 of these potholes in a square mile.

Early settlers were awed by the vast acreages of marshland found along the Mississippi River.

(Previous Spread) A typical early autumn view of an Iowa prairie glacial marsh. Several common wetlands communities can be seen: In the foreground a band of primarily grassland herbs that form a transition zone from uplands to wetlands vegetation; a brownish zone of senescent great river bulrush; a green zone adjacent to the water's edge composed of cattails and some bulrushes, and submerged plants in the open water area.

211

A small river with its associated gallery and flood plain forest winds its way across the central Iowa countryside.

THIS MOSAIC of prairie and wetlands acted as a huge sponge, soaking up runoff from winter snows or heavy rains. In turn, these drained into a series of creeks and rivers that carried the excess water eastward to the Mississippi River, but allowed some to escape westward to the Missouri River.

Major rivers flowing eastward now bear the names Des Moines, Raccoon, Skunk, English, Iowa, Cedar, Wapsipinicon, Maquoketa, Volga, Turkey, Yellow, and Upper Iowa. Looking west, we find the Nodaway, Nishnabotna, Boyer, Soldier, Maple, Little Sioux, Big Sioux, Floyd, Ocheyedan, and Rock. Much of our history is captured in these names that may always be there to remind us of our past.

Nature's forces — often quite violent — left their signatures for us to ponder. Heavy spring rains resulted in floodwaters with tremendous power that altered river courses, leaving old riverbeds or scoured-out wet areas along the river channels. Extensive wetlands were created along the Mississippi and Missouri as well as other inland rivers.

Marshes, lakes, and rivers, Iowa's common wetland types, have influenced the state's development and even our present-day lives. Though most travel by early settlers was by wagon and horseback, river courses were important for transportation of goods and supplies as settlements developed. Some of the oldest towns in Iowa — Dubuque, for example — were established along the Mississippi River. Other towns and cities that grew up along major inland rivers were Fort Dodge, Ottumwa, Iowa City, Cedar Rapids, Waterloo, Iowa Falls, Mason City, and our capital city on the banks of the Des Moines and Raccoon rivers.

Rivers served not only as a source of transportation, but also provided the essentials for man's existence. Water to drink was one of the main requirements. Wood for fuel and lumber for housing came from wooded lands along rivers, where low, wet areas protected trees from raging prairie fires that continually nipped the expansion of young timber seedlings. Plentiful wildlife such as turkey, deer, squirrels, ducks, geese, and fish served as food. Beavers, muskrats, and mink provided valuable fur that could be traded to European markets. All of these essentials to life were offered along the water courses and associated wetlands.

Not unlike the rivers, our large natural lakes provided the same provisions for survival. Water, abundant wildlife and fish, and sheer beauty attracted settlements like Clear Lake, Spirit Lake, and Storm Lake. These cities are very proud and protective of the waters at their back doors, and numbers of summer visitors verify the lure of these lakes.

Basins of former prairie marshes drained for agriculture frequently still hold water after spring rains.

213

Pioneers gradually settled the vast prairie-pothole region of north-central and northwest Iowa, where they plowed the prairie to raise food crops and exploited the almost endless wildfowl populations. However, they left virtually undisturbed the extensive wetlands. At that time, wetlands were not viewed as valuable potential agricultural lands, but more as a hindrance to farming and travel and as spawning grounds for the hated mosquito. It wasn't until after the Federal Swampland Acts of 1850 and 1860 that extensive areas were drained.

A series of events that occurred before the turn of the century has had an effect on the wildlife we may see on our wetlands today. Giant Canada geese once nested in the marshlands throughout northern Iowa, but settlers robbed their nests for eggs, captured the young, and shot the adults. Such exploitation, along with drainage of their nesting areas, caused the giant Canada goose to become extinct in the wild in the early 1900s. In the early 1960s biologist Harold Hanson of the Illinois Natural History Survey documented the existence of these large Canada geese. Additional research showed that a few farmers had private goose flocks that matched the descriptions of the giant goose. Tracing the lineage of these birds revealed their ancestry. They were descendants of wild birds that once nested in Iowa. Young geese captured in the wild were penned and domesticated for egg and meat production. Offspring of these geese were kept to replenish flocks, and some flocks were kept by the same families for more than 60 years. The Iowa Conservation Commission bought some of these genetically pure birds and returned them to the wild. Today, more than 3,000 giant honkers return to our marshlands each spring to mate and rear their young. Their story reminds us of man's influence on his environment and the bounty offered by our wetlands.

Larry Stone

(Above) **Giant Canada geese return each spring to their ancestral homeland to nest.**

(Right) **Snow geese stop and rest on Iowa marshes during their spring and fall migration to and from their Arctic nesting grounds.**

(Far Right) **Over 450 species of native plants are found in Iowa wetlands.**

Iowa Conservation Commission, Ken Formanek

Description of Iowa Wetland Types

Carl Kurtz

WETLANDS are low areas where water stands or flows continuously or periodically. They are often referred to as swamps, sloughs, marshes, potholes, lakes, bogs, wet meadows, and seeps. Usually wetlands contain plant-life characteristic of such areas. While most definitions of wetlands refer only to the shallow water areas with vegetation, we have broadened ours to include natural lakes, rivers, river oxbows, overflow areas, and manmade areas such as reservoirs, lakes, and farm ponds.

Water-saturated soils in these low areas are normally without oxygen and are described as anaerobic. Because plant roots require oxygen for respiration and this oxygen is normally obtained from air spaces in the soil, most plants can live in water-saturated soils only for very brief periods. Anaerobic soils and the presence of one or more members of a small group of plants able to tolerate and grow in such soils are universal features of all wetlands. Wetland plants have various anatomical, morphological, and physiological adaptions that enable them to live either partly or completely submerged. The most important and widespread of these adaptions is a system of interconnected air spaces in the leaves, stems, and roots that allows oxygen to diffuse to the roots from the leaves, thus making it possible for the roots to live in anaerobic soils.

Wetlands also are home to many different groups of animals that are able to find food and shelter in them. These animals also show a variety of adaptions for life in the wetland environment. Animals found in Iowa wetlands include muskrats, mink, ducks, geese, shore birds, songbirds, turtles, fish, salamanders, and many different invertebrate groups.

The key feature used to classify all wetlands is their water regime or hydrology. (Where does their water come from? Where does it go? How constant is the water level?) Four basic types of wetlands are found in Iowa: palustrine, lacustrine, riverine, and seepage. The only type of wetland not found in Iowa is a tidal wetland.

Arrowhead or duck potatoe is a common emergent in many types of Iowa wetlands.

Arnold van der Valk

Palustrine wetlands occupy shallow basins with small watersheds. They have marked fluctuations in water level: seasonal fluctuations, reflecting rainfall patterns and annual fluctuations, reflecting long-term drought cycles. In periods of drought, annual fluctuations can be so extreme that the wetlands may be free of standing water for one or more years. Most palustrine wetlands, once common in the northern half of Iowa on the recently glaciated areas, have now been drained, but some can still be found in northwest Iowa. Palustrine wetlands are often called prairie potholes or prairie glacial marshes.

Lacustrine wetlands are found in shallow, protected areas of lakes. They are generally less subject to water-level fluctuations than palustrine or riverine wetlands. Although Iowa has few large lakes, good examples of this wetland type may be found along the shores of Spirit Lake, Clear Lake, and many smaller Iowa lakes. Wave action that can uproot plants restricts lacustrine wetlands to sheltered areas of large lakes.

Riverine wetlands, which are associated with rivers, are not common in Iowa, except for those found in the backwaters of the Mississippi and in clear-water trout streams of northeastern Iowa. Most Iowa rivers today are too turbid to support the growth of aquatic plants, and they are either shaded out or buried under the settling load of suspended material. Plants that occasionally do become established are often scoured out by floods. In the few rivers where plants can take hold, their growth is often luxurious. The flowing water constantly supplies them with new sources of nutrients.

Seepage wetlands form in areas where groundwater surfaces, but where water volume is too small to create a stream or creek. These wetlands have a perpetually saturated soil, but may have little or no standing water. Since their water source is an aquifer, it often has a very different chemical composition from that of water in neighboring wetlands which have a surface-water source. Iowa's best-known seepage wetlands are the fens of northwest Iowa, *e.g.*, Silver Lake Fen. These fens are found in small areas where the ground is saturated by alkaline water discharging from an aquifer that flows through calcareous limestone and dolomite deposits. The soil in these fens is a mixture of precipitated carbonates and organic matter, and it supports the growth of many wetland species including a number restricted to this wetland type in the state: arrow grass, beaked sedge, and grass of parnassus. Another type of seepage found in eastern Iowa is the hanging bog, about which very little is known.

Wetland Communities

Arnold van der Valk

WETLANDS are usually composed of one or more plant communities, which are characterized by the growth form of their dominant species. In Iowa, five communities commonly are found: wet meadow, emergent, floating-leaved, free-floating, and submersed. These communities commonly overlap and may also interlock. The distribution of these communities in most wetlands is largely controlled by water depth, with the exception of the free-floating community. The normal pattern in lacustrine and palustrine wetlands, moving from shore to deeper water, is wet meadow, emergent, floating-leaved, and submersed. Free-floating plants may be found anywhere, but most typically they are found as an understory in the emergent community.

Wet meadow communities are found where the soil is normally saturated and is covered with standing water only in spring. Sedges or grasses like blue joint or manna grass are the dominant species. Usually a sprinkling of mints, polygonums, and other annuals are also found.

In emergent communities cattails, bulrushes, burreeds, arrowheads, and common reed are the dominant species of plants. These tall, upright plants, which can reach a height of several feet, normally grow in standing water less than three feet deep, but they can tolerate one or more years without standing water, although their growth is much reduced in such dry periods.

In most Iowa floating-leaved communities pondweeds dominate, but in others scattered across the state, waterlilies are the dominant species. Only three species of water lily are found in Iowa: the white, the yellow, and the American lotus, which exists primarily in the Mississippi River Valley, although it has been transplanted elsewhere, *e.g.*, Lilly Lake in the Amana Colonies.

Only a few, small — usually less than a half inch — free-floating plants are found in Iowa, and they belong to the group of aquatic plants called duckweeds. Among these free-floating plants in Iowa is a species of *Wollfia*, the smallest flowering plant in the world. Although most free-floating plants float on the surface of the water, a few actually float below the surface. Free-floating plants may grow luxuriantly in many Iowa farm ponds, and often their growth shades out other submersed plants there.

In Iowa's submersed communities, pondweeds, bushy pondweeds, coontails, water milfoils, and bladderworts are common. These plants can grow in water only a few inches deep to water several feet deep, and they are often found growing as an understory in emergent and floating-leaved communities. Members of this community are important as food for certain waterfowl.

Most Iowa wetlands are mosaics of the five communities, and the same species often, though not always, may be found in lacustrine, palustrine, or riverine wetlands. Seepage wetlands, on the other hand, are usually a mixture of wet meadow and emergent communities with a rudimentary submersed community present occasionally.

One minor wetland-community type has not been mentioned — peat land. Peat lands have organic soil composed of decomposing plant parts. Although they are quite common farther north in Minnesota and Wisconsin, only a few exist in Iowa; Deadman's Lake Bog in Pilot Knob State Park is the best example. On this floating mat of decaying vegetation is found a host of plants characteristic of peat lands across North America, including pitcher plants, sundews, sphagnum moss, and several heaths.

Sago pondweed and other submersed plants are a major source of food for waterfowl in all types of wetlands. Sago pondweed is one of the most common submersed plants in North America.

Wetland communities —
characteristic vegetation
- **Wet meadow** — *sedges and grasses*
- **Emergent** — *cattails, bulrushes, common reeds*
- **Floating-leaved** — *water lilies*
- **Free-floating** — *duckweeds, Wollfia*
- **Submersed** — *pondweeds, coontails, bladderworts*

Wetland Types
- **Palustrine** — *shallow basins*
  Seasonally flooded basin — Type I
  Fresh meadows — Type II, waterlogged soil
  Shallow fresh meadows — Type III, 6 inches deep in water
  Deep fresh marshes — Type IV, 6 inches to 3 feet deep
  Open fresh water — Type V, usually under 10 feet deep
  Shrub swamps — river flood plains
- **Lacustrine** — *shallow, protected lake areas*
- **Riverine** — *associated with rivers*
- **Seepage** — *groundwater surfaces*

Six Classifications of Palustrine Wetlands

PALUSTRINE WETLANDS may be the ones most commonly envisioned in people's minds when they hear the word wetland. They are the beautiful prairie marshes, potholes, and shallow lakes. Past work has dealt mostly with their benefits to wildlife and, consequently, they have been classified according to these benefits along with the associated vegetation.

In 1956, Samuel P. Shaw and C. Gordon Fredine authored *Wetlands of the United States, Their Extent and Their Value to Waterfowl and Other Wildlife*, published by the U. S. Fish and Wildlife Service, Department of the Interior as Circular 39. Shaw and Fredine's classifications placed Iowa's palustrine wetlands into six types.

Type 1 includes seasonally-flooded basins. The land is periodically flooded in periods of heavy rain or runoff from snows. In these periods the soil is waterlogged, but usually is well enough drained so it can be farmed most years. These areas can be found in upland depressions or in overflow bottomlands. Vegetation varies due to the length of time it is inundated, and typical plants are smartweed, wild millet, fall panicum, sedges, beggars tick, ragweed, and barnyard grass. Type 1 areas are quite valuable to breeding water-fowl because they offer abundant food and provide numerous areas for breeding pairs to seclude themselves during the early nesting period. These wetlands are also used extensively by migrating waterfowl in both spring and fall.

Fresh meadows make up the Type 2 classification. The soil usually is without standing water in most of the growing season, but is waterlogged within a few inches of the surface. In spring and after heavy rains, Type 2 areas hold water and provide breeding space for waterfowl. In some years, nesting waterfowl use them.

Vegetation is characterized by prairie cordgrass, reed canary grass, reedgrass, manna grass, sedges, rushes, and mints. Sometimes Type 2 areas are cut for hay in mid-to-late summer when surface water is gone.

Soil in shallow fresh marshes, Type 3 wetlands, usually is waterlogged in the growing season, and often is covered by six inches or more of water. These wetlands usually hold water in the early spring nesting and brooding-rearing periods for waterfowl and often dry out in late summer. Vegetation includes grasses, bulrushes, spikerushes, cattails, arrowhead, giant burreed, smartweed, and sedges.

Type 4 is composed of deep fresh marshes. Basins are covered with from six inches to three feet or more of water in the growing season. Common vegetation includes cattails, bulrushes, reeds, spikerushes, and burreed. In more open areas with deeper water are pondweeds, watermilfoil, coontails, waterlilies, and duckweeds. Type 4 areas provide nesting waterfowl with a dependable water supply and in most years, guarantee ducks a safe place to rear their young. The emergent vegetation provides waterfowl with cover from predators.

Open fresh water, Type 5, includes shallow ponds and lakes. Water — usually less than 10 feet deep — is fringed by emergent vegetation. Generally, these wetlands are deeper and have more open water than Type 4 marshes. Vegetation includes bulrushes, cattails, and reeds around the shoreline, plus pondweeds, naiads, coontail, watermilfoil, and waterlilies.

Waterfowl use these areas for brood-rearing, especially in late summer, when shallow, less permanent wetlands dry up. Ducks, geese, and other migrating birds use Type 5 wetlands as rest areas during migration.

Type 6, shrub swamps, most commonly occur in river flood plains, where floods have scoured out low areas. Overflow areas in the growing season are covered with six inches or more of water. Vegetation includes willows, buttonbush, and maples. Many acres of overflow and shrub swamps exist along interior Iowa rivers. They are important for nesting wood ducks and, to a lesser extent, mallards and blue-winged teal.

Larry Stone

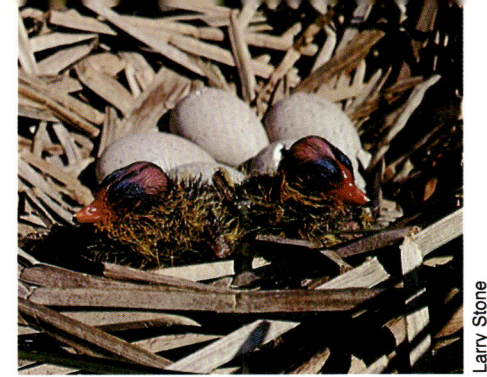

Young coots make their world debut.

Bob Coyle

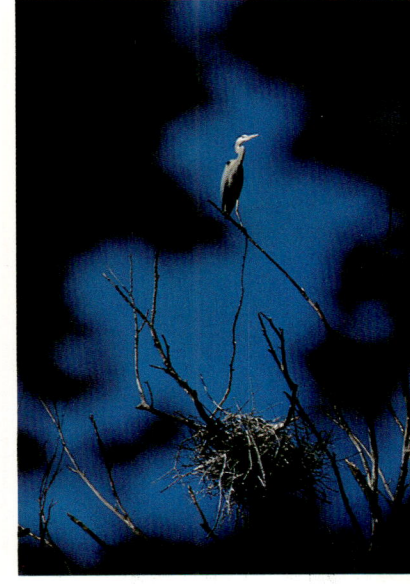

(Above) ***A stately blue heron surveys his watery domain.***

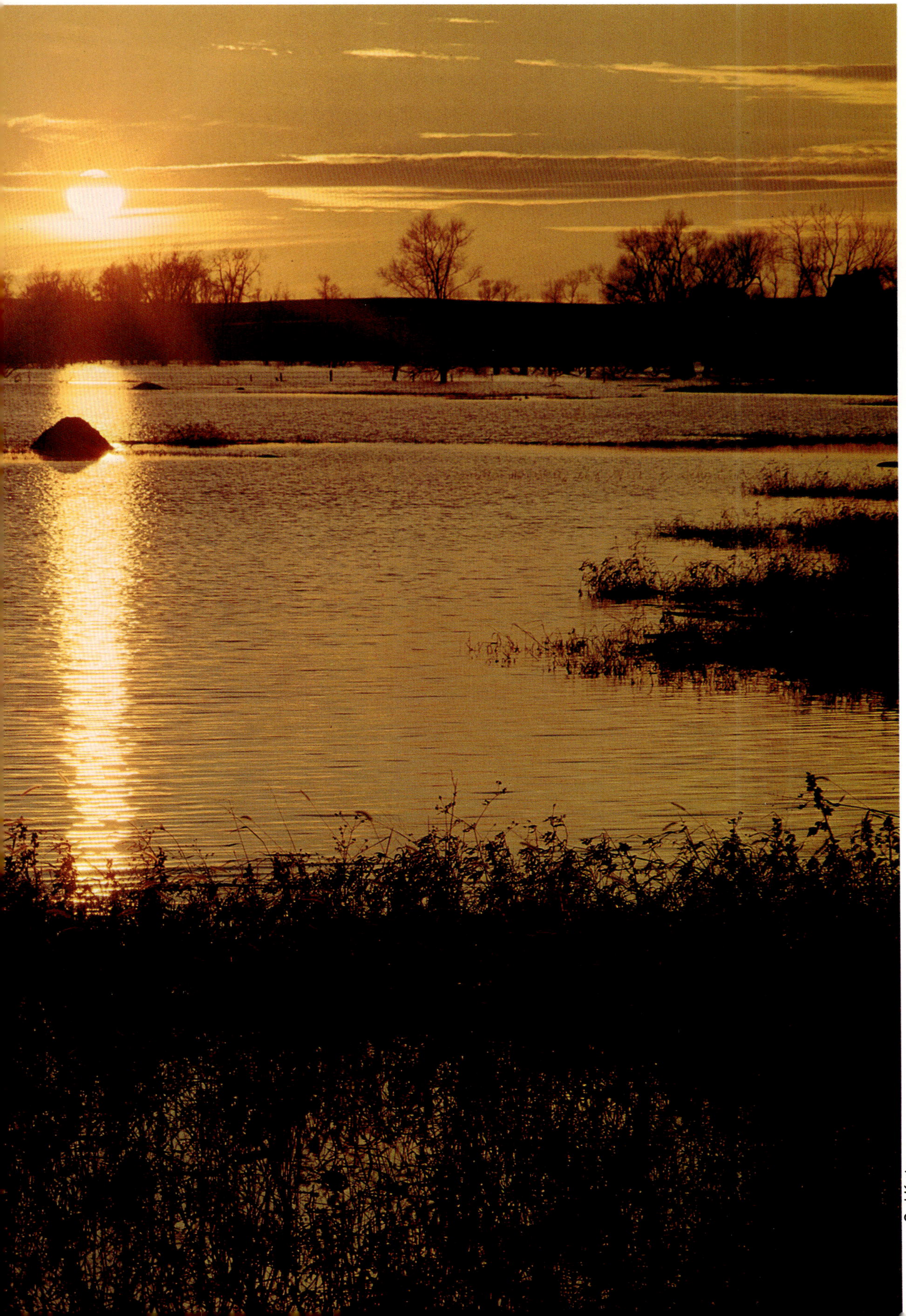

Carl Kurtz

(Left) ***A muskrat lodge on Hendrickson Marsh (Type 3 marsh) in central Iowa is a certain indicator of the presence of the most important mammal found in our state's marshes.***

Big Wall Lake in the semi-marsh stage showing about 50 percent water and 50 percent emergent plants. This is the ideal stage of the marsh cycle for wildlife.

Carl Kurtz

(Below) Muskrats are beginning to open up a dense marsh by their feeding and lodge-building activities. Note the open water areas around each lodge.
(Right) Yellow-headed blackbirds nest in cattails or bulrushes when plants are in standing water.

Iowa Conservation Commission, James S. Hansen

Carl Kurtz

Life of a Wetland

IOWA WETLANDS, as mentioned, are subject to annual fluctuations in water depth caused by cyclical changes in annual rainfall. Palustrine wetlands undergo cyclical changes in the dominant plant communities in response to these water level fluctuations and associated changes in muskrat populations.

The cycle begins in the lake or open-water stage. Water levels are high at this stage, and the wetland is dominated by submersed plants. A narrow fringe of emergents may also ring the shore. This open-water condition remains fairly stable until a drought period begins. In Iowa, serious droughts occur in 20-year cycles. The last was in 1977 and 1978, and the one before that occurred in 1957 and 1958.

When a wetland goes dry, seeds of many emergents and of a host of annuals germinate. The seeds of the emergent plants, which lay dormant in the marsh soil while standing water was present, now germinate and new seedlings grow rapidly among the dense cover of annuals that usually dominate dry marsh. When the drought is broken and rains come, the basin refloods, and the annuals — unable to tolerate flooding — die out. Emergents remain as the dominant plants.

The once open lake-like marsh now has turned into a sea of green plants. Dense stands of cattails, bulrushes, and other emergents hide the water. Little wildlife is present at this stage.

Muskrats move into the dense marsh, which provides plentiful food and house-building material. As muskrat populations increase, marshes open up, providing a mixture of open water and vegetation. A 50-50 open-water-to-vegetation ratio is the most desired marsh stage for the widest variety of wildlife. Dramatic shifts in plant communities are accompanied by similar shifts in animal populations. The more diverse the plant communities, the more attractive the area is to wildlife. A densely-vegetated marsh has the fewest species. Many species of birds — including red-winged blackbirds, bobolinks, meadowlarks, and other more upland-dwelling birds — are present in the upland grasses and along the edge of the marsh, regardless of vegetation density. Marsh wrens, bitterns, and rails tolerate more dense marsh vegetation.

As muskrats and high water open up the marsh, the variety of wildlife grows. The long-billed marsh wren, yellow-headed blackbird, Virginia rails and sora increase, and new faces appear on the scene — black terns, American coots, pied-billed grebe, mallards, blue-winged teal, redheads, ruddy ducks, wood ducks, least bitterns, mink, and raccoon. Muskrats multiply rapidly under optimum conditions; within two to five years, a muskrat population explosion occurs. In late summer and early fall, house-buildng can deplete most of the emergent vegetation. When open water exceeds 70 percent of the wetland, the number of species decreases and a drastic reduction occurs in the number of animals of a particular species, too.

It is the diversity of plant communities and structure that provide the variety of homesites for most birds — tall plants like phragmites or cattails, shorter bulrushes and burreed, down in height to arrowhead. Along with muskrats, high water and wind action will uproot mats of cattail and bulrush and wash them to the shoreline where they either die or reroot. The cycle continues until the marsh returns to the open-water stage, where it will remain until nature starts the process all over.

The time span for a cycle depends upon the type of marsh bottom, the water depth, and control of muskrat populations.

(Right and Below) ***The draining of Iowa's wetlands has destroyed more than 95% of our state's wetland acreage.***

Courtesy Delta Waterfowl Research Station

Man on the Scene

AFTER GLACIAL ACTION created our wetlands, a gradual change began. Shallow lakes became shallower still with the deposition of plant material and siltation from runoff. Shallow lakes changed to deep-water marshes, then to shallow-water marshes, then to wet meadows, and eventually to uplands. Over several thousand years this slow process gradually changed marshes to prairie. Nature's slow manner of change is seldom detected in a man's lifetime; however, man's changes have accelerated erosion and hastened the conversion of marshes to wet meadows.

Although the first human inhabitants of Iowa did little to alter its features, European immigrants pushed the frontier westward, determined to tame the wilderness. They built towns, plowed the prairie, drained lakes and marshes, and straightened rivers. Man's actions have overshadowed the geological changes that created and altered our wetlands over the past 10,000 years.

Tom C. Cooper

Plight of the Prairie Wetlands

AN ESTIMATED six million acres of prairie and wetland existed in the early 1800s. It is difficult to determine the exact acreage of wetlands, but we believe that at least a third of the area would be classified as wetland. Writings indicate that in those days wetlands were held in low esteem and considered a menace to land development. In 1850 and 1860, Congress passed the Swampland Acts, which granted 1,196,392 acres of public-domain wetland to Iowa for swamp reclamation. According to the accounts published in the U. S. Fish and Wildlife Service's publication *Wetlands of the United States*, land was turned over to the counties, where it was bartered for things such as public buildings and bridges. Some counties even bargained with immigration companies, selling the land for 25 to 75 cents an acre, providing the company put settlers on it. In some cases, land was sold by county commissioners to themselves for nominal amounts; other counties gave wetlands to railroad companies.

The event which drastically changed our wetlands was the establishment of drainage districts by the Iowa Legislature which gave the county boards of supervisors jurisdiction and authority to establish drainage districts and levees to drain, straighten, widen, deepen, or change any natural water course whenever this action is of public utility or conducive to public health, convenience, or welfare. In this same act, it declared the drainage of surface waters from agricultural lands and all other lands shall be presumed to be a public benefit and conducive to its public health, convenience, and welfare.

Two or more owners of lands described in a petition for drainage may file to drain a wetland or alter a stream course, but it takes the owners of 70 percent or more of the land in that petition to block such action. Consequently, this law provides a convenient vehicle to drain all wetlands and describe it as conducive to public health and welfare. The establishment of drainage districts was the most influential action in altering our wetlands.

Wetland inventories conducted by the U. S. Department of Agriculture estimated 930,000 acres of wetlands in 1906 and 368,000 acres in 1922. In this period, farmers became aware of the richness of drained water basins for growing crops. Draining increased, and ditches were dug to drain large areas. The more acreage that was drained, the more impetus there was for accelerated drainage. And so it went — pothole by pothole, marsh by marsh.

By 1940, most of our marshes, sloughs, and shallow lakes had been drained. Logan Bennett, who studied blue-winged teal in northwest Iowa, estimated that only 50,000 acres of prime marshland remained by 1938. His estimates however, did not include large sovereign lakes or other wetland types. A wetland inventory published in 1955 by Grady Mann showed 138,000 acres of water habitat. Mann's estimate includes wetlands along river systems and seasonally-flooded areas.

The most recent wetland survey conducted by wildlife biologists of the Iowa Conservation Commission identified 26,470 acres of natural marsh, all but 5,000 acres of which is publicly owned. In addition, 32,886 acres of sovereign lakes are owned by public agencies. Other wetlands include 10,000 acres of marsh created by artificial impounding for wildlife management and approximately 40,000 acres of river oxbows and overflow wetlands. Most of this latter acreage is privately owned and is endangered by clearing and landscaping done to create more cropland.

Tiling has aided the drying process. Areas that flooded temporarily in spring and after heavy rains were tiled, and this eliminated much of Iowa's water storage capacity — our natural sponge. No longer would these temporary soughs hold water for nesting ducks or retard runoff. Tile carried water as rapidly as possible to drainage ditches or creeks and on to rivers which flowed into the larger Mississippi and Missouri rivers.

Even though 95 percent of our wetlands have vanished, we still have about 110,000 acres of marshes, sloughs, lakes, and riverine wetlands

Tom C. Cooper

Reservoirs such as Redrock are needed today to store spring runoff that was formerly held by Iowa marshes.

— and close to 60 percent of this acreage is publicly owned. How were these areas preserved in the face of an aggressive and demanding agricultural system? The two most important events were, first, the declaration in 1935 of 65 lakes and marshes as sovereign lands of the State of Iowa and, second, the passage of the Pittman-Robertson Act of 1937, a federal law that imposed an 11 percent excise tax on all sporting arms and ammunition. For every dollar of state funds, the federal government returns three dollars of these taxes to the state for wildlife management, research, and habitat restoration. With these additional funds, the Iowa Conservation Commission actively pursued the purchase of wetlands. It bought marshes in eminent danger of drainage; and in some cases it bought drained lakebeds and restored them.

An article on wetlands by Richard Bishop, which appeared in a symposium entitled *Perspectives on Iowa's Declining Flora and Fauna*, describes man's influence as follows: "Natural phenomena have changed river courses and left oxbows as signatures to the force of nature, but natural changes are dwarfed by the magnitude of changes caused by modern machines and technology. Channelization of the mighty Missouri River is the most dramatic example of channel straightening. This once wide, wandering river was converted to a fast-flowing narrow drainage ditch. Inland rivers once meandered across Iowa creating a great drainage system. The winding nature of these river courses provided valuable habitat for fish as well as a wide variety of birds and mammals. However, as other wetlands which acted as water storage bodies were drained into the river systems and water-impeding vegetation was removed from the landscape, the twisting rivers could not cope with additional runoff and severe flooding resulted. Stream straightening allowed water to escape faster and also provided additional farmland where river bends and bottomland hardwoods once existed. The 6,851 miles of inland streams is

This prairie marsh has been preserved in public ownership and it will provide future generations an opportunity to look at our past and also preserve the natural flora and fauna of our wetlands.

Carl Kurtz

much less than half that which once existed when Iowa was first settled. Only 1,637 miles were designated as meandered streams in 1935. Much of the meandered portions of these rivers were altered prior to the 1935 designation that gave state ownership to these stream beds up to the high-water mark. Current vigilance protects these river portions from further degradation."

Most channelization occurred in the early 1900s, but it has continued on unmeandered rivers to the present day. Permits from the U.S. Army Corps of Engineers are now required before any alteration of navigable waters may occur. Little data are available on the miles of un-straightened water courses that remain, but they are truly a unique remnant of the past and need further protection.

Old river channels now cut off from the stream itself are called oxbows and are valuable areas for fish and wildlife. An estimated 40,000 acres of oxbows and overflow areas remain in inland river flood plains. Less than half of this acreage is permanent water. Rivers periodically inundate low areas and recharge oxbows. Clearing bottomland timber and filling wet areas for additional agricultural development continues to decrease this acreage.

Wetlands adjacent to or within the border rivers themselves often are overlooked. An estimated 324,785 acres constitute riverbeds of our 619 miles of border rivers. While the Missouri River lost most of its valuable backwaters and marshes, the creation of locks and dams for navigation on the Mississippi created some excellent river marshes in its upper portions. However Allamakee and Clayton counties boast the most valuable and picturesque river ponds and marshes, additional wetlands border the main channel down to Louisa County. The upper Mississippi still offers some of the finest wetlands in the state and is heavily used for recreation by hunters, fishermen, pleasure boaters, and sightseers. While much of this acreage is publicly owned, marshes and lakes within the confines of the river are threatened by siltation and deposition of spoil from channel dredging for navigation.

Recreational demand for boating, fishing, hunting, and camping have provided impetus for construction of numerous small lakes and reservoirs. In addition, four large flood-control reservoirs (30,250 acres) have been built by the U.S. Army Corps of Engineers. These man-made lakes total 47,562 acres, most of which have been constructed in the southern half of Iowa where few natural wetlands exist. These impoundments provide excellent recreational opportunities and reduce demand on our natural lakes. We can expect wetland construction of this nature to continue, and water acreage to increase.

Farm ponds gained popularity in the late 1930s and early 1940s and construction has continued through the present day. According to the 1973 Soil Conservation Service survey, some 47,700 ponds totalling 49,000 acres were built. Most farm ponds are in the more rolling terrain of southern Iowa, where the main purpose is to retard erosion and provide water for livestock. As concern for protecting our valuable topsoil heightens, we can expect to see additional incentives for landowners to build farm ponds.

Construction of periodically flooded wetlands and marshes — primarily waterfowl hunting areas — is creating first-class water areas that are used by a variety of birds in migration. Artificial marshes of this kind probably will gradually increase in number as long as waterfowl hunting is allowed.

Two programs were in operation to save prairie marshes. The first was initiated in 1972 when a law was passed that required all waterfowl hunters to purchase a $1 state duck stamp. In 1979, the law was changed to require hunters 16 years and older to purchase a $5 stamp. Approximately 15 percent of present duck stamp funds are given to Ducks Unlimited in Canada to create waterfowl production areas. The remainder is spent in Iowa on wetland acquisition and development.

The second is a cooperative state and federal program using funds from the federal duck stamp which is required of all waterfowl hunters 16 years or older. The U.S. Fish and Wildlife Service has bought two waterfowl production areas in Iowa with these funds and, when recent budget restrictions are lifted, acquisition may continue.

The two programs do not supply enough funds to purchase wetlands in immediate danger of drainage, let alone buy drained land for reclamation. Sportsmen cannot bear this burden alone. Public awareness of the value of these wetlands is vital. If public support is not forthcoming, the only water areas remaining may be those already in public trust.

In the Marsh

MEN OF THE MARSH and river have long been known for being a different breed. A little standoffish, idealistic maybe, but however you describe them, they have a certain air. They seem to possess a deep appreciation for the intricate, interwoven complexity of plants, animals, and water. One man who spent much of his life on the backwater marshes of the Mississippi River hunting, trapping, and fishing said: ". . . Once you have sensed her beauty and taken of her bounty, you will never be free of her compelling lure or a deep love to possess her." While most people are not as deeply affected by the marsh, they can enjoy its beauty, bountiful wildlife, and sense her moods. Let's listen to the annual moods of the marsh. When March and April winds melt the ice along the shallow marsh edge, another life cycle begins. Some of the first to return are red-winged blackbirds and mallard ducks. Close behind, a host of other ducks — pintail, green-winged teal, shoveler, wigeon, scaup, redheads, and canvasbacks — follow. Snow geese, Canada geese, and white-fronted geese can also be seen. Frogs soon serenade the homecoming and the announcement of spring. Yellow-headed blackbirds, Virginia and sora rails, coots, terns, herons, marsh hawks, more ducks, and a host of wading birds arrive shortly after.

No other habitat seems so alive. The excitement in the calls of marsh birds tells of the urgency and importance of home and a new breeding season. It is amost impossible to keep from being swept up in this excitement. Each calling bird proclaims his greatness. Newly arriving birds sweep low over the marsh surveying for a new home. Earlier arrivals run off intruders into their newly established territories.

Small mammals are active also. Muskrats busily swim along, appearing to be going somewhere in a hurry. Mink dart along the marsh edge, looking for a meal at this new time of plenty. Raccoon tracks show where they have searched for frogs and crayfish. Other animals — red fox, badger, skunk, opossum, ground squirrel, and meadow voles — can be seen in the uplands along the marsh.

Green cattail shoots spring up from the old root stalks, giving the marsh a greenish cast while marsh iris lift purple heads. Spring has arrived, and the birds are somewhat quieter as they go about the business of raising families.

Weather changes are more acute in the marsh, and you become intimately aware of the changing moods. Cattails tell of shifting winds, and the air and birds announce a coming storm.

Hot summer days find the marsh more subdued, except for the chatter of coot and rails, the flights of blackbirds, and the dipping and diving flight of the tern. Broods of ducklings can be seen in open-water areas in early morning or late evening busily eating a high protein diet of insects. This tranquil scene may best be appreciated at dawn's first light when the coolness of nighttime still clings. The buzzing of millions of insects can almost deafen you and make your stay uncomfortable, but that is part of the marsh.

Before changes in leaf color announces autumn, the marsh tells you that something is about to happen. Ducks testing their newly acquired flight feathers zoom restlessly across the marsh to join other ducks sitting in a favorite cove or along a mud bar. Blackbirds stream from their cattail roosts in an almost never-ending fashion. Muskrats actively chew off cattail stems and tow them away to be added to a winter home. Soon what is probably the most compelling of all of man's association with the marsh comes. When the southward migration of birds is in full swing, hunting season for ducks and geese begins.

In the wind's chill through the darkness of predawn, coots, rails, blackbirds, lesser yellowlegs, and gabbling ducks converse across the marsh. The tone of their calls is different from that of spring — they sense the coming winter and the need to move south.

Alex B. Thiermann

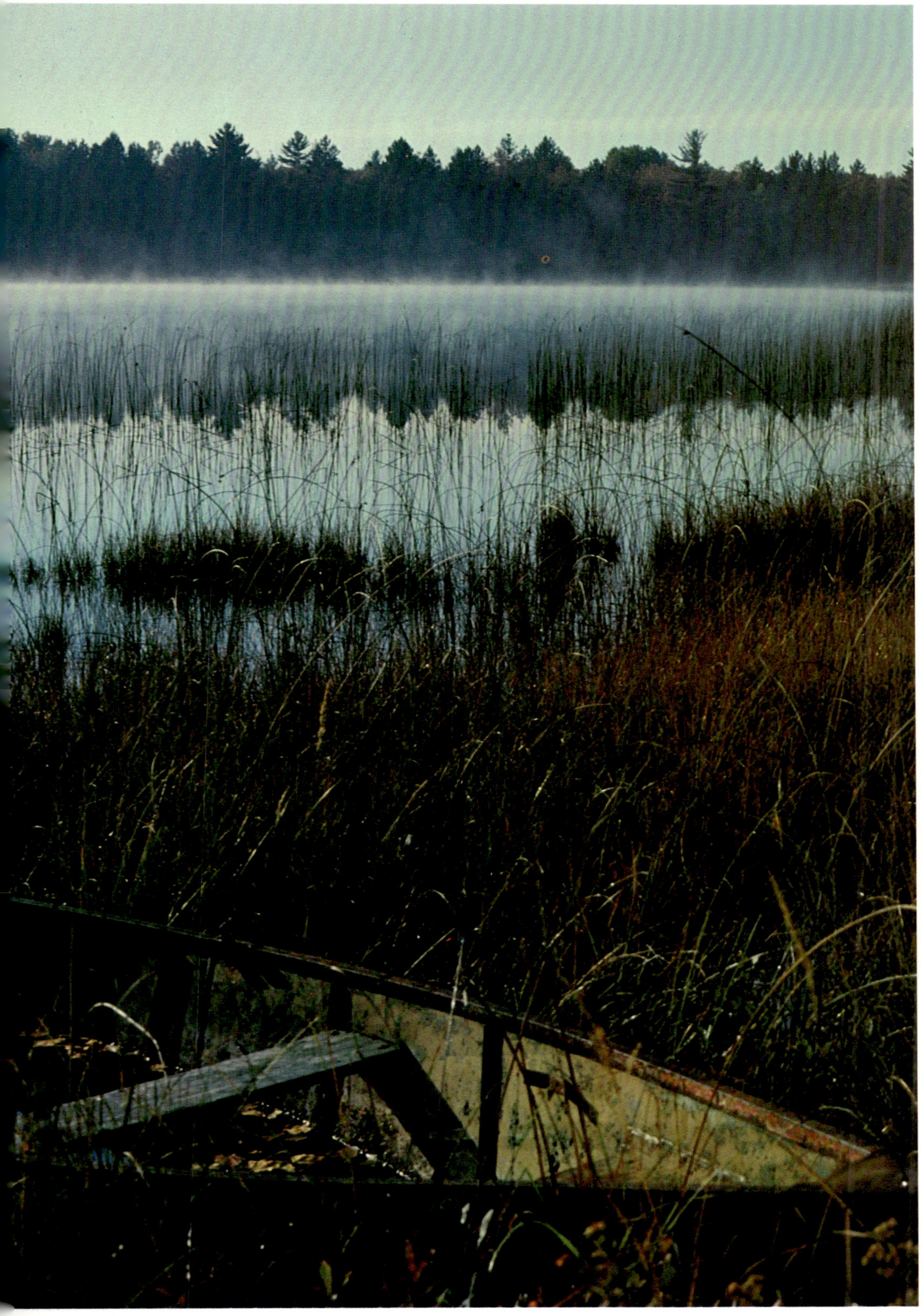

Alex B. Thiermann

Carl Kurtz

Alex B. Thiermann

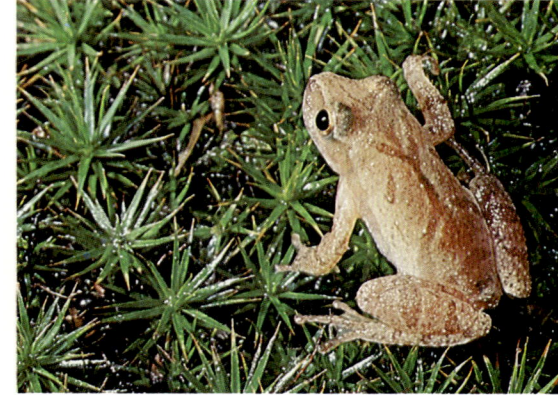

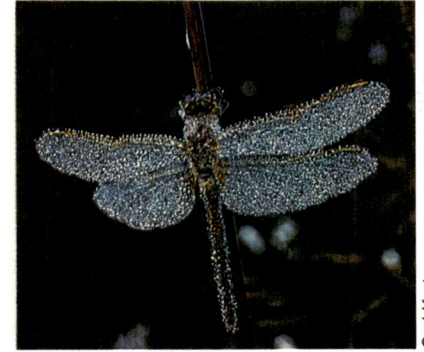

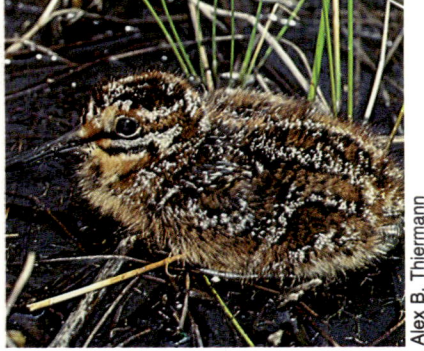

Marshes can be recreated by flooding low lying areas as has been done in this case.

Carl Kurtz

(Left)
***Tranquility at sunset**—There is a need to revive and replenish man's soul and to inspire one's inner energies and abilities.*
(Below)
The remnants of our wetland heritage provide recreational opportunities for all Iowans.

Iowa Conservation Commission, Ken Formanek

Future of Iowa's Wetlands

THE FUTURE does not need to be bleak. While most of our watery real estate has either been destroyed or altered by man, we have created an unrivaled agricultural system. What is most important now is that we protect what remains and secure the future of our natural resources.

Ninety-five percent of our prairie wetlands have been drained, but we need also to realize that to lose what remains would be an even greater tragedy. What can be done? More money is needed to make a major impact and to prevent further drainage. Sportsmen who have shouldered the major burden in the past need help from the general public, who can urge lawmakers to fund sound conservation projects to save our remaining wetlands. If money were available, drained basins could be bought, tile lines could be broken, and, with minor dirt work and a structure to control the water level, a marsh could be restored.

Most rivers have been drastically altered and will never return to their natural state; however, we still have several very alluring river corridors. If corridors could be bought along major scenic rivers in our state, a portion of these waterways could be preserved. Even with man's changes, they remain beautiful. We should strive to protect at least a few segments of our wildest and free-spirited rivers.

Preservation of wetlands is important. They serve as water-holding bodies to retard runoff and recharge groundwater supplies. Wise use of groundwater is becoming more and more important. Holding water on the land provides water for livestock as well as water supplies for towns and industry, and reduces erosion-causing runoff. Wetlands also make valuable outdoor classrooms. While many older Iowans may have rural backgrounds, our young rapidly increasing urban population does not. The need to educate them is great.

Recreational demands are also increasing, and water-related sports are at the top of the list. Whether it is fishing, water skiing, pleasure boating, canoeing, hunting, photography, or birdwatching, an increasing human population will make an ever increasing demand on remaining wetlands. We must not misuse what we have left. We still can protect and reclaim some wetlands.

CHAPTER TEN
AQUATIC LIFE
BY RICHARD BOVBJERG

To the visitor on the shores of an Iowa lake the sight is one of beauty: the mysterious beauty in the depths, the beds of aquatic vegetation, the sudden swirl of a fish tail, the ripple marks on sandy bottom, the insects quietly slipping out of the water onto reeds and into the air. The mysteries enhance the beauty. However, the lake is not really a mystery but the normal home for hundreds of kinds of plants and animals.

Consider what a lake would be like without this life. Lake Okoboji would be a giant tank, sterile and uninteresting. No green on the shoreline rocks; no gardens of plants hiding the fish, no fish, no glitter of damsel fly wings, and the bottom a smooth layer of sand and silt. More desolate than the desert or arctic wastes.

In this chapter we will examine lakes and streams the way we are fortunate to find them, rich in life and vigor. We invite you to see lakes the way a fish sees them; we invite you to see lakes in your mind's eye or by going there and looking carefully. There is no substitution for getting wet; the reknowned biologist Louis Agassiz said "Study nature not books."

During floods, oxbows, bays and flood plains become temporary lakes with a great richness in life adapted to that short life, as in the case of the dense bloom of duckweeds seen here in the backwaters of the Mississippi River.

(Previous Spread)
Woodland ponds such as this in southeast Iowa often show distinct zones of grasses, sedges, cattails, and rushes. Mats of green duckweed float freely on quiet waters.

Iowa's Natural and Artificial Lakes

THE LAKES OF IOWA (see Chapter 3) are restricted to the great Des Moines Lobe of the latest glaciation, that is, except for the several large reservoirs now impounded by flood control dams of large rivers. These dozens of lakes are variable; some are large like Spirit Lake or Okoboji, some are deep and some shallow; they range in size down to large ponds with permanent water. But whatever the size of the lake, we can discover very little if we just stand on the shore. We need to look at various parts of the lake to see something of what is there and how it works.

Patches of bladderwort prosper and bloom bright yellow in prairie marshes, ponds, and shallow bays in lakes. These plants are covered by numerous small bladders that are used to trap very small invertebrates.

(Top)
Damselflies mate after emerging from quiet waters where they grow and mature.
(Above)
Green filamentous algae may cover rocks of streams and lake margins. Within this algal mat lives a sheltered world of microscopic life.
(Right)
Picturesque Iowa streams, such as Prairie Creek in Marshall County, are home to a multitude of species specialized to hold on in rapid water.

The Shoreline of the Lake

SANDY SHORES are very poor in life. This is a zone where waves shift the sand, grinding the grains to create an abrasive habitat that can shelter very few types of plant or animal, but there are microscopic plants, animals, and bacteria that can survive here. Then there are, of course, the land animals that come to feed along the shore.

The rocky shores of lakes are different. There are sturdy creatures living here, even in storms. Pick up a rock, examine it closely, top and bottom, (using a hand lens if you have one). Then return it to its original place! It is solidly covered with living stuff. This is not "scum, slime, moss"; it is a community of living things with dozens of species of plants and animals. You immediately see that the rock's top is green and the bottom often stained black. The top is an algal garden, food for the small animals crawling over this green surface. The black underside often sits in a stagnant depression which may have almost no oxygen and there bacteria live and generate the foul smell of rotten eggs, a sulfurous byproduct of their metabolism.

The carpet of algae is attached to the rock so firmly that wave shock does not remove it. The shallow water and bright light assures that this algal mat is very productive. The species vary from season to season but in the summer all the major types may be found. The blue-green algae grow rapidly, often forming dark patches of film on the rock. The green algae are beautiful and delicate filaments that often cap rocks with a head of green hair waving about in the swirling waters between rocks. Many species of a third type of algae, the diatoms, may be present. These do have green pigments but the color is often masked by other pigments so that they appear brown or tan. Often the diatoms form a very thick, slick coating on the rocks.

Like the more familiar green plants on land, these algae are producing sugars, starches, fats, and oils, as well as proteins. This production is powered by light energy in the process of photosynthesis which uses the raw materials in the water: carbon dioxide, water, and minerals. In the process, oxygen is released; photosynthesis is the world's most important chemical process since it not only furnishes the world with all of its oxygen but all of its food.

Insects and snails feed on this rapidly growing vegetation. Predators such as dragonfly larvae (immature stages), small fish and leeches feed on the insects and snails.

In addition to the green plants, the herbivores and predators, dead plant and animal materials, in large chunks and small shreds, wash ashore. This detritus is food for many more species of animals. At night the crayfish venture out of their rocky crevices and feed on just about everything. So do the lovely ribbonlike flatworms that glide about on the rock surface; these small worms are about as long as your fingernail and a pair of eyes in a pointy head make them look like little ghosts. Also very efficient feeders on detritus are the caddis flies. These larvae spin webs of many kinds and build cases around themselves that create water currents through sieve-like strainers, to catch the food brought to them. There are many of these insects that attach to rocks; one of the most unusual is the size of a split pea and cements sand grains in a snail shell shape.

All inhabitants of the rocky shore have features in common; adaptations to this special place. They must withstand wave shock, exposure to air between waves, heat and cold, and the change of seasons. Some species remain on the rock during the winter, covered with ice. They can make it through such cold times by being in an inactive form like the tiny tough cells of the algae, cysts. Other animals migrate out to deeper water during the winter and back to shore in the spring. These animals of the shore live in water highly aerated like stream water and require high oxygen like the stream species do.

A Barren Area

AWAY FROM SHORE, in shallow, sand or gravel bottom areas where one might swim, we seldom see living things. This is a barren area of shifting sand where plants do not survive well. One does see an occasional fish or school of minnows very clearly in this open area. In early summer dense black balls of young bullheads are very conspicuous. Clams, or mussels, burrow and slowly crawl in the gravel bottom showing only their siphons. These siphons are openings for both incoming and outgoing water currents that bring fresh water and detritus to the mouths and gills of the buried clams.

Vegetation Flourishes

OUT FROM THE SWIMMING AREA is the region most people avoid. The beds of vegetation growing up from silty bottoms frighten swimmers but this underwater world is lovely. Swimming through this garden is akin to strolling through a sunlit forest, the same quiet and repose.

One can only be surprised by the productivity of these large aquatic plants. Each year they may grow to the height of corn, or more. These are flowering plants that are rooted in the muck; other members of their families live on land. Most folks call these plants sea weed but the plants here are not at all related to the actual sea weeds.

These aquatic plants are highly adapted to living in shallow waters. While they retain the vascular tissues of land plants (that microscopic tubing that runs throughout plants carrying water and nutrient), they do not have the woody aspect that land plants do. The land plant must be tough enough to remain upright but the water plant sways gently in the water, buoyed up by it. Bring home a bit of stem and cut it with a razor. A hand lens will show how spongy the stem is inside. This is unlike a tree twig that you might cut in comparison.

American lotus is a waterlily in Iowa, restricted almost exclusively to areas along the Mississippi and Missouri rivers. The seeds of this plant were collected in the fall by Indians who then ground them into flour.

Carl Kurtz

Bays of the Lake

IN QUIET BAYS, there may be tiny floating plants, duck weed, which form mats of bright green along the shore. Flowering plants such as the pond buttercup may also live in sheltered bays. Some of these plants are pollinated by wind and some by insects, as on land. Seeds and fruit are also produced and as on land, they disperse and start the next generation. Excess of production is food for the plant-eating animals of the water.

All of the crop of up to 20 or 30 species of plants grows without added fertilizer, pesticides, or cultivation. The bottom is rich in mineral nutrient, again, like the forest floor on land. Each year the massive crop dies back and disintegrates to detritus. Then the bacteria and fungi go to work decomposing the complex materials of life down to carbon dioxide, water, marsh gases, nitrogen, phosphorus, and other elements. They complete endless cycles of these elements vital to life — these basic substances are ready in the muck for the growth of next year's plants. And there is an excess; the bottom materials build up over the centuries adding to the organic silt deposits.

Very often aquatic plants are draped with mats of filamentous algae, diatoms, and later in the summer they are covered with rubbery gobs of blue-green algae. The green algae may form sheets that cover the bottom and many mats break loose to form large floating rafts. They contain bubbles of oxygen in the daytime. Eventually they die and disintegrate, adding to the detritus of the bottom.

Yellow water-lily is common statewide in marshes, lakes, and occasionally along slow-flowing streams.

Part of the microscopic world of life on a submerged boulder, this green, filamentous, algal strand even has unicellular life growing on it.

David B. Czarnecki

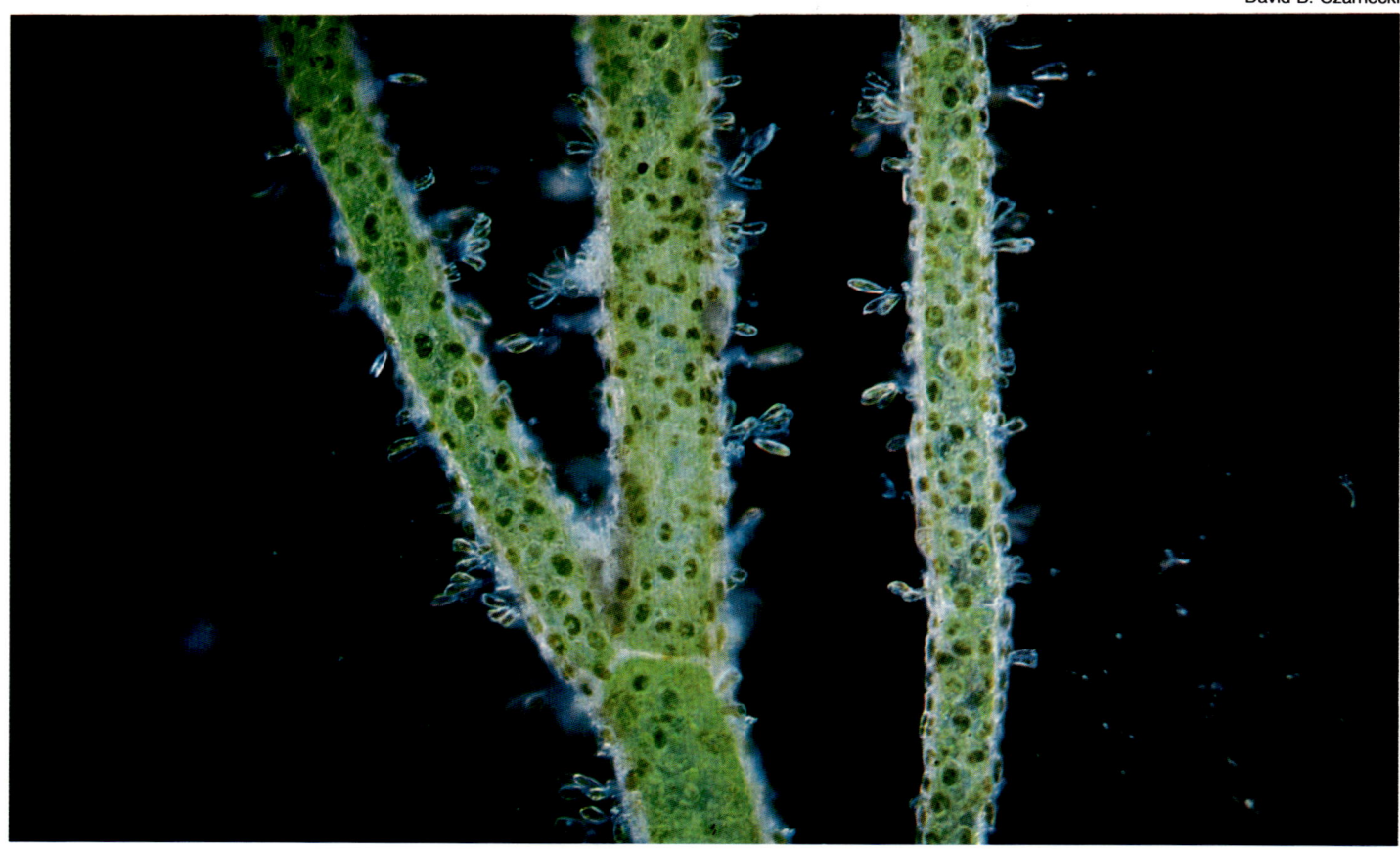

Food For Fish

THIS LUSH GARDEN of rooted plants, duck weed and algae supports an extensive fauna. It has been noted that many fish seek these areas, not because they eat the plants but because fish feed on the animals that feed on the plants: the food web again.

The smallest animals are the protozoans, one cell only, which swim and crawl in the algal growth on the rooted plants. Some swim by means of the cilia covering the cell; some swim by means of longer whip-like flagallae; some crawl along amoeba fashion, with the contents of the cell flowing this way or that. Utterly astonishing are those which are stationary, glued to a leaf by a long stalk which can relax to extend and contract into a spring-like coil. The cell on the end eats bacteria and shreds of detritus in the water, sucking these bits into the cell with a ring of beating cilia.

Many types of microscopic worms also live on plant leaves. Very tiny round worms can be seen only by the thrashing about that they do in the water, forming a figure S first this way then the other. Here, too, we see the spooky, gliding little flatworm that we also saw on the rocks of the shore. The same for several kinds of leeches and their prey, snails. Some of these snails are very small, about the size of a grain of wheat. They may also be the food of several fish. A green caddis fly larva secretes a clear substance that forms a case around itself resembling the spiked leaflet of a coontail plant.

Crustaceans may be so small as to be barely visible or as large as the crayfish. When these stay suspended in the water we refer to them as plankton (drifters). Aquatic plant gardens have small crustaceans (sometimes called water fleas but they are not parasites). Most are filter feeders on algal cells, protozoans, and bacteria. Many of these have an incredible habit of slowly rising at dusk and sinking at dawn. The value of this to their survival is that invasion of the surface waters (where food is plentiful) during the darkness makes them less visible to predators. This migration has been found in lakes all over the world and in all oceans.

Larger than plankton is a very common crustacean, the flat little greenish scud which darts about among the plants in huge numbers. Shake a few leaves in your hand and there will be several small scuds scurrying. They may be the size of a rice grain. They swim and crawl on the leaves of plants and along the bottom. They eat detritus, algae, small animals, almost anything. But in turn, they are food for other animals, especially fish.

This lovely looking specimen may be an algal nuisance. A colony of blue-green algal filaments, that to the naked eye look like a pinhead, can blow into bays of lakes and cover them.

Insects of the Lake

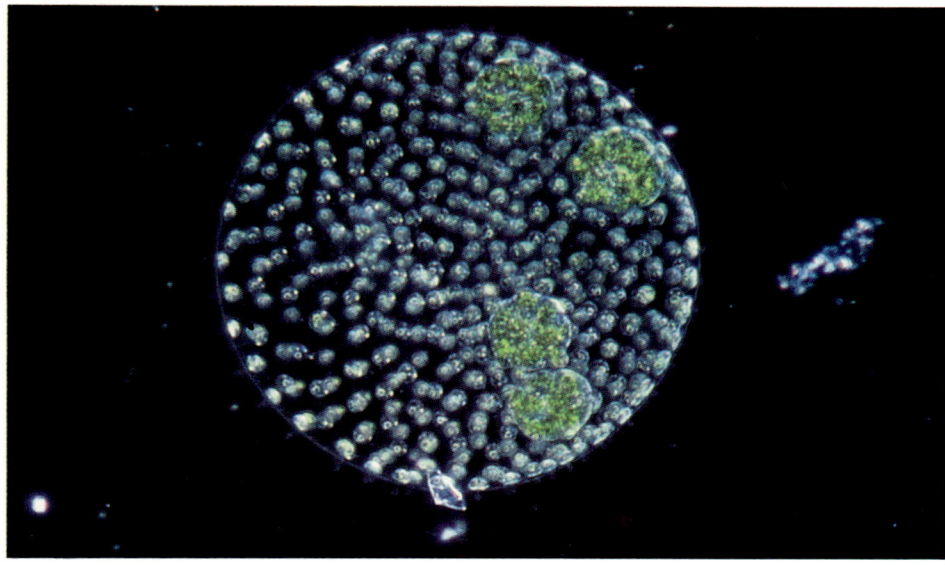

MOST OF THE INSECTS are immature larval stages of adults that we see emerging from the water. This list would include dragonflies, damselflies, many kinds of flies and midges. Some of these, like the fly larvae, burrow and feed on the muck of the bottom. They are present in countless numbers; every handful of muck would have many. The large dragonfly larvae are swift swimmers; some are jet propelled with a stream of water. These are voracious predators, even able to take some very small fish; they have a folding lower jaw which can flip out like a flash.

Some insects are adapted to this garden region even as adults; they normally do not leave the water, though some can fly like the giant water bug that resembles a huge cockroach. Several kinds of beetles hunt prey, propelled by legs shaped and used like paddles. The water scorpion with its gangly legs, crawls about with the tip of its abdomen acting as a snorkel for fresh air. Usually water boatmen and backswimmers are very numerous; these too have oar-like legs for swimming. On the water surface in protected bays the whirly-gig beetles skim the surface in circles. Catch one of these and take a close look at the eyes; they are double, half for watching under water and half for seeing out of water. Also on the surface are the water striders which stalk their prey on stilted legs that can detect the movements of prey.

Mosquitoes are not found in large numbers in the lake. The larvae (wrigglers) require very shallow, quiet water; they must have this for their snorkels to operate in obtaining air. Further, they are so fragile and obvious to predators that they are prey to any small predator in the water, both insect and fish. If there are mosquitoes near lakes, they have usually emerged from puddles in the low areas near the shore (not to mention from the half-filled, discarded cans stranded along the shore).

This planktonic jewel is just visible as it slowly rolls about in quiet waters. This sphere of green cells is a parent colony — a womb to the developing colonies within.

Rivers and bays of lakes spew mayflies into the countryside in spring evenings. The immature stages in the water are morsels for fish.

Jerry D. Leonard

Larger Forms of Life

SMALL BODIES of water without large fish have many kinds of amphibians, frogs, toads, and salamanders. But in larger lakes these would be eaten by the many fish prowling along the shore. One seldom sees frogs in large lakes. One does see turtles however; these reptiles are also found in ponds.

Although one would usually go to marshes to look for muskrats, larger lakes may have them in sheltered, pond-like bays. They burrow in the bank but find all the food they need in the shallow water gardens. The beaver may be here as well, though more likely to be seen in rivers. They build shelters on remote shores, cutting young willows for the purpose. There are also birds that are usual along the shores of lakes and there are many land birds that may go to the shore for part of their food.

Carl Kurtz   Jim Wee

Iowa sloughs, ponds, and bays of lakes are noted for their muskrats which still are being trapped for their pelts.

Turtles abound in Iowa's wetlands and lake margins. They live in the water, but are air breathers and must lay their eggs up on the bank.

Nyla Hunt

Iowa's lakes and streams offer the patient fisherman a variety of good eating. This is Little Wall Lake in Hamilton County.

The Middle of a Lake

THERE ARE RELATIVELY FEW animals that can survive in the open water region of a lake, only about a dozen planktonic crustacea. One or two species are huge by comparison and are predators on the smaller types. As in shallow water species, some of these migrate up and down, night and day. They have traits that allow them to stay suspended. They dart about, resisting sinking. But their structure also slows sinking; they are light in weight with little shell material; they often have oil that is lighter than water, and spines and legs slow the rate of sinking. They are normally down below the lighted layer of water and they are glass-clear.

The food web here is rather restricted, not plentiful enough to attract fish for feeding. The predators are plankton themselves, they eat smaller animal plankton which feed on planktonic algae. Again three basic types of algae are found here. Neither the total volume of living stuff nor the number of species is large. This is an impoverished region of the lake, a tough environment with no place for an organism to rest. They are at the mercy of currents although some specialize in living at deeper strata where currents are less prominent.

In shallow lakes, some light may get to the bottom. Some algae may grow here even when rooted plants cannot. This is a habitat of decomposition and in deeper, dark areas, that is all that goes on. It is not just the silt particles from eroding shore that collect on the bottom of the lake, but also the dead particles of lake plants and animals collect here. This is food for some detritus feeders and for molds and bacteria. The rich ooze of deeper lakes may be highly organic. The bottom ooze is in fact very rich in nutrients. The final decomposition products include the very minerals needed for plant growth. In the times of circulation of lakes, these minerals can be distributed to all levels of the lake and become the nutrient for the plants of the lighted upper layers. The cycling of elements is in fact best seen in the lake ecosystem. Much, of course, also comes in each year from the surrounding land.

In the deeper lakes, like West Okoboji, the bottom environment is severe. Not only is it full of decomposition gases, but during the summer there is little if any oxygen. This greatly restricts the kinds of animals that can survive here, leaving only a few types of insect larvae and worms. These have to be able to live without oxygen. Those that can make it in this region may be in very high numbers. They are especially adapted to living in this soft ooze, the consistency of chocolate pudding, cold and dark.

The Lake: An Ecosystem

A LAKE IS the classical ecosystem (ecological system): a body of water, the included community of living things, and the interrelatedness between water and life. The lake basin and water can be measured and described. So too can the community, species by species. It has already been made clear that the life is dependent on the environment and in turn the water is altered by the presence of life, interrelatedness.

However, one part of the lake is different from another; we have considered how this is so. The green gardens of shallow waters differ from the algae of the open lake. The top of the lake differs from the bottom, differs in characteristics of water and differs in the living things present. But it is still all the same water; it circulates from top to bottom and shore to shore. An oxygen atom released from a green algal cell in the center of the lake may be taken into the gills of a bullhead spawning in shallow water. Vice versa with a molecule of carbon dioxide. The fine organic pudding of the deep forms from remains of life all over the lake; drifting clouds of detritus slowly rain down to the bottom in the center of the lake. Some fish swim from side to side. Over the years, even snails, at a snail's pace, could move from one shore to another. So both physically and ecologically, the lake is an ecosystem of interrelated parts.

The lake, large or small, is part of a basin in the landscape. The kind of lake and what happens in the lake are affected by the surrounding land area. Even before Iowa was farmed, there was some surface runoff into the lakes, some in streams flowing into lake bays; and a great deal of water flows into lakes through the soil as ground water. This is a form of spring water seeping into shallow areas. Whether surface water or ground water, the impact of the land is important. If the soils are rich the waters will be rich. Iowa's lakes are richer in life than the impoverished waters of states like Minnesota and Wisconsin where ground water filters through a thin soil layer of gravel and pine needles. Our ground waters filter through very deep layers of black soil rich in plant nutrients. These nutrients ensure an enriched lake; this is natural eutrophication (enrichment).

There is another way the lake ties into the surrounding land. The willows and poplars around the lake shed their leaves in the fall. Many of these fall into the lake, a new carpet of food for the lake community. Pollen from miles about is part of the ooze at the bottom and food for small creatures. Lake bottoms are cored and the vegetation history of the entire region may be traced through these layers of pollen from the past.

But the reverse is also true; the lake returns matter and energy to the land. Midges, mayflies, and caddis flies emerge from the lake in clouds. Anyone with a light on at night in June knows something of the enormous numbers of insects leaving the lake. They mate, lay eggs in the shallow water but end their lives as prey for land animals. In the evening, birds and bats gorge on these insects; the spider webs fill. These insects are part of the lake as larvae and part of the terrestrial systems as adults.

Lakes also maintain and provide a reservoir of water without which no land species can exist.

Lakes Are Structured

Looking back over this discussion of lake plants and animals, it is so obvious that any one creature or any one species is not where it is in some random pattern. Human communities are structured; downtown, schools, airport, and homes are not randomly placed; so with natural communities. From top to bottom life is stratified in a lake; it is also in zones from the shore. Each species is where it is because its requirements are met and the extremes of the environment can be tolerated. We have emphasized this by considering one part of the lake at a time. The fisherman knows this; time is not wasted randomly searching for fish. It is known where one finds bullheads or any other species.

Impounded lakes are river-lake hybrids. Red Rock Reservoir, like all impoundments, shows the problems of siltation and water level fluctuation that exposes mud flats and inhibits plant growth.

Carl Kurtz

The Iowa River lies between the rushing trout streams of northeast Iowa and the meandering prairie streams of western Iowa.

Carl Kurtz

The Life of Iowa's Rivers

Pikes Peak State Park offers Iowans a good view of flood plain and abandoned channels of the Mississippi River near McGregor.

Iowa is uniquely bordered by two of the great rivers of the world, the Missouri and Mississippi. In between one finds the state divided into many land forms *(see Chapter 1)*. The landscape dictates the type of river. In the northeast, with forested regions of greatly dissected hills and bold outcrops of rock, one finds swift streams, plunging rapids, and generally clear cold water. To the westward on the gently rolling prairie landscape one finds meandering rivers cutting through rich black soils. While some of these were once clear waters, now silty through runoff from agriculture, some were always silty waters when the river level was high.

Any river is very different from a lake and the life is different as well. We are comparing standing and running waters. The animals in running water have many adaptations to the current, in their structures, functions, and in their behavior. Obviously all parts of the life cycle must contend with the flow of water. Like the need of lake plankton to resist sinking to the bottom, so stream animals must resist dislodgment and being tumbled and crushed downstream.

Iowa's glacial landscape, now agricultural but once prairie, is drained by rivers cutting into rich black soil. These have always carried a silt load at highwater, but this has been heightened when the plough goes all the way to the river bank.

Holding on in Current

Several structural adaptations are used for holding on in moving water. Most forms are streamlined in shape, low and gently curved so that the water flows over them easily. They have many ways of holding on. Some actually glue themselves with a sticky web material like the caddis flies. The gliding foot of the snail or the flatworm clings to rocks. Clams, fly larvae and mayfly larvae may burrow in the gravel bottom. Most have legs that jab into crevices, some have actual suckers like the leeches. There are a host of crevice dwellers who do not actually face the problem of current. On the downstream edge and underside of rocks there is dead water with only gentle water movement. Here small animals can walk and even swim about without struggling against current. Eggs are often laid here; female crayfish brood their young in these crevices between and under rocks.

"Holding on" for fish is special; it is done largely by powerful swimming and use of the quiet places in the current such as in little embayments or overhanging banks with fallen logs making small dams. Some fish can use their fins to wedge against crevices. The shape of fish is different from those in lakes. There is no place in fast water for fish which are flat from side to side like sunfish; this is the home of fish which are more round or square in cross section, like the pike, trout, and minnows.

Plants have the same problem. Many clear water streams have beds of rooted plants whose roots have underground runners connecting them. Such plants have long, grass-like leaves that flow freely with the current without resisting the pull. Mosses cling tightly to rocks and old logs in streams; they have masses of tiny, fibrous rhizoids. The algae cling to the rocks by gluing on. Diatoms form sheets of colonies in a gelatinous film or there may be masses of filamentous green algae. The bottom cell of the filaments is a special holdfast cell.

There is even a microscopic world on the rocks. In the algal covered film there exists a community free of current because the thin layer of water here is trapped in the algal mats. This is like the interior of a forest, dark, windless and quiet. In this algal forest on the rocks are microscopic rotifers swimming, small scuds crawling, protozoans, worms, and juvenile snails grazing on the algae. Even those refugees from the seas, bryozoans and sponges, cling to rocks in streams. Any of these small things would be dashed to death if they were not in this microscopic shelter on the rock surface. Within this layer of quiet water they spend their lives, feeding, breeding, and staying home.

Functions of River Animals

Iowa is on the migratory path of many species of waterfowl.

Steve Zavodny

FOOD GATHERING must be different in river animals. Only the powerful swimmers can hunt prey; the rest rely on the current bringing food to them on an endless watery belt-line. The black fly and caddis fly larvae build nets at the mouth of their cases. This net gathers detritus and small tumbling organisms dislodged from their perches. The animals gather food from the net with jaws, legs, or with a sieve-like mouth apparatus. There are of course grazers on the algae covering the rocks. A vast number of stream animals are omnivorous, eat anything that comes along. A crayfish may eat leaves, scrape rocks for the algae, eat dead pieces of fish. The clams, wedged into the gravel of the stream bottom, have only their tips exposed with siphons pumping water and detritus food. They are living pumps.

Several species of fish, including some minnows and darters, glue eggs to the leeside of rocks. When the immature hatch, they are in the quiet water next to a rock. Crayfish carry eggs and the very young on the abdomen of the mother. Insects lay their eggs in rafts on the rock. Snail eggs are in gelatinous sacs attached to the rock. Many species have larval stages in the egg; the hatchlings are well along in development before facing the rigors of the stream. There is little place here for a species with fragile immature stages.

Even so, many animals are washed downstream and recover their place by instinctive upstream orientation and movement. Fish are capable of much upstream swimming and even some snails slowly march upstream. The clams have a remarkable life history and some clam, or mussel beds, remain in the same place over years even though the immature individuals are swept downstream. With luck, some of these are carried into the gills of fish; here they clamp on and become parasites. The fish then swim all over, which means wide dispersal of the tiny clams when they finally drop from the fish gills to take up a mature existence.

Carl Kurtz

Food From the Shores

SOME OF THE ALGAE and rooted plants grow rapidly and are grazed as fast as they grow. This is the first link in the food chain of the river. But the productivity is often less than in a lake. Streams are shaded by trees and silty water allows far less light to penetrate; light is the key to productivity. Light is the ultimate source of energy for any ecosystem.

Much of the food base must be organic material washed in from the banks of the river. Recall that much of the feeding is on detritus. Much of the detritus comes from the land. Leaves shower into the river in the fall; seeds and fruits fall into the river where the current grinds them to detritus fragments, food for all sorts of animals. The detritus also includes animal material from the shore. Insects, birds, even mammals drown in the water and add their carrion to the food chains.

In times of flood not only a new load of silt is introduced but plant debris from forests, grasslands and farm land. This input is added to the production of the river.

Tom C. Cooper

(Left)
Western and northern Iowa were once dotted with prairie potholes and sloughs.
(Above)
Duckweed on the pond and autumn color create this quiet spot in northeast Iowa.

247

Rivers Change

A sudden abundance of aquatic life fills oxbows and woodland ponds in the spring.

Carl Kurtz

THE CLASSICAL RIVER has its headwaters in upland or mountain springs. Several Iowa rivers originate in northern Iowa or Minnesota; they flow southerly and easterly to the Mississippi or westerly to the Missouri. None starts in mountains but they do show some of the obvious changes from small brooks to large rivers. Brooks and springs are often summer dry but streams that would be called creeks or larger are almost never totally dry. As tributaries come together, the volume, width, and cutting powers increase. The larger rivers have formed flood plains on which they meander in serpentine loops, occasionally cutting off a loop which then becomes an oxbow pond.

The life in flowing waters changes as the river enlarges downstream. The coldwater spring and brook are constant environments but very small. The water is chilly even in summer. Springs and brooks bubble along and are well aerated; they are also shallow and often vegetation filled. The flora and fauna are special, often with species known only from such small waters. There are few species but these may be in very large numbers. Marsh plants sometimes invade shallow brooks and they often have a type of water cress. They invariably have algae that are suited to cold water. Brooks are too shallow for a large variety of animals, species are small: flatworms, scuds, snails, insect larvae.

Downstream, the numbers of species increases, if the river is not polluted. The environment has different habitats and therefore different types of plant and animal species. There are rapid stretches, riffles or cascades, where specially adapted species are different from the life in the deeper, slower pools of the river. The center of the stream is different from the margins. The deeper outer margin of the river bend is an abrasive, eroding rush of water while the shallow water of the inside bend is gently depositing sand and silt. The forms of life must therefore differ on those two sides of the same river.

The varied habitats of a river support a rich variety of life.

Saylorville Lake is one of four major reservoirs in Iowa offering extensive recreational facilities. The reservoirs have also created a rich environment for some fish and other aquatic life.

Impounded Rivers

IOWA HAS a large number of dams across its rivers. At one time every town had a mill on a dam; then these gave way to local hydroelectric dams and plants. When large power lines swept across the state, these smaller plants become obsolete but the dams remain. Following World War II, the U.S. Army Corps of Engineers started a program of flood control projects on major rivers like the Des Moines and Iowa rivers.

These reservoirs are lake-like in their depth, increased width, and quiet water. They remain rivers in their general serpentine form and they continue to flow of course. If the dam spillway is over the top, then water is drawn along the surface of the impoundment. This changes the temperature picture of such reservoirs. Not only are temperatures sometimes strange, but the ups and downs regulating water flow also greatly change the volume and shoreline of such a lake. Silt carried by the upstream river is deposited in these lakes when the water velocity slows. The bottoms are thick with fine silt — Iowa's topsoil. Various figures have been given for silting in of these lakes, 100 years is conservative; our reservoirs will finally be silted in and relatively useless as reservoirs. They become then broad marshes with a river cutting through them.

The life of reservoirs is a lake-river hybridization. Lake fish are often stocked. The algae and planktonic crustacea are those of lakes. But rooted vegetation of lakes have a hard time growing in shallow water where depth fluctuates violently. Often, the insects and other small animals may exist in great numbers when conditions are just right. At other times they are killed off by a draw down of the lake level. A variety of life from both lakes and rivers may come and go in our reservoirs.

Water cress may fill springs, brooks, and seepage areas — food to snails, insects, or crayfish.

The Future

HUMAN IMPACT on our waters has been tragic. Our water resources are the first thing we pollute. We cut down the bottomland forests for farming; this deprives us of the protective green belt along the rivers. We straighten the meanders of long stretches to stabilize farmland but increase the downstream scouring of the channel. We dam and turn rivers into silt-laden lakes. And we dump in the river.

We dump poisons from factories; first, raw sewage, later treated sewage; from farms come agrichemicals and topsoil; from industry poisons and hot water. All of these or any of these reduces the number of kinds of life in a river or lake and reduces the capacity of the water to cleanse itself. Engineers used to claim that the "solution to pollution is dilution"; they no longer say that and attempts are being made to restore our waters. It goes slowly.

One of the primary causes of extinction in both plant and animal species is the loss of habitat. Preserving and restoring our rivers, ponds, and lakes will insure survival of the diverse varieties of life found in Iowa's waters.

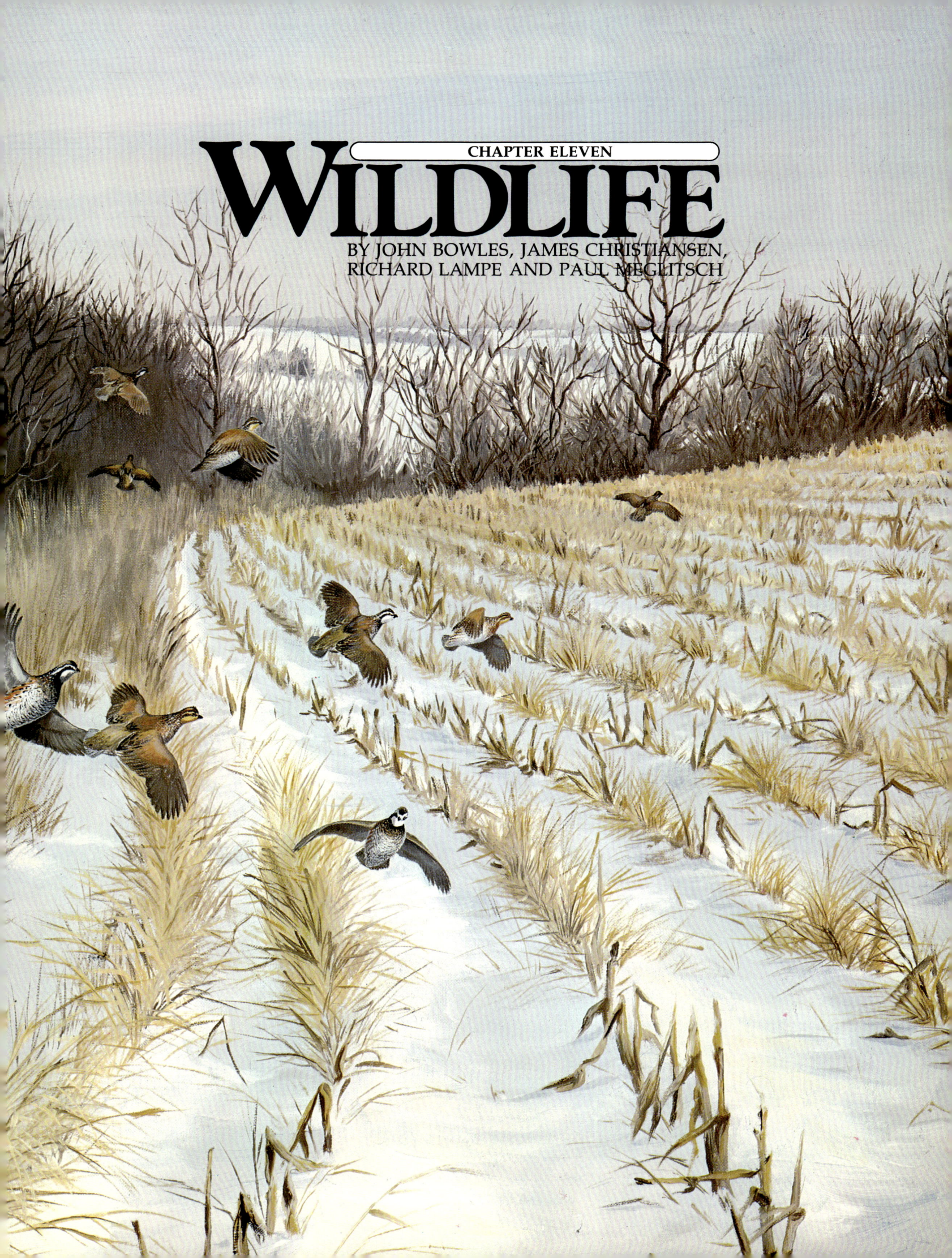

CHAPTER ELEVEN
WILDLIFE
BY JOHN BOWLES, JAMES CHRISTIANSEN, RICHARD LAMPE AND PAUL MEGLITSCH

"Deer and elk were grazing on the meadow... The woods were vocal with the music of the birds. Squirrels, quail, prairie chickens, wild turkeys, and other game were found in great abundance." (Joliet and Marquette, 1673, on the Mississippi River). Following settlement, drainage and cultivation of ponds, marshes, and sloughs drastically reduced habitat for aquatically adapted species in Iowa. Here, snow geese are seen during a stop at DeSoto Bend National Wildlife Refuge as they rest and feed. As its name implies, this is a refuge amid intense cultivation and hunting pressure.

(Previous Spread) "Quail Country," ©1973 by Maynard Reece. Courtesy of the artist and Mill Pond Press, Inc. Without adequate winter cover in the form of brushy fencerows or wooded field margins, quail are unable to survive. Other marginal areas, such as grassy roadsides, are important nesting sites. Destruction of these "wasteland" regions has a severe effect upon quail and many other wildlife populations.

Carl Kurtz

WHAT A SIGHT it must have been for the early explorers, trappers, and settlers when they saw the diverse and complex fauna in what came to be called Iowa. We shall never know exactly what it was like then, but fortunately vivid images of that land have been captured in the writings of early Europeans who traveled the waters, sought refuge in the forests, or crossed the grasslands of the interior of North America. These men, women, and children sought a new way of life in a land that contained a complex of grasslands, savannahs, deciduous forests, and wetlands.

Imagine paddling up the meandering Des Moines River through the flood plain forest and seeing thousands of passenger pigeons in the trees and wapiti (elk) and deer in the clearings. Even a fleeting glimpse of a mountain lion, a small group of bison, or a bear was possible then. Aquatic animals were abundant and easily caught or trapped in those years. Or think about driving a covered wagon across the wetlands and tall-grass prairies of northern Iowa and looking westward to see more of the same. Above you "geese, swans, ducks, pigeons and blackbirds often came in clouds" (H. A. Bennett, 1927).

Yes, the Iowa of the early settlers abounded with animals — not just game, but many species that made up the total complex of the diverse fauna. Each species was peculiarly adapted to the Iowa environment. Each was able to survive the long, cold winters and, with the warmth of spring and summer, reproduce in sufficient numbers to insure survival until the next reproductive season.

But all animals affect their environment and, in turn, are affected by it. The simple act of living constitutes an interaction between plants and animals and between animals of the same and different species. Beavers build dams, deer browse, cowbirds lay their eggs in nests of other birds, bull snakes eat rodents, and earthworms form burrows as they eat their way through the soil. These things animals did when the settlers arrived in Iowa just as they do now.

Iowa today, however, is not like Iowa then. Otter no longer live in our inland waters, pronghorns do not graze along the Big Sioux River, and swallow-tailed kites do not nest in trees along the wooded waterways of what once were vast stretches of tall-grass prairie. Changes have occurred.

As this young red fox cub explores the area surrounding the den site, such as this hollow log, or frolics with littermates, it is developing behavior required for its survival to adulthood. Although predators in general are persecuted because of their carnivorous existence, creatures such as the red fox play an important regulatory role in an ecosystem. Often they prey on the old, young or diseased, leaving the healthy.

IN EARLY SETTLEMENT DAYS, animals for fur and food were plentiful. Not only were settlers well supplied, but they in turn supplied a ravenous eastern market that took any meat and fur from the west. Thus "hundreds of farmers in North-Western Iowa became trappers, and for a year or two more money came into our section from shipments of furs than from the produce of farms" (H. A. Bennett, 1927).

Many of us know about the demise and extinction of the passenger pigeon in the past century (the last one was seen in Iowa in 1879). Few, however, know that elk herded or bunched and thus were easy prey for settlers, especially during severe snow and ice storms. In fact, most elk were killed off in Iowa by the 1860s, and the last published state record was from Lyon County in December, 1871. Deer, beaver, and otter were virtually gone by 1900 as the unrestricted onslaught continued.

Fear, justified or not, and misunderstandings often play a part in the demise of animals. Then, as now, there was paranoia about certain species and an often unreasonable desire to get rid of them. Circular wolf and rattlesnake hunts were frequent, and often smaller "varmits" were slaughtered. The last documented gray wolf record was from Butler County in "about the winter of 1884-85" (J. B. Bowles, 1975). Timber rattlesnakes now occur only locally and massasauga and prairie rattlers are nearly extinct. By 1880, black bears were gone and the last reported shooting of a mountain lion was on an island in Rush Lake, Osceola County, in about 1909.

As easy as it is to be critical of the early settlers for their unremitting slaughter of particular species, nothing has affected the total fauna more than the habitat changes resulting from cultivation. Forests were cleared, prairie sod broken and wetlands drained. Yet agriculture has provided a few species with a consistent food supply. The surge in deer population in the past two decades is in part due to thousands upon thousands of fields of corn. So agriculture has drastically altered the environment for wildlife.

Post-Glacial History of Iowa's Fauna

Carl Kurtz

Although resting in the early morning dew, this adult dragonfly will spend much of its life on the wing, often in pursuit of flying prey. The aquatic juvenile stages, called nymphs, are voracious predators. These nymphs survive the cold winters now, just as they did in Iowa thousands of years ago during times of glaciation.

IOWA TODAY is quite different than it was in the period of early settlement by Europeans. But that was only a hundred or so years ago. Vegetation is different now, but certainly the climate has not changed much in the last century.

What was Iowa like 12,500 years ago as the last glacier, the Wisconsin, receded? What animals could have survived in those totally different climatic, vegetational, and environmental conditions? We have no settlers' journals to read. Instead, we must use fossil records and meager data from archaeological digs in Iowa and adjacent states.

Many animals, however, left no record of past existence in Iowa. This is especially true of those with delicate skeletons, such as fish, amphibians, some reptiles, and the many species of insects and other invertebrates. Thus, we must study the current distributional patterns and adaptive mechanisms that allow them to live in conditions similar to those that probably followed the retreat of the Wisconsin glacier. Any such reconstruction is necessarily speculative and subject to constant revision as more data become available.

At the height of glaciation some tundra probably existed south of the ice, along with spruce, fir and other cold climate trees. Under such conditions, it is not surprising to realize that caribou, muskox, and probably even collared lemmings lived in Iowa. Cold water from the melting glacier provided stream, bog, and shallow-lake habitat for the hardiest of pioneer amphibians. Northern leopard frogs and western chorus frogs that now occupy much of Canada must have been present then. The hardy tiger salamanders likely were among the first tailed amphibians to lay their eggs in Storm Lake or Spirit Lake or other bodies of water left by glacial melt. Meanwhile, the always aquatic mudpuppy, unable to move to isolated pools was limited to the drainages of the Missouri and Mississippi rivers and thus could establish itself only in a few of Iowa's lakes.

Reptiles, too, are limited by colder conditions, so only those tolerant of low temperatures could have

The western painted turtle, a common and beautiful occupant of Iowa's marshes and streams, entered the state from the southwest almost on the heels of the receding glacier. It survived the warm, dry period that followed and became one of few reptilian species to prosper under the agricultural practices of man.

survived in Iowa then. Wood turtles probably moved from the cold streams to feed on gooseberries and blackberries. Blandings and painted turtles, as well as the common snapper, must have found their way into the mid-continent's glacial lakes. Certainly the eastern garter snake entered from the east and its newly formed western subspecies from the west, perhaps following the frogs and salamanders on which they often feed. The pencil-sized northern red-bellied snake and the beautiful smooth green snake established themselves in the forest meadows and along the edges of bogs or marshes. But not all animals were tolerant of those conditions. For example, few, if any warmth adapted lizards were present in the Iowa of 10,000 years ago.

As time passed, climate changed and so, also vegetation. Following glacial retreat, conditions were relatively warm and moist. Deciduous forest trees, such as oaks and hickories, entered Iowa from the eastern forests gradually replacing the tundra and spruce-fir vegetation. Such woodland conditions were more hospitable for animals present in eastern North America. Tree frogs, like spring peepers and gray tree frogs, must have been numerous in Iowa then, along with the American toad. Also many kinds of snakes and small mammals such as voles, fox squirrels, and white-footed mice were present. All these animals were adapted to the conditions of the deciduous forest of Iowa around 8,000 years ago.

But nowhere does climate become fixed, and Iowa became drier and, perhaps, warmer still. We know that by 6,000 to 7,000 years ago, the western grasslands had expanded into and well beyond the eastern border of Iowa in response to climatic changes. Most likely drying deciduous forests were burned by ever reoccurring fires that were so essential to maintenance of the prairies. So too, the species composition of Iowa's fauna changed. Animals suited to grasslands and more tolerant of the warm dry climate of the west entered and survived — often at the expense of the deciduous forest animals. Wes-

Gray treefrogs may not have entered Iowa until the last five or six thousand years. You will know they are here, however, if you ever walk near an Iowa marsh in late spring. Males inflate their black throats, often while clinging to vegetation overhanging the water, and release an unnerving, ear-splitting, territorial call.

The western meadowlark is more common in grasslands of western Iowa than its eastern counterpart. Interglacial environments undoubtedly isolated eastern and western populations sufficiently to allow speciation. The two species continue to remain reproductively isolated despite absence of geographical and ecological barriers.

(Above Middle)
Disappearance of the gray wolf benefited the coyote by eliminating competition. Coyotes now are widespread in Iowa and probably are more abundant than prior to settlement.

(Above)
The western slender glass lizard a snake-like resident of southern Iowa, attains lengths of more than three feet. Though lacking legs, the nature of their scales, internal skeleton, movable eye lids, and external ear openings clearly distinguish them as lizards. They have suffered more than most from agricultural expansion.

tern box turtles, prairie rattlesnakes, bull snakes, western meadowlarks, grasshopper mice, and badgers are just some of the western grassland animals that found Iowa a suitable place to live. Subsequently, conditions became more mesic (moisture balanced) although there were periodic returns to a drier climate.

When climatic conditions change, existing flora and fauna are never totally replaced. Species vary in tolerance and adaptiveness to new conditions. Thus at least some animals continue to compete effectively for food, shelter, and other necessary elements. Still others are able to survive in local refuges — small "islands" of suitable habitat within the larger inhospitable region. Some perish.

In Iowa a few northern boreal species have survived these changes. The masked shrew, southern bog lemming and meadow jumping mouse have long been a part of Iowa's fauna. Likewise, some grassland species have survived either integrated into the existing fauna or in refugia. The 13-lined ground squirrel, for example, is widespread but the plains pocket mouse, spadefoot toad, massasauga rattler, and yellow mud turtle are found only where special local conditions permit survival.

When Europeans arrived, the flora and fauna present reflected this biogeographical history, forming a complex biota of different geographical origins. Some species were widespread, and others were of more local or restricted occurrence. Still others only wandered into the state from time to time. Some of Iowa's animals are even post-settlement arrivals, being introduced to the North American continent either deliberately or by accident and many have become a part of the fauna of our state.

Because of flight, birds are able to take advantage of abundant food in north temperate and even Arctic regions, yet flee south to avoid the harsh winter. Spectacular numbers of a species may collect as they funnel into the same corridor or flyway. Here, geese are seen as they pass through Iowa on their way south. The "V-shaped" formation reduces the resistance that each bird encounters as it flies, but forces the lead bird to increase its exertion. As a result, the lead position is rotated between members of the group.

©1980 Annie Griffiths

The daytime activity, size and coloration of the bald eagle make it an easily observed species. Our excitement at viewing our national symbol certainly has ensured its survival in Iowa and elsewhere. Can our selection of species worthy of protection be based solely on such criteria?

Alex B. Thiermann

The snowy owl is an infrequent winter guest in Iowa. Its striking white plumage allows it to blend into the snow-covered winter landscape, thereby avoiding detection. A bird of northern latitudes, this owl occasionally migrates south when winter populations of its food (small mammals) are low.

Adaptations to Iowa

BUT WHY are some animals able to survive only locally, albeit in refugia, while others are more tolerant of a broader range of conditions? What are the special adaptations that allow some to survive and compete only in grasslands or forests or wetlands, while others can survive almost anywhere? In fact, how can these animals even tolerate Iowa's midcontinental climate with its cold, snowy winters and warm humid summers? And why have some animals like muskrat, starlings, corn borers, and coyotes survived the onslaught and harrassment of man while others have not? How is it possible that some species are numerous despite drastic habitat changes brought about by today's highly mechanized agriculture while others are rapidly declining? What factor or factors have contributed to the decline of barn owls — was it loss of hollow trees or disappearance of haylofts suitable for nesting? Or are other factors involved? Why have starlings increased so dramatically since they first appeared in Decatur County in 1922?

Few answers are forthcoming, because at best the totality of adaptive features — including structural, physiological, and behavioral — and the complex of environmental requirements for any species is poorly known, at best. We know, for example that hormones, often in response to seasonal or climatic factors, control sex differences and behaviors necessary for reproduction and survival. Similarly, hormones are involved with preparation for migration in certain birds. We also know that feather pigments make a brooding female inconspicuous in one habitat but visible in another. But how do these factors relate to the survival or decline of various species in the state?

Sometimes human interference can be documented and a single factor identified, such as the negative effect of DDT on the shell thickness and nesting success of some predatory birds and herons. Likewise, high water turbidity such as in the Mississippi River can be shown to adversely affect many aquatic organisms. Nevertheless, it is difficult to assign increasing turbidity of Iowa's rivers and streams to the disappearance or decline of any specific animal.

In characterizing the survival and distributional patterns of Iowa animals, we must consider the nature and distinctiveness of the climate. And perhaps nothing is more typical of Iowa than the midcontinental nature of its climate. While hot, humid, cloudless summer days are uncomfortable for humans, they are ideal for production of corn — as well as for chiggers, mosquitoes, and mayflies. Cold winters, however, are difficult times for most animals, and many are unable to cope with the low temperatures. But it is not just seasonal extremes to which animals must adjust. Temperature, precipitation, depth of frost-free ground are only some aspects of climate that vary daily and from year-to-year. Thus some years may have exceptionally mild winters and so mortality is relatively light while others may be considerably more devastating to populations.

Winter is a difficult season because food is scarce and shelter limited. Iowa's animals show three primary strategies for surviving these adverse conditions: migration, dormancy, and continued activity in a protected environment.

Migration is the most spectacular strategy, often involving flights of hundreds or thousands of miles. In our part of the world, fall migration is a shift south, and some creatures, like the northern junco, move into Iowa for the winter from more northerly breeding zones, while others, like the snow bunting and the snowy owl only appear this far south during extreme cold or food shortage. We see, in the autumn, aggregations of monarch butterflies, kettles of hawks or flocks of geese moving southward. Great changes in behavior and internal physiology are a part of migration in birds and insects, as well as bats.

Dormancy is another very widely used strategy, applicable to invertebrates as well as vertebrates. In its simplest form, dormancy results from remaining in one stage of the life cycle, a quiescent stage, until the next

White-tailed deer were hunted to extremely low numbers during the 1890s and early 1900s. From deer captured in Nebraska, Minnesota, and Wisconsin, captive herds were raised and deer reintroduced throughout the state. This effort plus establishment of a hunting season led to the present widespread occurrence of deer.

spring. Thus crickets and grasshoppers deposit eggs in the upper layers of the soil, while many species overwinter in plant tissues. Those insects with complex life cycles rest as larvae or pupae.

Dormancy poses many problems. Unable to escape, the dormant animal is exposed to predation. Thus hiding is a normal part of the preparation for dormancy in most animals, whether the mother deposits eggs in inconspicuous places or adults seek reclusion. Invertebrates may burrow in the soil or plant tissues. Mammals seek the protection of a burrow, a nest, or perhaps, a hollow limb.

Dormancy poses special problems for warm-blooded animals. While fuel must be burned to maintain body heat, there are limits to the amount of fuel that can be stored. Fat is the most compact fuel for storage so hibernators must feed actively and accumulate fat rapidly during the late summer and autumn. The rate of heat loss depends on the surface area to body weight ratio. Thus the relatively large woodchuck can move into its burrow to overwinter without arousing until spring. The smaller ground squirrels, however, must combine hibernation with other strategies; they often store food in their burrows, and when body temperatures fall too low, awaken long enough to eat some of their stores. Still smaller creatures may remain active all winter, hidden beneath the surface litter and snow. For many of these animals a layer of dried leaves and stems of winter plants beneath the snow provide shelter and food. Dormant grasses provide matting for shallow-burrowing animals. For many bird species, dead trees provide cavities for shelter and overwintering insects for food.

Deep burrowers, of course, may be little affected by the cold. The immature cicadas need make no preparations; the roots they require are all around them. Ant colonies remain active, and in some cases store considerable food against winter scarcity.

Aquatic animals especially face severe problems of survival in winter. Whereas beaver and muskrat store food and are able to remain quite active in houses or burrows, fish must seek refuge in warmer deep water, often reducing their activity. Frogs also must move to warmer conditions, burrowing into the mud of a pond or river bank.

For those animals able to survive the Iowa winter, production of young is the next important hurdle. While there probably are as many strategies as there are species, each species is adapted for precise timing of reproduction to maximize survival of offspring.

Most insects, clams, crayfish, and other animals that do not care for their young lay thousands of eggs. Conditions for hatching must be exact as untended eggs will freeze, dry out or not develop if temperatures are too high. Such developmental factors plus low survival after hatching make it necessary for a large number of eggs to be laid in order for a few to develop into breeding adults.

In the spring, what sight and sound could be more impressive than the courtship of the American toads as they gather in ponds to mate and lay their eggs. The eggs develop quickly and soon the pond is teeming with tiny black tadpoles. By early

Raccoons, such as this subadult, have expanded their range in Iowa in response to cultivation. Agricultural areas that once were prairie, now provide adequate food and shelter for raccoons. In winter, raccoons may den in hollow trees, caves, cellars, and haylofts. Alone or in groups, they sleep through the coldest time of winter.
©1980 Jim Brandenburg

The northern water snake must raise its body temperature in order to feed. Soon after the first rays of sun strike a log on the water's edge, these snakes align themselves to take maximum advantage of the radiant heat. Such gathering places provide opportunities for males to meet females where they may forget the cold water and become entangled in courtship.

June, thousands of tiny black toads hop about the land. But few survive to grow, mature, and reproduce as they are important food sources for other animals.

In spring, birds fly north, returning to their nesting grounds. Some migrants, such as the peregrine falcon and the double-crested cormorant, no longer nest in Iowa; suitable habitat is gone here. Others, like the giant Canada goose which once nested in Iowa, have been encouraged to nest again in suitable places. Great horned owls hatch their young early enough in the spring to allow adequate time for growth before the next winter sets in. And who has not been thrilled by the male cardinal singing lustily on a bright early spring day.

Richardson's ground squirrel has recently entered the northwestern corner of Iowa. It is a western species that occupies short grass habitat and therefore is slowly spreading into overgrazed pastures. Commonly called the "flicker-tail", this ground squirrel has a light brown coloration without stripes, is colonial, and forms large burrow entrances.

Alex B. Thiermann

The great horned owl is a long-time Iowa resident. Unlike most raptors, it seems to be more widespread now. This increase may be due to a lack of competition and greater availablity of hollow nest trees. It is one of the few animals that has benefited by man's activities.

(Far Left)
The yellow warbler, now a common summer resident along waterways, forest edges, and thickets in Iowa's towns, times its reproductive cycle so young will be fully grown for fall migration south. Habitat loss and increasing parasitism by brown-headed cowbirds, however, are taking their toll on this colorful, vociferous warbler.

(Left)
The eastern pipistrelle is one of the smaller insect-eating bats in Iowa. It may be found roosting in caves or forested areas in the eastern two-thirds of our state. The absence of caves in western Iowa probably limits its occurrence there.

Some birds, such as the many migrant warblers, sing loudly in the tree tops on their way north to nest in Minnesota, Michigan, and Wisconsin. The male red-wing blackbirds arrive in Iowa a week or two before the females. They can be heard in the cattails or shrubs, announcing the limits of their territories and hoping to attract females.

Intricate timing of reproduction to maximize success is achieved in an entirely different way by long-tailed weasels. After about two weeks, the development of the embryo is greatly decreased and the dormant embryo remains in the uterus. Implantation into the uterine lining does not occur until spring, about a month before birth in April or May. In little brown bats, however, mating occurs in fall and winter, and the sperm in the female reproductive tract become dormant. Fertilization does not actually occur until spring before the females have returned to their summer maternity colonies. Young are born in early summer and begin to fly by early July.

Spring and summer are times when insects which have overwintered in various stages of development emerge or are hatched. Native species, such as the rhinocerus beetle which has remained in its pupation chamber, is stimulated to develop into an adult when the weather warms up.

Farmers know well that many introduced insects have adapted to the Iowa climate. The European corn borer, for example, first introduced into Boston in 1917, quickly spread to the major corn producing states. Aided by the increase in its food supply and decline in the practice of crop rotation, the larvae of this moth have become major agricultural pests. Corn borers usually overwinter as caterpillars in the stems of the food plants, including corn. In spring, they pupate in the stem and emerge as adults 10 days later. The females lay about 2,000 eggs and the larvae then bore into the new stem or ear of corn. They have two cycles, one in spring and one in late summer.

Perhaps no emerging summer animal evokes more consternation and is less understood, however, than the chigger. The chigger is the immature stage of the tiny red harvest mite which lives underground. The young stages (chiggers) emerge in summer, often in large numbers, as any picnicker knows. They collect on moist grass and attach to the thin-skinned areas of many mammals. Here they bite into the skin with their tiny mouth parts, causing skin irritations. However, they do not burrow into the skin, so any treatment is really too late and can be useful only to alleviate itching caused by the bite.

Inevitably, summer merges into fall, the time of breeding for many animals. For deer, it is the rutting season as they must mate then to ensure birth of the fawns in spring, the season of new growth. The velvety nubbins have grown to bony antlers as the bucks prepare for the competition for does. But the breeding season is short and by early winter, the bucks have lost their antlers. All attention must now be given to winter survival.

Land Use and the Future of Iowa's Animals

THE ALTERNATING PATTERN of cold and often snowy winters and hot humid summers has occurred in Iowa for thousands of years. Inevitably, the minor variations in length and severity of the cold or periods of drought have had adverse effects on some species. Others have benefited, however. Thus the environment of Iowa in the 1800s was a dynamic one, just as it now is.

To be sure, the native North Americans hunted, cleared land for agriculture, built fish traps, and probably set some of the fires that helped maintain the prairies. With the coming of European man, however, all animals faced a new and continuing challenge — one with as great an impact as the great glaciers or the warm, dry "xerothermic" period of the past.

The decline and disappearance of species hunted or trapped for food, fur, or out of fear is easy to document. There is even some public concern now when severe seasonal weather, coupled with minimal cover causes death to game animals, such as pheasants. Likewise, there is some outcry when a bald eagle is shot or deer taken illegally with the aid of off-road vehicles and high-powered rifles. But inevitably, our life style and ever increasing population place pressure on the land and take their toll of animals through loss of habitat.

Good quantitative information on the animals of our state, especially invertebrates, is meager, at best. Nevertheless, an Iowa Academy of Science symposium in 1980 on "Perspectives on Iowa's Declining Flora and Fauna" resulted in a bleak report. Current habitat change, specifically the loss of forest and brush, is contributing to the steady decline of many species.

There is no question that private and governmental efforts to protect lands by placing them in parks and preserves is beneficial and necessary for preservation of our diverse flora and fauna. However, simply protecting small tracts of land may not be enough. Habitat fragmentation is a serious problem for species that need large areas in order to survive. Caves and other sites for over-wintering animals also need protection.

Likewise, thinning of timber, especially along streams, can cause detrimental effects on nesting of birds such as the ovenbird, scarlet tanager, and rufous-sided towhee.

Efforts to manage timber by removal of dead or dying trees takes away major summer and winter habitat for many of our forest animals. It is easy to visualize habitat loss when a ravine of trees is bulldozed, but think about the profound effects of the increased pressure to cut firewood from our state's diminishing woodlots and forests.

Inevitably, our life style and population growth dictate continued onslaught on our land, our plants and our animals.

Perhaps no Iowan stated this better than did H. A. Bennett (1927) when he said, "The interests of man and beast have rarely been compatible. Iowa in its primitive state was ideal for wild creatures, but not for civilized man. Therefore, the latter . . . has sought to adapt primitive Iowa to the service of his needs and desires. By cutting of timber, the draining of swamps, and straightening of streams, man has rendered Iowa more habitable and productive for man. Yet every step forward in the adaptation of Iowa to the better satisfaction of the wants of its people have been a step backward from the standpoint of the interests of the creatures of field, forest, and stream."

The complex of animal species found in Iowa today is, of course, not the same as it was when the Wisconsin glacier retreated, or when Europeans settled our state. One can only speculate about the future. Without concerted effort by our citizens, we face a future with fewer animals and we will be a state that has lost much of its natural heritage.

Tom C. Cooper

Game species, such as the white-tailed deer seen here, are likely to survive because we have valued their presence and protected them with sanctuaries and hunting seasons. Many other less visible species have not been so fortunate.

PART III
Man in Iowa

the north is too cold,
the west too barren,
the south too hot, and
the east too bloody.
Iowa is just right.

— Old Mesquaki Indian Saying

CHAPTER TWELVE
EARLY IOWANS

BY LARRY J. ZIMMERMAN
AND DUANE C. ANDERSON

FOR AT LEAST 12,000 YEARS the people of Iowa have faced many obstacles as they have gradually changed from the earliest hunters and gatherers to the farmers, factory workers and business executives of our present day society. Decisions (often unconscious) made by people of the past helped them to adapt to changing conditions and to survive. Details of the challenges peoples of the past faced, as well as their responses to them, are recorded sketchily in archaeological deposits in Iowa's soils, and in the case of the past few hundred years, with greater clarity in historical documents. These evidences are the subject of archaeology and are the focus of this chapter.

Ice Age Climate

Projectile point styles changed through time. Large lanceolate spear points were used by Paleo Indians prior to 7000 B.C. They were replaced by corner-notched, side-notched and stemmed forms in the Archaic and Woodland periods. The bow and arrow came into use ca. A.D. 300 as reflected by smaller projectile points found in large quantities in refuse associated with villages of the Late Prehistoric period.

When humans first entered Iowa, they came to land vastly different from the climate and topography we see today. They came to the region during the time of the last advance of the Pleistocene glaciers, the so-called Wisconsin glaciation. These peoples were descended from those who had crossed the Bering Land Bridge (Beringia) early in Wisconsin times, perhaps as early as 30,000 years ago. These people probably came to the New World from Asia at various times throughout the Wisconsin period. At this time ice sheets covered major parts of the Northern Hemisphere and, as they grew, they also locked up thousands of cubic miles of ocean water *(see Chapter 2)*. Sea level was lowered worldwide by as much as 600 feet, and many areas of land formerly covered by water were exposed.

The Bering Straits area was one such land mass exposed, and a land bridge some 1,300 miles wide was formed linking the two continents. Many species of animals, including humans, migrated across Beringia. It was ice free, although swampy, and provided an open passage to the interior of Alaska. Two ice sheets, the Cordilleran on the west and the Laurentide on the east, formed a continuous ice mass during much of the Wisconsin advance. During brief intervals of glacial retreat, however, an ice-free corridor may have appeared along the eastern flank of the Rocky Mountains, and several waves of migration may have flowed along this corridor.

When these peoples entered Iowa 12,000 years ago, they were already familiar with the Ice Age environment. At the time of their entry into our state, ice occupied northcentral Iowa (the Des Moines Lobe) and tundra extended out from the ice, where it gave way to a forest of spruce and fir. The regions near the ice were certainly cold, with temperatures nearly 11 degrees centigrade lower than modern temperatures. In July it would have been somewhere on the order of 10-12 degrees C, compared with about 24 degrees C. today. By the time Iowa had significant human populations, the final retreat of the glaciers had begun, and temperatures gradually moderated. When the Des Moines Lobe ice melted, a number of lakes and ponds were left behind. Many of these prairie potholes are still present in northcentral Iowa counties.

The ancient hunters had met the challenge of the Ice Age long before they migrated into the state. Their ancestors were hunters who stalked the large game animals that had accompanied the spread of the glaciers. In Europe and Asia, hunting cold-adapted, big game species — including mammoth, mastodon, musk ox, caribou, and bison — had become the subsistence mainstay. The first people to arrive in North America simply expanded their hunting ranges and drifted into the New World without knowing they had left the plains and tundras of Asia.

In Iowa, these Paleo-Indians left few remains, and we know little of them except by inference from sites discovered elsewhere. They are included in a complex known as the Llano Culture. In Iowa we recognize them through the large, fluted lance points — called Clovis points — they left behind at places like the Rummels-Maske Site on Hare Run in Cedar County. In other states, these points and other artifacts are found in association with the remains of large, extinct game species such as horse, camel, bison, mastodon, and particularly, mammoth. These places are usually kill sites, where the animals were dispatched, or butchering sites, where the animals were prepared for use as raw materials and food.

The second of the Paleo-Indian cultures in Iowa is part of a widespread complex known as Folsom Culture. These peoples are represented in Iowa only by a few scattered finds of their small, fluted projectile points recovered from the surface of the ground. We know little about them, except that their life was probably much like that of their Llano predecessors. In place of mammoth (extinct about 11,000 years ago), they concentrated more on a large species of now-extinct bison. Grasslands began to replace conifer forests by this time, and the uniform Ice Age environment was gradually transformed into a number of distinct regional habitats across the upper middle west.

The Plano Culture

Al Elder

THE LAST Paleo-Indian complex in Iowa is the Plano Culture. The people lived much like their Folsom predecessors. The mainstay of their subsistence was bison, but other animals including elk, deer, and smaller game were also taken. Gathering of wild plant foods probably received more emphasis as well. The Plano people continued the trend of settling into more local habitats and populations began to increase slightly. Consequently, more variety in artifact forms, especially spear points, began to appear. The characteristic fluting of the Clovis and Folsom points was abandoned, but many exhibit great skill in manufacture with long thin flakes running diagonally across the point. The best-known site for this period in Iowa is Horizon III at the Cherokee Sewer Site. There two cultural layers (dating circa 8,400 years old) were found buried over 20 feet below the modern ground surface. Each layer represented a site where bison were butchered and processed after a kill had been made nearby. In such places, bones were stripped of meat and broken for marrow. Fires were kindled for cooking and presumably warmth as the kills were probably made in late winter. Stone tools were manufactured at the site, and the presence of end scrapers indicates that hides were prepared for tanning.

Occupation of such sites was short, for it was necessary to move on when the food supply dwindled. Throughout a yearly cycle, the people occupied many different places over a fairly broad territory. Spear points in use included leaf-shaped ones reminiscent of earlier periods, as well as stemmed and notched styles that were making their appearance late in the Paleo-Indian era.

Contrary to common stereotypes, hunting and gathering peoples were not necessarily always "on the verge of starvation." Based on studies of contemporary hunting groups like the Kung San of Africa, it is believed that ancient hunters actually devoted very little time to making their daily living, probably spending only three to five hours each day working. The rest of their time was spent in leisure and other pursuits, including gossip, games, and religious activities.

Surviving in this affluent lifestyle must have had its costs. Hunting and gathering peoples must maintain low population densities and remain nomadic or they can very easily over-hunt and over-gather the resources in an area. Hunting and gathering groups rarely exceed 10 percent of the so-called carrying capacity of their environment. This usually means a population density of less than one person per square mile. To maintain such low population levels, fairly rigid controls must be placed on births through sex taboos, birth control, abortion, infanticide, and occasionally geronticide. The attitude of hunting and gathering peoples may have been that these methods are preferable to watching a child starve because overpopulation caused a decline in standard of living.

Most cultures are delicately balanced with their technological level, population, and environment. If any one factor changes, the others must also change. So it was with the Paleo-Indian peoples. Their technology remained roughly the same, but the environment changed as the glacial period ended. As the ice sheets retreated, many of the large game animals died out. Some scholars suggest that the animal's disappearance was caused by disease or failure to adjust breeding seasons, while others think that the Paleo-Indians over-killed the big-game species. Whatever the case, the environment did change and Iowa's ancient cultures had to adjust accordingly.

(Previous Spread)
MA-MA-WA-CHI'S *wickiup as it appeared on the Mesquaki Indian Settlement near Tama in 1905.*
Courtesy State Historical Society

Office of the State Archaeologist of Iowa

Excavations at the Cherokee Sewer Site in 1976 revealed four cultural horizons. The man standing above the crew is on an Archaic level dated 4350 B.C. that was buried 9 feet below the ground surface at the time the site was discovered. The crew is working on a second Archaic level dated 5450 B.C. At the lower left workers are excavating the upper of two Late Paleo Indian levels dating 7450 B.C. Each of the cultural horizons originally represented areas where bison were butchered and processed after being killed at a nearby site.

Regional Environments

WITH THE DISAPPEARANCE of Ice Age animals that were the focal point of Paleo-Indian life, people faced a climate that was generally warming, peaking by around 6,000 years ago at temperatures warmer than today's, and then moderating to resemble modern day temperatures. Vegetational patterns were much like modern ones, with prairie grass uplands and wooded river valley lowlands. Modern forms of bison fed on the grasslands, and the woodland provided a wealth of animal and plant material. Adaptation to these conditions resulted in a veritable technological explosion between 8,500 and 3,000 years ago in the Archaic Period. Abundant wild seeds and nuts provided excellent protein sources. Upper levels of the Cherokee Sewer Site and the Simonsen Site in northwestern Iowa demonstrate that hickory nuts, goosefoot, and hackberry were used. Seeds of sunflower, marsh elder, lamb's quarter and other common plants may also have been collected. Animals available included deer, elk, and small game such as rabbits and rodents. Ducks, geese, prairie chickens, and other birds were plentiful. Aquatic resources included fish, turtle, and shellfish. New technologies were required to exploit this huge variety of resources. Hunting still occupied an important place in the Archaic subsistence pattern and, in western Iowa, large, well-organized bison hunts were probably important seasonal activities.

Tom Dunstan

The most common spear points were medium sized, triangular, and notched on the corner with concave bases to aid in hafting. A hunting device known as the "atlatl" or spear-thrower was in use. It consisted of a shaft of wood perhaps two feet long fitted with a bone or antler hook at one end and finger loops or handles at the other. The end of the spear was placed on the hook, and the spear was hurled with the thrower. The effect was to lengthen the reach of the arm and thus increase both velocity and range of the spear. Sometimes weights were attached to the thrower to increase velocity. In the late Achaic Period in eastern Iowa, these weights

Drawing by Jim Buckels, based on photographs by Toby Morrow

Milling stones first appeared in Iowa at the Cherokee Sewer Site 7400 years ago. At first the handstones and grinding slabs were used to process wild seeds and plant materials. Later farming cultures used similar artifacts to process corn into flour. This example is a typical milling stone used by the Oneota people of the Late Prehistoric period.
Courtesy State Historical Society, Charles R. Keyes Collection

Bison replaced the mammoth as a major food source of our early people.

Al Elder Photos

The banded slate gorget was probably an item of personal adornment.

Ground stone tools make their first widespread appearance in the Archaic Period. The winged bannerstone left is believed to have functioned as a weight on the spear thrower or "atlatl."

Archaeologists learn about the past through experimentation. Here the spear thrower or "atlatl" is demonstrated. Note the arch in the spear in the middle drawing caused by the force exerted by the handle which serves to extend the arm. This device, in widespread use in the Archaic period, was in use for several thousand years prior to the introduction of the bow and arrow ca. A.D. 400.

often took the form of beautifully shaped artifacts called bannerstones. Archaic hunters and gatherers also used other kinds of chipped stone artifacts, including blades, scrapers, choppers, notched flakes, and drills.

One of the Archaic people's more important innovations involved production of ground-stone artifacts. Seeds and nuts had become increasingly important, and ground-stone tools were needed to process them into flour. Manos (hand stones) and metates (milling slabs) were in use by 7,200 years ago at the Cherokee Sewer Site to process the nuts or seeds. The techniques of pecking and grinding stone led to the development of a whole new class of tools, including grooved axes, hammerstones, and bannerstones that were extremely important for Archaic and later cultures across North America.

Bone utensils also became important. Some were used to butcher animals, scrape and sew hides, and probably also in the maufacturing of baskets. At the Cherokee Sewer Site, a hollow bird-bone flute was found; it is one of the earliest artifacts of its kind in the United States. A copper artifact, hammered from native copper in boulders from the Lake Superior region, has been found at the Olin Site in Jones County along with Archaic projectile points. The presence of these copper artifacts indicates that trade was increasing in importance throughout the region.

Archaeologists know more about the daily life of the Archaic people because more sites have been excavated. Sites like Soldow in Humboldt County, Hill and Lungren in Mills County, and the Cherokee Sewer in Cherokee County apparently were campsites. Each contained hearths that were the centers of activity, surrounded with utensils or tools, animal bones, and flint chips. Such sites were the focal point for food processing, as well as the manufacture of stone and bone tools important to the continued success of the group. Since the Archaic people had no pottery, they probably heated stones in their firepits to use in roasting pits or to drop into water-filled hide containers or tightly woven baskets in order to boil cooking water.

Housing Varied with Seasons

ARCHAIC PEOPLE were nomadic and followed a seasonal round of hunting and gathering activities. As certain foodstuffs became available, they moved to places where the materials were most accessible. Each group probably had a fairly well defined territory that contained the resources needed to sustain it through all four seasons. This territory was known to the group's neighbors and may have consisted of a small drainage system and a segment of a larger river unit.

While we know little of Archaic Period housing, it probably varied with the seasons. Small, impermanent structures with wood frames covered by hides or woven mats may have been built. During the more vigorous season, rock shelters were used in eastern Iowa. Some of these may have served the group as year-round base camps. While the group usually stayed within its own territory most of the year, small bands may have gotten together each season to conduct religious rituals, exchange marriage partners, socialize, and play. These gatherings probably occurred when certain foods, like hickory nuts, were plentiful or a communal hunt was to be carried out.

Because they had a very general form of subsistence and because, like the earlier Paleo-Indian people, they controlled their population, the Archaic people probably lived a relatively trouble-free and stable existence, perhaps the most idyllic in Iowa prehistory. Archaic people saw little change in the 6,000 years that their culture flourished.

Iowa Archaeological Sites

Pottery became widely distributed during the Woodland period. The Middle Woodland vessel shown above left exhibits the zoned and stamped design typical of the Hopewell Period. The horizontal designs around the neck and the vertical lines on the body were produced by pressing a cord-wrapped stick into the moist clay before firing. By Late Woodland times ceramic vessels were thinner walled and often more elaborately decorated. This lower vessel shows the impression of a fabric bag that was pressed into the moist clay before firing. Such artifacts provide detailed evidence of the weaving techniques that were in use during the Effigy Mound Period.

Al Elder
Courtesy State Historical Society, Charles R. Keyes Collection

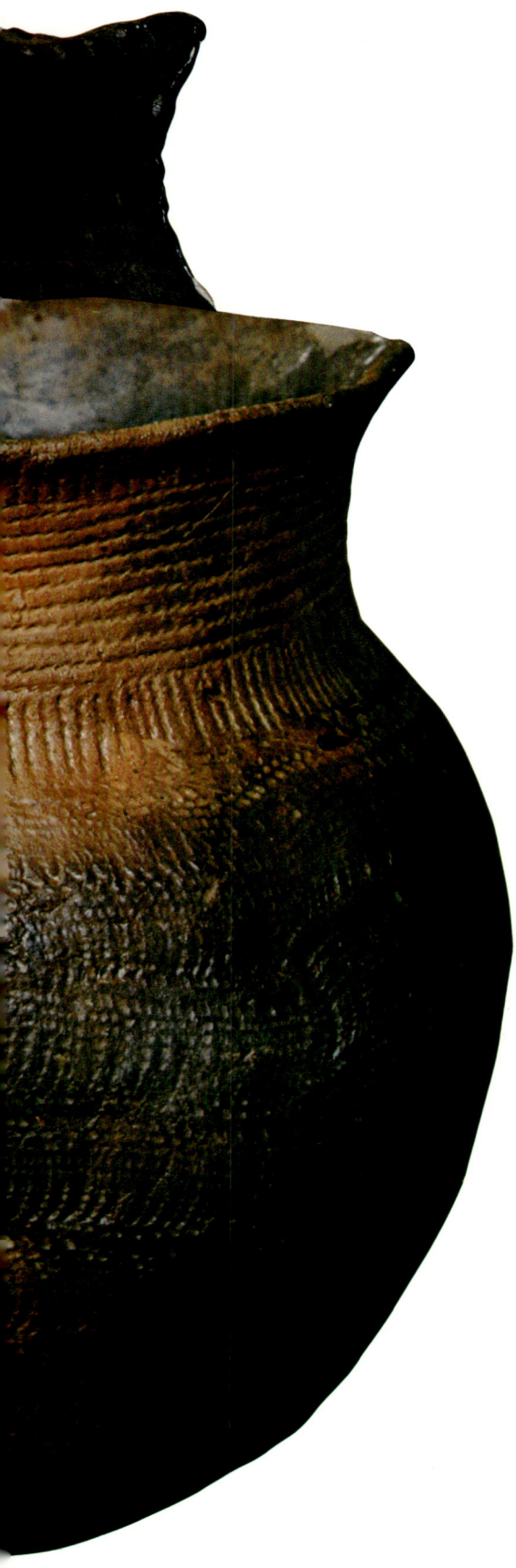

Adjusting To New Ideas

THE PALEO-INDIAN and Archaic peoples probably did little to alter the natural environment. As a result, an optimum population size was ultimately achieved, and it was probably maintained until new technological developments and religious practices developed elsewhere spread into Iowa, disrupting the stable pattern. These changes in the Archaic life-way marked the beginning of the Woodland Period around 2,500 years ago. The disruption caused by new ideas continued throughout Iowa's prehistoric period and into the historic era. Indeed, such disruption continues into the present day.

In many respects, early Woodland populations were transitional, for they lived much the same sort of life as the Archaic people before them. Hunting and gathering were the subsistence pattern; band size was probably still rather small, but growing, and artifacts made resembled those used in the Archaic. But the changes that were beginning to take place were inspired by the populations to the East and South, as well as in Mexico, where groups were expanding in size, influence, and social complexity. Their influence was felt first in our state in the form of burial grounds as exemplified by certain mounds in the Turkey River Mound Group in Clayton County. There some mounds contain burials covered with iron oxide (red ochre), so-called turkey tail points and cylindrical copper beads. While some may regard the artifacts as Archaic, mound burial is a hallmark of the Woodland tradition. Although Red Ochre people apparently did not make pottery, it was introduced shortly thereafter, marking the beginning of the Woodland Period in Iowa.

The first pottery probably imitated baskets or leather containers. Marion Thick pots, the first ceramic type in Iowa, used large amounts of grit or fiber temper mixed with clay to make forms that were thick, straight walled, with flat bottoms. Later Woodland ceramic forms were thinner walled with finer temper and cone-like in shape with incised or scratched triangular designs. On many vessels, a paddle wrapped with cord was slapped against the moist clay to thin the walls of the pot. A distinctive cord-roughened texture resulted and covered the exterior of the vessel. Occasionally, single strands of cord were pressed into the wet clay in intricate patterns. On the whole, the people gave evidence of increased skill in working with ceramics in the medium of fired clay.

Approximately 500 B.C. an elaborate woodland cultural complex called Hopewell developed in Ohio and Illinois and spread its influences into eastern Iowa and eventually out onto the Great Plains. Hopewell has been defined as a widespread Woodland burial cult that imposed itself on many local Woodland groups. While some villages such as the Smith and Wolfe sites in Iowa have been excavated, most archaeological investigation has focused on the burial mounds. The sites were composed of mounds containing burials both in and out of log tombs; some also contain cremations. With the burials are incredibly varied and often beautiful grave offerings. These include elaborately carved mica sheets from Appalachia, Great Lakes copper ornaments, Rocky Mountain obsidian, conch shells from the Gulf Coast, carved effigy pipes, and special mortuary pottery. These grave goods suggest that the individuals buried in the tombs were people of high status, perhaps like the "shaman," or holy man, and his retainers. It seems that those buried within the tombs had access to exotic goods obtained along trade routes of the so-called Hopewell Interaction Sphere. Imitations of Hopewell Cult objects appeared along trade routes and have been found as far west as Glenwood in Mills County.

The Hopewell complex in some ways represents a dramatic shift in the culture of Iowa Woodland people. First, the fact that important persons were buried in mound-covered log tombs and that these people had access to the elaborate goods acquired from the trade routes indicates that some sort of social stratification had begun. Evidently wealth — at least the exotic goods — was controlled by

One of the more spectacular groups of effigy mounds in Iowa is the Marching Bear group in the South Unit at Effigy Mounds National Monument. The bird, linears and bears were temporarily outlined with lime for the photograph.

Courtesy of Luther College in cooperation with the National Park Service. Photo by Al Zarling.

Nyla Hunt

To the visitor, burial mounds appear as subtle, but recognizable, low relief features. These are the Fish Farm Mounds north of Lansing.

a few individuals. These wealthy individuals, who perhaps controlled religious and political subsystems of Hopewell Woodland Culture, were treated with respect in death and probably in life as well. Building burial mounds is in many respects a social control mechanism. Some of the mounds are sizeable and would have required considerable effort to construct. That these respected people controlled the villagers in both death and life seems apparent.

In Iowa and parts of Minnesota, Wisconsin, and Illinois, mound building took a slightly different direction as the Hopewell complex began to decline about A.D. 500. The intensity of Hopewell influence decreased, and large villages like those of southeastern Iowa were replaced by smaller, less sedentary campsites reminiscent of the Archaic pattern. Mounds were still built for burials, but exotic items usually were absent. A smaller version of the conical form of the Hopewell mounds was built, but linear or oblong mounds also were made. Some mounds were constructed in forms shaped like animals. These "effigy mounds" included forms like birds and bears, built along the ridgelines separating river and stream drainages of the wooded and rugged driftless area of northeast Iowa. A number of these mounds may be found in our state's only national monument, north of McGregor in Clayton County. These mounds were probably made by groups of related families who gathered in times of abundance to solidify social ties as well as to renew their relationships with the environment and supernatural world. In addition to occasionally serving as burial places, the mounds may have delineated hunting and gathering territories as well as being of religious significance.

Throughout the Woodland Period, people continued to live as hunters and gatherers in a world of abundance, but they also lived in a world that was changing. Mound building, perhaps symbolic of intensifying changes in the social and technological realms, became an ongoing facet of life, a collective rite of solidarity that served to reproduce social relationships, the social order, and the universe itself. The effigy mounds in particular served as metaphors for abundant and renewable natural resources around the territories of each people.

The adjustments that began to occur in the Woodland Period were small in terms of the intensive changes to come. By the end of the period, much of the material culture had changed, and social relationships had seen some reordering. People had begun to modify their environment by building large mounds with sizeable villages nearby. Perhaps the most important modification — one that would change culture dramatically — was the growing dependence on domesticated crops by the end of the Woodland Period. The immense costs as well as the assumed benefits from raising rather than collecting foodstuffs were to cause a major restructuring of the native world.

Food Production

THE IMPACT OF CULTURES elsewhere in North America on those in Iowa was felt in the Woodland Period. The origin of pottery, the development of some species of domesticated plants, and the entire Hopewell complex came from outside our state.

Around A.D. 800, the cultures of Mexico began a huge expansion based on their use of corn, beans, and other domesticated crops. Mexican cities (like Teotihuacan) were urban centers. They sent out traders, missionaries, and colonists to other parts of Mesoamerica and North America. Cities like Cahokia, with perhaps 20,000 people, developed along the Mississippi River near the site of modern St. Louis.

These cultures influenced the Woodland people living along the drainages that eventually feed the Mississippi River. In Iowa, such influence was felt primarily along major river systems. At the headwaters of the Des Moines River in northwestern Iowa and southwestern Minnesota, a late Woodland complex felt the influence of these Mississippian pressures for change. Sometime shortly after A.D. 900, a group called the Great Oasis Culture emerged. This complex has been discovered in many areas throughout western Iowa. The people lived in villages with varying numbers of rectangular lodges. The floors of such structures were dug perhaps a foot and a half into the ground. Walls were constructed of vertical posts interwoven with sticks and plastered with mud. The roofs of the structures were grass thatching that probably formed a rounded dome. An entryway extended outward from the narrow end of the house. A central fireplace formed the focal point for family activities. The Great Oasis people used a variety of plants and animals such as deer, elk, bison, wolf, coyote, rabbit, gopher, mouse, moles, frogs, turtles, snakes, and a variety of birds. Bison, deer and elk were probably the most important items hunted. The people also grew crops consisting of corn, sunflower, and squash, and collected plants including goosefoot, pigweed, clover, hackberry, and walnut.

Stone tools of the Great Oasis people retained many Woodland characteristics, like stemmed and corner-notched points. Much of the material used for these tools must have been traded from places like the Bijou Hills in southern South Dakota and the Knife River in North Dakota. Pottery is perhaps the most distinctive product of the Great Oasis Culture. One common vessel type has high, outflaring rims with intricate triangular designs incised into them. The body of the pots was globular, very thin-walled and had cord-marking reminiscent of earlier Woodland pottery.

In the same area as the Great Oasis people, we find evidence of another group that has been labeled the Mill Creek Culture. They lived along the Big and Little Sioux rivers in northwestern Iowa, in large, rather permanent villages. While their origin is not known, they are related to both Mississippian cultures and those in the Middle Missouri River region of southeastern South Dakota. They are well-known for their extensive and well-made bone and pottery industries and for trade goods such as shell ornaments from the Gulf of Mexico, snail shell beads from the Southeast, gaming pieces called chunkey stones, and trade pottery presumed to be from the Cahokia Center near the site of modern day St. Louis.

This house model resembles houses used by the Great Oasis and Mill Creek people. While most probably had a covered entrance, other structural details are representative including thatched roof, mud plastered walls, and outside storage pits.

Courtesy Sanford Museum, Cherokee

Great Oasis villages seldom reflect long occupation. Mill Creek sites, on the other hand, often exhibit deep trash middens. Debris at the Brewster Site in Cherokee County (below) had accumulated to a depth of 6 feet.

Villagers Move Away

As many villages such as the Phipps and Brewster sites were occupied for long periods, middens (trash deposits) measuring up to nine feet deep accumulated. Most of the late Mill Creek sites were fortified, indicating that deteriorating climatic conditions around A.D. 1250 brought with them raids from neighboring groups. The difficulties they faced proved to be too much of a challenge, for they, and their Great Oasis neighbors, moved out of the state by A.D. 1300.

A similar response was also made by the earthlodge builders of southwestern Iowa, known as the Glenwood Culture. Their affinities were with central plains horticulturists, and their primary occupation in Iowa was limited to areas in the loess hills of Mills County.

These people lived in scattered hamlets, consisting of a few houses often situated on the transition between forest and prairie. Deer and small game were hunted, and principal garden crops were corn, beans, squash, and sunflowers. Clay pipes and toggle-headed harpoons represent two artifact forms unique to the Glenwood Culture. Interestingly they represent the only late prehistoric culture for which trade can be documented with a people known as the Oneota. This fact was recognized through pottery vessels found at the Kullbom Site.

The Oneota first appear in Iowa about A.D. 1000 in the archaeological record and are known for their versatility and their longevity throughout our state. They appear to be more mobile than Mill Creek, Great Oasis, and Glenwood peoples, and in some cases are suspected of conducting raids that were, at least in part, responsible for driving other groups away. In the prehistoric period, they are known for globular pots that sparkle with ground clam shell which was mixed with the clay as a strengthening agent. Other hallmarks of Oneota culture include pipestone tablets with animal designs scratched onto the surface, and fine disc and elbow pipes made of pipestone (Catlinite). The Oneota were the only people to persist into the period of recorded history, and from that time on, they became known as the Ioway and closely related Oto tribes. While the Mill Creek, Great Oasis, and Glenwood cultures had met the challenge of food production by A.D. 800-900, they apparently lost their competitive edge during the more severe climate of the Pacific episode by A.D. 1200-1300 and, under pressure from the Oneota, they moved out of Iowa.

The Mill Creek people were involved in trade with the Mississippian center called Cahokia located near present-day East St. Louis, Illinois. Trade items found on Mill Creek sites include effigy bowls, hooded water bottles, and chunkey stones. Trade ceramics often feature ground clam shell as a tempering agent as opposed to grit tempered ceramics made locally on Mill Creek sites.

Al Elder Photos
Courtesy State Historical Society

The Oneota Culture is characterized by globular shell tempered pottery with wide handles and broad trailed lines. The Oneota people are the prehistoric ancestors of a number of Siouan speaking tribes including the Ioway, Oto, Winnebago, Kansa, Missouri, Osage and others. Pots like the one shown above often have a capacity of several gallons.

Acculturation and Assimilation

The first record of the Ioway in written documents appears in 1676, when a number of tribesmen called on the French at Green Bay, Wisconsin. By 1685, they were visited in one of their villages by Nicolas Perrot who found both earthen and metal pots in use — indicating that they had already traded for objects of Euro-America manufacture. Soon metal axes and knives, glass beads, silver (Jesuit) finger rings, and muskets found their way into Ioway culture. The fur trade disrupted the aboriginal lifestyle at first, and the Ioway adjusted well by moving from one place to another over our entire state. In addition to Euro-America influence, the Ioway were receiving new traits from Plains tribes who probably introduced the horse to the Ioway before 1700. Ultimately, the Ioway included the tipi among the house types they constructed and used other Plains artifacts. In addition, they continued to cultivate gardens of corn, beans, and squash.

As Euro-America pressure on Ioway land increased, the Ioway were pressed into signing a series of treaties, ceding lands in Missouri and Iowa. In 1830, the Ioway were moved to an area in northwestern Missouri where they remained until 1836, when they were placed on the Nemaha Reservation on the Nebraska-Kansas border.

Little reference is made to disease among the Ioway in the historic period, but they, like other better-documented tribes, probably sustained heavy losses to smallpox, measles, influenza, and other diseases to which they had little or no resistance. In spite of all the difficulties, the Ioway met the chaʼlenge of acculturation and assimilation. Like adjustments made by other cultures in the face of change, the costs were high. Many Ioway people survive today, but the language, the arts and crafts, and the tribal religion exist for the most part only in books and museums.

At the same time the Ioway were involved with the fur trade in Iowa, two new groups moved in from the Great Lakes region — the Sac and Mesquaki (sometimes called the Fox).

Tom C. Cooper

Each August young and old Indians from Iowa and surrounding states gather for a four-day pow-wow on the Mesquaki Indian Settlement near Tama.

By 1735, they had established permanent villages in Iowa and Illinois along the Mississippi River. In time, areas they occupied were desirable for Euro-America settlement. In 1804, William Henry Harrison persuaded a group of Sac and Mesquaki into signing a treaty in St. Louis, giving up lands east of the Mississippi. Although the treaty was illegal and the groups remained, another treaty with the same provision was signed in 1829. This set up the well-known conflict called The Blackhawk War, in which Chief Blackhawk's people were killed by the American army.

Because of the close association between the Sac and Mesquaki, both groups were blamed for the Blackhawk War. Keokuk, a Sac, was made chief of both groups by the government because he spoke against joining Blackhawk. This caused a good deal of friction between the groups. Ultimately both groups sold all their land by the Treaty of 1842. At that point, all were expected to go to the Sac and Fox Reservation in Kansas. Unlike the Ioway and the Sac, the Mesquaki did not accept reservation life. Many never went to Kansas in the first place, even though government troops were used to round them up. From 1846-1856, many Mesquaki returned to Iowa. In 1856, the Iowa Legislature passed a law allowing the Mesquaki to remain in Iowa. In time they bought 3,200 acres of land near Tama which has become the Mesquaki Settlement of today. Now approximately 1,000 live at the settlement.

In the time since, the Mesquaki have weathered many changes, in-including smallpox, government programs, missionary activity, and boarding schools. Despite these many difficulties, they have retained much of their language, arts and crafts, customs, and beliefs. They not only met the challenge of acculturation and threat of assimilation, they have learned to cope with the age of agriculture and industrialization. They stand with the rest of Iowa's citizens, ready to meet future challenges.

Corn, squash, beans and sunflowers were the principal garden crops raised by the Late Prehistoric villagers. Many of the varieties raised by historic tribes have survived to the present day and form the basis for interesting research. The corn illustrated here is red flour corn. The box on the right contains charred corn kernels from the McKinney Oneota Site, Louisa County. Bottom row, l to r, corn, squash, beans, and sunflower.

Agriculture and Industrialization

The coming of European and other peoples to the woodlands and prairies of Iowa has been well documented by historians and represents a dramatic change of perspective toward Iowa's natural heritage. While intensive horticultural production marked the advent of Mississippian Culture (A.D. 900), intensive agricultural production marked the coming of Euro-American peoples.

Agriculture is distinguished from horticulture primarily by the use of the plow. The horticulture of the Indian villagers relied primarily on human muscle power transmitted through implements like digging sticks and hoes. Actual modification of the environment is minimal, and most garden plots were on flood plains near river courses. The plow, on the other hand, employed first the power of domesticated draft animals and, eventually, highly mechanized tractors. With the plow, Iowa's peoples were able to break the deep prairie sod and convert vast lands that had been unusable by Indian horticulturists to farmland capable of producing great surpluses. Conversion of Iowa land to agriculture included deforestation of timberlands, drainage of extensive northcentral Iowa wetlands, and many other modifications of the landscape.

Tahcoloquoit was a Sac-Fox chief who visited Washington D.C. in 1837. He was part of a larger, delegation of Sac and Fox which included 26 warriors, 4 women, and 4 children.

Making Informed Decisions

The prehistoric record of people in Iowa suggests some clear trends that have importance for us today and, more importantly, for tomorrow. As cultures adapted to Iowa's natural and social environments, they became increasingly complex. These changes brought about a progressively improved quality of life — a standard few of us today would wish to give up. As we have seen through Iowa's history and prehistory, however, our present standard of living has not come without cost. Over the millenia, we have greatly increased our population and thus our demand for natural resources. As we have modified our environment and depleted these resources, the prospect that we will reach a point where our environment cannot renew itself becomes very real. Our social and ideological systems frequently are outstripped by technological changes instituted by forces that seem outside our control, forces which seem to take little note of our aspirations or our traditions.

Iowa's prehistoric and early historic cultures provide records of peoples' attempts to come to grips with the consequences of their modes of production. Every human system contains structural contradictions; that is, parts of the system work against each other. These contradictions reveal themselves as people cope with the physical and social environments and cause stress in the system. In retrospect, many of the peoples of Iowa's past met these challenges remarkably well, and in so doing they formed new relationships among cultural and environmental features. In this way they forged new cultural self-identities in order to salvage some success, order, security, and harmony for their lifetime.

Modern science and mass communication have broadened our perspective, giving us a means to "manage by objective," meeting head on challenges such as soil erosion, water pollution, energy conservation, and overpopulation. We can learn from the past that we, too, must examine the contradictions in our own cultural systems so that our future will be successful, orderly, and secure.

Painting from *North American Indian Portraits* by James Horan. Courtesy Crown Publishers, Inc.

CHAPTER THIRTEEN
EXPLORATION & SETTLEMENT
BY LOREN N. HORTON AND DOROTHY SCHWIEDER

Courtesy Dubuque County Historical Society

Bob Coyle

Mitch Schearer

IN THE SUMMER OF 1673, French explorers Louis Joliet and Father Jacques Marquette traveled down the Mississippi River past the land that was to become the State of Iowa. They recorded their observations of lush green countryside and abundant wildlife. They particularly noted the hospitable treatment accorded them by the local natives.

Approximately 150 years later, as exploration of the region became more frequent and systematic, countless other individuals rediscovered Iowa's natural hospitality in the form of fertile land, sufficient rainfall, and a generous growing season.

The history of Iowa in the 19th century is largely the history of white immigration and settlement. Most newcomers came seeking land, and they were not disappointed. After white settlement began in 1833, word traveled fast that the Iowa region offered great agricultural opportunities. Within 35 years, settlements dotted the entire state. Those who settled here soon came to know the good life that the Native Americans had known before them. The land proved itself to be so abundantly fertile that, by 1900, Iowa had lived up to its prophecies of becoming one of the nation's most productive agricultural areas.

This log cabin, constructed at Living History Farms, is representative of the 1840 period. Many pioneers who settled in Iowa after 1833 first lived in log cabins. Traditionally seven logs high with wood shakes for a roof, most cabins measured approximately 16 by 18 feet. The primitive construction reflects the urgency with which these first structures were erected. On the first warm day of spring, all family members gladly moved outside to continue their tasks or to simply enjoy the welcomed sunshine.

(Previous Spread) "Early Settlers Crossing Mississippi River to Mines at Dubuque." Painted by John E. McBurney in 1923, this mural may be seen at the Fred W. Woodard Riverboat Museum at the Port of Dubuque.

Indians in Iowa

HISTORICAL RECORDS indicate that, before white settlement in Iowa, at least 17 different Native American groups resided here. These groups included the Potawatomi, the Winnebago, the Oto, and the Missouri. The dominant tribes, however, were the Ioway, the Sac, the Fox (Mesquaki), and the Sioux. The Ioways were one of the first major tribes to settle in the region; it is believed that they migrated from the Southwest in the 1600s. They lived in several different parts of Iowa — their last residency being in southeastern Iowa. In the 1820s, the Ioways were decisively defeated by Sac and Fox. In 1838, they sold their Iowa land and moved to a reservation in Kansas.

Both the Sac and Fox, the dominant tribes in the area, had resided originally in the Great Lakes region. Forced from there by French traders, the two tribes relocated in Illinois. In 1829, the federal government demanded their removal to Iowa to clear western Illinois for white settlement. After all Sac and Fox had been removed from Illinois in 1832, a group of about 400 Sac, led by Chief Black Hawk, returned to claim their Illinois village of Saukenauk. A three-month campaign ensued in which the Illinois militia pursued the Indians northward along the eastern side of the Mississippi River. The Indians surrendered at Bad Axe River in Wisconsin. Less than 200 of Black Hawk's followers survived the campaign known as the Black Hawk War. The federal government punished the Indians for their part in the war by taking from them a strip of land in eastern Iowa known as the Black Hawk Purchase. Following that, both Sac and Fox signed several land treaties with the federal government. They relocated in Kansas, Missouri and Oklahoma in the 1830s and 1840s.

The Santee Sioux, a small part of the Sioux nation in the Great Plains, moved into the region in the early 1700s. They lived in extreme northwestern and northern Iowa until 1851, when they relinqished their Iowa land to the federal government and relocated in Minnesota and the Dakotas.

Courtesy Dubuque County Historical Society

Iowa continues to be the home of the Fox or Mesquaki Indians. In the 1850s, Mesquaki who had relocated in Kansas expressed a desire to return to Iowa. Arrangements were made with the Iowa government for the Indians to obtain land in Tama County. The Indians collected $735 for their first land purchase. The Mesquaki then began returning from Kansas. Tribal leaders also sent out word to other Mesquaki who had not yet left Iowa to gather at the newly acquired camp. Eventually the Mesquaki bought additional land, and today their Settlement contains approximately 3,200 acres and about 1,000 members.

The French were the first white men to view the Iowa region. In summer, 1673, Joliet and Marquette, along with five companions, traveled down the Mississippi River, taking careful notes on the area's geography and making contact with local Indian tribes. The Frenchmen visited the Illini Indians, an Illinois tribe which was hunting temporarily on the Iowa side of the river in southeast Iowa. Toolesboro, a site maintained by the State Historical Society of Iowa, now commemorates their visit. The Frenchmen traveled south as far as present-day St. Louis before returning to Montreal to report their findings to the government of New France. Several years later the French explorer Sier de LaSalle claimed the Mississippi Valley for Louis XIV, the French king, and named the entire area Louisiana in his honor.

In 1762, fearful that the region might fall to England, France secretly transferred Louisiana to Spain. During its tenure, the Spanish govern-

(Left)
"Julien Dubuque and Mesquaki Chief at Mines of Spain." This mural, located at the Fred W. Woodard Riverboat Museum at the Port of Dubuque, depicts the harmonious and cooperative relationship between Dubuque and the Mesquaki in the late 1700s and early 1800s.

(Above)
Five modern day voyagers carry a birch bark canoe to their evening campsite during a re-enactment of the 1673 voyage of Frenchmen Marquette and Joliet. Re-enacted in 1973, on the 300th anniversary of the original exploration, the participants retraced the voyage of the early Frenchmen, using the same type of boats and wearing the same type of clothing as the original explorers.

ment made three large land grants in the Iowa area. The first was to Julien Dubuque, a French Canadian, who had gained permission from the Fox Indians to mine and trade in the area around what today is the city of Dubuque. Dubuque married an Indian woman, Petosa, the daughter of the Fox Chief Peosta. In 1796, the Spanish government granted Dubuque title to certain lands in the area. By the time he died in 1810, Dubuque had transferred most of his holdings to Auguste Chouteau, a St. Louis fur entrepreneur. The claim, however, later proved to be worthless.

The second grant from the Spanish government went to Louis Honore Tesson of St. Louis, who was given land in present day Lee County. In the late 1700s, Tesson obtained about 100 apple trees from Missouri and planted them on his Iowa land. Basil Giard received the third Spanish grant, this for land in Clayton County in the Marquette vicinity.

In 1803, the United States bought the Louisiana Territory from France, which had reclaimed the area three years earlier. All or part of 13 states, including Iowa, would later be carved out of the Louisiana Purchase. Also in 1803, President Thomas Jefferson commissioned Meriwether Lewis and William Clark to investigate the newly acquired area. Jefferson specifically ordered the men to travel up the Missouri River, to search for its source, and to record physical features along the way. The explorers also were instructed to make contact with local Indian tribes. The expedition caused great interest in the newly acquired territory.

The Establishment of Forts

FOLLOWING the Lewis and Clark Expedition, the federal government built a series of forts along the Mississippi River. The government's intention was twofold: to protect the area against the British in Canada and to keep white settlers out of Indian territory. In 1809, Ft. Bellevue (later renamed Ft. Madison) was built in extreme southeastern Iowa. In the next 20 years, Ft. Armstrong on Rock Island, Ft. Crawford near Prairie Du Chien, Wisconsin, and Ft. Atkinson in extreme northeastern Iowa were established. Ft. Atkinson differed from the other forts in that it was built to protect the Winnebago from neighboring Indians. The federal government had moved the Winnebago out of Wisconsin and relocated them in Iowa between lands held by the Sioux and the Sac and Fox. In the 1840s, at the confluence of the Des Moines and Raccoon rivers, the government built the second Ft. Des Moines (the first had been situated on the Mississippi River, but later was abandoned).

In the first half of the 19th century, the federal government concerned itself with negotiating land treaties with Indian tribes before relocating them in the West. Thus it followed a policy established in the late 1700s — land would be acquired from the Indians through treaty-making, thus insuring the legality of the transactions. Treaty-making marked the first step in a procedure that ultimately resulted in land being sold or granted to individual white landowners.

The first treaty concerning Indians in Iowa, the Treaty of 1804, was negotiated unscrupulously. Federal authorities visiting in St. Louis discovered the presence of five members of the Sac tribe. The Indians, in St. Louis on other matters, were approached by the authorities about signing a treaty for the sale of 51 million acres, mostly in western Illinois and northeastern Missouri. After much drinking and dining, the Indians agreed to sign the treaty, although they had no tribal authority to do so. As a result of this treaty, the Sac and Fox were eventually relocated in Iowa. The next major land treaty to affect the state came in 1832 after the Black Hawk War. In what has been called the Black Hawk Purchase, the Sac and Fox were punished for their role in the war by being forced to surrender a strip of land approximately 50 miles wide in extreme eastern Iowa.

In 1830, the federal government inaugurated the Indian Removal Policy. The purpose, it was said, was to separate Indians and whites because continued interaction would be injurious to the Indians. All Indians would be moved west of the Mississippi, the government first decreed, thus allowing whites the land east of the river. Eventually the policy was altered so that many tribes found themselves relocated even further west, beyond the Missouri River.

In the next two decades, the federal government continued to negotiate treaties with Indian tribes in Iowa. In 1837, the Sac and Fox sold a triangular-shaped area in southeastern Iowa. In 1842, they sold a huge area in southcentral and central Iowa. This land deal did not take place without considerable anguish for the Indians. The federal government approached tribal leaders in 1841 with a offer of $1 million plus sufficient money to cover Sac and Fox trading debts (totalling $350,000) to buy the tribes' last remaining lands in Iowa. The Indians declined the offer, saying it would be impossible for them to exist in the new areas. Wapello, a Fox chief, responded to the officials: ". . . This is all the country we have left, and we are so few now, we cannot conquer other countries. You now see me and all my nation. Have pity on us. We are but few and are fast melting away." One year later, the Indians sadly requested the return of the federal officials. This time they faced the inevitable. With huge debts and few resources, they agreed to the government's terms. In late 1845, following the completion of the treaty, federal troops removed the Sac and Fox from their Iowa homeland.

Few government facilities were built in early Iowa. Fort Atkinson is unique for being established to regulate the relationships of Indian groups with each other. This is a scene from the annual historic celebration held in late September at the fort in Winneshiek County.

Al Elder

The Land and the Settlers

IOWA'S LANDFORMS were shaped by glaciers and other prehistoric phenomena. These natural features — significant to geologists, botanists, and others who study them — had a profound influence upon the first European explorers and an even more dramatic impact upon the first Europeans to settle permanently on the land that became Iowa.

Lightly glaciated sections of the state often were settled later than other areas, which were more easily cleared and cultivated. Prehistoric Lake Calvin in southeastern Iowa was coveted for its fertile farmland, not because it was an interesting geological feature. The flat prairies of northcentral Iowa contained some of the richest farmland in the nation, possibly the world. High present-day land prices indicate this vividly.

The lure of mineral deposits drew Iowa's first permanent white settler to the area that became our first major urban settlement. The lead mines at Dubuque were well-known for decades before the government bought the Indian land and opened it for legal white settlement. The Black Hawk Purchase of 1832 made it legal for settlers to pour into the area west of the Mississippi River after the stroke of midnight June 1, 1833. More than 1,500 people came to the Dubuque mines area by early summer of that year. It was Iowa's version of a rush — not as huge as the California Gold Rush, to be sure, but a Lead Rush of significance to our state.

Other mineral resources later became important, but none created quite the excitement caused by the lead mines in and around Dubuque. Coal throughout the central and southcentral regions, gypsum in the northcentral area, and even iron in Allamakee County are natural resources that attracted Europeans and Americans to Iowa between 1833 and the end of the century.

Other natural features also proved important. Hardwood trees along eastern Iowa streams furnished building and fencing materials and fuel. Softwood trees from stream flood plains (called bottoms by the settlers) also were useful. Native birds and animals provided the settler with some food, but mainly with irritation. These creatures were obstacles to overcome so they would not interfere with domestic animals and fowl or with the crops. In an effective if not systematic way, many species of wild animals and birds went the way of the native inhabitants — killed or pushed out. Forests, prairie grasses, and flowers fared no better. They also interrupted the smooth flow of farming, and farmers cut down the trees and plowed up the prairie sod. When today's visitors find it hard to imagine what the land must have looked like in the 1820s, it is because Iowa settlers reacted to their environment and acted upon it. They changed and adapted some features; others they simply eliminated. The face of the landscape was never the same after immigrants finished imposing a civilized pattern upon the land. Many names recall the earlier days, the natural features, and the original inhabitants, however. Think of Poweshiek, Decorah, Pilot Knob, Prairie City, Red Oak, Skunk River, Raccoon River, Maquoketa, Lime Springs, Winnebago, Sioux Rapids, Sulphur Springs, West Branch, Long Grove, Big Rock, Linn Grove, Pilot Rock, Pilot Mound, Pilot Grove, Cedar Rapids, Waukon, Bowen's Prairie, Low Moor, Grand Mound, Muscatine, Wapello, Highland, Maple Hill, Coon Rapids, Tama, and countless others.

The Federal Land Office authorized survey of the Iowa region in the mid and late 1830s. Field notes of the first surveyors contain frequent references to the desirability of certain parcels of land for farming. The Loess Hills area, however, along the Missouri River in western Iowa, was avoided at first. Now we know that this region is very fertile and desirable. The first settlers also avoided the marshes and wetlands of the northcentral and northwest parts of the state. After they were drained, these lands became the most desirable crop land in the state. Settlers who clung to the hills and valleys of southeastern and southcentral Iowa eventually wound up with the poorest land in the state.

Tom C. Cooper

A towboat approaches the locks on the Mississippi River at Bellevue. Today barge traffic on the Mississippi represents a major form of transportation for the state of Iowa.

Rivers in eastern Iowa served as arteries of transportation. Iowa settlers were never out of touch with the civilized East; regular packet service by steamboat was available before there were any legal residents of the area. The first settlers could come in with relative ease on riverboats. Large groups could bring considerable quantities of goods and furnishings along with them. Later, when farmers began producing cash crops, a ready national market was available by shipping to St. Louis, Cincinnati, or other busy river ports.

Migration patterns of settlers from the east, even from Europe, tended to be up the Mississippi River by boat; or down the Ohio River and then up the Mississippi; or up the St. Lawrence River, through the Great Lakes and then overland from the present site of Chicago or other lake towns. Because water travel was cheap, the Erie Canal was a much more feasible route for getting to Iowa than was the National Road to Vandalia.

When settlers first moved into extreme southeastern Iowa, they stopped along rivers and streams. Settlements appeared in the 1830s all along the Mississippi River and, a decade later, settlement crept up the major river valleys — the Des Moines, the Iowa, and the Cedar. All of these were negotiated by steamboat, some a remarkable distance. These latter rivers were rarely navigable in a commercial sense, but there were many schemes of dredging, building locks, and other technological adventures. None of these materialized, however, and Iowans never fell prey to the canal craze that swept residents of states to the east. Railroad development in Iowa began in 1853, rendering canal-building unnecessary.

Early Iowa settlers experienced a transitional zone — technologically as well as geographically. Just as the swell of settlement rose in Iowa, railroads supplanted steamboats as the major carriers of goods and people. Lines stretched west from Chicago to the Mississippi. Dubuque, Lyons, Davenport, and Burlington all vied to be the state's eastern terminus of a transcontinental railroad. Railroad lines reached Iowa City and Cedar Falls before the Civil War broke out. Ten years later, Iowans claimed that no place in our state was more than 10 miles from a railroad. That boast was also a signal that natural geographical features had become less important. For instance, the state's western rivers — such as the Big Sioux, Maple, Soldier, Boyer, Nishnabotna, and Nodaway — were never significant to settlement patterns. In a small way, settlers laid out farms along their banks, but the railroad depot was a far greater lure than a river. Iowa's flat prairies allowed for easy railroad construction, and the hundreds of thousands of settlers who came to or moved through Iowa during the 19th century generally traveled by railroad. When they came by horse and wagon, their roads were often along routes originally surveyed for railroad right-of-ways. The railroads were granted more than 4 million acres of Iowa land (out of a total of 36 million), and settlers arrived by the thousands to buy it. Farmers considered railroads to be their salvation in the early years, just as they resented the economic dominance of the railroads later in the 19th century. However one considers them in Iowa history, railroads were very important.

Iowa's Ethnic Heritage

IOWA'S SETTLERS came primarily from the Northeast and the South. In 1850, the greatest number of Iowa residents had been born in the eastern states of Ohio, Indiana, Pennsylvania, New York, and Illinois, or the southern states of Kentucky, Virginia, Tennessee, Missouri, and North Carolina. Southerners dominated Iowa politics for the first two decades, and they were economically and socially powerful, too. They tended to be concentrated in Lee and Dubuque counties. Other heavy migration came from the Cincinnati area and from Pennsylvania. By 1870, southern influence was less visible because, by then, only Virginia and Missouri ranked in the top 10 states providing population for Iowa. Some later immigration came from the middle Atlantic states, but very few people came directly from the east to Iowa in the early years. Census evidence indicates a New England origin for many Iowa settlers, but there often was a lengthy stop-over in other states before they reached Iowa.

In eastern states, potential settlers could purchase maps and guidebooks on Iowa, as well as receive information from settlers newly arrived in the Hawkeye State. An example of the literature available was *Northern Iowa: Containing Hints and Information of Value to Emigrants*, published by the Dubuque and Pacific Railroad in 1858. The book proclaimed Iowa was one of the healthiest and one of the best watered states in the Union. It asserted, moreover, that Iowa had fewer criminals and paupers because of the mavelous opportunities offered by the region's physical resources.

Iowa's early population growth was quite rapid, increasing almost 350 percent between the federal censuses of 1840 and 1850, and another 250 percent between 1850 and 1860. Iowa's population almost doubled between 1860 and 1870. After that, percentage figures were not as spectacular, but actual numbers of increase remained impressive.

Increasingly, throughout the mid-1800s, Iowa attracted foreign-born people from northern and western Europe. Beginning in the 1840s,

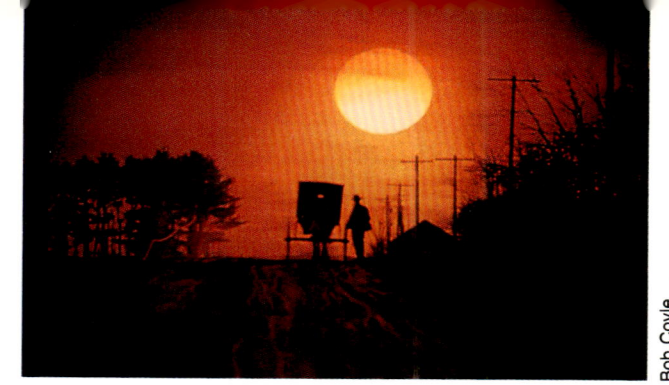

A Kalona Old Order Amishman stands by his buggy, silhouetted against the setting Sun.

Bob Coyle

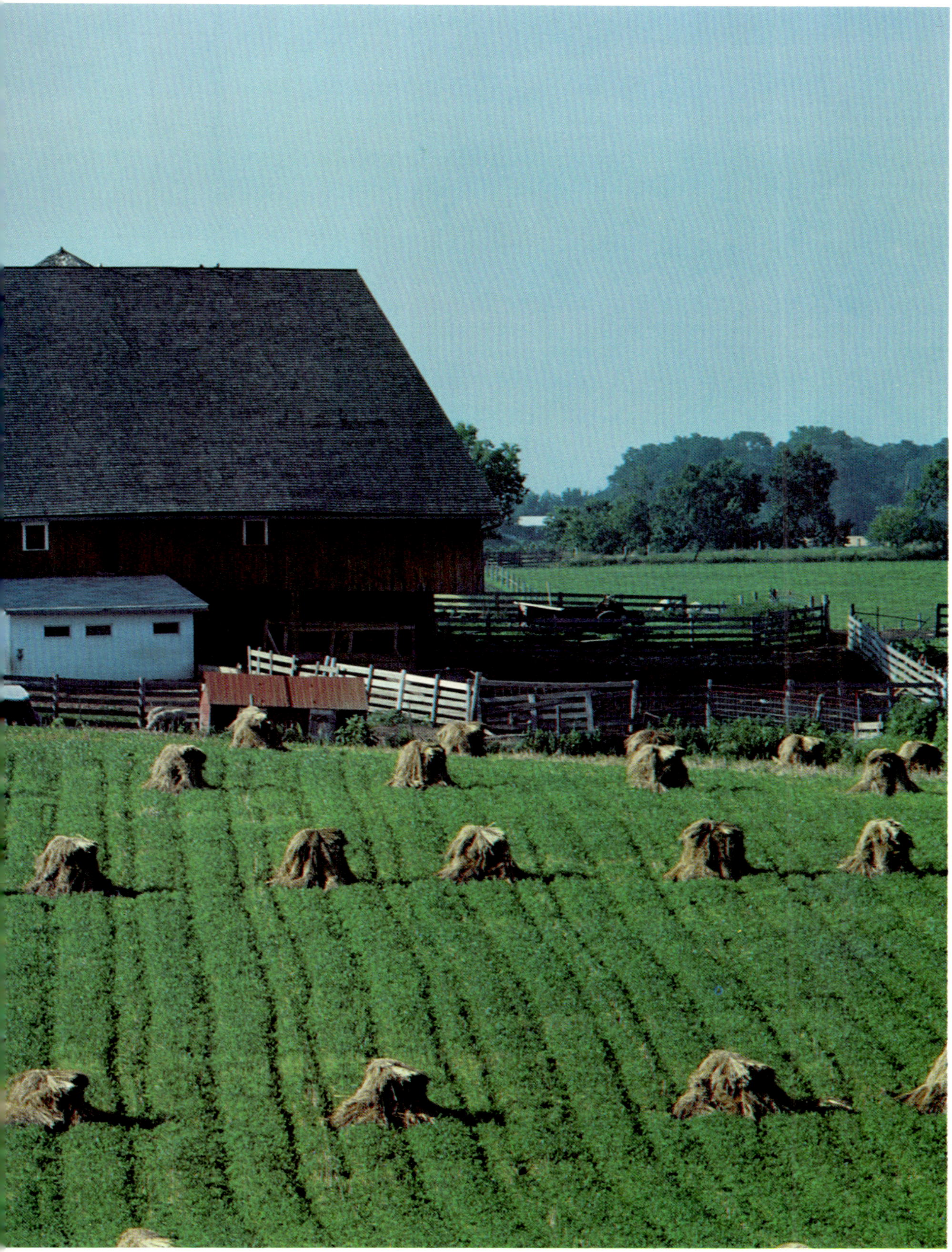

Present-day farming methods by the Amish near Kalona and other communities are reminiscent of mid-to-late 19th century. The use of horsepower was a significant factor in changing Iowa from a natural wilderness to the cultivated farmland we see today. This is a field of shocked oats north of Kalona.

Tom C. Cooper

Each year residents of Pella celebrate their Dutch heritage with a Tulip Festival. Dressed in their native garb, a mother and child view the colorful array of tulips to be seen at tulip time.

hundreds of Irish and German immigrants arrived in Dubuque, Clinton, Burlington, and Muscatine. In 1847, some 800 Dutch immigrants arrived to settle in Marion County. The tempo of foreign-born settlement accelerated in the 1850s; by 1865, immigration was in full swing. The Iowa General Assembly created a Board of Immigration in 1869 to encourage foreign immigration to Iowa, and the board soon published *Iowa: The Home for Immigrants*, providing social, economic, and geographical information about our state. The General Assembly provided for 65,000 copies to be printed in English, German, Dutch, Swedish, and Danish. By 1870, 18 percent of Iowa's residents were foreign-born. German-born settlers ranked highest, with Irish, English, and Scandinavians ranking next in importance. Generally, the foreign-born settled in northern Iowa and along the Mississippi. Immigrants from the same country tended to cluster in particular areas. Even today many Iowa communities have colorful ethnic characteristics. Among the most visible ethnic groups are Norwegians in Winneshiek and Story counties, Danes in Shelby and Audubon counties, Czechs in Tama and Linn counties, and Dutch in Sioux and Marion counties. Today you can see Danish and American flags flown side by side in the town of Kimballton in Audubon County.

While most newcomers traveled and settled in family units, Iowa also attracted several communitarian societies. In the early 1840s, Amish families from Ohio and Pennsylvania settled near Kalona in Johnson County. (Today they are known as Old Order Amish.) In the 1850s, the Community of True Inspiration settled in Iowa County. They erected seven villages and developed both agricultural pursuits and industrial operations. Known today as the Amana Colonies, the villages have retained some of their original architecture and industrial flavor. In the same decade, a small group of French Icarians moved from Nauvoo, Illinois, to Adams County. While the Amish and Amana people were religious communitarians, the Icarians em-

Norwegians at Decorah celebrate their heritage each year with a Nordic Fest. Young people in Norwegian costumes perform folk dances. Visitors have the opportunity to appreciate ethnic food and folk art.

Political Development in Iowa

POLITICAL SUBDIVISIONS in Iowa began as early as 1824, when the United States government acquired a parcel of 119,000 acres in what is now Lee County. This became known as the Half-Breed Tract, although it always had as many white squatters as it did descendants of mixed parentage. The early Spanish Land Grants of Dubuque, Tesson, and Giard did not establish a formal subdivision under American land law. After the Louisiana Purchase in 1803, Congress placed the area within the District of Louisiana. There officials assigned it to the Indiana Territory for administration purposes. From 1805 to 1812, Iowa was part of the Territory of Louisiana; from 1812 to 1820, it was part of the Territory of Missouri. Between 1820 and 1834, Iowa existed in political limbo, without territorial status, governed directly by the national government. In 1834, it was attached to the Territory of Michigan and, in 1836, to the Territory of Wisconsin. Not until 1838 was it organized as the Territory of Iowa and, in 1846, it became the 29th state. In this somewhat haphazard history of jurisdictions, officials conducted surveys and laid out subdivisions.

The first official survey was done between March 1832 and March 1833 in the Half-Breed Tract. The general survey of public lands began in the fall of 1836.

Townships are numbered from Prime Meridians and Base Lines. Each township is 36 square miles. The 36 sections within a township are numbered consecutively, beginning at the northeast corner. Section 16 was withheld from sale to support public schools. All township surveys were completed for the whole state in 1858, and all townships were subdivided into sections by 1860.

The government officially closed the Land Office Surveying District for Iowa June 30, 1866. In 1838, land offices for the sale of public lands had been established in Burlington and Dubuque. In the following years officials opened additional offices at Fairfield, Marion, Iowa City, Chariton, Fort Des Moines, Council Bluffs, Fort Dodge, Sioux City, and Decorah. The

phasized economics.

Settlers came to our state for many reasons. Farms were cheap or free. Land was fertile, generally well drained, and not so heavily forested that it was difficult to clear. Although Iowa lies in a transitional zone between the heavily forested regions to the east and the relatively treeless plains to the west, early settlers discovered sufficient resources to survive. Moreover, by the time the government opened the land, settlers had lived in the Grand Prairie area in Illinois, where they learned to break the dense root network of the prairie sod and to use mowed prairie grass for hay. Settlement proceeded rapidly in Iowa, and newcomers soon found themselves close to transportation routes and to markets. They found sufficient water power for lumber and grist mills. They discovered that the entire area had been well mapped and scouted before any permanent settlement. And they soon learned that there was relatively little danger from the Native Americans.

Survey proceeded rapidly. Sales and title deeds could be acquired quickly, cheaply, and legally. Preemption laws were regularly passed for squatters — who could be protected by claims clubs in the meantime — and veterans' bounty warrants were common. These warrants were issued as payment for military service, and they enabled former soldiers to acquire public land free. Although the warrants led to much speculation, they also led to much farm operator ownership. Because towns on the urban frontier in Iowa existed simultaneously with or before the farming hinterland, a ready need existed for food supplies and for craftsmen and professionals to provide support services.

Our state illustrates well many of the generalizations that can be made about the American frontier. Iowa was not the first to achieve territorial or statehood status west of the Mississippi River, but it was the first to be a part of normal and general migration patterns. Settlers coming here used the rivers as transportation routes. As noted earlier, steamboat packet service was well established before permanent settlement. It was easy even for large groups of settlers to arrive here with large amounts of baggage and equipment, and it was fairly easy to ship out bulk commodities for cash income. People were never out of contact with the settled areas of the east, and they were never in danger of starving. In Iowa, no one had to live out of contact with a settled area — unless he did so by choice. The political and legal institutions — modeled after those in the East — never had to be developed indigenously. Survey was by the familiar square-mile pattern, developed in the 1780s.

297

Tom C. Cooper

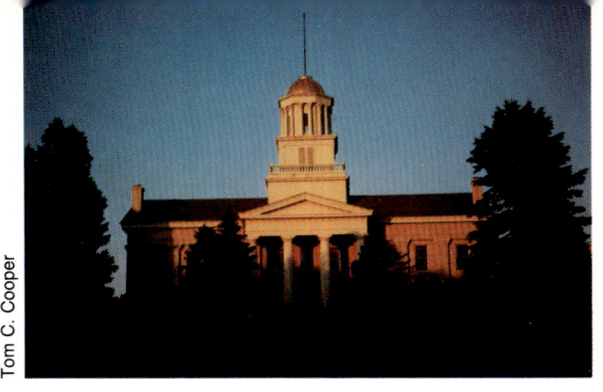

Known as "Old Capitol," this structure served as Iowa's territorial capitol and the first state capitol. Completed in 1842, the structure was designed by John Francis Rague of Springfield, Illinois. Old Capitol is located on the University of Iowa campus.

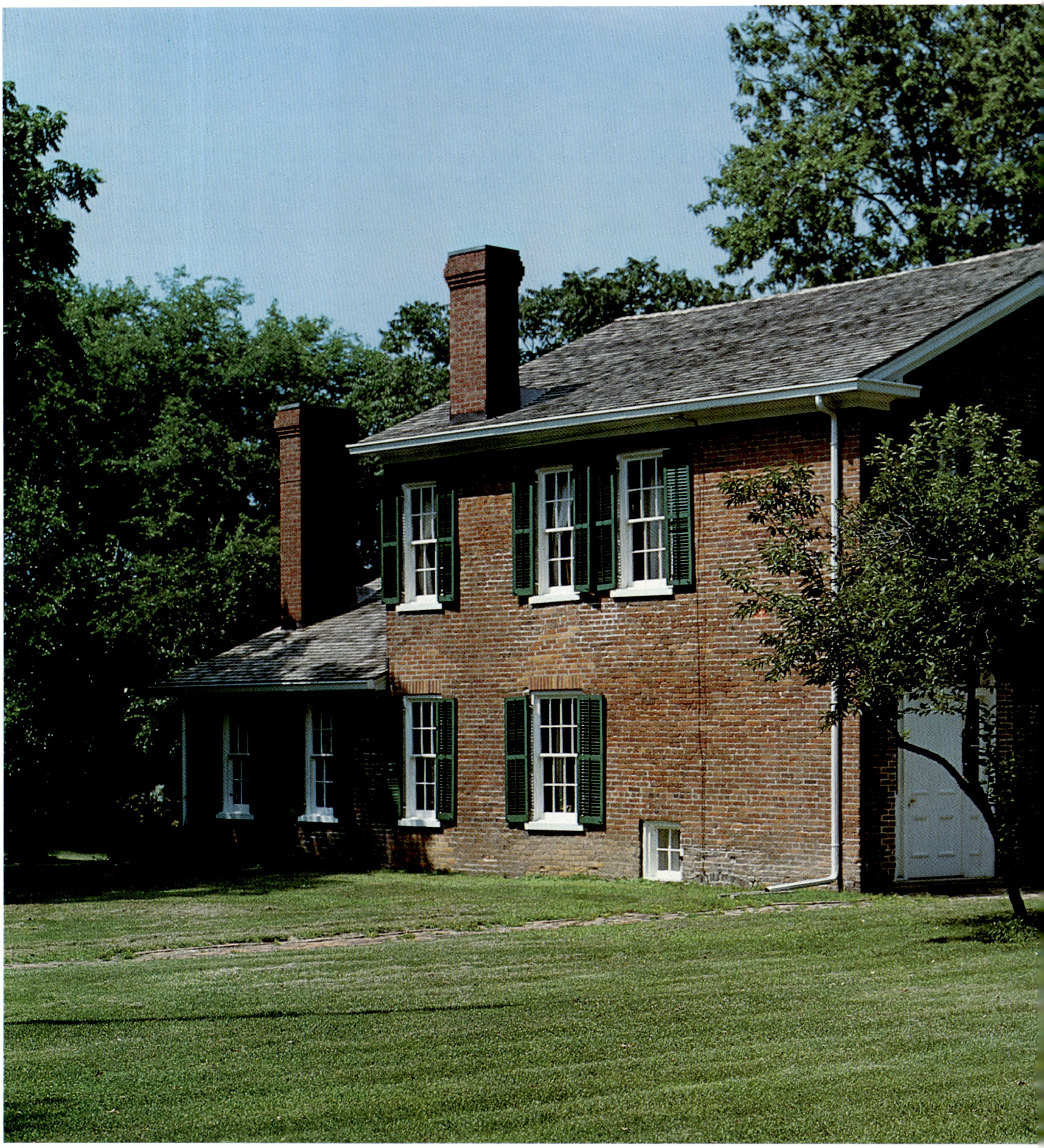

Al Elder

This is Plum Grove, in Iowa City, the home of Iowa's first territorial governor, Robert Lucas. Today the site is administered by the State of Iowa.

last land office to be opened in Iowa was at Osage in 1856. Under the Wisconsin Territory administration, officials divided the area west of the Mississippi River into two counties, Du Buque and De Moine. In 1836, De Moine County was additionally subdivided into 7 new counties and, in 1837, Du Buque County was further subdivided into 14 new counties. Later various acts created new counties, often before any settlement had been made in the area. The biggest division at any one time was in 1851, when 45 counties were created. The last county — Humboldt — was created in 1857. Boundaries and names underwent changes in the years following, but the total of 99 counties has remained the same. Some of the counties to experience name changes were: Slaughter to Washington, Fox to Calhoun, Wahkaw to Woodbury, Yell to Hamilton, Kishkekosh to Monroe, Risley to Webster, Buncombe to Lyon. The names of Cook, Bancroft, Crocker, Belknap, and Grimes were proposed from time to time, but none became permanent.

Boundary disputes, conflicts over seats of government, and various other minor problems plagued Iowa in the early territorial years. Both Belmont and Burlington served as the capital of the Wisconsin Territory, and the Territory of Iowa had designated capitals of Davenport, Burlington, and Iowa City. Davenport, however, never actually functioned in that capacity. A long and tangled dispute with Missouri over the boundary between the two states reached the courts in 1837. Litigation over the next 14 years resulted in at least four possible boundary lines. The United States Supreme Court issued a final decree in 1851 to settle the matter. When Iowa was proposed for statehood, controversy erupted over the western and northern boundaries. A compromise was reached, with the aid of Senator Stephen A. Douglas of Illinois, and the Constitution of 1846 included a description of the present boundaries when Iowa was admitted to the Union in December of that year.

Just as Iowa exemplifies many general aspects of the American frontier, our state is illustrative of many national political and economic trends. Democrats controlled the state government for the first few years, but with the national development of the Republican Party, domination passed to it. Iowa remained Republican from 1854 until 1932. In fact, the town of Crawfordsville in Washington County claims to be the birthplace of the national Republican Party. Slavery was the issue that apparently caused the shift in party alignment. A new state constitution was ratified in 1857 and, although it was not the reason for the decline of the Democratic Party influence, it marks a convenient dividing line between times of Democratic and Republican party dominance.

The Civil War (fought from 1861 to 1865) was a powerful force for change in Iowa. Our role in financing, supplying and fighting the war should not be minimized. Although there was little concentration of capital here, Iowans contributed more than $300,000 to bond sales. Our state's population reached roughly 675,000 in 1860, but Iowa still furnished almost 80,000 volunteers and draftees for 49 infantry and 9 cavalry regiments. Almost 13,000 Iowans died on active duty in the war. Although Iowa had always had tremendous potential for food production before the war, agriculture was still largely subsistent, rather than commercial. Also, transportation was inadequate for bulk agricultural commodities. Iowa managed to furnish huge amounts of food supplies for the Union armies, however, and this had a major impact on the outcome of the Civil War. At this time, commercial farming became common, and transportation networks were improved, paving the way for a great burst of transportation and communication building in the postwar years.

After the Civil War, obvious blocks of political power existed in our state. The Republican Party and its allies — such as the Grand Army of the Republic, a veterans' organization; the railroads, and perhaps the grain elevators, meat packers, and temperance forces — controlled the

*(Right)
James B. Weaver was an Iowan who ran as presidential candidate for the Greenback Party in 1880 and for the Populist Party in 1892.*

power in Iowa. While this was an era of unparalleled corruption nationally, Iowa was spared the extremes of this behavior. The railroad corporations, however, did control many office holders, and this delayed railroad regulation.

To counteract the power of corporations in both government and political parties, Iowa's farmers joined protest organizations. The first of these was the Patrons of Husbandry, known commonly as the Grange. Social, educational and charitable needs led to creation of the Grange, but the economic depression of 1873 caused the group to become politically active and to demand railroad rate regulation and cooperative buying and selling of goods.

Continued dissatisfaction over economic conditions gave rise to the Greenback Movement of the 1870s and 1880s. This was a national political movement to force currency reform to help the agricultural debtors. An Iowan, James B. Weaver, was the presidential standard bearer for the national Greenback Party in 1880. He polled few votes, and the party faded. Within a few years, the Populist Party replaced the Greenback Party. Weaver, the Populists' candidate for president in 1892, did remarkably well for a third-party candidate; he won more than a million popular votes and carried the electoral votes of five states. The Populists fused with the Democrats in 1896 and faded out of the mainstream of politics.

The Republicans were successful in keeping Democrats out of office in the decades after the Civil War, partly by use of a campaign tactic they called "waving the bloody shirt." By identifying the rival party with the Confederate states of the Civil War, the Republicans succeeded in branding the Democrats as disloyal and treasonous. No Democrat won election from Iowa to the U.S. Senate in the decades after the war. Only one Democrat was elected Governor of Iowa from 1858 until 1933; Horace Boies served from 1890 to 1894. State politics tended to be dominated by such nationally prominent Iowans as Senator William B. Allison and Senator James Harlan. Harlan, the first

Iowan to serve in a president's cabinet, was named Secretary of the Interior by Abraham Lincoln. These men replaced the prewar leaders. One of the latter, Democratic Senator George Wallace Jones, was unjustly discredited for his college friendship with Confederate President Jefferson Davis.

The Republican Party leaders remained powerful from the time of the Civil War until the end of the 19th century. Radical agrarian reform movements such as the Grange, Greenback Alliance, and Populist movements did not break their control. Not until the Progressive movement at the turn of the century were these leaders successfully challenged — this time from within their own party. Issues such as railroad reform, temperance, women's suffrage, and free coinage of silver dominated the platforms of all political parties of the time. These issues were not resolved in these decades, but they did shape the thought and ways of life of a majority of Iowans in the latter part of the century.

This is the National Cemetery at Keokuk where both Union and Confederate soldiers are buried.

(Far Left)
James Harlan was a U. S. Senator from Iowa during the Civil War. Harlan was the first Iowan to serve in a president's cabinet.

(Left)
George Wallace Jones. U. S. Senator from Iowa during the 1850s.

At Living History Farms in Des Moines, a young woman prepares a pie for the oven. The woman portrays a pioneer homemaker of the 1850s. Living History Farms presents a view of Iowa agriculture in the 1840s, and 1900 as well as presenting the farm of today and tomorrow.

Mimi Dunlap

Life on Iowa Farms

AFTER THE CIVIL WAR, Iowa agriculture underwent continual change. Our state's farmers had raised large quantities of wheat for the war, moving nationally from eighth to second place in wheat production. After the war, however, settlers moving into the Great Plains were to become the major wheat producers. Our farmers then began to listen to such prominent state agriculturists as James "Tama Jim" Wilson and Henry C. "Uncle Henry" Wallace (father of F. D. Roosevelt's vice president), men who advocated that Iowa farmers reduce their reliance on wheat and diversify their agricultural operations. Wilson served as U.S. Secretary of Agriculture under Presidents McKinley, Theodore Roosevelt, and Taft, and he urged Iowa farmers, "Raise corn always in preference to wheat. Learn how to convert corn into pork, beef, and wool by the cheapest and most economical means." The farmers responded by growing more corn and, in turn, feeding corn to hogs. In the 1870s, Iowa's farmers gained first and second places, respectively, in national corn and hog production. Our state continued to be among the nation's major producers of corn and hogs throughout the remainder of the century.

Although crop production saw changes in this period and farmers continued to buy larger and more expensive farm machinery, the farmer's daily life changed little. Work was dictated by the seasons. Farmers butchered hogs for home use in January. Cold weather was also the time to repair fences, cut firewood, and cut and store ice. In March and April, farmers prepared fields for spring planting. In June, they sheared sheep. They cut hay and harvested winter wheat and oats in July. In September, hogs were brought in from the fields to be fattened for sale in November and December. In late November, farmers began to harvest corn; many spread out the work of corn-picking and husking over several months.

In similar fashion, farm women's work changed little before the turn of the century. The four seasons clearly determined women's responsibilities. In the cold winter months, women sewed and mended; each family member's clothing was made at home. Butchering was a family task, and it was regarded as hard work. Each part of the hog was used — brains, head, liver, heart, feet, and back bones, as well as the more choice parts of the animal. If winter weather permitted, families spent more time visiting relatives and socializing. Springtime activities often began with soap-making. Kerosene had replaced candles and purchased yard goods had replaced hand-weaving, but soap-making was still done at home. Spring also marked the time to clean the chicken coop and set hens in preparation for hatching of chicks. Eggs were important to the family, both as food and as a source of in-

By the latter part of the 19th century, Iowans were solidly established on the land. They were proud of their homes, farms, and towns. Views such as this, showing Sioux City (from the 1875 Andreas Atlas*), were common methods of showing accomplishments.*

come. The general view that "egg money was grocery money" prevailed. In spring, farm women and children planted large vegetable gardens. Many families also maintained fruit trees. Farm wives also followed the traditional practice of spring housecleaning: old carpets were taken up, dirty straw was carried out, rugs were beaten on the clothesline, and floors were scrubbed. Fresh straw then went on the floors, and the women tacked the rugs back in place.

Summer and fall brought another round of responsibilities for farm women. First came endless hours of weeding the garden and putting up fruits and vegetables. Women also faced hard work in preparing for the threshers. Farmers belonged to threshing rings in which five or six farm families went together to purchase a threshing machine and then cooperated in threshing each family's grain. Threshing crews stayed at each farm for several days. Women were required to prepare a large noon meal as well as a mid-afternoon snack.

Fall was the time for making molasses and for bringing in the last of the garden produce. In 1885, a northeastern Iowa teenager, Sarah Kimball, recorded some fall activities: "Saturday lots of work to do for mother and I. We churned, made bread, dressed a chicken, made sweet pickles, made up a pail of apples into apple sauce, cleaned my bird cage, then the room and did the work upstairs and it was nearly milking time." Many farm families also made large amounts of sauerkraut. Apples and potatoes were stored for the winter. After the first frost, several varieties of nuts were gathered from nearby timber areas. Some tasks were not delegated to a particular season. Throughout the year, women helped milk cows, churn butter, and made cheese. Farm families were nearly self-sufficient in regard to food needs.

Although farm families were not shut off from neighbors, they relied heavily on their own members for social activities before 1900. Trips to town to attend social functions were limited; the family's social life revolved around the rural church and the rural school. Farm life appears to have been largely local. Farm diaries mention few state or national events, concentrating instead on local affairs. For the most part, farm families looked to their own members and to their neighbors for help in time of need.

By 1900, Iowa held an enviable position among the states. Our state's fertile soil and abundant rainfall had marked Iowa farmers as among the nation's most productive. In fact, of the state's 36 million acres, 26 million are rated Grade A.

Educational institutions had developed rapidly, and Iowans could be proud of both their public school system and their system of higher education. Iowans could boast of a few large cities like Des Moines and Cedar Rapids, but most Iowans continued to live either on farms or in small towns.

A few industries — like Quaker Oats in Cedar Rapids — and coal mining in central and southern Iowa developed in the late 1800s, but for the most part, Iowa remained unindustrialized at the turn of the century. Iowans continued to be strong proponents of Republicanism. U.S. Senator Jonathan P. Dolliver said in 1885, "Iowa will go Democratic when Hell goes Methodist." Indeed, that sentiment prevailed through 1900. For most Iowans, an abundant lifestyle stemming from a bountiful land characterized their existence in 1900.

As the 20th century matured, Iowa continued to grow. The state's contribution to the nation remained high, and our fortunes paralleled those of the nation as a whole. Iowans carried their share of the burdens of the nation's major wars — World Wars I and II, the Korean War, and Viet Nam. Our citizens suffered through the Great Depression, as did their brothers and sisters in other states.

In the last quarter of the century, our state continues to progress and prosper, but like the other 49 states, our future is wrought by new and demanding challenges.

Carl Kurtz

CHAPTER FOURTEEN

EVOLUTION of a CONSERVATION ETHIC

BY WILLIAM FURNISH

Carl Kurtz

UNTIL THEY WERE DISTURBED by Europeans, the land and its living things tended to maintain a balance. The first people to inhabit this area we now call Iowa had little impact on its resources. They existed harmoniously with other living things, taking only what they needed, and their population was regulated by what the land could support.

A description of our state by Lt. Albert M. Lea, quoted in *Sketches of Iowa and Wisconsin* by John Plumb, Jr., 1839, tells us what drew eastern immigrants to this region:

"The general appearance of the country is one of great beauty. It may be represented as one grand rolling prairie, along one side of which flows the mightiest river in the world, and through which numerous navigable streams pursue their devious way towards the ocean. In every part of this whole district, beautiful rivers and creeks are to be found, whose transparent waters are perpetually renewed by the springs from which they flow. Many of these streams are connected with lakes; and hence their supply of water is remarkable uniform throughout the seasons. All these rivers, creeks and lakes are skirted by woods, often several miles in width, affording shelter from intense cold or heat to the animals that may there take refuge from the contiguous prairies. These woods also afford the timber necessary for building houses, fences and boats . . . .

"Taking this Territory, all in all, for convenience of navigation, water, fuel and timber; for richness of soil; for beauty of appearance, and for pleasantness of climate, it surpasses any portion of the United States with which I am acquainted."

This is a view of what greeted settlers coming into Iowa in the 1800s: compass plants, nodding heads of Canada wildrye, and big bluestem grass. The photograph was taken at sunrise on a native prairie in western Marshall County.

(Previous Spread)
A sunrise silhouettes the island on Pine Lake near Eldora in Hardin County.

Conquer the Land

IOWA'S EARLY SETTLERS were agriculturists whose occupancy caused major changes in this state. Forests were cleared, swamps drained, and prairie sod broken up. In farmers' minds, virgin territory represented a wasteland to be conquered and converted into productive acreage. Wholesale slaughter of wildlife by market hunters was a major industry. Mining and farming destructively altered the state's terrain.

The first assessment of our natural resources was made in the interest of mining in the Dubuque area by David Dale Owen (1807-1860), who was commissioned by the federal government to do the survey.

Under the primitive conditions that existed in 1839, Owen's accomplishments were remarkable. Orders were not received in Indiana until mid-August, but he completed the work that year. A month was required to assemble an expedition and reach the base camp. After about 60 days of surveying, field work was ended by the approach of a fierce blizzard. Eleven thousand square miles had been examined, and a report was submitted to Congress by the following February. A map was drawn of the entire region, with an outline of areas devoid of mineral interest. Many specimens collected in the field were identified. The report was a good combination of pure and applied science. Owen predicted that a work force of thousands at Dubuque would meet a substantial part of the world's need for lead. He also found good fertility in the soils.

In 1852, Owen published the results of an additional three-year survey of the Chippewa Land District, an area about the size of New York State bordering Dubuque on the north. This account drew admiration from Europe, as well as prestigous eastern scientists. Owen had insisted upon the highest quality reproduction then available. He personally directed the printing of 8,000 copies. The work is considered a classic and was particularly significant in presenting Lyell's English classification scheme for rock layers in the Mississippi River Valley region. Thousands of mineral and fossil specimens he carefully collected and catalogued served as a nucleus of original collections at the Smithsonian Institution (they were later destroyed by fire).

After Iowa was granted statehood in 1846, the legislature on three different occasions established a geological survey to map our state in detail and to describe the natural resources. The first of these, the Hall Survey, carried out in the 1850s, resulted in the publication of two volumes.

In the following decade, the 1860s, Charles A. White resurveyed with an emphasis on the coal-bearing south-central part of the state. White's home was in Burlington, and he had broad interests as a naturalist. Through his efforts and those of his assistant, Orestes St. John, a major contribution to the knowledge of our state's resources was printed.

Another team of scientists followed as a result of White's activities. A volunteer laboratory assistant in this party was Frank Springer, then a young law student. Springer later became a lawyer and practiced in New Mexico, where he became an eminent jurist and figured prominently in obtaining statehood for that territory. Over the years, Springer devoted much of his spare time to the study of crinoids, Iowa's official state fossil.

Detail of a rock wall projecting from a limestone bluff along the Upper Iowa River in Winneshiek County, northeast Iowa.

Carl Kurtz

Collecting Crinoids

AN ASSOCIATE of Springer's was Charles Wachsmuth, described by Aldo Leopold as that "peculiar old German storekeeper given to scrambling around the Mississippi bluffs" (see Chapter 1). No Burlington resident could imagine why distinguished foreign visitors came to see Wachsmuth. Crinoids were the answer. The two men — Springer and Wachsmuth — authored a series of monographic studies impossible to equal today. Wachsmuth proved to be the scholar, and Springer participated directly on extended vacations each year. Funds from his law practice in New Mexico and astute land investments there financed the studies. Their greatest work, on certain kinds of crinoids abundant around Burlington, was published only days after Wachsmuth's death. Springer continued work in Washington and left an endowment there to preserve his collections and support research. Duplicate collections were donated to the Agassiz Museum (Museum of Comparative Zoology) at Harvard and to the University of Iowa, his alma mater.

Another avid crinoid collector, B. H. Beane (1879-1966), of Le Grand, became well known for his painstaking work. His collections can be seen in museums all over the world but the rarest and best pieces are on display at the Iowa State Historical Museum in Des Moines (see Chapter 1).

In the 1870s, a scientist appeared on the Iowa scene who displayed remarkable talents and diverse interests. W. J. McGee (1853-1912) was perhaps the first to define supply limits of critical materials, such as water and wood, and recommend control of waste. He was even accused by some of opposing development.

McGee was born into a large farm family in Dubuque County. He was a sickly child, and his formal education ended at 14. His mother, who had been a teacher, encouraged him to continue to study on his own. He mastered mathematics, Latin, and German, and went on to study law and surveying. He then completed a 12,000 square-mile survey of his home

309

area, wrote articles for newspapers and journals, and gave a speech about a forest-bed in the glacial drift to a national convention of the American Association of Scientists.

Recognition of his abilities came when he was called to Washington in 1883 to work for the Federal Survey. In 1894, he left the Survey to go to the Bureau of Ethnology and became its director in 1895. He was invited to arrange exhibits on anthropology for the Louisiana Purchase Exposition in 1903 in St. Louis and stayed on there to be the director of the Public Museum.

McGee was called back to Washington in 1907 by President Theodore Roosevelt to be assistant chairman and secretary of the Inland Waterways Commission and researcher on ground water for the Bureau of Soils.

In this position McGee became not only a philosopher on preservation of our natural resources, but also an active and successful promoter of new programs. Gifford Pinchot, an adviser to Roosevelt and director for the National Forests, believed that the use of our natural resources must be controlled and that they could most effectively be preserved under one program of management. After talking to McGee about this, Pinchot described what followed.

"McGee became the scientific brains of the new movement. With his wide general knowledge and highly original mind, we developed — as I never could have done alone — the breadth and depth of meaning which lay in the new idea. McGee had constructive imagination. It was McGee, for example, who defined the new policy as the use of the natural resources for the greatest number for the longest time. It was McGee who made me see, at long last and after much argument, that monopoly of natural resources was only less dangerous to the public welfare than their actual destruction."

Carl Kurtz

A male American goldfinch feeds his mate on their nest in a Canada thistle. The goldfinch is Iowa's official bird.

Herds of bison and elk once roamed Iowa's prairies.

Conservation Is Born

IT WAS at McGee's suggestion that President Roosevelt and Pinchot called the new movement "Conservation." Conservation became a full-fledged philosphy nationally at that time. Roosevelt, Pinchot, McGee and many others, must be credited for the birth of this principle.

McGee received many honors in his lifetime, and Cornell College awarded him a doctorate in 1901. He wrote well over 100 papers and books, of which possibly the most significant were related to an interpretation of glacial deposits in Iowa. He is remembered as having good insight about matters of national interest, as an expert on anthropology, a renowned geologist, and a leader of conservation policy. He regarded water supply as a key issue and foresaw an eventual shortage. His assessments of nonrenewable resources, fuels and minerals, can be considered realistic today — 80 years later — in most of the subjects he surveyed.

An Iowan, lawyer, and politician, Maj. John F. Lacey (1841-1913), was the first member of Congress to "make the cause of the wild birds and beasts particularly his own." The *John F. Lacey Memorial Volume*, published by the Iowa Park and Forestry Association in 1915, says:

"At first he was treated by some of his colleagues with good-natured raillery and taken every way but seriously. But, like the good soldier that he was, in more causes than one, he enlisted not for three months' service, nor one year, nor three years, but during the period of the war. From that moment down to his last day in Congress, he was never elsewhere than on the firing line."

Major Lacey visited every state in the Union and all its territories and possessions. He acquainted himself with every national wonder in the country and every Indian Reservation. He fathered and secured enactment of laws that preserved Yellowstone Park, the Petrified Forest of Arizona, Crater Lake in Oregon, Yosemite Park in California, our national forest preserves and many archeological sites.

The killing of wild game was totally unrestricted at that time, and wildlife was being slaughtered faster than it was renewing itself. Major Lacey began his fight in a effort to save the vanishing birds. In an address to the Iowa Federation of Women's Clubs at Waterloo in 1905, he said: "We have a wireless telegraph, a crownless queen, a thornless cactus, a seedless orange, and a coreless apple. Let us now have a birdless hat."

He was successful in the passage of what was named the Lacey Game Bill, December 25, 1900. Among other things, his act restricted interstate commerce of wild game, and it was commended by sportsmen and naturalists alike. He followed this with other legislation, including a Federal Bird Refuge Law in 1906, an enabling act and $15,000 by which the first national bison herd was established in Yellowstone National Park, and he was instrumental in the creation of the Wichita National Bison Range and Herd in Oklahoma. Lacey-Keosauqua State Park in Van Buren County honors him.

Another illustrious Iowan, William T. Hornaday (1854-1937), also fought nationally for wildlife and maintained connection with Iowa naturalist groups. He received his education at Iowa State Univesity, prior to becoming a taxidermist and collector for Ward's Natural Science and the U.S. National Museum. He donated a large collection of exotic birds and mammals to the Natural History Museum in Iowa City. In 1905, he helped form and became president of the American Bison Society, without which the buffalo would probably have become extinct. He wrote several influential books for conservation including *Our Vanishing Wildlife* in 1913 and *Wild Life Conservation* in

1914. Hornaday was builder and Director of the New York Zoological Park.

Many other nationally famous Iowans contributed to the conservation and study of the natural resources of the state. For example, there has been a tradition to appreciate nongame birds. The White Survey (1870) included a catalogue by J. A. Allen of birds in our state. Many outstanding scholars in natural history received their start with bird studies; McGee was one. Charles Rollin Keyes of Des Moines (*not* the Cornell archeologist) joined in preparing a collection in 1889; later he became the most prolific writer ever known in the general field of earth history. Paul Bartsch, internationally famous for his work with snails, was an ornithologist and prepared a thesis at the University of Iowa in this field (1899). Carroll Lane Fenton, best known for his study of Devonian fossils in the Rockford area and co-author with his wife of popular books on science, was a well-rounded naturalist who published on the birds of Floyd County. Ira Gabrielson was basically an expert in this same field before his career in wildlife administration. T. C. Stephens of Sioux City and Bert Bailey of Cedar Rapids were bird specialists who participated actively in the Conservation Association.

Several others are noteworthy. Rudolph Anderson published a comprehensive bird catalogue in 1906 and this was revised by Philip DuMont in 1934. The lists include 364 species, plus a possible 18 more. Various museums in the state contain important bird collections. The Natural History Museum in Iowa City is recognized as a repository in this field. The D. H. Talbot Collection of the 1880s is an important resource for information. Material from Iowa collections made by Bond, Bartsch, Anderson, and Gabrielson has been preserved there also. Similar studies in Iowa continue today. Species threatened in years of widespread DDT application appear to be recovering. The beaver, whitetail deer, and wild turkey have been restored spectacularly by restocking. Perhaps flocks of sandhill cranes will be seen and heard again.

The loess hills of western Iowa coupled with adequate rain create a green carpet of vegetation.

Larry Stone

County Surveys

The Iowa Geological Survey became active during the late 1800s and early 1900s. Its designated purpose was to analyze all natural resources, including wildlife and vegetation. In the time Samuel Calvin was director, the entire state was covered, county by county, until Iowa was considered to have the best fund of knowledge in the union. His career as a professor was equally outstanding. Calvin was to become the most distinguished member of his profession ever to be associated with the state.

The county surveys in Iowa were mostly conducted by college and university teachers, who received a few hundred dollars to work during the summers near their home. W. H. Norton of Cornell, J. A. Udden of Augustana, and several others participated. Some were not qualified by prior experience, *e.g.*, Bohumil Shimek (1861-1937) of the University of Iowa Botany Department. His assignment in the state mapping program involved Harrison and Monona counties on the Missouri River, considered then to be remote and otherwise unattractive. Characteristically though, he found matters of interest, for it was a good place to study glacial deposits and prairie flora in western Iowa. He named the Nebraskan glacial epoch in 1909, but is best known for a systematic diagnosis on how the Loess Hills were formed. Along the way it was necessary to become an authority on land snails, because these little shells were the common fossils of the loess. Shimek is generally acknowledged now as the one who demonstrated how these deposits were piled up by the wind, rather than having accumulated in water as was supposed. International recognition was received because of this research. In 1914 he was awarded a doctorate and appointment as exchange professor in Prague. He later exerted influence to see Czechoslovakia become a nation.

Shimek was one of the founders and a major contributor to the original magazine *Iowa Conservation*. Its avowed purpose was to help in the creation of state parks and, in 1917, he submitted a list of beauty spots or natural areas that could logically be considered. Shimek State Forest in Lee and Van Buren counties has been named in his honor. He was involved in forming the group called "The Association."

The Association was created in 1901 by a small group of concerned naturalists, who first called it the Iowa Park and Forestry Association. Louis H. Pammel, an Iowa State University botany professor, convened the meeting in Ames. He and Thomas H. Mac-Bride (1848-1924) of Iowa City served as secretary and president, alternating these positions. Proceedings of yearly sessions were issued by the two men with help from the State Horticultural Society. Additionally, a *Lacey Memorial Volume* was issued in 1915, after the Congressman's death. A Mississippi Valley National Park of 5,000 to 15,000 acres was visualized for the McGregor-Prairie du Chien region at the mouth of the Wisconsin River. At the 1916 meeting, a resolution specifically requested purchase of this land by the Federal Government. By 1917, the Association had shifted emphasis to a summer convention and the publication of a quarterly journal entitled *Iowa Conservation*. G. B. MacDonald, head of Forestry at ISU, was the secretary. Pammel and MacBride were still active, but the former was now chairman of the new State Conservation Board and the latter President Emeritus at the University of Iowa.

A dynamic individual, Rev. George Bennett, directed a membership drive and solicited sponsors. Also, the state park movement showed promise of final success as nine areas had been selected for acquisition. About 100 other beauty spots or natural areas were also being considered. A legislative act made this possible by authorizing the State Fish and Game Warden, together with an Executive Council (The Board), to spend funds from Fish and Game Protection. Fifty thousand dollars a year was to be available. The act further stipulated that donations could be received and necessary improvements made in the public areas. All these activities so stimulated The Association that, by 1920, the membership had reached more than 700. An outgrowth of the regular summer convention at McGregor Heights in 1919 was a "School of Wild Life." This gathering involved faculty from state institutions and other experts as the instructors. Pammel, G. F. Kay, Shimek, Stephens, and C. R. Keyes presented the first program.

In May, 1920, Backbone State Park in Delaware County was dedicated. A purchase of 1,200 acres had been authorized in 1918. Thousands attended the program, and 15 speeches were given, interspersed with musical selections. Difficulty of access made a parade impractical. Gov. W. L. Harding accepted for the State. A second dedication occurred in October, 1920, at Lacey-Keosauqua in Van Burean County. Acquisition of 1,300 acres there was aided by local support. This new park was particularly gratifying to MacBride, who had been reared nearby. In February, 1921, the State accepted 168 acres at Anamosa on the Wapsipinicon River. Twenty-one thousand dollars was raised by subscription for this purchase.

Promotion for an Iowa national park at McGregor continued. The State was represented at a Mississippi Valley Association meeting in Chicago and at a Conservation Congress of the Upper Valley States in the Twin Cities. Henry C. Wallace, new Secretary of Agriculture, was expected to exert favorable influence. Paul Bartsch, an Iowan who had become Curator of Mullusca at the Smithsonian, endorsed the park idea enthusiastically. In January, 1921, the First National Park Conference was held in Des Moines. Fully half of the states and several government agencies were represented. Although direct reference to the McGregor park proposal was withheld, a certain reluctance on the part of the federal government became apparent. Stephen H. Mather, National Park Service Director, brought greetings from Interior Secretary John Barton Payne and described several tracts newly acquired by the service. He next expressed hearty approval of local jurisdiction for park areas; almost all proposals were thought to be of local interest and better handled by such capable State Boards as that in Iowa. Meanwhile, an offer by Mrs. Martha Buell Munn to donate 150 acres of river bluff including Pike's Peak was contingent upon favorable action by the U.S. Congress. Although the period of anticipation was past, most of this area eventually became public land: Pikes Peak State Park, Point Ann, Yellow River Forest, Effigy Mounds Monument, the Federal Wildfowl Refuge, and Wisconsin's Wyalusing Park. A wildlife school at McGregor prospered for several years, and the magazine persisted until 1928, its last issues with Rev. Bennett as editor and publisher. The Association's purpose had been accomplished.

A view from Pikes Peak State Park looking toward the mouth of the Wisconsin River as it joins the Mississippi River. This area was once proposed as a national park.

Tom C. Cooper

Early morning light reddens the drying grass in this autumn scene of the reconstructed prairie display at the entrance to the Ledges State Park in Boone County.

Carl Kurtz

Resource Protection

MACBRIDE, the first president of The Association, was perhaps the most influential person in Iowa to sense the need for resource protection and in setting in motion machinery toward that end. MacBride was an original member of the Iowa Academy of Science and a moving force in its reorganization in 1887. He was a founder of a Lakeside Laboratory on West Lake Okoboji, still used by classes from Iowa's universities for study. It was his article on county parks (1895) that led to the system of state parks we have today.

MacBride, in expressing his great appreciation for Iowa's natural resources and immense fertility said:

"Here nature asks for nothing but defense — only for protection. In nature, as in social life, great things grow. We speak of parks and wildlife and summer splendor, and Iowa responds. In this interim of our advance, let us teach our people reverence for the silent power and magnificence of nature as she works incessantly for our good."

Shimek, in a memorial article, appropriately referred to MacBride as "distinctly the father of conservation in Iowa." Lake MacBride and the adjacent state park now bear the name of this early naturalist.

Pammel, who succeeded MacBride as president of the Iowa Park and Forestry Association, was the first president of the State Board of Conservation Association and twice was president of the Iowa Academy of Science. He was one of the founders of the American School of Wildlife. In his lifetime, he published more than 400 scientific articles. He was committed to the preservation of Iowa's natural areas and presented many descriptive pamphlets and other articles about them. Pammel State Park in Madison County was named for him.

Our Iowa prairies nearly slipped away without preservation and probably would have without the efforts of Ada Hayden (1884-1950). As a young girl, she was responsible for the maintenance of a small tract of prairie on her parents' farm. From this she developed an early interest in botany and conservation. She attended Iowa State University and there was influenced by Pammel. She was the fourth person to receive a doctorate in botany from Iowa State and the first woman.

Hayden found and documented more than 100 tracts of native prairie and described 32 she considered suitable for preserves. As a result of her work, four were purchased, including one in Howard County that bears her name. Her report continues to be of value in locating prairies.

Charles E. Bessie (1845-1915) had a reputation as the most influential Nineteenth Century botanist west of the Mississippi. He was at Iowa State University for 14 years. He wrote textbooks, organized classification systems, and pioneered the use of the microscope in botany.

In 1870-71, Bessie participated in Iowa's first Farm Institute at Nevada in Story County. He was Institute president for several years. Bessie initiated agricultural research at Iowa State and was influential in the development of land-grant colleges. He established Iowa State's herbarium and collected and catalogued plant specimens from across the state.

Courtesy J. N. "Ding" Darling Foundation

Ding Darling

TURN-OF-THE-CENTURY awareness of the need to preserve our natural heritage was largely led by men of the academic world. Other influential voices joined with theirs in the early 1900s, however, and one of the most vocal was that of Jay N. "Ding" Darling, a journalist. Darling came to Sioux City with his parents when he was 10 years old. He attended Beloit College, Wisconsin, but returned to Sioux City for his first newspaper job there. One of his cartoons about the local school board president resulted in his being fired. Gardner Cowles, president of the *Register and Leader* in Des Moines gave him his next job and also more freedom to express himself. By 1911, his success there brought him a job with the *New York Globe*, followed by national syndication in 1916.

A crippling of his right hand caused him to seek help from a Sioux City native in 1919 for surgery. Beloit College conferred a doctorate upon Darling in spite of difficulties during his student days there. His interest in Iowa conservation was renewed and, in 1931, he became a member of the newly constituted Iowa State Fish and Game Commission.

Cartoonists are allowed a certain license. They can indulge in humorous ridicule if a sense of propriety is maintained. "Ding" had it. His insight, combined with an artistic talent and hard work, exerted a strong influence. As a commissioner, he helped initiate a wildlife research and training program at Iowa State and personally paid a part of the costs. He knew how to get things done and established himself as a leader.

Secretary of Agriculture Henry A. Wallace asked Darling to join a committee in Washington to form a restoration program for migratory fowl. Acquisition of large refuges was recommended. After a period of skepticism and inaction, Wallace appointed Darling director of the Biological Survey to get things moving. Success was finally obtained when a $6 million appropriation was slipped through Congress in the summer of 1934. Other victories involved stricter rules on hunting: shorter seasons, reduced limits, no bait or live decoys,

Ken and Brenda Formanek

and plugs in repeating shotguns. He was also instrumental in instituting a Federal Duck Stamp Act, passed in 1934.

Outside of government, Darling was able to solicit funds from gun and powder manufacturers to train scientists in wildlife research. The National Wildlife Federation was created with Darling as first president. Many of his cartoons on conservation are still relevant today.

A friend of Darling's and a fellow Iowan, Herbert Hoover, also worked at the national level in the early 1900s to conserve natural resources. Hoover can be said to have been a leader in the field of ecology. He first recognized that oil pollution was a major threat and worked for controls when he was Secretary of Commerce. In 1921, Hoover called a conference of Fish Commissioners from the Atlantic and Gulf states. He was chairman of this first conference on Pollution of Waters. Congress never passed the strict legislation that Hoover pressed for, even after his testimony on the seriousness of oil pollution and the deplorable condition of America's streams and waterways. Hoover believed no industry should be allowed to exist unless it could prove it would not pollute. As president, he was able to act on some of his conservation interests. The government worked to develop inland waterways for navigation and flood control. The Bureau of Reclamation started to build Hoover Dam on the Colorado River. The Hoover administration added 3 million acres to national parks and monuments, and enlarged the national forests.

Aldo Leopold

Another nationally known Iowan, native born Aldo Leopold (1887-1948), began his career as an employee of the U.S. Forest Service. Leopold was born in Burlington and grew up in a home on the bluffs over-looking the Mississippi River. His interest in nature grew from watching birds following the Mississippi Flyway, hunting with his father and brothers along the river, and studying the native trees and plants that grew on the grounds of his home.

Leopold conducted game surveys for the Sporting Arms and Ammunition Manufacturers Institute. He researched environment and habitat manipulation and published a text on game management that is still used today as a major reference in this field. In 1933, he became the first full-time professor of game management in the country. *Sand County Almanac*, published soon after his death, is the best known of his writings.

The Leopold family has continued to contribute to the naturalist field. Aldo's brother, Fred, has been instrumental in providing nesting habitat for and breeding of wood ducks.

A student of Leopold's, Paul L. Errington (1902-1962), became head of the wildlife program started at Iowa State by Darling. Errington was internationally recognized for his work on population dynamics of fur and game species in North America and Northern Europe.

Each of the individuals mentioned in the preceding pages and many others contributed to the knowledge and preservation of our natural heritage. Without their dedication and work much more would have been lost.

A yellow-headed blackbird clings to a cattail.

Saving the Pieces

BY DEAN ROOSA

In his famous essays on *Round River**, Aldo Leopold said that the first premise of intelligent tinkering is: Save the pieces. In tinkering with a smoothly running watch, no one would discard even the smallest part; in tinkering with smoothly-running ecosystems, Leopold's warning is even more important. Save the parts!

In tinkering with Iowa's native ecosystems, have we saved the parts? Have we saved at least an example of each native community-type in the state?

In the past century, it was found that Iowa had a rich potential for food production, thanks to the black topsoil which formed from hundreds of years' buildup of prairie plant roots. By the turn of the century, the nearly 30,000,000 acres of Iowa's prairie was basically gone, and today only a few thousand acres remain. Forests, never abundant in Iowa, were cut over, and today only about one fourth remain. Wetlands, some 6,000,000 acres at the close of the past century, had diminished to 138,000 acres by 1955, and today only about 26,000 acres — less than one percent of the original — remain. As these losses occurred, numerous species found Iowa no longer fit for their existence — and they vanished.

As the native character of our state was rapidly being lost, a few naturalists' voices were raised in protest — thus the first call to "save the pieces."

The early efforts of T. H. MacBride, Bohumil Shimek, L. H. Pammel and Ada Hayden are detailed in the previous section. However, it was not until the era of the mid-1950s to mid-1960s that systematic attempts at saving natural areas occurred. In this period, legislation created the county conservation board system. All but one of Iowa's counties now have boards and many have professional staffs. These boards have been instrumental in preserving natural areas in many counties.

In 1965, in response to recommendations of the Governor's Advisory Committee on Outdoor Resources, the legislature created the State Preserves Advisory Board. The

Carl Kurtz

seven members, appointed by the Governor, have the responsibility of establishing a statewide system of protected areas of natural, archaeological, geological, or historical significance. Once dedicated, these areas are afforded the highest protection possible.

A brief description of selected preserves follows:

White Pine Hollow: 712-acre woodland, Dubuque County. Perhaps the most significant woodland in Iowa. Contains many rare species of plants, boreal moss communities, a relict white pine stand, and rare land snails.

Mossey Glen: 80-acre native prairie, Howard County. It is unusually rich in species; a spectacular event is the annual blooming of the shooting star, a prairie wildflower.

Hayden Prairie: 240-acre native prairie, Howard County. It is unusually rich in species; it is also known for the annual blooming of shooting star.

Kalsow Prairie: 160-acres, Pocahontas county. Probably no place in Iowa epitomizes the tall-grass prairie like this remnant.

Cayler Prairie: 160-acre prairie remnant, Dickinson County. It serves as an outdoor labortory for students from the Lakeside Laboratory, a field school of the state's universities.

Silver Lake Fen: 10 acres, Dickinson County. Waters heavily laden with carbonates and sulfates flow gently upward where they are discharged and form pools down the slopes. These pools contain unusual vascular plants and rare algae. On the wet

*©Copyright 1953, Oxford University Press, Inc.

(Left)
Sand prairies are among Iowa's most unusual communities and contain a complex of very characteristic plants. Sand lovegrass, shown here, is one such sand-loving plant.

(Below)
A remnant from an earlier climatic period, the Bluffton Fir Stand contains a large population of balsam fir and other disjunct species.

spring marl are found such unusual plants as arrow grass, bog twayblade, hooded ladies' tresses and leafy northern green orchid.

Freda Haffner Kettlehole Preserve: 100-acres, Dickinson County. This is the best example of a glacial kettlehole in Iowa. At the bottom is a soft-water marsh which contains unusual bryophytes and vascular plants; the dry rim of the kettlehole provides good habitat for soil lichens and mosses.

Turin Loess Hills Preserve: 200-acres, Monona County. The loess hills of western Iowa are a unique landform. This preserve is located in the heart of these hills in Monona County.

Gitchie Manitou: 93-acres, Lyon County. The area is noted for the ancient bedrock and some of the rarest plants in the state.

Woodman Hollow: A botanical treasure located adjacent to the Des Moines River in Webster County. This preserve contains large populations of unusual ferns.

Pilot Knob: 369-acres, Hancock County. This area contains the only sphagnum bog known to occur in Iowa.

The National Park Service regularly surveys the United States for outstanding examples of representative natural communities. In Iowa, there are five (three are state preserves). They are Cayler Prairie, Hayden Prairie, White Pine Hollow, Dewey's Pasture/Smith's Slough (these two state-owned tracts epitomize the prairie pothole complex), and Goose Lake (also known as Anderson Lake; a 140-acre pothole).

These areas represent successful efforts to preserve the variety of Iowa's habitats. Looking back to the 1800s, it appears that it would have been so easy to save substantial areas — some of them the finest examples of our state's native habitats. And in another 100 years, it may be easy to look back at our present efforts and ask, "Why, when it could have been so easy, didn't they save the pieces — these precious, irreplaceable pieces?"

As in the past, it will be the efforts of concerned groups and, ultimately of concerned individuals, that will determine if Iowa in the 1980s will accept the responsibility for "saving the pieces."

Priceless Areas

Necessary ingredients for successful rearing of young red-tailed hawks are a woodland edge, a grassy hunting area, and freedom from excessive human disturbance. Shown here in early June, these young hawks are about six weeks old and nearly ready to leave the nest.

NO PRESERVATION program is without critics. Many feel areas dedicated as preserves are "locked up," never to be used again. Others feel preservation is a tool used by those wishing to stop progress. Scientists and far-sighted planners, however, realize these areas are priceless as natural laboratories, as "benchmarks" against which to assess environmental change. We are just beginning to understand the ecological needs of sensitive nongame species; some need fairly large unbroken tracts of woodland, some need a buffer against human intrusion, some need the heavy duff which results from years of nondisturbance. But mostly, we do not understand the needs of sensitive wildlife.

Preservation of undisturbed areas are our only hope of understanding natural processes of an ecosystem and are valued for teaching and research purposes. They serve as a genetic reservoir which may be of inestimable value in the future. All of our cultivated crops and domestic animals descended from wild species. We dare not tinker too boldly without saving the pieces.

But why bother? Is there an intrinsic value in carefully setting aside these small, unique areas? The reasons, not always obvious, are many and varied. Historical and cultural perspectives can be gained from these preserved communities. These communities have developed and matured, some for over a million years. Before settlement by European man, these communities maintained a fairly stable existence with their human inhabitants. These natural communities represent the land settlers faced as pioneers in a new country. These areas are also points of reference, allowing us to see how the land has changed in the tenure of agricultural and industrial man. They serve as outdoor museum pieces: examples of communities which were much more widespread early in our history.

The most compelling reason for such preservation is for the future. Here the reasons are even more profound: these areas are essential for

Larry Stone

The pink lady's-slipper, shown here, once grew in woodlands in many parts of Iowa. Because of its beauty, people could not resist picking it. It is now one of our rarest plants, known from only three locations in northeast Iowa.

our understanding of the dynamics of different types of natural systems, especially as more sophisticated methods of community analysis are developed. Maintenance of natural diversity — the key to a healthy environment — is dependent upon protection of each native community type. Species diversity — protection of a broad array of species in a community — is important because some of these species will undoubtedly prove of great value to future societies. The unique genetic information stored and reproduced by native species may have value to future generations by aiding in the treatment of disease, by contributing to our quality of life, or by increasing the variety of food plants available to man.

Another reason for establishing fully-protected natural areas is for the protection of those species which have suffered most at the hand of man — those species we now term "endangered."

Many species have vanished from Iowa in the past 100 years. The large herbivores, the buffalo and elk, were first to go, followed by the carnivores, the black bear, gray wolf, and mountain lion. Some, like the deer, beaver, and wild turkey, nearly vanished, but have been re-established and now flourish as a result of good wildlife management. However, the declining trend continues, as evidenced by the near disappearance of the red-shouldered hawk in the early 1960s, the near loss of the spotted skunk in the past two decades, the near depletion of the least tern and peregrine falcon, and the almost total loss of the lovely pink lady's-slipper orchid.

Facing Extinction

MANY PEOPLE are concerned, but others feel it not important, saying that species become extinct naturally. This is true, but consider the following: extinction in the "natural" world occurred at a rate of about one species per 1,000 years; by 1950, this rate was a species every 10 years — now it is a species each year. Natural extinction is a process for culling the species which cannot adapt to natural changes; man has so drastically altered our planet that today's extinctions are those species which cannot adapt to man's technology.

Many of the surviving species have been forced into small refuges almost like islands in a hostile environment. Some have adapted well and thrive; others have vanished or their habitat which supplies the needs of a species; some species have narrow, specialized niches while others have broad, general niches. The latter have adapted well and thrive; the former have vanished or have become greatly reduced in number. Animals or plants which become endangered, in addition to having specialized niches and being unable to adapt, may have some of the following characteristics: they compete with humans for space or food; have low numbers of offspring and a long juvenile period; exist at the top of a food chain, are prized for their beauty or the beauty of their pelt.

We must relate the species to their environment; each species is part of an ecosystem which contains an exceedingly large number of different kinds of organisms. This diversity helps to provide stability for natural ecosystems, a balancing of nature's forces. This large number of organisms exhibit a nearly infinite range of sensitivity. A few cannot tolerate even subtle changes in their environment and, when such changes do occur, the more tolerant organisms increase in response to decreased competition. Increases in the populations of house sparrows, starlings, and certain blackbirds are easily observed examples. Each time an organism is removed, the ecosystem or community becomes less stable, less complex, and more vulnerable to disease and disorder. In this way, sensitive species may act as an "early warning system," heralding changes not yet felt by human populations. For example, our first indication that certain pesticides were disruptive to metabolic activities was from the effect on falcons and eagles. Consider the consequences if we had been obliged to wait until changes began occurring in humans.

Less obvious reasons compel our commitment to saving rare species. Each species has a unique genetic complement. Once a species is destroyed, man has no means of recreating it, despite our marvelous technology. We have no way of knowing what the future needs of many may be and this genetic resource may be of inestimable value to mankind. Many people, out of strong moral conviction, simply respect the right to existence of all living things. They feel a deep appreciation for the wild and rare treasures of nature and feel a grave sense of responsibility for the preservation of the richness of our natural heritage for future generations. Who can put a price tag on the sight of a northern harrier coursing the fields, the call of an upland sandpiper, the beauty of pink lady's-slipper, or the knowledge that Iowa yet has places wild enough to harbor prairie rattlesnakes and bobcats?

Some people take an emotional approach to saving rare species. Emotion alone, however sincere, will not save rare species. It must be coupled with research to learn the ecological parameters of each species and the translation of this knowledge into management. This management may range from leaving the species alone to propagating it in captivity. Some will defy attempts to learn their secrets easily. A few, whose problems are complex, subtle, and tied to the entire community, may never be fathomed or may have world-wide implications as in the case of the bald eagle and the DDT ban. Our goal in learning the secrets of their ecological needs is to apply this knowledge to their well-being and hopefully remove them from the "endangered species" list.

Realism must be present in an endangered species program — the realism that we cannot save everything, that we must have priorities, and that extinctions will occur in spite of our best efforts. A goal of a well-conceived endangered species program is to prevent needless, premature extinctions.

Preserving Habitats

IT IS FUTILE to speak of endangered species without centering on endangered habitats; only by protecting buffered tracts which include a rare species' habitat can we insure adequate space and long-term survival. Frequently this preserved habitat is suitable for many other native wildlife species including game and other species known to be directly beneficial to man. These areas, or parts of them, may be compatible with other uses such as hiking, photography, educational purposes, hunting, or simply as wild places for man's comfort and appreciation — a refuge for a rare and fragile species may also provide respite for city-weary mankind. This is where the private citizen can help. Only about two percent of Iowa's land is publicly owned. This is not enough to provide space for recreation and protection of rare species; it is certainly not enough land to adequately minister to the needs of future generations. Only by public support for increased appropriations for land acquisition in the next few years can we find and acquire sufficient land to provide safe habitat for our endangered co-inhabitants of earth.

Pat Duncan

Tom Dunstan

A common scene in Iowa decades ago was the dance of the greater prairie chicken. It last nested in Iowa in the early 1950s, and now is a rare sight.

The bobcat, once fairly common in our woodlands, has been pushed to the brink of disappearance. There are now only scattered reports of this predator whose preservation adds excitement to the Iowa landscape.

(Opposite)
All of the ingredients of the barn owl's habitat seem to occur in Iowa. There are sufficient numbers of abandoned barns for nesting, enough small mammals for food, and public awareness of its usefulness, yet it is one of Iowa's rarest species, with only two reported nestings in the past decade.

Iowa's Endangered and Threatened Flora and Fauna

IN 1975, the Iowa legislature passed a law providing protection for endangered and threatened species in our state. Since that time, the Iowa Conservation Commission and State Preserves Advisory Board have compiled lists of endangered species, embarked on a research program to determine how best to protect them, and acquired land to protect certain species.

Some examples of critically endangered species are —

the red-shouldered hawk, once common, now reduced to a few nesting sites along major rivers,

Iowa Pleistocene snail, known from only a few small areas in the northeast corner of Iowa,

golden saxifrage, known from perhaps only seven sites in the world and six are in Iowa,

prairie bush clover, known from only a few locations in northern Iowa, southern Minnesota and southwest Wisconsin;

monkshood, a beautiful flower found in a few sites in northeast Iowa, southeast Wisconsin and single sites in Ohio and New York,

Illinois mud turtle, occurs in a few locations in Iowa, Illinois and Missouri, with much of the population in Iowa.

Some of the preceding are examples why species become endangered — they require very narrow ecological conditions. However, there are various reasons why animals and plants come face to face with extinction — some have always occurred in low numbers and may disappear if we put added stress on them, and some, with a normally low reproductive potential, are pushed to the brink when pressure of man's existence is exerted.

We cannot afford to risk losing a species from our state or from the world. No one can say for certain that one or some of these will not be of great value to the human race in generations to come. Aside from this practical aspect, we simply should have the reverence for the life of all species and recognize their right to exist.

A list of endangered and threatened species in Iowa follows.

One of the most thrilling sights in Iowa is the migration of broad-winged hawks through our state. A few stop to nest, generally preferring a site deeper in the woodland than other hawks. This young broad-winged hawk has left the nest, but is not old enough to be self sufficient.

Northern wild monkshood is known from less than 20 places in the world, mainly in the Driftless Area of Iowa and Wisconsin.

E — Endangered
T — Threatened

Plants

- E — Purple Cliffbrake
- E — Glandular Wood Fern
- E — Marginal Shield Fern
- T — Oak Fern
- E — Limestone Oak Fern
- E — Rusty Cliff Fern
- E — Western Cliff Fern
- T — Water Horsetail
- T — Meadow Horsetail
- E — Dwarf Horsetail
- E — Woodland Horsetail
- E — Running Clubmoss
- E — Round-branched Clubmoss
- E — Crowfoot Clubmoss
- T — Shining Clubmoss
- E — Rock Clubmoss
- E — Leather Grape Fern
- E — Least Grape Fern
- E — Adder's-tongue Fern
- E — Cinnamon Fern
- E — Meadow Spike-moss
- T — Rock Spike-moss
- E — Water Willow
- T — Adoxa
- E — Eared Milkweed
- E — Wooly Milkweed
- E — Mead's Milkweed
- E — Forked Aster
- E — Water Marigold
- T — Dwarf Dandelion
- E — Spreading Goldenrod
- E — Bunchberry
- E — Sundew
- T — Persimmon
- E — Waterwort
- T — Buffalo Berry
- E — Bearberry
- E — Prince's Pine
- E — Huckleberry
- E — Shinleaf
- E — Low Sweet Blueberry
- E — Velvet-leaf Blueberry
- E — Fragrant False Indigo
- E — Rattle Vetch
- E — Prairie Bush Clover
- E — Silky Prairie Clover
- E — Twinleaf
- E — Northern Lungwort
- E — Bog Birch
- T — Spreading Yellow Cress
- T — Fragile Prickly Pear
- T — Kalm's Lobelia
- T — Twinflower
- E — James' Cristatella
- E — Field Chickweed
- E — Poverty Grass
- E — Pinweed
- T — Erect Dayflower
- T — Post Oak
- T — Fringed Gentian
- E — Rough Water Milfoil
- E — Mermaid Weed

Carl Kurtz

- E — Mare's Tail
- E — Northern St. John's Wort
- E — Blue Giant Hyssop
- T — Pagoda Plant
- E — Humped Bladderwort
- E — Flat-leaved Bladderwort
- E — Small Bladderwort
- E — Water Willow
- T — Poppy Mallow
- T — Glade Mallow
- T — Red False Mallow
- E — Meadow Beauty
- E — Bogbean
- T — Water Shield
- T — Blue Ash
- E — Golden Corydalis
- E — Pink Milkwort
- E — Fameflower
- E — Rough-seeded Fameflower
- E — Monkshood
- T — Goldenseal
- T — Waxy Meadow Rue
- T — Three-toothed Cinquefoil
- T — Canada Plum
- E — Shining Willow
- T — Bog Willow
- T — Grass of Parnassis
- T — Sullivantia
- E — Round-stemmed False Foxglove
- E — Pale False Foxglove
- E — Yellow Monkey Flower
- E — Winged Monkey Flower
- E — American Brookline
- E — Kitten-tails
- E — Valerian
- E — Green Violet
- E — Summer Grape
- T — Winter Grape
- E — Clustered Sedge
- E — Crawford's Sedge
- E — Slender Sedge
- E — Intermediate Sedge
- E — Rocky Mountain Sedge
- E — Deep Green Sedge
- E — Purple Spike-Rush
- E — Dwarf Spike-Rush
- E — Tall Cotton-Grass
- E — Slender Cotton Grass
- E — Slender Fimbristylis
- T — Baked Rush
- E — Prairie Bulrush
- E — Tapegrass
- E — Alpine Rush
- E — Green's Rush
- T — Arrow Grass
- E — Nodding Wild Onion
- T — Rosy Twisted Stalk
- T — Bunchflower
- T — Putty-root
- T — Small White Lady's-Slipper
- E — Pink Lady's-Slipper
- E — Pale Green Orchid
- T — Round-leaved Orchid
- E — Green Orchid
- E — Prairie-fringed Orchid
- E — Hooded Ladies Tresses
- E — Buffalo Grass
- E — Rice Grass
- E — Slim-leaved Panicum
- E — Weak Bluegrass
- E — Tumble Grass
- E — Spear Grass
- T — Wild Rice
- E — Mud Plantain
- T — Large-leaved Pondweed
- T — White-stemmed Pondweed
- T — Vasey's Pondweed

Amphibians and Reptiles

- T — Stinkpot
- E — Illinois Mud Turtle
- E — Wood Turtle
- T — Ornate Box Turtle
- T — Red-eared Turtle
- T — Blanding's Turtle
- E — Five-lined Skink
- E — Great Plains Skink
- E — Western Slender Glass Lizard
- T — Diamondback Water Snake
- T — Yellow-bellied Water Snake
- T — Graham's Water Snake
- T — Western Earth Snake
- E — Black Rat Snake
- E — Speckled Kingsnake
- E — Northern Copperhead
- E — Prairie Rattlesnake
- T — Massasauga Rattlesnake
- T — Small-mouthed Salamander
- E — Blue-spotted Salamander
- E — Central Newt
- T — Plains Spadefoot
- T — Spring Peeper

Birds

- T — Eared Grebe
- T — Cooper's Hawk
- E — Red-shouldered Hawk
- T — Broad-winged Hawk
- E — Bald Eagle
- E — Northern Harrier
- E — Peregrine Falcon
- E — Upland Sandpiper
- E — Least Tern
- E — Piping Plover
- E — Black-billed Cuckoo
- E — Barn Owl
- E — Burrowing Owl
- T — Long-eared Owl
- T — Say's Phoebe
- T — Loggerhead Shrike
- T — Blue-winged Warbler

Fish

- T — Chestnut Lamprey
- T — American Brook Lamprey
- E — Lake Sturgeon
- E — Pallid Sturgeon
- T — Skipjack Herring
- E — Grass Pickerel
- E — Sicklefin Chub
- T — Lake Chub
- T — Gravel Chub
- T — Pugnose Shiner
- E — Blacknose Shiner
- T — Weed Shiner
- E — Silverband Shiner
- T — Topeka Shiner
- E — Pearl Dace
- E — Black Redhorse
- E — Starhead Topminnow
- E — Plains Topminnow
- E — Longear Sunfish
- T — Western Sand Darter
- T — Mud Darter
- T — Bluntnose Darter
- E — Least Darter
- E — Orangethroat Darter

Mammals

- T — Keene's Myotis
- E — Indiana Bat
- T — Evening Bat
- E — Plains Pocket Mouse
- E — Grasshopper Mouse
- E — Red-backed Vole
- E — Pine Vole
- E — Black Bear
- T — River Otter
- E — Bobcat

Iowa Tomorrow

BY LAUREN SOTH

WE TWENTIETH CENTURY Iowans inherited treasures of soil, rivers, lakes, woodlands and plant and animal life so abundant as to seem inexhaustible. They are not, we now know.

We have watched woodlands disappear and clear, clean water become scarce. One hundred sixty-six species of native Iowa plants are endangered or threatened, and 70 species have disappeared. Seventy-three species of fauna are endangered or threatened, and 28 species are already gone. But it is the loss of topsoil, our richest legacy, which is of greatest concern.

Topsoil — that carpet of fine earth particles created by sedimentation, glaciation, weathering, decay of prairie grasses and the composting of forest vegetation; deposited on our land by water and wind over multi-centuries of time; life-giving resource bestowed upon Iowa most generously — does disappear with use. This natural factory for food production washes and blows away under intense cultivation. We started with a layer of topsoil 16 inches deep on the average. It is now skimmed off to half that. We have not yet learned how to use this factory most efficiently without depreciating its substance. But we are learning.

As trustees of the soil and other gifts of Nature for future Iowans and Americans (and world humanity), we are under obligation to maintain these resources in good, working condition. Preserving our heritage of resources usually does not mean non-use but different use — a park instead of a lumbering enterprise; a lumbering enterprise based on sustained long-term production instead of a wipe-out; a living museum of prairie grasses and flowers instead of another corn field. For our most precious natural heritage, the Iowa soil (with accompanying temperatures and rainfall), conservation means economic use on a multi-generational time scale.

We developed the Iowa land for farming on a short-time scale — that is, thinking ahead only one to three generations. If you wore out one farm, you could move west for a virgin one. That mood didn't last long, but the reluctance to look far ahead in land use did. More profit could be made by continuous corn and soybean growing. New yield-increasing technology, especially chemicals, made it possible. The chemicals disguised the effects of soil erosion and replaced soil fertility.

Most farming family members in modern industrial societies do not consider themselves permanent farmers — any more than members of lawyer families or drugstore families consider themselves inevitable lawyers or pharmacists. People are mobile as to geography and in their educational and work choices. True, some farm families hold to strong traditions of continuity in operating the family farm through the generations. But these are exceptions in a society of constantly changing technology and job opportunities.

To preserve the Iowa soil heritage, therefore, we must take a societal view of the economics of land management, such as that being taken by the Iowa Natural Heritage Foundation. Society can look farther ahead than an individual or family can look toward maintaining the soil as a sustainable, permanent resource. Where the private and the public interests collide, as they sometimes do in matters of the natural endowment, then the public interest takes precedence. The land and other natural resources are, in a sense, common property even when privately owned.

Iowans have taken a proud lead in the nation toward curbing the waste of their soil inheritance. The state government has taken action to supplement federal programs and assist private land owners to make investments for holding the soil in place. This is most appropriate for a people in charge of the nation's premier agricultural land dominion.

Holding soil in place within tolerable natural replacement rates requires more than building terraces and farming on the contour or practicing no-till farming or conservation tillage. It also requires long-term retirement of hilly and fragile lands from cultivation and planting them to grass and trees. It requires frequent rotation of grass and grain on erosive land, plus reliance on Nature's own conservation system, including return of plant and animal wastes to the land.

Such a mode of operating Iowa farmland assumes a many-generational scheme of land-use planning — beyond the range and capacity of most family farm owners. Indeed, such long-term planning sometimes is uneconomic for an individual owner. Unfortunately, exploitation of the land or "mining" it, is often good business for owners looking a mere 30 to 40 years into their future use of the resource.

That is why society must take a hand in research, education, technical assistance and financial aid concerning the common heritage of natural resources.

Epilogue

One person can make a difference—
One person will watch topsoil wash and blow away; another person will change farming methods to reduce erosion.

One person will watch windbreaks disappear from age and neglect; another person will plant new trees.

One person will ravage timberlands for firewood; another person will leave some deadwood and cover for wildlife habitat.

One person will watch birds and animals starve in a bitter winter; another person will feed our wildlife.

What can one person do? Look around and learn about our natural heritage. Programs are begging for help. And please, like so many great Iowans, make a personal decision to practice wise resource management.

One person can become involved in local, state or national organizations striving for policies that will preserve and enhance our natural resources.

Everyone of us counts. Together we can save, even improve, what is so special about this place we call home — Iowa.

Robert D. Ray
Robert D. Ray
Governor of Iowa, 1982

Bert Vogel

Authors

Duane C. Anderson
Dr. Anderson is State Archaeologist of Iowa. He has earned B.A., M.A. and Ph.D. degrees from the University of Colorado. He is the author of *Western Iowa Prehistory* (1975) and *Eastern Iowa Prehistory* (1981), both published by The Iowa State University Press; *Mill Creek Ceramics* (1981), published by the Office of the State Archaeologist of Iowa, and co-author of *The Cherokee Excavations: Holocene Ecology and Human Adaptations in Northwestern Iowa* (1980), published by Academic Press Inc.

Wayne I. Anderson
Dr. Anderson is professor and head, Department of Earth Science, University of Northern Iowa. He holds B.A., M.S. and Ph.D. degrees from the University of Iowa. He is the author of *Geology of Iowa: Over Two Billion Years of Change* (1982), published by The Iowa State University Press.

Roger W. Bachmann
Dr. Bachmann is a professor in the Department of Animal Ecology at Iowa State University. He has earned B.S. and Ph.D. degrees at the University of Michigan, and an M.S. from the University of Idaho.

Richard G. Baker
Dr. Baker is an associate professor in the Department of Geology at the University of Iowa. He received his B.A. degree at the University of Wisconsin, an M.S. from the University of Minnesota, and his Ph.D. from the University of Colorado.

Richard A. Bishop
Mr. Bishop is Wildlife Research Supervisor for the Iowa Conservation Commission. He was awarded a B.S. degree from Iowa State University, and an M.S. from the University of Arizona.

Richard V. Bovbjerg
Dr. Bovbjerg is a professor of zoology at the University of Iowa, and is director of the Iowa Lakeside Laboratory. He holds B.S. and Ph.D. degrees from the University of Chicago.

John B. Bowles
Dr. Bowles is professor of biology at Central College. He has earned a B.A. degree from Earlham College, an M.S. from the University of Washington and a Ph.D. from the University of Kansas. He is the author of *Distribution and Biography of Mammals of Iowa* published by Texas Tech University.

James L. Christiansen
Dr. Christiansen is professor of biology at Drake University. He holds a B.S. degree from Buena Vista College, an M.S. from the University of Utah, and a Ph.D. from the University of New Mexico.

Paul Christiansen
Dr. Christiansen is professor of biology at Cornell College. He earned a B.A. degree from the University of Iowa, an M.S. from the University of Oregon and a doctorate from Iowa State University.

Lawrence J. Eilers
Dr. Eilers is professor of biology, University of Northern Iowa. He holds B.A. and M.A. degrees from the University of Northern Iowa, and a Ph.D. from the University of Iowa. He is the author of *The Vascular Flora of the Iowan Area* (1971), and *Studies in Natural History* (1970), both published by the University of Iowa Press.

Thomas E. Fenton
Dr. Fenton is professor of agronomy at Iowa State University. He was awarded B.S. and M.S. degrees from the University of Illinois and a Ph.D. from Iowa State University.

William M. Furnish
Dr. Furnish is professor emeritus of geology at the University of Iowa. He holds B.S., M.S. and Ph.D. degrees from the University of Iowa.

David C. Glenn-Lewin
Dr. Glenn-Lewin is an associate professor of botany at Iowa State University. He has earned an A.B. degree from Knox College and a Ph.D. from Cornell University.

Benjamin F. Graham
Dr. Graham is professor of biology at Grinnell College. He holds B.S. and M.S. degrees from the University of Maine and a doctorate from Duke University.

George R. Hallberg
Dr. Hallberg is chief, geological studies at the Iowa Geological Survey. He earned a B.S. degree from Augustana College and a doctorate from the University of Iowa.

Paul J. Horick
Mr. Horick is senior groundwater geologist for the Iowa Geological Survey. He holds a B.A. degree from Augustana College and an M.S. from the University of Iowa. He is the author of *The Minerals of Iowa* (1974), published by the State of Iowa.

Loren N. Horton
Dr. Horton is acting director of the State Historical Society. He holds B.A. and M.A. degrees from the University of Northern Iowa and a Ph.D. from the University of Iowa. He is the author of *Recent History of the United States* (1971), published by the University of Iowa Press; *Census Data for Iowa* (1973) and *The Character of the Country* (1976), both published by the State Historical Society.

Otto W. Knauth
Mr. Knauth served as science editor for the *Des Moines Register*. He retired January 1, 1982, after 33 years with the Des Moines paper. Earlier in his career he was employed by the *St. Joseph (Mo.) Gazette*.

Richard P. Lampe
Dr. Lampe is associate professor of biology at Buena Vista College. He has earned a B.S. degree from Buena Vista College, an M.A. from the University of Kansas and a Ph.D. from the University of Minnesota.

Paul A. Meglitsch
Dr. Meglitsch was professor emeritus of biology at Drake University. He held B.S., M.S. and Ph.D. degrees from the University of Illinois. Professor Meglitsch was co-author of *Introductory Biology* (1939) and co-author of *General College Zoology* (1940), both published by the Chicago Planograph Corp., co-author of *Introductory Biology* (1949), published by D. Van Nostrand Corp., and author of *Invertebrate Zoology* (1967), published by Oxford University Press, Inc.

Dr. Meglitsch died Feb. 21, 1982.

Gerald A. Miller
Dr. Miller is an associate professor and extension agronomist at Iowa State University. He holds a B.S. degree from Virginia Polytechnic Institute and State University, and M.S. and Ph.D. degrees from Iowa State University.

Jean C. Prior
Mrs. Prior is senior research geologist for the Iowa Geological Survey. She holds a B.A. degree from Purdue University and an M.S. degree from the University of Illinois. She is the author of *A Regional Guide to Iowa Landforms* (1976), published by the Iowa Geological Survey.

Dean M. Roosa
Dr. Roosa is State Ecologist for the State Preserves Advisory Board. He received B.A. and M.A. degrees from the University of Northern Iowa and a Ph.D. from Iowa State University.

Carl Kurtz

Water flows gently over limestone ledges near the Mississippi River in northeast Iowa. This autumn scene is in Lenth Hollow in Clayton County.

Dorothy A. Schwieder
Dr. Schwieder is an assistant professor in the Department of History at Iowa State University. She earned a B.A. degree from Dakota Wesleyan University and M.S. and Ph.D. degrees from Iowa State University. Dr. Schwieder is the author of *A Peculiar People: Iowa's Old Order Amish* (1975), published by The Iowa State University Press.

Holmes A. Semken
Dr. Semken is professor of geology at the University of Iowa. He has earned B.S. and M.S. degrees from the University of Texas and a Ph.D. from the University of Michigan. He is co-author of *The Cherokee Excavations: Holocene Ecology and Human Adaptations in Northwestern Iowa* (1980), published by Academic Press, Inc.

Robert H. Shaw
Dr. Shaw is a distinguished professor of agronomy at Iowa State University. He earned B.S., M.S. and Ph.D. degrees from Iowa State University.

Daryl D. Smith
Dr. Smith is professor of biology at the University of Northern Iowa. He was awarded a B.A. degree from the University of Iowa, an M.S. from the University of South Dakota and a Ph.D. from the University of Iowa.

Lauren Soth
Mr. Soth served as an editorial writer and editorial page editor for the *Des Moines Register* until his retirement in 1975. He continues to write for the *Des Moines Register and Tribune Syndicate*. In 1956, he was awarded a Pulitzer Prize for writing on agricultural economics and was instrumental in paving the way for a visit to Iowa by Russian Premier Nikita Khrushchev in 1959. Mr. Soth holds B.S. and M.S. degrees from Iowa State University.

Lois Hattery Tiffany
Dr. Tiffany is professor of botany at Iowa State University. She has earned B.S., M.S. and Ph.D. degrees from Iowa State University.

Arnold van der Valk
Dr. Van der Valk is associate professor of botany at Iowa State University. He holds a B.S. degree from the University of Windsor, an M.S. from the University of Alberta and a Ph.D. degree from North Carolina State University.

Paul Waite
Mr. Waite is State Climatologist in the Iowa Department of Agriculture and an adjunct professor at Drake University. He holds a bachelor of education degree from Western Illinois State University and an M.S. from the University of Michigan.

Larry J. Zimmerman
Dr. Zimmerman is associate professor of anthropology at the University of South Dakota. He has earned B.A. and M.A. degrees from the University of Iowa, a master of philosophy and a doctorate from the University of Kansas. Dr. Zimmerman is the author of *Prehistoric Locational Behavior* (1977), published by the State of Iowa; co-author of *Sources of South Dakota Prehistory* (1981), published by the *South Dakota Archaeological Society*, and *The Crow Creek Site Massacre* (1981), published by the U.S. Corps of Engineers.

Index

A

Adair County 52
Adams County 34, 296
adaptation 259, 322
Afton 50
Aftonian 50
Age of Dinosaurs 15
Age of Mammals 41
agrichemicals 77, 93, 237, 249, 322
Agriculture Adjustment Act 91
Alden 32
alfalfa 140
algae 23, 34, 70, 129, 149, 153, 234 illus, 235, 237, 238, 238 illus, 239 illus, 241, 242, 245-249, 318
Allamakee County 21, 202, 225, 292
Allen, J.A. 312
Allison, William B. 300
alluvial deposits 65, 73, 75, 83, 85, 127
alluvium 65, 73, 75, 83, 85, 127
Amana Colonies 217, 295, 296
American Forestry Association 204, 205
American lotus 205, 217
Ames 75, 101, 205
Ames High School Preserve 178
amphibian 131, 240, 255
Anamosa 27, 314
Anderson Lake 319
Anderson, Rudolph 312
aquatic life 70, chapter 10, 230-249
aquatic plants 215-218, 233, 236-238, 241, 242, 245, 247-249
aquifers 65, 72, 73, 75, 76, 216
Arbor Day 205
Archaic people 271-275
armadillo 54
arrow arum 127
arrow grass 129, 216, 319
arrowhead 271 illus
artesian 73, 75, 76
Arctic shrew 54
artifacts 270-273, 275, 278, 279, 279 illus
ash 140, 195, 201
aspen 132, 197 illus, 201
aster 142, 168, 171, 173, 177
atlatl 272 illus
Audubon County 52, 296

B

Backbone State Park 27, 204, 314
backswimmers 239
bacteria 84, 86, 235, 237, 238, 241
Bad Axe River 288
badger 226, 257
Bailey, Bert 312
bald eagle 127, 259 illus, 264, 322
balsam fir 146, 154, 202
Balltown Ridge 57, 83 illus
barge 69, 69 illus, 259, 293 illus
barnyard grass 218
Bartsch, Paul 312, 314
basalt 19
basswood 124, 131 illus, 186
bat 131, 242, 259, 263, 263 illus
beaked sedge 216
Bealer's Quarry 27 illus
beans 278, 279, 282
Beane, B. H. 30, 32, 309
bear 54, 253, 254, 321
bearberry 133, 154
beard tongues 142
beaver 45, 54, 55, 213, 240, 253, 254, 260, 312, 321
bedrock Chapter 1, 8-41, 48, 50, 57, 59, 65, 71-73, 75, 83, 85, 86, 319
Beeds Lake State Park 64 illus
beetles 239, 263
beggers tick 211
Belmont 299
Bellevue 76, 293
Bellevue State Park 27, 133
bellflower 142
bellwort 142, 143 illus
Bennett, Rev. George 313, 314
Bennett, H. A. 264
Bessie, Charles E. 315
big bluestem 125, 161, 166, 166 illus, 167, 169, 173, 306 illus
Big Creek Lake 70
Big Sand Mound 157, 173
Big Sioux River 127, 128, 213, 253, 278
Big Wall Lake 220 illus
bigtooth aspen 197 illus, 201
birch 54, 132, 154, 156 illus, 200 illus, 202
Bixby State Park 27
bison 54, 253, 270-272, 278, 311, 311 illus, 321
see also buffalo
bittern 129, 221
black cherry 144
black walnut 122
blackberry 143, 256
blackbird 129, 253, 263, 322
black-eyed Susan 176 illus, 177
Blackhawk, Chief 288
Blackhawk County 134, 167 illus
Blackhawk Purchase 288, 290, 292
Blackhawk War 281, 288, 290
bladderwort 147, 147 illus, 217, 235 illus
blazing star 167 illus, 168, 168 illus, 173, 177
blue flag iris 171, 175
blue heron 219 illus
blizzard 67, 97, 109
bloodroot 142, 144, 144 illus
bluebell 142
blue beach 197
blue cohosh 144
blue-green algae 235, 237
blue joint-grass 166, 171, 217
Blue Lake 70
bluets 169
blue-winged teal 218, 221, 223
Bluffton 23
Bluffton Fir Stand 154, 319 illus
Board of Immigration 296
bobcat 322, 323 illus
bobolink 129, 221
bog 53, 81, 129, 132, 147, 186, 189, 215, 216, 255, 319
bog-bean 129, 130, 157
bog cotton 129, 157
bog twayblade 319
bog willow 132
Boone County 102, 112, 113, 130, 191 illus, 192 illus, 193, 194, 205-207, 315
boxelder 189, 195
Boyden 107
Boyer River 213
brachiopods 24, 27, 29, 30, 34
Brewster Site 279
Brooklyn 112
brown creeper 127
Brush Creek Canyon State Preserve 38 illus
bryoza 24, 30
buckbrush 197
Buena Vista County 65
buffalo 211, 272 illus, 311 illus, 321
see also bison
buffalo grass 126, 157
bulrush 157, 211 illus, 217, 218, 221
bullhead 236, 242
bumblebee 141 illus
bunchberry 133
bunch flower 171
Burlington 32, 61, 75, 296, 297, 299, 308, 309, 317
Burlington formation 30, 32
burreed 217, 221
Butler County 29, 254
buttercup 122, 168, 171, 175
butterfly 127, 128, 141 illus, 259
butternut 143
buttonbrush 218

C

caddis flies 235, 238, 242, 245, 246
Cahokia Center 278, 279
Calhoun County 20, 299
Calvin, Samuel 313
Camanche 112
Cambrian 16, 21
camel 54
Cambrian-Dresbach Aquifer 73, 76
Cambrian-Ordovician Aquifer 73, 76
Canada geese 214, 214 illus, 216
Canada thistle 310 illus
Canada wildgrass 166
Canada wildrye 306 illus
Canada yew 131, 146, 154, 157, 202
Canadian anemone 175
cancer-root 145
canvasback duck 226
carbon dioxide 235, 237, 242
carbonates 23, 24, 28, 32, 57, 75, 129, 216
Cardiff Giant 39, 39 illus
cardinal flower 142
caribou 270
Carlile Formation 39
carnivorous plants 141, 147
catkins 197, 199
catsteps 57
cattail 157, 211 illus, 217, 218, 221, 226
cave 24 illus, 55, 187 illus, 202
Cayler Prairie 157, 318, 319
Cedar County 134, 135, 270
Cedar Falls 75
Cedar Rapids 75, 112, 213, 303, 312
Cedar River 26 illus, 27, 62 illus, 67, 132, 134, 135, 213
Cedar Valley Formation 28
Cenozoic 12, 15, 41
Centerville 65
cephalopod 24, 27
Cerro Gordo County 28, 29, 65, 88, 211
Chariton 297
Chariton River 65
Charles City 179
chenopods 54
Cherokee 104
Cherokee County 48, 52, 211, 273
Cherokee Sewer Site 271 illus, 272, 273
chestnut, American 202
chestnut blight 202
Cheever Lake 157
Chickasaw County 49
chigger 259, 263
chipmunk 55
Chippewa Land District 308
choke cherry 143
Chuck-will's-willow 127
cicada 260
Civil War 299
clam 236, 245, 246, 260
clay 12, 28, 34, 48, 72, 73, 75, 82, 83, 86, 275, 279
Clayton County 10, 23, 61, 157, 225, 275, 277, 289
Clear Lake 104, 211, 213, 216
Clements, Frederick 163
climate 11, 86, Chapter 5, 94-115, 185
Clinton 73, 75, 76, 112, 296
clubmosses 37, 183
coal 12, 15, 34, 34 illus, 36 illus, 37, 183, 292, 303, 308
Cold Water Cave 24, 24 illus, 57
colluvium 83
compass plant 174 illus, 177, 306 illus
Conard, Henry 202
cone 146
coneflowers 175, 177
conifer 146, 154, 186, 191, 202, 270
see also pine and forests
conodonts 29, 34
conservation 89, 91-93, 205, 207, 229, 283, 310-312, 315-318, 319, 321, 322, 326
coontail plant 218, 219, 238
coot, American 219 illus, 221, 226
copper 19, 273, 275
coral 11, 15, 24, 27, 28, 34
coralberry 197, 199
Coralville 65
cormorant, double breasted 261
corn 82, 92, 99-101, 140, 263, 273, 278, 279, 282, 301
corn borer 259, 263
corn smut 149
Cornell College 311, 313

cottonwood, eastern 185, 204
Council Bluffs 61, 73, 99, 297
cowbird 250, 263
coyote 257 illus, 259
crane 123
Crawfordsville 299
crayfish 226, 235, 238, 245, 246, 260
cricket 260
Cresco 75
cretaceous 38, 39, 72, 73, 75
crinoid 14 illus, 27, 30, 30 illus, 31, 32, 308, 309
crustacean 238, 241, 249
cut-leaved goldenweed 169
Czechoslovakian 296

D

dairy 54, 166, 177
Dakota Formation 39, 75
Dallas County 23, 211
dam 64, 68, 69, 70, 225, 234, 245, 249
damselfly 233, 234 illus
Danish 296
Darling, J. N. "Ding" 89, 316 illus, 317
Davenport 299
DDT 259, 312, 322
Deadman's Lake Bog 217
Decatur County 259
Decorah 72, 203, 297
Decorah shale 72
deer 54, 55, 189 illus, 213, 250, 260, 263, 264, 264 illus, 272, 278, 279, 312, 321
Delaware County 314
Delta Queen 68 illus
Democratic Party 300
Des Moines 24, 32, 59, 61, 65, 75, 130, 131, 161, 297, 301, 303, 312, 309
Des Moines County 29, 30, 50, 196
Des Moines Lobe 52, 59, 129, 234, 270
Des Moines River 12, 18, 41 illus, 65, 67, 69, 192 illus, 213, 249, 278, 290
Des Moines Series 34, 37
DeSoto Bend National Wildlife Refuge 134, 252
detritus 235, 237, 238, 241, 242, 246, 247
dewberry 143
Dewey's Pasture/Smith's Slough 319
Devonian 16, 27, 28, 75
diatom 235, 237, 245
dickcissel 131
Dickinson County 59, 65, 170, 178, 318
dinosaur 15
Disciseda 129
dodder 145
dog-tooth violets 200
dogwood 198
Douglas 72
Dolliver, Jonathan P. 303
Dolliver State Park 13, 34, 131

Larry Stone

dolomite 24, 27, 30, 57, 133, 216
dolostone 71-73, 75, 76
dragonfly 227 illus, 235, 239, 255 illus
Driftless Area 57, 192, 277
dropseed 166, 169
drought 70, 97, 99, 104, 109, 115, 216, 221
Dresbach Aquifer 76
Dubuque 23, 25, 57, 68, 69, 75, 76, 83, 88, 107, 170, 213, 287, 289, 292, 296, 308
Dubuque County 146, 157, 203 illus, 204, 294, 297, 299, 309, 318
Dubuque, Julien 289
ducks 123, 211, 213, 215, 218, 221, 223, 225, 226, 229 illus, 250, 272, 317
Ducks Unlimited 225
duck stamp 225
duckweed 217, 218, 231 illus, 233 illus, 237, 238, 247 illus
Dutch elm disease 149, 153, 196
Dutchman's breeches 142, 199, 199 illus
DuMont, Philip 312
dwarf birch 132

E

eagle 259 illus, 322
earth tongues 129
earthstar 134, 149, 151
eastern pipistrelle bat 263
echinoids 32
Echo Valley State Park 27
ecosystem 55, 77, 241, 242, 247, 254, 318, 320, 322
edible plants 140, 141, 143, 198
Effigy Mounds National Monument 274, 276 illus, 277, 314
elderberry 144
Eldora 73, 157, 203
elk 250, 254, 272, 311 illus, 321 see also wapiti
elm 54, 186, 196, 202, 205
Elm Lake 130, 157
endangered species 127, 134, 321-325
energy 34, 97, 99, 100, 111, 114
English River 213
equator 11, 15, 34
erosion 21-23, 28, 38, 41, 57, 72, 82, 89, 91-93, 107, 109, 111, 126, 185, 222, 225, 327
Errington, Paul L. 317
Estherville 109, 157
extinct 45, 54, 55, 189
evaporates 28
evergreen
  see pines
European elm bark beetle 196

F

falcon, peregrine 261, 321, 322
fall panicum 218
Falling Spring 72 illus

false rue anemone 122
fameflower 126, 157
Fayette County 38, 49, 72
Federal Swampland Act 214, 223
Federal Wildlife Refuge 314
fen 129, 154 illus, 216
Fenton, Carroll Lane 312
ferns 37, 122, 132, 134, 135, 142, 147, 147 illus, 183, 198, 203, 319
fertilizer 70, 93, 237
field milkwort 177
fir 122, 186, 203, 255, 270
fire 163, 165, 170, 189, 196, 213, 245, 256
fish 13, 28, 34, 213, 215, 224, 225, 233, 235, 236, 238-240, 242, 245, 246, 249, 255, 260, 272
Fish Farm Mounds 277 illus
fishing 69, 89
flatworms 235, 238, 245, 248
Flint Creek Valley 61
flood 49, 70, 96, 99, 102, 107, 109, 194, 196, 247
flood control 65, 70, 234, 249
flood plain 47, 49, 82, 83, 183, 189, 194, 196, 218, 224, 225, 233, 247
floodwaters 196
flowered beard tongue 169
Floyd County 28, 179, 312
Floyd River 213
fly-amanita 200 illus
fog 102, 104, 114 illus
Folsom Culture 270
forecasts 97, 99
forests 34, 37, 45, 53-55, 122, 122 illus, 124-126, Chapter 8, 180-207, 227, 229, 249, 270
forts 290
Fort Atkinson 290, 291 illus
Fort Madison 73, 290
Ft. Armstrong 290
Ft. Bellevue 290
Ft. Calhoun 99
Ft. Crawford 290
Ft. Des Moines 290
Ft. Dodge 12, 39, 69, 213
Ft. Dodge Formation 39
fossils 10-12, 14-16, 24, 28, 29, 34, 39, 45, 48, 53-55, 61, 183, 186, 280
fox 55, 226, 254 illus
Fox Indians 186, 189, 281, 283, 288-290
Franklin County 29, 64, 211
Freda Hafner Kettlehole Preserve 59, 178
frog 109, 226, 227 illus, 240, 255, 256
frost 101 illus, 104, 109
fruit 53, 237, 247
fuel 183, 192, 206, 213
fungi 84, 86, 129, 145, 149, 153, 196, 198, 237

G

Gabrielson, Ira 312
gabbro 19
Galena Group 23, 24, 25 illus, 62

gaura 169
geese 123, 127, 211, 213, 214, 214 illus, 215, 218, 226, 250, 258 illus, 259, 261, 272
Genevieve Formation 30
gentian 72, 176 illus, 177
geologic column 16, 17
geologic timetable 12, 15
geode 32, 32 illus
Gilmore City 32
Gilmore City Formation 30, 32
gingko 205
Gitchie Manitou State Preserve 20, 20 illus, 61, 126, 157
glaciation 15, 41, Chapter 2, 42-61, 65, 68, 72, 81, 83, 84, 125, 170, 185, 186, 192, 222, 232, 234, 270
Glenwood 275
Glenwood Culture 279
Glenwood Shale 24, 70
goat's beard 131
golden alexander 171, 175
golden plover 123
goldenrod 167 illus, 168, 172, 173, 176 illus, 177
goldfinch 310 illus
gooseberry 198, 200, 202, 256
goosefoot 186, 272
Goose Lake 130, 131 illus, 157, 319
Gower Formation 27
grain 100, 140
grama grass 130, 166, 169, 170
Graneros Formation 39
Grange 300
granite 15, 19
grasshopper 260
grasslands 81, 270, 272, 282
  see also prairies
grass of parnassus 129, 216
gravel 41, 65, 71-73, 75, 236, 242, 247
great horned owl 261, 262 illus
Great Oasis People 278, 279
green ash 195
Greenback Party 300
Greene County 112
Greenhorn Formation 39
green-winged teal 217
Greiner, William H. 92
Grinnell 112
ground cherry 143
ground squirrel 128, 226, 257, 260, 261, 261 illus
groundwater 10, 54, 65, 66, 70-72, 216, 229, 242
grouse 122, 127
gypsum 12, 28, 29, 292

H

habitat 53, 61, 127, 129, 131-135, 192, 194, 196, 206, 224, 226, 235, 248, 249
hackberry 189, 205, 272
hail 96, 97, 102, 104, 107, 109
Half Breed Tract 297
Hamilton County 130, 131, 241, 299
Hampton Formation 30, 32

Tom C. Cooper

Hancock County 30, 59, 129, 151
hanging bog 216
Hardin County 36, 73, 109, 131, 146, 154, 157, 201, 203
Hardin County Greenbelt 154
Hare Run 270
Harlin, James 300, 301 illus
Harrison County 52, 61, 163, 313
Harrison, William H. 281
hawk 127, 135, 226, 259, 320, 321, 324
hawthorne 202
Hayden, Ada 315, 318
Hayden Prairie 157, 160 illus, 315, 318
hazelnut 143, 198
Hazen, Thomas 93
heath 217
Hendrickson Marsh 219, 219 illus
hepatica 122, 123 illus, 142, 200
herbivore 235
herons 226, 259
hibernation 260
hickory 124, 125, 131, 143, 194, 202, 203, 256
Hickory Grove Park 70 illus
Hill Site 273
Hinrichs, Professor Gustavus 99
Holocene 41
Honey Creek 108
Hoover, Herbert 317
Hopewell Interaction Sphere 275
Hopewell Woodland Culture 275, 277, 278
Hopkinton Formation 27
Hornady, William T. 311
hornbeam 198, 202
hornwort 148
horse 54, 270, 281
Howard County 157, 178, 315, 318
Hull, George 39
Humboldt 32
Humboldt County 30, 35, 75, 129, 273, 299
humus 86, 194
hunting 225, 229
hydroelectric power 65, 66, 68, 249
hydrologic cycle 66
hyphae 149, 153

I

Ice Age 12, 15, 41, 45, 47-52, 54, 55, 133, 154, 185, 186, 270, 272
ice cave 55, 133, 154
igneous rock 19, 48
Illini Indian Tribe 288
Illinoan 52, 135
Illinois 24, 30, 37, 51, 54, 161, 288, 290
Independence 28
Indian 69, 165, 236, Chapter 12, 268-283, Chapter 13, 284-303
Indian burial grounds 275-277, 276 illus, 277 illus
Indian grass 125, 161, 166, 170, 173
Indian pipe 145, 145 illus
Indiana bat 131

335

industry 65, 66, 68, 72, 77, 229
insect 84, 86, 100, 111, 140, 168, 169, 172, 202, 226, 233, 235, 237, 238, 241, 242, 246, 247, 249
insect larvae 169, 235, 238, 239, 241, 242, 245, 246, 248, 260
Iowa Academy of Science 206, 264, 315
Iowa Agricultural and Home Economics Experiment Station 88, 93
Iowa Arboretum 206
Iowa Basin 72
Iowa Board of Forestry Commissioners 206
Iowa City 28, 65, 99, 102, 122, 213, 299, 311, 313
Iowa Conservation Commission 64, 89, 131, 206, 214, 223, 224
Iowa Conservation Magazine 313, 314
Iowa County 296
Iowa Department of Soil Conservation 88, 91, 92, 225
Iowa Falls 157, 213
Iowa Farm Bureau 179
Iowa General Assembly 32, 89, 91, 296
  see also Iowa Legislature
Iowa Geological Survey 23, 126, 313
Iowa Horticulture Society 206, 313
Iowa Legislature 213, 281, 308, 313, 318, 324
  see also Iowa General Assembly
Iowa's Men's Reformatory 27 illus
Iowa Natural History Museum 311-313
Iowa Park and Forestry Association 311, 313-315
Iowa River 36, 65, 67, 68, 135, 157, 213, 245 illus, 249
Iowa State Conservation Board 313, 315, 318
Iowa State Fish and Game Commission 313, 317, 324
Iowa State Historical Museum 32, 309
Iowa State University 88, 99, 110, 114, 205, 311, 312, 315, 317
Ioway Indian Tribe 279, 280, 281
iris 141 illus, 171, 175
Irish 296
iron 292
iron oxide 23, 86, 275
iron sulphide 37
ironweed 141 illus, 171
ironwood 198, 202
irrigation 66, 68, 72, 73, 75
isopyrum 122

J

Jack-in-the-pulpit 142, 144, 144 illus
Jasper County 178, 203
Jefferson 112
Jemmerson Slough 157
Jewell 157

Johnson County 24, 28, 48, 148, 178, 296
Joliet, Louis 252, 287-289
Joliet and Marquette Expedition 252, 287-289
Jones County 27, 273
Jones, George Wallace 301 illus
Jordan 102, 113
Jordan Sandstone 76
junco 259
Junegrass 130, 166, 173
juniper 146, 170, 202
  see also red cedar
Jurassic 38, 39

K

Kalona 295, 296
Kalsow Prairie 157, 162 illus, 318
Kansan Glacier 50-52
Kansas 125, 161, 173, 281, 288
Kay, G. F. 314
Keokuk 32, 68, 75, 101, 300
Keokuk County 32
Keokuk Formation 30, 32
Keokuk National Cemetery 300 illus
Keota 23
Keswick 33
kettlehole 123, 125, 129, 130, 213 illus, 319
Keyes, Charles R. 312, 314
Kimballton 296
Kingston Site 275
Kossuth County 129
Kullbom Site 279

L

Lacey-Keosauqua State Park 311, 314
Lacey, Major John E. 311, 313
lacustrine wetlands 215-217
lady's-slipper 122, 130, 142, 171, 203, 321, 321 illus, 322
ladies' tresses 319
lake 53, 59, 66, 68-71, 123, 125, 129, Chapter 9, 208-229, Chapter 10, 230-249
Lake Calvin 135, 292
Lake Geode 66 illus
Lake Okoboji 54, 65, 70, 157, 211, 233, 234, 241, 315
Lake Rathbun 65
Lakeside Laboratory 315, 318
Lansing 76, 133
larch 54
larkspur 144
larvae
  see insect larvae
LaSalle, Sier de 288
lava 15, 19
lead 24, 25 illus, 272, 292
lead plant 177
least bittern 129, 221
Ledges State Park 34, 34 illus, 194, 205, 315 illus
Lee County 30, 289, 294, 297, 313
leeches 235, 238, 245
LeGrande 14, 30, 31, 309

legume 168, 175, 177
lemming 54, 55, 127, 157, 255, 257
Leopold, Aldo 32, 89, 309, 317, 318
Leopold, Frederic 317
levee 70, 127
Lewis and Clark Expedition 69, 112, 165, 289, 290
lichen 35 illus, 126, 127, 133, 134, 153, 198, 205 illus, 319
lightning 102, 106 illus, 107, 165
lignite 39
lily 142 illus, 143, 176 illus, 177 illus
Lily Lake 217
Lime Creek Formation 28
Lime Springs 157
limestone 8-9 illus, 12, 15, 22 illus, 23, 24, 26 illus, 27-29, 32, 34, 57, 71-73, 75, 194, 216
Linn County 27, 134, 196
little bluestem 125, 166, 169, 170, 173
Little Sioux River 213, 278
Little Wall Lake 239, 241 illus
liverwort 148, 198
livestock 99, 107, 109
Living History Farms 286 illus, 287, 301 illus
lizard 256, 257, 257 illus
llama 54
Llano Culture 270
lock 69, 225, 292-293 illus
locust 200, 202 illus
loess 47, 52, 57-59, 61, 72, 83, 86, 128, 130, 157, 184 illus, 185, 313
loess hills 57-59, 59 illus, 111, 127, 131, 157, 169 illus, 292, 312 illus, 313, 319
Loess Hills Wildlife Area 157
long-billed curlew 123
lotus, American 236 illus
Louisa County 135, 225, 282
Louisiana Territory 288, 289, 297
louseworts 175
Lucas, Governor Robert, home 298-299 illus
lumber 183, 206, 207, 213, 292
Lungren Site 273
lungwort 133
Luxemburg 203
lycopod trees 37
Lyon County 20, 61, 254, 299, 319

M

MacBride, Thomas H. 89, 189, 313-315, 318
MacDonald, G. B. 313
Madison County 34, 315
magma 15, 19
magnesium 27
Malcom 112
mallard ducks 218, 221, 226
mammal 15, 39, 41, 55, 219, 224, 226, 247, Chapter 11, 250-265
mammoth 45, 54, 55, 270
Manson 18, 20 157
Manson Disturbed Area 20

maple 122, 124, 125, 157, Chapter 8, 180-207, 218
Maple River 213
Maquoketa 76, 131
Maquoketa Caves State Park 27, 187 illus
Maquoketa Formation 24, 27
Maquoketa River 313
mannagrass 217, 218
mare's tail 129, 159
Marion County 91, 183, 277, 296
Marion thick pots 275
marmot 55
Marquette 69 illus, 289
Marquette, Father Jacques 252, 287-289
marsh 53, 59, 66, 131-133, Chapter 9, 208-229, 236, 240, 249, 319
Marshall County 14, 195 illus, 234, 234 illus, 307
Marshalltown 68
marsh hawk 226
marsh iris 226

Alex B. Thiermann

marsh wren, long billed 221
Mason City 28, 213
mastodon 45, 54, 55, 270
mayapple 142, 144, 144 illus
mayfly 239 illus, 242, 245, 259
McCraney Formation 30
McGee, W. J. 309-312
McGregor 61, 68, 245, 277, 313, 314
McKinney Oneota Site 282
meadow beauty 134
meadowlark 221, 257, 257 illus
Mediapolis 28
Melephany Springs 72 illus
mentzelia 157
Mertensia 122
Mesozoic 12, 15, 20, 38, 39, 41
Mesquaki Indians 281, 288, 289
Mesquaki Settlement 280 illus, 281, 281 illus
metamorphic 15, 19, 47
meteorite 20
Michigan 19, 112, 263
migration 55, 125, 127, 128, 135, 218, 225, 226, 238, 259, 270
Milford 178
milkweed 162 illus, 168, 171, 172 illus, 177
millett 218
mills 249, 297
Mill Creek people 278, 279
Mills County 273, 275, 281
mine 12, 24, 25 illus, 292, 308
mineral 20, 21, 24, 32, 37, 52, 65, 82, 83, 86, 148, 185, 193, 195, 235, 237, 241, 242, 308
Mines of Spain 289, 292
mink 213, 215, 221, 226
Minnesota 19, 20, 48, 52, 67, 68, 75, 129, 161, 242, 248, 260, 263, 277, 288
minnow 236, 245, 246
mint 168, 173
Mississippian 16, 30, 32, 73, 75
Mississippian Culture 278, 282
Mississippi River 23, 30, 32, 47, 49, 58, 59, 61, 65, 67, 68, 68 illus, 70, 70 illus, 75, 77 illus, 99, 183, 192, 196 illus, 210 illus, 213, 216, 217, 223, 225, 226, 233 illus, 245, 245 illus, 248, 255, 259, 278, 281, 288, 290, 292, 293, 293 illus, 313, 314 illus
Missouri 30, 37, 59, 161, 281, 290, 294, 299
Missouri River 47, 49, 58, 59, 61, 65, 68-70, 73, 75, 83, 112, 134, 165, 185, 192, 213, 223, 225, 236, 245, 248, 255, 289, 290, 292, 313
Missourian Series 34
Missouri Tribe 288
Missouri Valley 163
Moine Creek 38 illus
Monarda 142
monkshood 124, 154, 324, 324 illus
Monona County 52, 59, 61, 313, 319
Monroe County 299

moonseed 144
moose 54
moraine 59, 129-131
morel mushroom 149 illus, 198
Morrowan Series 34
mosquitoes 172, 214, 239, 259, 263
moss 126, 130, 148, 148 illus, 198, 198 illus, 200, 203, 235, 245, 318, 319
Mossy Glen 157, 318
mountain 11, 15, 19, 24
mountain lion 250, 254, 321
mountain mint 160 illus
mouse grasshopper 127, 134, 157, 256
Mt. Hosmer 133
Mt. Pleasant 112
Mt. Simon Sandstone 76
Mt. Vernon 157, 205
mud 21, 24, 28-30, 278
mudpuppy 255
mudstone 20
muhlry grass 166, 169
Munn, Martha Buell, 314
Muscatine 28, 73, 75, 99, 104, 173, 203, 296
Muscatine County 135, 154, 157
Muscatine Island 134, 173 illus
mushroom 149, 149 illus, 150-153, 196, 198
    see also fungi
musk ox 45, 54, 270
muskrat 123, 132, 213, 219, 221, 226, 240, 259, 260
muskrat lodge 219 illus, 240 illus
mycorhizae 151

N

naid 218
national cemetery 300 illus
National Registration of Big Trees 205
National Weather Service 99, 113
native prairie 122, 124, 127, 161, 176, 178, 306 illus, 315, 318, 319
natural gas 23, 37
natural resources 41, 65, 77, 81, 89, 93, 100, 229, 249, 277, 308, 310-313, 315
Nature Conservancy 177
Nebraska 39, 41, 50, 125, 161, 173, 260, 281
Nebraskan Glacier 50-52, 313
needlegrass 173
Nemaha Reservation 281
nettle 145, 196
Nevada 315
New England Aster 142
Newell, William 39
Newton 75
nightshade 144
Nishnabotna River 213
nitrate 75
nitrogen 149
Nodaway River 213
Nora Springs 28
North Dakota 39, 129, 161, 278, 288
northern harrier 322

337

northern prairie grass 173
North Liberty 28
Northwood 75
Norton W. H. 313
Norwegian 296, 297

O

oak 54, 101, 122, 125, 129, 140, Chapter 8, 180-207, 256
oak wilt 153
O'Brien County 205, 211
Ocheyedan Mound 59
Ocheyedan River 213
Old Capitol 28, 298 illus
Olin Site 273
Oneota people 273, 279
oolite 23, 30
oppossum 226
orchid 122, 129, 130, 132, 142, 171, 203, 319, 321, 321 illus, 322
Ordovician 16, 23, 24, 27
Osage 299
Osceola County 59, 211, 254
Oskaloosa 161
Oto Tribe 279, 281, 288
otter 54
Ottumwa 213
outcrops 170
Owen, David Dale 23, 25, 308
owl 129, 131, 259, 259 illus
oxbow 59, 65, 123, 127, 135, 215, 223-225, 248
ox-eye 175
oxygen 21, 85, 149, 186, 196, 215, 235, 241, 242
Ozark Uplift 72

P

Page County 34
paleobotany 183
Paleo-Indian 15, 270-272, 274, 275
paleontology 30, 32
Paleozoic 12, 15, 19, 28, 38, 57, 72
Palisades Kepler State Park 26 illus, 27, 62 illus, 157, 205
palustrine wetlands 215-218
Pammel, Louis H. 203, 313, 314, 318
Pammel State Park 205, 315
paper birch 156 illus
parasite 141, 145, 196, 203, 238, 246
parhelia 134, 134 illus
parrot 189
parsley 168, 171
partridge pea 133, 173
Parvin, Theodore Sutton 99
pasque flower 130, 175, 175 illus
passenger pigeon 122
pawpaw 131
pea 100
Pearlette Ash 52
peat 37, 52, 53, 81, 130, 186, 217
pecan 127, 131, 203
Pecan Grove State Preserve 203, 205
peccaries 54

Alex B. Thiermann

pelican 123
Pella 65, 296
Pennsylvanian Period 32, 34, 37, 38, 75, 183
Permian 38
Perrot, Nicholas 281
pesticide 237, 259, 279, 312, 322
pheasant 264
Phipps Site 279
Phlox 122, 142, 175
photosynthesis 114, 183, 188, 235, 247
phragmites 221
Pictured Rocks 23
pied-billed grebe 221
pigeon 122, 250
pigweed 54, 186, 278
pike 245
Pikes Peak State Park 23, 60 illus, 61, 69, 70, 133, 134 illus, 245, 245 illus
pileated woodpecker 207 illus
Pilot Knob 59, 129, 157, 319
Pilot Knob State Park 217
Pilot Rock 48
Pinchott, Gifford 310, 311
pine 123, 131, 146, 154, Chapter 8, 180-207, 318
see also conifer
Pine Lake State Park 74 illus, 146, 188, 203, 304 illus
pine vole 55
pipestone 120, 279
pitcher plant 217
Pittman-Robertson Act 224
plankton 238, 239 illus, 241, 245, 249
Plano Culture 270, 271
Platteville Formation 24, 70
Pleistocene 41, 47, 48, 51, 52, 55, 57, 59, 185, 186, 270
plover 123, 134
plum 175, 189
Plum Grove 299
Pocahontas County 19, 32, 157, 318
poisonous plants 141, 144, 145, 171, 196, 198
Polk County 24, 211
pollen 53, 53 illus, 54, 55, 59, 111, 140, 186, 242
pollination 140, 141, 141 illus
pollution 70, 77, 89, 111, 115, 149, 248, 249
polygonums 217
pond 66, 68, 225, 230 illus, 234, 249, 270
pond buttercup 237
pondweed 217 illus, 218
poplar 196, 242
population 66, 131, 229, 271, 275, 283, 294, 299
Populist Party 300
porcupine grass 166
Post, Lennart von 186
Potawatomi Indians 288
Pottawattamie County 55, 91
pottery 273, 274, 274 illus, 275, 278, 279, 279 illus
powdery mildew 153
pow-wow 280, 280 illus
prairie 48, 53-55, 124, 128, 129, Chapter 7, 158-179, 183, 189, 207, 245
prairie avens 163 illus, 175
prairie bush clover 129, 167 illus, 175, 324
prairie chicken 123, 125, 211, 272, 323 illus
prairie clover 132, 170, 173, 175 illus, 177
prairie cordgrass 166, 218
Prairie Creek 234 illus
Prairie du Chien Group 23
prairie fire 124, 129, 163, 164 illus, 165, 165 illus, 170, 196, 213
prairie gay-feather 177 illus
prairie, hill 169, 170 illus, 171-173, 173 illus, 177, 318
prairie loosestrife 171
prairie marsh 225 illus
prairie phlox 162 illus
prairie potholes 10, 81, 125, 129, 157, 211, 213-216, 218, 223, 245, 319
prairie ragwort 175
prairie reconstruction 179 illus
prairie swale 177 illus
prairie smoke 132, 163 illus
Precambrian 12, 15, 18-20, 72
predator 218, 235, 238, 239, 241
Preparation Canyon 27
prickly pear cactus 126, 157, 157 illus, 173
pronghorn 54, 250
Prospect Hill Formation 30
protozoans 238, 245
pucoon 170, 175
puffball 127, 129, 149, 151
purple coneflower 175 illus

Q

quaking aspen 197 illus
quarry 12, 18, 27, 27 illus, 28, 30, 31 illus, 50, 70
Quaternary Period 41
quartz 21, 23
quartzite 12, 19, 20
Queen Anne's lace 144
quicklime 27, 28

R

rabbit 55, 272, 278
raccoon 207 illus, 221, 261 illus
Raccoon River 213, 290
radiometric dating 16, 19, 51-53, 55
ragweed 53, 173, 190, 218
ragwort 175 illus
railroad 297
rain 66-68, 70, 71, 81, 84, 85, 97, 97 illus, 104, 107, 109, 110, 110 illus
rainbow 98 illus, 102
raptor 128, 131, 261
raspberry 143
rattlesnake 128, 132, 254, 257, 322
rattlesnake master 177 illus
rattlesnake plantain 229
recreation 65, 69, 75, 225, 229

red cedar 26 illus, 122, 123 illus, 146, 170, 194, 202, 205
red fox 226
Red Ochre people 275
Red Rock Reservoir 65, 224 illus, 243 illus
Redfield 23
redhead duck 221, 226
red-winged blackbird 221, 226, 263
red-shouldered hawk 127
Reece, Maynard, painting 250
Reece's County Park 109, 200 illus
reed 217, 218, 233
reed canary grass 218
reedgrass 173, 175 illus, 218
reindeer 45, 54
relic 45, 124, 130, 154-157
Republican Party 299, 300
reservoir 65, 69-71, 215, 234, 242, 249
rhinocerous beetle 263
rhizoids 243
rift-valley 15, 19
Ringgold County 52
river birch 132
riverine wetlands 215-217, 223
Rockford 312
Rock River 213
rodent 54, 55, 254, 261, 272
rosette panic grass 166
ruddy duck 221, 226
rue anemone 122, 142
Rummel-Maske Site 270
rushes 37, 218, 233
Rush Lake 254
rust 153

S

Sac Indians 186, 189, 281, 283, 288, 290
sage 173, 177
sago pondweed 217 illus
salamander 131, 132, 215, 240, 255, 256
Salisbury Laboratories 179
sand 12, 21, 23, 30, 37, 65, 71-73, 75, 82, 83, 134, 173, 194, 233, 235, 236, 248
Sand Cave 23
sand dunes 157
sandhill crane 123, 312
sand lily 169
sand lovegrass 319
sandpiper 129, 322
sandstone 10 illus, 12, 13 illus, 18, 18 illus, 21, 21 illus, 23, 23 illus, 24, 34, 34 illus, 35 illus, 36 illus, 39, 57, 71-73, 75, 76
saprophyte 149
sassafras 131
savanna 129, 132, 196
savory-leaf aster 173
saxifrage 133, 154, 324
Saylorville Lake 65, 249 illus
scamp 226
Scandinavians 296
School of Wildlife 315
Scott County 135
scouring rush 154

scud 238, 245, 248
scurf pea 170, 177
sea lilies 14 illus, 27, 32
sea shells 11, 15
sea urchins 32
sedges 125, 125 illus, 130, 131, 168, 171, 198, 217, 218, 233
sediment 27, 28, 45, 47-50, 53, 58, 59, 68, 71, 72, 83, 91, 237, 249
sedimentary rock 16, 21, 23, 24, 28, 30, 32, 34, 39, 45, 48, 51, 57, 72, 83
seed 53, 101, 163 illus, 166, 177, 179, 194, 196, 198, 202, 221, 237, 247, 272, 273
seepage wetlands 215-217
sensitive fern 171, 171 illus
sewage 249
shale 12, 15, 24, 27-29, 32, 34, 39, 72, 73, 75
shark 11, 28
Shelby County 296
Shell Rock Formation 28
Shell Rock River 28
shelterbelt 97, 111
see also windbreak
Shimek, Dr. Bohumil 122, 163, 313-315, 318
Shimek State Forest 313
shinleaf 133, 154
shooting star 132, 142, 168 illus, 175, 318
shoveler duck 226
shrew 54, 257
shrub oxen 54
silicon 21
silt 30, 37, 47, 52, 58, 59, 72, 75, 82, 83, 86, 127, 134, 233, 235, 236, 248
siltstone 28, 34, 72
Silurian 16, 27
Silurian-Devonian Aquifer 73, 75
Silurian Escarpment 27, 57
Silver Lake Fen 154 illus, 216, 318
Simonson Site 272
Sioux City 59, 68, 73, 75, 127, 297, 302 illus, 312, 317
Sioux County 20, 107, 296
Sioux Indians 290
Sioux Quartzite 12, 20, 20 illus, 126, 157
skeleton weed 169
skunk 226, 321
skunk cabbage 135, 138 illus
Skunk River 67, 75, 213
Slater 98 illus
slough 59, 123, 125, 215, 223, 240, 245 illus
slough grass 160 illus, 171
sloth 54
smartweed 171, 218
Smith's Slough 319
snail 24, 133, 154, 235, 238, 242, 245, 246, 248, 278, 312, 313, 318, 324
snake 131, 134, 250, 254-257
sneezeweed 172
snow 97, 102, 104, 108 illus, 109, 111
snow bunting 259
snowgeese 127, 214, 226, 252 illus
snowy owl 259, 259 illus

339

sod 81, 194, 282
soil 48, 67, 77, Chapter 4, 78-93, 100, 101, 110, 124, 127, 148, 173, 185, 189, 194, 196, 225, 242, 245, 283
Soil and Water Resources Conservation Act 93
soil conservation 70, 89, 91, 92, 93, 283
Soil Conservation Districts 91
soil erosion 58, 70, 82, 84-86, 91, 92, 92 illus, 93, 107, 109, 111, 185, 225, 245, 283
Soldier River 213
Soldow Site 273
sora rail 129, 221, 226
South Dakota 39, 41, 129, 161, 278, 288
soybean 82, 140
Spanish needles 172
sparrow 129, 131, 134, 322
spear point 269, 269 illus, 270
Spencer 75
Spergen Formation 30, 32
sphagnum 129, 134, 157, 217
spider 242
spike rushes 218
Spirit Lake 61, 65, 157, 211, 213, 216, 234, 255
spore 29, 147, 148, 151
spring beauty 122, 142, 200
spring peeper 256
Springer, Frank 32, 308, 309
springs 57, 67, 242, 248
spruce 45, 53, 54, 186, 255, 256, 270
squash 278, 279, 282
squirrel 55, 101, 135, 192, 192 illus, 213, 256
Stephens, T. C. 312, 314
St. John, Orestes 308
St. Louis 32, 278, 281, 288, 289, 293, 310
St. Louis Formation 30
St. Peter's Rock 49 illus
St. Peter Sandstone 23, 24
stag-mouse 54
Stainbrook Geological Preserve 47
State Historical Society of Iowa 288
statehood 297, 299
starfish 32
starling 259, 322
Starr's Cave 61
Starr's Cave Formation 30
State Forest Nursery 206
State Preserves Advisory Board 318
State Quarry Formation 28
State Quarry Limestone 48
State Soil Conservation Committee 91
steamboat 69, 293
Ste. Genevieve 32
sticktights 172
stilt-legged deer 54
stinkhorn 151
stomata 67
stone, building 27, 28, 30, 32
Stone City 27
storm 67, 96, 102, 107, 109, 111, 112, 235

Storm Lake 65, 213, 255
Story City 75
Story County 70, 82, 88, 97, 98, 102, 113, 178, 296, 315
stratigraphy 50, 51
strawberry 143, 143 illus
sulphur 37
sundew 129, 147, 147 illus, 157, 217
sundog 102, 102 illus
sunfish 245
sunflower 27, 54, 168, 177, 186, 272, 278, 282
sunspot 115
surface water 65, 67, 70, 71, 77, 216, 223, 242
swales 59, 186
swallow-tailed kite 250
swamp 11, 15, 34, 37, 123, 125, 183, 215, 218
swamp saxifrage 171
swan 250
switchgrass 166
sycamore 127, 131, 205

T

Taconic Mountains 24
Tama 281
Tama County 88, 205, 288, 296
Taylor County 34
tern 129, 134, 221, 226, 321
Tertiary 41
Thayer 50
threshing 303
thunder 96, 102, 107
tick trefoil 177
tile 28, 34, 81, 125, 129, 223, 229
timber 122, 225
  see also forests
tipi 280 illus, 281
toad 127, 128, 240, 256, 257, 260, 261
toadflax 145
Toolesboro 288
topography 50, 51, 57, 59, 82, 85
topsoil 81, 82, 84, 86, 92, 93, 225, 249
tornado 96, 97, 102, 107, 109, 112, 113 illus
treaty 274, 288, 290
tree frog 256, 256 illus
Triassic 38, 39
trillium 142, 203
trilobites 24, 32
trout 133, 245
Tulip Festival 296
tulip-tree 205
tundra 54, 55, 256, 270
Turin 61
Turin Loess Hills State Preserve 157
Turkey River 23, 133, 213
Turkey River Mound Group 275
turtle 132, 134, 135, 157, 240, 240 illus, 256, 256 illus, 257, 272, 324
twinflower 154
Twin Springs State Park 146

U

Udden, J. A. 313
Umbillicaria 133
Union County 52
United States Army 99
United States Congress 93, 223
U.S. Army Corps of Engineers 65, 225, 249
U.S. Army Signal Corps 99
U.S. Department of Agriculture 81, 91, 99, 223
U.S. Department of Commerce 99
U.S. Game and Fish Wildlife Service 218, 223, 225
U.S. Geological Survey 66
U.S. Soil Conservation Service 88, 91
University of Iowa 28, 89, 122, 163, 309, 312, 313
Upper Iowa River 8 illus, 22 illus, 72, 123, 203, 213, 308

V

Van Buren County 311, 313, 314
vetch 175
viburnum 198
vines 196, 198
violet 173, 175
Virginia creeper 144, 186
Virgilian Series 34, 37
Virginia rail 129, 221, 226
volcanic 20, 24, 45, 51, 52
vole 54, 55, 129, 157, 226, 256
Volga River 213

W

Wachsmuth, Charles 32, 309
Wallace, Henry 89, 301, 314, 317
walnut, black 140, 143, 189
Wapello 32, 75, 290
wapiti 54, 250
  see also elk
Wapsipinicon Formation 28
Wapsipinicon River 132, 213, 314
warbler 261, 263 illus
Warsaw Formation 30, 32
Washington County 23, 29, 299
water boatmen 239
water bug 238
water cress 248, 249 illus
waterfall 23 illus, 70 illus, 72 illus, 73 illus
water flea 238
waterfowl 127-129, 217, 218, 225, 246
water hemlock 144, 172
water lily 157, 217, 218, 236 illus, 237, 237 illus
Waterloo 28, 75, 213
water milfoil 217, 218
water scorpion 239
water shield 132
water strider 239
weasel 263
Weaver, James R. 300, 300 illus
Webster County 13, 18, 35, 39, 299, 319

Alex B. Thiermann

weeping willow 205
wetlands 69, 123, 124, 129, 130, 183, Chapter 9, 208-229, 282, 318
wells 20, 21, 48, 51, 66, 71, 73, 75, 76
wheat 100
whirly-gig beetles 239
white birch 154, 203
White, Charles A. 308
white crane 123
white-fronted geese 226
White Pine Hollow State Forest Preserve 146, 146 illus, 157, 203, 204 illus, 318
white snakeroot 144
whitetop grass 130
wickiup 269 illus
wigeon 226
Wildcat Den State Park 34, 154, 203
wildflowers 122, 142, 144, 198, 200
wild geranium 142
wild ginger 142
wild grape 189, 198
wildlife 211, 213, 218, 221, 223, 226, Chapter 11, 250-265
wildlife habitat 89, 125, 131, 132, 134, 157, 206, 264, 317, 318, 320, 321-323
wild parsnip 144, 145
wild pea 177
wild quinine 171
wild rice 129, 157
wildrose 136 illus, 142, 168, 171
wild turkey 122, 213, 312, 321
willow 194, 218, 240, 242
Wilson, James 301
wind 47, 57-59, 83, 84, 96, 99, 102, 107, 109, 111, 112, 114
windbreak 97, 111, 206
Winnebago County 129
Winnebago Tribe 288, 290
Winneshiek County 10, 23, 24, 57, 72, 146, 154, 203, 291, 296, 308
Wisconsin 19, 24, 48, 217, 242, 260, 263, 277, 281, 288, 290
Wisconsin Dome 72
Wisconsin Glacier 52, 57, 59, 129-131, 185, 186, 211, 255, 256, 270
Wisconsin River 313, 314 illus
witch hazel 200
wolf 55, 254, 321
Wolfe Site 275
Wollfia 217
Woodbury County 299
woodchuck 260
wood duck 218, 221, 317
Wood, Grant 56 painting
woodland 48, 53, 54, 57, 124, 125, 128
   see also forests
Woodland People 275, 277, 278
wood lily 176 illus, 177 illus
Woodman Hollow State Preserve 18, 35, 319
worm 84, 238, 241, 245
wormwood 54
Worth County 129, 211
wren 129
Wright County 75, 123, 130, 132, 137, 157

Y

Yarmouth 50
yellow-headed blackbird 129, 221 illus, 226, 317, 317 illus
yellowlegs 226
yellow flax 170
Yellow River 213
Yellow River State Forest 133, 314
Yellow River Site 275
Yellow Spring Group 28, 29
yellow ox-eye 162 illus
yucca 127, 157, 169
yucca moth 169

Z

zinc 24

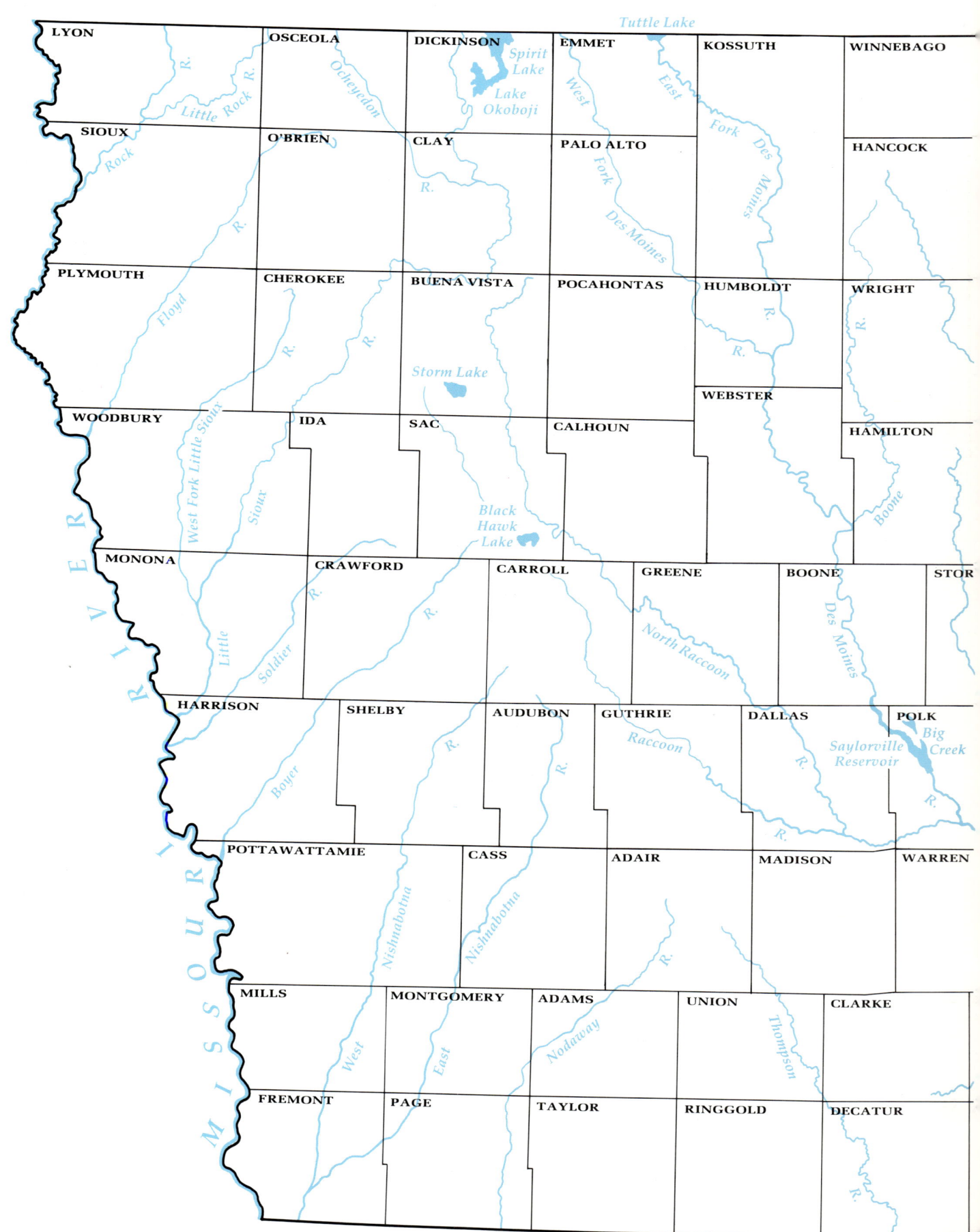